Frommer's®

2nd Edition

San Antonio & Austin

by Edie Jarolim

Macmillan • USA

ABOUT THE AUTHOR

Edie Jarolim was a senior editor at Frommer's in New York before she indulged her Southwest fantasies and moved to Tucscon, Arizona. She has contributed to numerous travel guides, and her articles have appeared in such diverse publications as the London *Guardian,* the *Wall Street Journal,* and *Bride's.* She was tickled to have the chance to write about two of her favorite cities in the state that spawned two of her favorite people, Ann Richards and Molly Ivins.

MACMILLAN TRAVEL

A Simon & Schuster Macmillan Company
1633 Broadway
New York, NY 10019

Find us online at **http://www.mgr.com/travel** or
on America Online at Keyword: **Frommer's**

ISBN 0-02-861584-0
ISSN 1080-9104

Editor: Jim Moore
Production Editor: Laura Uebelhor
Design by Michele Laseau
Digital Cartography by Jim Moore

SPECIAL SALES

Bulk purchases (10+ copies) of Frommer's and selected Macmillan travel guides are available to corporations, organizations, mail-order catalogs, institutions, and charities at special discounts, and can be customized to suit individual needs. For more information write to Special Sales, Macmillan General Reference, 1633 Broadway, New York, NY 10019.

Manufactured in the United States of America

Contents

List of Maps

AN INVITATION TO THE READER

In researching this book, I have come across many wonderful establishments, the best of which I have included here. I am sure that many of you will also come across appealing hotels, inns, restaurants, guesthouses, shops, and attractions. Please don't keep them to yourself. Share your experiences, especially if you want to comment on places that have been included in this edition that have changed for the worse. You can address your letters to:

Edie Jarolim
Frommer's San Antonio & Austin, 2nd Edition
Macmillan Travel
1633 Broadway
New York, NY 10019

AN ADDITIONAL NOTE

Please be advised that travel information is subject to change at any time—and this is especially true of prices. We therefore suggest that you write or call ahead for confirmation when making your travel plans. The authors, editors, and publisher cannot be held responsible for the experiences of readers while traveling. Your safety is important to us, however, so we encourage you to stay alert and be aware of your surroundings. Keep a close eye on cameras, purses, and wallets, all favorite targets of thieves and pickpockets.

WHAT THE SYMBOLS MEAN

✪ **Frommer's Favorites**

Hotels, restaurants, attractions, and entertainment you should not miss.

Ⓢ **Super-Special Values**

Hotels and restaurants that offer great value for your money.

The following abbreviations are used for credit cards:

AE	American Express	DISC	Discover
CB	Carte Blanche	MC	MasterCard
DC	Diners Club	V	Visa

Introducing San Antonio

Call it the Fiesta City or the Alamo City; each of San Antonio's nicknames reveals a different side of its character. Visitors come here to kick back and party, but they also come to seek out Texas's history—some would say its soul. They come to sit on the banks of a glittering river and sip cactus margaritas, but also to view the Franciscan missions that rose up along the same river more than two and a half centuries ago.

Amid San Antonio's typical Southwest sprawl, it is the winding downtown streets most visitors recall, whether they're ardent urban enthusiasts or folks who just get a charge out of briefly abandoning their cars. They recall those downtown streets—and that river. Few who come to San Antonio leave without a memory of a moment, quiet or heart quickening, sunlit or sparkling with tiny tree-draped lights, when that river didn't somehow work its magic on them.

1 Frommer's Favorite San Antonio Experiences

- **Recapturing Texas's Fight for Independence at the Alamo.** It's hard to imagine downtown's prime attraction as a battle site, surrounded as it is today by hotels and shops, until you step inside the Long Barrack, where Texas's most famous martyrs prepared to fight General Santa Anna's troups.
- **Attending a Mariachi Mass at Mission San José.** You're welcome to watch members of the congregation of this largest of the mission churches raise their voices in spirited musical prayer every Sunday at noon. Come early; seats are limited and this is a popular thing to do.
- **Strolling Along the San Antonio River.** Whether you opt to join the throngs at the restaurants and cafes of the Big Bend portion of the River Walk or get away by yourself to one of its quieter stretches, the green, lush banks of San Antonio's river can match your mood, day or night.
- **People-Watching at Market Square.** After an afternoon of shopping at the square's two lively Mexican markets, take a load off your feet at an outdoor table and sip a margarita or a soda. Among the colorful crowd, you'll see vendors from Mexico and locals who have been coming here since the days when animals and produce were still being sold in the stalls.

- **Seeing a Show at the Majestic Theater.** As it happens, the restored Majestic offers top-notch shows of all kinds, but it wouldn't matter if it didn't—the venue itself, one of the world's last atmospheric theaters, is worth the price of admission.
- **Climbing into a Treehouse at the Witte Museum.** You can recapture your youth (or enjoy your kids relishing theirs) at the Witte, where a new treehouse is one of the many terrific interactive science exhibits.
- **Pretending You're Rich in the King William District.** The gorgeous homes built by German merchants in the 19th century are eye-popping. You can't enter most of these opulent mansions (unless you're staying at one of the area's many B&Bs), but walk around with assurance and fantasize away.
- **Riding the World's Largest Wooden Roller Coaster at Six Flags Fiesta Texas.** If you're a fan of stomach-churning adventure, you've got to get this coaster under your belt. And while you're there, check out the new Joker—it's insane.
- **Buying a Piñata in Southtown.** This Hispanic neighborhood, adjacent to King William, is getting hip, but low-key stores carry traditional celebration items. If you're lucky enough to be in town for the Day of the Dead, this is definitely the place to be.
- **Ascending the Tower of the Americas in HemisFair Park.** It's a great way to get the lay of the land—no vantage point in the city is higher. And after dark, the lofty bar is a great place to sip a drink while overlooking the sparkling array of city lights.
- **Checking out the Headgear in Paris Hatters.** Even if you don't buy a Stetson, you should at least wander over to this San Antonio institution that has sold hats to everyone from the pope and Queen Elizabeth to Jimmy Smits.
- **Grooving to Jazz at The Landing.** Jim Callum and his band play cool jazz at a cool location—the River Walk. It's hard to get much mellower than this.

2 San Antonio Today

The ninth largest city in the United States (population: 1,084,700) and one of the oldest is undergoing a metamorphosis. For a good part of this century, San Antonio was a military town that happened to have a nice river promenade running through its decaying downtown. Now, with the downsizing and (by the year 2001) privatizing of Kelly Air Force Base and the continuing growth in tourism, the city is increasingly perceived by outsiders as a place with a terrific river walk—and, oh yes, it has a strong military presence, doesn't it?

Although the city's outlying theme parks and central area attractions are also benefiting from increased visitation, downtown is by far the most affected section. In 1996, the Downtown Alliance, a group of neighborhood property and business owners, published *A Strategic Plan for Entering the 21st Century,* which focuses on managed growth. Among the goals of the group are an improved north/south–east/west transit system, a new visitor and transportation center, more parking spaces, greater access to the river from the street, and additional green spaces and sidewalk canopies for shade. The city has already been given the nod to expand its convention center and to build an adjacent hotel with 1,000 rooms.

Middle-class residential growth still lags behind commercial development in this area. San Antonians who moved downtown in the last decade initially patted themselves on the back for their prescience in staking out an upward-bound section, but many are now beginning to second-guess the changes they helped bring about. Not only are there few residential services (the area has no major supermarket, for example), but the huge success of the riverside Southbank and Presidio complexes, opened in 1995, destroyed what little quiet there was at night along the developed sections of the river. The enactment of ordinaces that cut down on late-night noise and the opening up of a dialogue between residents and businesses have begun to resolve that friction.

This is not to suggest that there is no growth in any other business sectors. The city is attempting to take the sour order to privatize Kelly Air Force Base and turn it into lemonade by working to attract an aerospace firm to the large, well-maintained facility. Such a firm would be following the lead of other businesses: The big financial news in late 1996 was the merger of oil giant Diamond Shamrock and Ultramar, and the move of the huge new company's headquarters to San Antonio.

But for all its rosy outlook, San Antonio is facing some major problems. One of the worst droughts in the decade and a suit brought by the Sierra Club have forced the city to pay attention to what is likely to be its major concern in the future—water. Currently, the Edwards Aquifer is the city's only source of water; because it is underground, no one knows exactly how many years' supply it contains. And in late 1996, a U.S. district court judge ruled in favor of the Sierra Club, which wants to impose pumping limits on the aquifer in order to protect the endangered Barton Springs salamander. No matter what the ultimate outcome of the case—the judge's ruling is being appealed, so San Antonio is still pumping at full force—it's clear the city needs to find some alternate water sources.

In addition, although San Antonio and Austin are 80 miles and political light-years apart—among other things, Austin, which has the much-dammed Colorado River to drink from, thinks San Antonio is water greedy—the two cities are literally growing together. Although they are still far from melding to form the single, huge metropolis that futurists predict, the increasing suburban sprawl and the growth of New Braunfels and San Marcos, two small cities that lie between San Antonio and Austin, are causing a great deal of congestion on I-35, which connects all four cities. San Antonio's Metropolitan Planning Commission has just been alloted the funds to study this problem; one of the solutions that's being considered is a light rail commuter train.

3 A Look at the Past

The history of San Antonio is the stuff of legends, that of the Alamo being but the most famous of an amazing lot. If it were a movie, the city would be an epic with an improbably packed plot, encompassing the end of a great empire, the rise of a republic, and the rescue of the river with which the story began.

ON A MISSION

Having already established an empire—the huge Viceroyalty of New Spain, which covered, at its high point, Mexico, Guatemala, and large parts of the southwestern United States—by the late 17th century, Spain was engaged in the far less glamorous task of maintaining it. The remote regions of east Texas had been coming under attack by the native Apache and Comanche; now with rumors of French forays into the Spanish territory flying, search parties were dispatched to investigate.

Dateline
- **1691** On June 13, saint day of Anthony of Padua, San Antonio River discovered and named by the Spanish; governor of Spanish colonial province of Texas makes contact with Coahuiltecan Indians.
- **1718** Mission San Antonio de Valero (later nicknamed the Alamo) founded; *presidio* San Antonio de Béxar established to protect it and other missions to be built nearby.
- **1720** Mission San José founded.

continues

- **1731** Missions Concepción, San Juan Capistrano, and Espada relocated from East Texas to San Antonio area; 15 Canary Island families sent by Spain to help populate Texas arrive in San Antonio and establish the first civil settlement.
- **1793–94** The missions are secularized by order of the Spanish crown.
- **1820** Moses Austin petitions Spanish governor in San Antonio for permission to settle Americans in Texas.
- **1821** Mexico wins independence from Spain.
- **1835** Siege of Béxar: first battle in San Antonio for Texas independence from Mexico.
- **1836** The Alamo falls after 13-day siege by Mexican general Santa Anna; using "Remember the Alamo" as a rallying cry, Sam Houston defeats Santa Anna at San Jacinto.
- **1836–45** Republic of Texas.
- **1845** Texas annexed to the United States.
- **1861** Texas secedes from the Union.
- **1876** Fort Sam Houston established as new quartermaster depot.
- **1877** The railroad arrives in San Antonio, precipitating new waves of immigration.
- **1880s** King William, first residential suburb, begins to be developed by German immigrants.
- **1939–40** Works Progress Administration builds River Walk, based on plans drawn up in 1929 by architect Robert H. H. Hugman.
- **1968** HemisFair exposition—River Walk extension, Convention Center, Mansión del Rio, and Hilton Palacio del Rio completed for the

continues

On one of these search parties in 1691, regional governor Domingo Teran de los Ríos and Father Damian Massenet came upon a wooded plain fed by a fast-flowing river. They named the river—called Yanaguana by the native Coahuiltecan Indians—San Antonio de Padua, after the saint's day on which they arrived. When, some decades later, the Spanish Franciscans proposed to build a new mission halfway between the ones on the Rio Grande River and those more recently established in east Texas, the abundant water and friendliness of the local population brought the plain near the San Antonio River to mind.

And so it was that in 1718, Mission San Antonio de Valero—later known as the Alamo—was founded. To protect the religious complex from Apache attack, the *presidio* (fortress) of San Antonio de Béxar went up a few days later. In 1719, a second mission was built nearby, and in 1731, three ill-fated east Texas missions, nearly destroyed in attacks by both the French and the Indians, were moved hundreds of miles to the safer banks of the San Antonio River. The year 1731 was significant for another reason: In March, 15 weary families arrived from the Spanish Canary Islands with a royal dispensation from Philip V to help settle his far-flung New World kingdom. Near the protection of the presidio, they established the village of San Fernando de Béxar.

Thus within little more than a decade, what is now downtown San Antonio became home to three distinct, though related, settlements: a mission complex; the military garrison designed to protect it; and the civilian town known as Béxar (pronounced Bear) until 1837, when it was officially renamed San Antonio. To irrigate their crops, the early settlers were given narrow strips of land stretching back from the river and from the nearby San Pedro Creek; centuries later, the paths connecting these strips, which followed the winding waterways, were paved as the city's streets.

REMEMBER THE ALAMO

As the 18th century wore on, the missions came continuously under siege by hostile Indians, and the mission Indians fell victim to a host of European diseases against which they had no natural resistance; by the end of the 1700s, the Spanish mission system itself was terminal. In 1794, Mission San Antonio de Valero was secularized, its rich farmlands redistributed. In 1810, recognizing the military potential of the thick walls of the complex, the

Spanish authorities turned the former mission into a garrison. The men recruited to serve here all hailed from the Mexican town of San José y Santiago del Alamo de Parras; the name of their station was soon shortened to the Alamo.

occasion, along with Tower of the Americas and other fair structures.

- **1988** Rivercenter Mall opens.
- **1993** Alamodome, huge new sports complex, completed.
- **1995** Southbank and Presidio complexes open on the river.

By 1824, all five missions had been secularized and Spain was once again worried about Texas. Apache and Comanche roamed the territory freely; with the incentive of converting the native populations eliminated, it was next to impossible to persuade any Spaniards to live there. So, although the Spanish were rightly suspicious of Anglo-American designs on their land, when *empresario* (land agent) Moses Austin arrived in San Antonio in 1820, the government reluctantly agreed to allow him to settle some 300 Anglo-American families in the region. Austin died before he could see his plan carried out, and Spain lost its hold on Mexico in 1821, when the country became independent; but Moses's son, Stephen, convinced the new government to honor the terms of the original agreement.

By 1830, however, the Mexicans were growing nervous about the large numbers of Anglos descending on their country from the north. They had already repealed many of the tax breaks they had initially granted the settlers; now they prohibited all further U.S. immigration to the territory. When, in 1835, General Antonio López de Santa Anna abolished Mexico's democratic 1824 constitution, Tejanos (Hispanic Texans) and Anglos alike balked at his dictatorship and a cry rose up for a separate republic.

The first battle for Texas independence fought on San Antonio soil fell to the rebels; Mexican general Martín Perfecto de Cós surrendered after a short, successful siege on the town in December 1835. But it was the return engagement, that glorious, doomed fight against all odds, that forever captured the American imagination: From February 23 through March 6, 1836, some 180 volunteers—among them Davy Crockett and Jim Bowie—serving under the command of William Travis, died trying to defend the Alamo fortress against a vastly greater number of Santa Anna's men. One month later Sam Houston spurred his troops on to victory at the Battle of San Jacinto with the cry "Remember the Alamo," thus securing Texas's freedom.

AFTER THE FALL

Ironically, few Anglos came to live in San Antonio during Texas's stint as a republic (1836–45), but settlers came from overseas in droves: By 1850, Mexicans and Anglos were outnumbered by European, mostly German, immigrants. The Civil War put a temporary halt to the city's growth—in part because Texas joined the Confederacy and most of the new settlers were Union sympathizers—but expansion picked up again soon afterward; the coming of the railroad in 1877 set off a new wave of immigration. Riding hard on its crest, the King William district, a residential suburb named for Kaiser Wilhelm, was developed by prosperous German merchants.

Some of the immigrants set up Southern-style plantations; others opened factories and shops; and more and more who arrived after the Civil War earned their keep by driving cattle. The Spanish had brought longhorn cattle and *vaqueros* (cowboys) from Mexico into the area; now Texas cowboys drove herds north on the Chisholm Trail from San Antonio to Kansas City, where they were shipped east. Others moved cattle west, for use as seed stock in the fledgling ranching industry.

Over the years San Antonio had never abandoned its role as a military stronghold. In 1849, the Alamo was designated a quartermaster depot for the U.S. Army; in

Impressions

> *From all manner of people, business men, consumptive men, curious men, and wealthy men, there came an exhibition of profound affection for San Antonio. It seemed to symbolize for them the poetry of life in Texas.*
> —Stephen Crane, *Patriot Shrine of Texas* (1895)

1876, the much larger Fort Sam Houston was built to take over those duties. Apache chief Geronimo was held at the clock tower in the fort's Quadrangle for 40 days in 1886, en route to exile in Florida; Teddy Roosevelt outfitted his Rough Riders—some of whom he recruited in San Antonio bars—at Fort Sam 12 years later.

As the city marched into the 20th century, Fort Sam Houston continued to expand. In 1910, it witnessed the first military flight by an American; early aviation stars like Charles Lindbergh honed their flying skills here. From 1917 to 1941, four air force bases—Kelly Field, Brooks Field, Randolph Field, and Lackland Army Air Base—shot up, making San Antonio the largest military complex in the United States outside the Washington, D.C., area. Although Kelly is being gradually downsized and privatized, the military remains the city's major employer today, with the tourism industry nudging it closely from behind.

A RIVER RUNS THROUGH IT

As the city moved further and further from its agrarian roots, the San Antonio River grew less and less central to the economy; by the turn of the century, its constant flooding made it a downright nuisance. When a particularly severe storm in 1921 caused it to overflow its banks, killing 50 people and destroying many downtown businesses, there was serious talk of cementing the river over.

In 1925, the newly formed San Antonio Conservation Society put on a puppet show warning the city council against killing the goose that was laying the golden eggs of downtown economic growth. And in 1927, Robert H. H. Hugman, an architect who had lived in New Orleans and studied that city's Beaux Carré district, came up with a detailed plan for saving the waterway. His proposed River Walk, with shops, restaurants, and entertainment areas buttressed by a series of floodgates, would render the river profitable as well as safe, and also preserve its natural beauty. The Depression intervened, but in 1941, with the help of a federal Works Project Administration (WPA) grant, Hugman's vision became a reality.

Still, for some decades more, the River Walk remained just another pretty space; not until the 1968 HemisFair exposition drew record crowds to the rescued waterway did the city begin banking on its banks. In the next 20 years, commercial development of the Big Bend section took off, culminating in the huge Rivercenter shopping and hotel complex in 1988; the South Bank complex, anchored by a Hard Rock Cafe, and Presidio Plaza, featuring Planet Hollywood, are the latest of the riverside entertainment meccas. Instead of falling victim to the city's suburban spread, the place where San Antonio began was revitalized by its river—just as the Conservation Society had predicted.

4 The Lay of the Land

Three geographical zones meet in San Antonio: The Balcones Fault divides the farms and forests of east Texas from the scrubby brushland and ranches of west Texas, and the Edwards Plateau drops off to the southern coastal plains. Frederick Law Olmsted's description in his 1853 *A Journey Through Texas* is more poetic. San Antonio, he writes, "lies basking on the edge of a vast plain, through which the river winds slowly off beyond where the eye can reach. To the east are gentle slopes toward it; to the north a long gradual sweep upward to the mountain country, which comes down within five or six miles; to the south and west, the open prairies, extending almost level to the coast, a hundred and fifty miles away."

5 Multiculturalism

It may be a buzzword on academic campuses, but multiculturalism is very real in San Antonio. As the only major city founded before Texas won its independence from Mexico, its history encompasses diverse groups with distinct goals: Spanish missionaries and militia men, German merchants, southern plantation owners, western cattle ranchers, and Eastern architects. All left their mark not only on the city's culture and cuisine but more tangibly on its winding downtown streets.

With its German, southern, western, and, above all, Hispanic influences—the city is nearly 60% Mexican American—San Antonio's cultural life is immensely rich and complex. At the New Orleans–like Fiesta, for example, San Antonians might break confetti eggs called *cascarones,* listen to oompah bands, and cheer rodeo bull riders. Countless country-and-western ballads twang on about San Antone—probably because the name rhymes with "alone"—which is also America's capital for Tejano music, a unique blend of Mexican and German sounds. And no self-respecting San Antonio festival would be complete without Mexican tamales and tacos, Texan chili and barbecue, southern hush puppies and glazed ham, and German beer and bratwurst.

The city's buildings also reflect its multiethnic history. After the Texas revolution, Spanish *viga* beams began to be replaced by southern Greek Revival columns, German *fachwerk* pitched roofs, and East Coast Victorian gingerbread facades. San Antonio, like the rest of the Southwest, has now returned to its Hispanic architectural roots—even chain hotels in the area have red-clay roofs, Saltillo tile floors, and central patios—but updated versions of other indigenous building styles are also popular. The rustic yet elegant Hill Country look, for example, might use native limestone in structures that combine sprawling Texas ranch features with more intricate German details.

6 Local Flavor

San Antonio may be multicultural, but when it comes to ethnic food, Mexican rules. The city has come up with its own versions of classic south-of-the-border recipes; even people who are familiar with Mexican fare are likely to come across some dishes here that they don't recognize. At Market Square, you might see vendors selling funnel cakes—huge, puffy concoctions of fried dough topped with powdered sugar—so-called because the dough is poured into the hot fat through a funnel, or *gorditas* (literally, little fat ones)—fried cornmeal cakes topped with cheese, lettuce, tomatoes, salsa, refried beans, and other tasty possibilities. At almost every Mexican restaurant, you'll find some version of *pico de gallo* (chopped tomatoes, onions, and chiles) on the table; it's usually a bit chunkier than salsa. (Did you know that more jars of salsa than ketchup are consumed in the United States today?) In addition to the usual enchiladas, tamales, and quesadillas, you'll also come across *chalupas,* or open-faced tacos; because the fried corn tortilla isn't folded over, the usual fillings can be piled high on top. And though you may already know the joy of huevos rancheros for breakfast, San Antonio is a great place to be introduced to *chilaquiles*—corn tortillas scrambled up with eggs, cheese, and chile peppers.

But good as they are, updated versions of Mexican food are not what gives the city its claim to culinary fame. For details on San Antonio's role in the history of chili, that American food classic, see chapter 5.

7 Recommended Books & Films

BOOKS

Before Frederick Law Olmsted became a landscape architect—New York's Central Park is among his creations—he was a successful journalist; his 1853 *A Journey Through Texas* includes a delightful section on his impressions of early San Antonio. William Sidney Porter, better known as O. Henry, had a newspaper office in San Antonio for a while; two collections of his short stories, *O. Henry's Texas Stories* and *Time to Write*, include a number of pieces set in the city, among them "A Fog in Santone," "The Higher Abdication," "Hygeia at the Solito," "Seats of the Haughty," and "The Missing Chord."

O. Henry wasn't very successful at selling his newspaper, the *Rolling Stone*, in San Antonio in the 1890s, but there's a lively literary scene in town today. Resident writers include Sandra Cisneros, many of whose powerful, critically acclaimed short stories in *Women Hollering Creek* are set in the city; novelist Sarah Bird, whose humorous *The Mommy Club* pokes fun at the yuppies of the King William area; and mystery writer Jay Brandon, whose excellent *Loose Among the Lambs* kept San Antonians busy trying to guess the identities of the local figures fictionalized therein.

FILMS

For a bit of the myth surrounding the city, you might want to rent *The Alamo*, starring John Wayne, or *San Antonio*, starring Errol Flynn, though neither was shot in town (the 1935 *Fall of the Alamo*—not available on video—was). A number of early aviation movies used Fort Sam Houston as a location, among them the 1927 silent film, *Wings*, the first film to receive an Academy Award for best picture. Some of the better-known films set in San Antonio are *The Getaway* (1972), *Sugarland Express* (1973), *Race with the Devil* (1975), and *Cloak and Dagger* (1983). *Ace Ventura: When Nature Calls* (1995) was filmed in and around the city; the African safari park scenes were shot just outside San Antonio. The recent remake of *Lolita* (1996), starring Jeremy Irons and Melanie Griffith, was shot largely in the area, as was *Selena* (1997), based on the life of the Tejano star. The strongest claim to accuracy of setting comes in the miniseries *Rough Riders*, which details the career of Teddy Roosevelt. The Menger Hotel, where Roosevelt recruited a number of men, was called into service again for the tube version of the events.

Planning a Trip to San Antonio

Spontaneity is all well and good once you get to where you're going, but advance planning can make or break a trip. San Antonio is becoming more and more popular; it's best to book your vacation here well in advance. If you're thinking of coming for April's huge Fiesta bash, try to reserve at least 6 months ahead of time to avoid disappointment.

Most tourists visit San Antonio in summer, though it's not really the ideal season: The weather can be steamy, and restaurants and attractions tend to be crowded. That said, there are plenty of places to cool off around town, hotel rates are generally lower, and some of the most popular outdoor attractions are open only—or have far more extended schedules—this time of year. (If sights such as Sea World and Six Flags Fiesta Texas top your roster of things to do, call ahead to check when they're closed.) Consider visiting during the week: San Antonio is the single most popular destination in the state for Texans, many of whom drive in just for the weekend.

1 Visitor Information

Contact the **San Antonio Convention & Visitors Bureau (SACVB),** P.O. Box 2277, San Antonio, TX 78298 (☎ 800/447-3372 or e-mail sacvb@ci.sat.tx.us), for a useful pretrip information packet, including a visitors' guide and map, lodging guide, detailed calendar of events, arts brochure, and SAVE San Antonio booklet with discount coupons for a number of hotels and attractions. You can get pretrip information on-line at the SACVB's new Web site, **www.sanantoniocvb.com.** If you want to find out about hotel room availability before you leave, call the bureau's lodging line (☎ 800/858-4303).

Phone the **Texas Department of Tourism** (☎ 800/8888-TEX) ahead of time to receive the *Texas State Travel Guide,* a glossy book chock-full of information about the state, along with a statewide accommodations booklet. The **Texas Travel Information Center** has a toll-free number (☎ 800/452-9292) to call for the latest on road conditions, special events, and general attractions in the areas you're interested in visiting; traveler counselors will even advise you on the quickest or most scenic route to your intended destination. On-line, you'll find the Texas Department of Transportation at www.traveltex.com. *Texas Monthly* magazine, another good source of information, can be accessed at **www.texasmonthly.com.**

What Things Cost in San Antonio	U.S. $
Taxi from the airport to the city center	14.00
Streetcar ride between any two downtown points	.50
Local telephone call	.25
Long-neck beer	2.00
Double at the Fairmount (very expensive)	185.00
Double at the Ramada Emily Morgan (moderate)	100.00
Double at the Best Western Town House Motel (inexpensive)	65.00
Lunch for one at Zuni Grill (moderate)	10.00
Lunch for one at Schilo's (inexpensive)	5.00
Dinner for one, without wine, at Biga (expensive)	25.00
Dinner for one, without wine, at La Calesa (moderate)	14.00
Dinner for one, without wine, at Earl Abel's (inexpensive)	8.00
Coca-Cola	1.00
Cup of espresso	2.00
Roll of ASA 100 Kodacolor film, 36 exposures	6.00
Admission to the Witte Museum	4.00
Movie ticket	1.50–6.25
Ticket to the San Antonio Symphony	14.00–42.00

2 When to Go

CLIMATE

Complain to San Antonians about their city's heat on a sultry summer day and you're likely to be assured that it's far more humid in say, Houston, or anywhere in east Texas. This may be true—but it won't make you feel any less sweaty. From late May to early September, expect high temperatures and high humidity with some regularity.

Fall and spring are prime times to visit; the days are pleasantly warm and, if you come in late March/early April, the wildflowers in the nearby Hill Country will be in glorious bloom. Temperate weather combined with the lively celebrations surrounding Christmas also make November and December good months to come. January and February can be a bit raw—but if you're from up North you probably won't even notice.

San Antonio's Average Monthly Temperature & Rainfall

	Jan	Feb	Mar	Apr	May	June	July	Aug	Sept	Oct	Nov	Dec
Avg. Temp. (°F)	52.0	54.5	60.8	68.2	75.3	81.9	84.0	83.8	79.3	70.5	59.7	53.2
Rainfall (in.)	1.66	2.06	1.54	2.54	3.07	2.79	1.69	2.41	3.71	2.84	1.77	1.46

THE FIESTA CITY

San Antonio's nickname refers to its huge April bash, but it also touches on the city's tendency to party at the drop of a sombrero. It's only natural that a place with strong southern, western, and Hispanic roots would know how to have a good time: elaborately costumed festival queens, wild-and-wooly rodeos, and Mexican food and mariachis are rolled out year-round. And where else but San Antonio would something as potentially dull as draining a river turn into a cause for celebration?

SAN ANTONIO CALENDAR OF EVENTS

January

- **Miller Lite River Bottom Festival and Mud Parade,** River Walk. When the horseshoe bend of the San Antonio River Walk is drained for maintenance purposes in early January, San Antonians cheer themselves up by electing a king and queen to reign over such events as Mud Stunts Day and the Mud Pie Ball at Kangaroo Court Restaurant. ☎ 210/227-4262.
- **San Antonio CineFestival,** Guadalupe Cultural Arts Center. The nation's oldest and largest Chicano/Latino film festival is held for 5 days in late January or early February. More than 70 films and videos are screened. ☎ 210/271-3151.

February

- **Stock Show and Rodeo,** Joe and Harry Freeman Coliseum. Starting in early February, San Antonio hosts more than 2 weeks of rodeo events, livestock judging, country-and-western bands, and carnivals. ☎ 210/225-5851.

March

- **St. Patrick's River Dyeing.** Are leprechauns responsible for turning the San Antonio River into the green River Shannon? Irish dance and music fill the Arneson River Theatre from the afternoon on. ☎ 210/497-8435.

April

- **Starving Artist Show,** River Walk and La Villita. Part of the proceeds of the work sold by nearly 1,000 local artists go to benefit the Little Church of La Villita's program to feed the hungry. ☎ 210/226-3593.
- ✪ **Fiesta San Antonio.** What started as a modest marking of Texas's independence more than 100 years ago is now a huge celebration, with an elaborately costumed royal court presiding over 10 days of revelry: parades, balls, food fests, sporting events, concerts, and art shows.
  Where: All over town. **When:** Starting the third week of April. **How:** Call 210/227-5191 for details on tickets and events.

May

- **Cinco de Mayo,** Market Square. On the weekend closest to the Fifth of May, Mexico's independence from France is celebrated with music, food booths, and more. ☎ 210/207-8600.
- ✪ **Tejano Conjunto Festival.** This annual festival, sponsored by the Guadalupe Cultural Arts Center, celebrates the lively and unique blend of Mexican and German music born in south Texas. The best *conjunto* musicians in the nation perform here.
  Where: Rosedale Park, 340 Dartmouth St. **When:** Four days in mid-May. **How:** Call 210/271-3151 for schedules and ticket information.
- **Return of the Chili Queens,** Market Square. Memorial Day weekend sees the annual celebration of chili, said to have originated in San Antonio, with music, dancing, craft demonstrations, and, of course, chili aplenty. ☎ 210/207-8600.

June

- **Fiesta Noche del Rio,** Arneson River Theatre. Every Thursday, Friday, and Saturday from June through August, a colorful revue celebrating Latin culture is held on one side of the river while the audience claps from the opposite bank. ☎ **210/226-4651.**

July

- **Contemporary Art Month,** Blue Star Arts Complex. You can pick up a calendar of the more than 70 events that celebrate the city's creative community throughout July. ☎ **210/227-6960.**

August

- **Texas Folklife Festival,** Institute of Texas Cultures. For 4 days in early August, ethnic foods, dances, crafts demonstrations, and games celebrate the diversity of Texas's heritage. ☎ **210/558-2300.**

September

- **Fiestas Patrias.** On the weekend nearest September 16, Mexican independence from Spain is celebrated at La Villita, the Arneson River Theatre, and Guadalupe Plaza. For schedules of events, call the San Antonio Convention and Visitors Bureau (☎ **800/447-3372**).
- **JazzSAlive,** Travis Park. Bands from New Orleans and San Antonio come together for a weekend of hot jazz in late September. ☎ **210/207-8486.**
- **Great Country River Festival,** River Walk. Late September is also a time for Texas two-stepping to the free country-and-western bands that play at the Arneson River Theatre and up and down along the river. ☎ **210/227-4262.**

October

- **Oktoberfest,** Beethoven Home. San Antonio's German roots show at this early October festival with food, dance, oompah bands, and beer. ☎ **210/222-1521.**
- **Inter-American Bookfair and Literary Festival,** Mexican Cultural Institute. Forty international publishers gather for poetry and fiction readings, workshops, panel discussions, and book exhibits. ☎ **210/271-3151.**

November

- ○ **Lighting Ceremony and River Walk Holiday Parade.** On the Friday following Thanksgiving Day, trees and bridges along the river are illuminated by some 50,000 lights; Santa Claus arrives on a boat during the floating river parade. ☎ **210/227-4262.**
- **Fiestas Navidenas,** Market Square. On weekends between Thanksgiving Day and Christmas, the Mexican market hosts piñata parties, a blessing of the animals, and surprise visits from Pancho Claus. ☎ **210/207-8600.**

December

- **Rivercenter Christmas Pageant.** River barges in the Rivercenter complex are the untraditional setting for the traditional Christmas story on December weekends leading up to the holiday. ☎ **210/225-0000.**
- **Fiesta de las Luminarias,** River Walk. On the weekends before Christmas, the River Walk is lit up by thousands of candles. ☎ **210/227-4262.**
- **Las Posadas,** River Walk. Singers walk along the river searching for lodging in a moving multifaith rendition of the Christmas story. ☎ **210/224-6163.**

3 Tips for Travelers with Special Needs

FOR TRAVELERS WITH DISABILITIES

An excellent resource for travelers with any type of disability is **Travelin' Talk,** P.O. Box 3534, Clarksville, TN 37043 (☎ **615/552-6670;** fax 615/552-1182). Whether you want general information about transportation in San Antonio, or have specific questions for an individual in town with a similar impairment, the organization can refer you to a local resource. Members receive a quarterly newsletter and get a discount on the huge *Travelin' Talk* directory, which lists, among many other things, travel agents and tour operators who specialize in working with the disabled. Membership fees are on a sliding scale.

The Disabled Accessibility Information number in San Antonio is **210/207-7243.**

FOR GAY & LESBIAN TRAVELERS

San Antonio's gay and lesbian community is fairly large, but not very visible. For information on community events and for referrals, call the **Gay & Lesbian Switchboard** (☎ **210/733-7300**); if there are no volunteers staffing the line, you'll get a recording with some referral numbers. **Lesbian Information San Antonio** (☎ **210/828-LISA**) focuses on gay women's events around town. You can pick up a copy of the lesbian newspaper, *Woman Space,* at **Textures Bookstore,** 5309 McCullough (☎ **210/805-8398**), also a good resource for lesbian literature and information on gay happenings around town.

FOR SENIORS

By joining the **American Association of Retired Persons (AARP),** 601 E St. NW, Washington, DC 20049 (☎ **202/434-2277**), those over age 50 can get good discounts on many hotels, rental cars, and sights; an Amoco Motoring Plan offers trip-routing information and emergency road service. (Always remember to ask about these discounts in advance—for example, when you're booking a room or renting a car, not when you're checking out or returning the vehicle.)

The nonprofit **Elderhostel,** 75 Federal St., 3rd Floor, Boston, MA 02110 (☎ **617/426-7788**), has a variety of inexpensive and interesting study programs, including room and board, for ages 60 and older; they're becoming very popular, so book early. Among the many classes offered in San Antonio in 1996 were "The Making of Texas Heroes: Myths and Realities on the Frontier" and "San Antonio: A Close Look at Its Art, Architecture, and Culture."

FOR FAMILIES

Those who travel frequently with children will glean some useful hints from the *Family Travel Times* newsletter, Travel with Your Children, 40 Fifth Ave., New York, NY 10011 (☎ **212/477-5524;** fax 212/477-5173), offering both general and destination-specific information. An annual subscription (four issues) costs $40; you can order back issues, including the one devoted to San Antonio (March 1994), at a discount if you are a member. The free monthly *Our Kids* magazine, published in San Antonio, includes a calendar that lists daily activities oriented toward children; you can find it in San Antonio at many downtown hotels, HEB supermarkets, Target, Toys R Us, Barnes & Noble, or order it in advance from the publisher, 8400 Blanco, Suite 201, San Antonio, TX 78216 (☎ **210/349-6667;** fax 210/349-5618).

FOR STUDENTS

The **Council on International Educational Exchange (CIEE),** 205 E. 42nd St., New York, NY 10017 (☎ **212/822-2600**), offers a variety of discounts on airfares, rail fares, and accommodations; send for the organization's *Student Travels* magazine for details. You don't have to be a student—or even a youth—to join **Hostelling International—American Youth Hostels,** P.O. Box 37613, Washington, DC 20013 (☎ **202/783-6161**), which gives its members discounts at its dorm-style hostels around the world, and also offers rail and bus travel discounts in many places. San Antonio is not a college town, and there's no general gathering place for college-age folks. The city's major universities, Trinity, 715 Stadium Dr. (☎ 210/736-7011), and St. Mary's, 1 Camino Santa Maria (☎ 210/436-3011), are private, as is Incarnate Word College, 4301 Broadway (☎ 210/829-6000). The best source of local information for student visitors is probably the San Antonio International Hostel, 621 Pierce St., San Antonio 78208 (☎ 210/223-9426).

4 Getting There

BY PLANE

THE MAJOR AIRLINES   The major domestic carriers serving San Antonio are **America West** (☎ 800/235-9292), **American** (☎ 800/433-7300), **Continental** (☎ 800/525-0280), **Delta** (☎ 800/221-1212 or 800/221-1212), **Northwest** (☎ 800/225-2525), **Southwest** (☎ 800/435-9792), **TWA** (☎ 800/221-2000), **United** (☎ 800/241-6522), **USAir** (☎ 800/428-4322), and **Western Pacific** (☎ 800/930-3030). **Aerolitoral** (☎ 800/237-6639), **Aeromar** (☎ 210/829-7482), **Continental** (☎ 800/231-0856), and **Mexicana** (☎ 800/531-7921 or 210/525-9191) offer international service. Smaller commuter airlines that fly into San Antonio include Air Tran, American Eagle, ASA, and Conquest.

Because San Antonio isn't a hub, service to the city has often been circuitous, but Southwest now offers nonstops from Los Angeles, Nashville, and Orlando, and Continental has introduced nonstop service from Newark.

FINDING THE BEST AIRFARES   The lowest standard fares to San Antonio require a 14-day or 21-day advance purchase, a stay-over Saturday night, and travel during the week. With these restrictions, prices from New York to San Antonio can run as low as $314; from Chicago, $298; and from Los Angeles, $144. If you're departing from one of the cities that Southwest services, you're likely to get the lowest rates on that airline. Remember that all the airlines run seasonal specials; look out for them as soon as you start thinking about taking a trip.

SAN ANTONIO'S AIRPORT   The two-terminal **San Antonio International Airport** (☎ 210/207-3411), about 13 miles north of downtown, is compact, clean, well marked—even cheerful. Among its various amenities are a postal center, ATM, foreign-currency exchange, game room, and some well-stocked gift shops. Each terminal hosts an unstaffed branch office of the City of San Antonio Visitor Information Center (see "Visitor Information," in chapter 3) with an electronic panel on which you can pull up descriptions of selected area hotels and a phone that will connect you directly to any of them you choose. Advantage, Alamo, Avis, Budget, Dollar, Enterprise, Hertz, and National all have desks at both of the airport terminals.

Loop 410 and U.S. 281 south intersect just below the airport. If you're renting a car here (see "By Car" in "Getting Around," in chapter 3), it should take about 15 to 20 minutes to drive downtown via U.S. 281 south.

Most of the hotels within a radius of a mile or two offer **free shuttle service** to and from the airport (be sure to check when you make your reservation). If you're staying downtown, you'll most likely have to pay your own way.

VIA Metropolitan Transit's bus no. 2 is the cheapest (75¢) way to get downtown but also the slowest; it'll take from 40 to 45 minutes. (If you have a long layover at the airport, VIA's Loop 550/551 Limited express bus [$1.50] can bring you to the nearby North Star and Central Park malls and let you shop the time away.)

Star Shuttle (☎ 210/341-6000), with a booth at each of the terminals, offers van service from the airport to the downtown hotels for $6 per person. It runs around the clock, but if you're arriving after midnight you'll need to call 24 hours in advance to prearrange pickup.

There's also a cab queue in front of each terminal. The flag-drop charge on taxis is $1.60; add $1.30 for the first and each additional mile. It should cost you about $13 to $15 to get downtown, including the 50¢ airport departure fee; from 9pm to 5am there's an additional $1 after-hours charge.

BY CAR

As has been said of Rome, all roads lead to San Antonio. The city is fed by four interstates (I-35, I-10, I-37, and I-410), five U.S. highways (U.S. 281, U.S. 90, U.S. 87, U.S. 181, and U.S. 81), and five state highways (Hwy. 16, Hwy. 13, Hwy. 211, Hwy. 151, and Hwy. 1604). In San Antonio, I-410 and Hwy. 1604, which circle the city, are referred to as Loop 410 and Loop 1604. All freeways lead into the central business district; U.S. 281 and Loop 410 are closest to the airport.

San Antonio is 975 miles from Atlanta; 1,979 miles from Boston; 1,187 miles from Chicago; 1,342 miles from Los Angeles; 1,360 miles from Miami; 527 miles from New Orleans; 1,781 miles from New York; 1,724 miles from San Francisco; and 2,149 miles from Seattle. The distance to Dallas is 282 miles, to Houston 199 miles, and to Austin 80 miles.

BY TRAIN

The San Antonio **Amtrak** station, 1174 E. Commerce St. (☎ **210/223-3226**), provides service three times a week—east to Miami via Houston, Lafayette, and New Orleans and west to Los Angeles via El Paso and Tucson. There is also thrice-weekly service between San Antonio and Chicago via Austin, Fort Worth, Dallas, Little Rock, St. Louis, and Springfield. Call **800/872-7245** for current fares, schedules, and reservations. The station is located in St. Paul Square, on the east side of downtown near the Alamodome. You can pick up a public VIA streetcar from here to the major hotel areas; cabs are also available in this area.

BY BUS

San Antonio's **Greyhound** station, 500 N. St. Mary's St. (☎ **210/270-5824**), is located downtown about two blocks from the River Walk; buses come and go from all directions to the busy 24-hour terminal. Look for Greyhound's 14-day advance specials, 3-day advance companion special (if you book a round-trip at least 3 days in advance, a companion rides free), and other promotional discounts. For all current price and schedule information, call **800/231-2222**. The station is within walking distance of a number of hotels, and many public streetcar and bus lines run nearby.

3 Getting to Know San Antonio

For visitors, San Antonio is really two cities. Downtown, site of the original Spanish settlements, is the compact, eminently strollable tourist hub. The River Walk and its waterside development have revitalized a once-decaying urban center that now buzzes with hotels, restaurants, and shops. And thanks in large part to the San Antonio Conservation Society, many of downtown's beautiful old buildings are still intact; some house popular tourist attractions, while others are occupied by the large businesses that are increasingly trickling back to where it all began.

The other city is spread out, mostly low-rise, and connected by freeways—more than its fair share, in fact. San Antonio's most recent growth has been toward the northwest, where you'll find the sprawling South Texas Medical Center complex and, farther out, the ritzy new Dominion Country Club and housing development and the large theme park, Six Flags Fiesta Texas; two new resorts are also planned for this area. The old southeast section, home to four of the five historic missions, remains largely Hispanic, while much of the southwest is taken up by Kelly and Lackland Air Force Bases. Whether you fly in or drive in, you're likely to find yourself in the northeast at some point: Along with the airport, this section hosts the Brackenridge Park attractions and many of the best restaurants and shops in town.

You'll probably want your own wheels if you're staying in this second San Antonio; downtown, where public transportation is cheap and plentiful, a car tends to be more of a hindrance than a help.

1 Orientation

VISITOR INFORMATION

The main office of the **City of San Antonio Visitor Information Center** is across the street from the Alamo, at 317 Alamo Plaza (☎ 210/270-8748). Hours are 8:30am to 6pm daily, except Thanksgiving, Christmas, and New Year's, when the center is closed. Two unstaffed satellite offices with brochures are located in Terminals One and Two of the San Antonio International Airport; they both have phones that will connect you to the main office.

Publications such as the free *Fiesta,* a glossy magazine with interesting articles about the city, and *Rio,* a tabloid focusing on the River

Impressions

We were already almost out of America and yet definitely in it and in the middle of where it's maddest. Hotrods blew by. San Antonio, ah-haa!
—Jack Kerouac, *On the Road* (1955)

Walk, are available at the Visitor Information Center, as well as at most downtown hotels and many shops and tourist sights. Both of these advertising-based tourist publications list sights, restaurants, shops, cultural events, and some nightlife. Also free— and not ad-driven—is San Antonio's alternative paper, the *Current*. It's pretty skimpy, but it's a good source for nightlife listings. Check out the *Current's Visitors Guide to the Alamo City*, published four times a year and available at most River Walk hotels, restaurants, and bars for its offbeat takes on the standard tourist attractions and its suggestions for unusual things to do around town.

Arguably the best state-oriented magazine in the country, *Texas Monthly* contains excellent short reviews of restaurants in San Antonio, among other cities; its incisive articles about local politics, people, and events are a great way to get acquainted with Lone Star territory in general. You can buy a copy at almost any local bookstore or newsstand.

CITY LAYOUT

Although it lies at the southern edge of the Texas Hill Country, San Antonio itself is basically flat. As noted above, the city divides into two distinct districts: a compact central downtown surrounded by a western-style, freeway-laced sprawl. Neither section is laid out in a neat grid system; many of downtown's streets trace the meandering course of the San Antonio River, while a number of the thoroughfares in the rest of town follow old conquistador routes or 19th-century cattle-drive trails.

MAIN ARTERIES & STREETS   Welcome to loop land. Most of the major roads in Texas meet in San Antonio, where they form a rough wheel-and-spoke pattern: I-410 traces a 10- to 15-mile circumference around downtown, and Hwy. 1604 forms an even larger circle around them both. I-35, I-10, I-37, U.S. 281, U.S. 90, and U.S. 87, along with many smaller thoroughfares, run diagonally, but not always separately, across these two loops to form its main spokes. For example, U.S. 90, U.S. 87, and I-10 converge for a while in an east–west direction just south of downtown, while U.S. 281, I-35, and I-37 run together on a north–south route to the east; I-10, I-35, and U.S. 87 bond for a bit going north–south to the west of downtown.

Among the most major of the minor spokes are Broadway, McCullough, San Pedro, and Blanco, all of which lead north from the city center into the most popular shopping and restaurant areas of town. Fredericksburg goes out to the Medical Center from just northwest of downtown. When locals refer to the Strip, they mean the stretch of North St. Mary's between Josephine and Magnolia, known for its nightlife.

Downtown is bounded by I-37 on the east, I-35 on the north and west, and U.S. 90 on the south. Within these parameters, Commerce, Market, and Houston are important east–west thoroughfares. Alamo and Santa Rosa are major north–south streets, the former on the east side, the latter on the west side.

FINDING AN ADDRESS   Few locals are aware that there's any method to the madness of finding downtown addresses, but in fact directions are based on the layout of the first Spanish settlements, when the San Fernando cathedral was at the center of town: Market is the north–south street divider and Flores separates the east from the west. Thus, South St. Mary's becomes North St. Mary's when it crosses Market, where the addresses start from zero in both directions. North of downtown, San Pedro is the east–west dividing line, although not every street sign reflects this fact.

There are few such clear-cut rules in loop land, but on its northernmost stretch, Loop 410 divides into east and west at Broadway; at Bandera Road, it splits into Loop 410 north and south. Keep going far enough south and I-35 marks yet another boundary between east and west. Knowing this will help a little in locating an address, and will explain why, when you go in a circle around town—you probably won't do this voluntarily—you'll notice that the directions marked on overhead signs have suddenly shifted.

STREET MAPS   The Visitor Information Center (see "Visitor Information," above) and most hotels distribute the free street maps published by the San Antonio Convention and Visitors Bureau (SACVB). They mark the main attractions in town and are useful enough as a general reference, especially if you're on foot; they even indicate which downtown streets are one-way—a bonus for drivers. You Are Here, a San Antonio company, publishes a color souvenir map of downtown that's less distorted and more detailed than the SACVB's map; you can pick one up at Booksmiths, 209 Alamo Plaza, or Alamo News, 511 E. Houston St. But if you're going to do much navigating around town, you'll need something better. Both Rand McNally and Gousha's maps of San Antonio are reliable; you'll find one or the other at most convenience stores, drugstores, bookstores, and newsstands.

NEIGHBORHOODS IN BRIEF

Downtown   Site of San Antonio's three oldest Spanish settlements, this area includes the Alamo and other historic sites, along with the River Walk, the Alamodome, the convention center, the Rivercenter Mall, and many high-rise hotels, restaurants, and shops. It's also the center of commerce and law; many banks and offices, as well as most government buildings, are located here. Once seedy and largely deserted at night, it has rebounded with a vengeance—the recent proliferation of bars and clubs catering to younger crowds resulted in a 1996 city ordinance restraining the volume of outdoor noise.

King William   The city's first suburb, this historic district directly south of downtown was settled in the mid- to late 1800s by wealthy German merchants who built some of the most beautiful mansions in town. It began to be yuppified in the 1970s and, at this point, you'd never guess it had ever been allowed to deteriorate. Only two of the area's many impeccably restored homes are generally open to the public, but a number have been turned into bed-and-breakfasts.

Southtown   Alamo Street marks a rough border between King William and Southtown, the adjoining commercial district. Long a depressed area, it's now becoming trendy, thanks to a Main Street refurbishing project and the opening of the Blue Star arts complex. You'll find a nice mix of Hispanic neighborhood shops and funky coffeehouses and galleries here.

Monte Vista   Immediately northwest of downtown, Monte Vista was established soon after King William by a conglomeration of wealthy cattlemen, politicos, and generals who moved "on to the hill" at the turn of the century. A number of the area's large houses have been split into apartments for students of nearby Trinity University and San Antonio Community College, but many lovely old homes have been restored in the past 20 years. This is still a somewhat transitional area, but quickly heading upscale.

Fort Sam Houston   Built in 1876 to the northeast of downtown, Fort Sam Houston hosts a number of stunning officers' homes. Much of the working-class neighborhood surrounding Fort Sam is now run-down, but renewed interest in restoring San Antonio's older areas is beginning to have some impact here, too.

Alamo Heights Area   In the 1890s, when construction in the area began, Alamo Heights was at the far northern reaches of San Antonio. It has slowly evolved into one of the city's most exclusive neighborhoods, and is now home to wealthy families, expensive shops, and trendy restaurants. Terrell Hills to the east, Olmos Park to the west, and Lincoln Heights to the north are all offshoots of this moneyed area; the latter is home to the Quarry, once just that but now a ritzy golf course. The greater portion of these neighborhoods share a single zip code ending in the numbers "09"— thus the local term "09ers," referring to the area's yuppie residents.

Medical Center   The characterless neighborhood surrounding the South Texas Medical Center—host to the majority of San Antonio's hospitals and medical facilities, including the University of Texas Health Science Center—is one of the more recently established. Most of the homes are condominiums and apartments, and most of the shopping and dining is in strip malls.

Far Northwest   In the next few years, two high-end resort hotels, one of them a Westin, will join The Dominion, an exclusive residential enclave, and La Cantera, a toney new golf course, in the far northwest part of town. This area, just beyond Six Flags Fiesta Texas and near the public Friederich Park, promises to be San Antonio's next prime growth area.

2 Getting Around

BY PUBLIC TRANSPORTATION

BY BUS   San Antonio's public transportation system is visitor friendly; though prices have gone up a lot in recent years, they're still reasonable. Among the 99 regular bus routes that **VIA Metropolitan Transit Service** runs around town is no. 7/40, the VIA Vistras Cultural route, which stops at many popular tourist attractions: the McNay Art Museum, the San Antonio Botanical Gardens, the San Antonio Zoo, the Witte Museum, the San Antonio Museum of Art, Alamo Plaza, La Villita, HemisFair Park, the King William Historic District, the Yturri-Edmunds House and Mill, the Buckhorn Museums and Bar, and San Antonio Missions National Historical Park. The cost is 75¢ for regular routes (including the cultural one), with an additional 10¢ charge for transfers, and $1.50 for express buses (10¢ for transfers); call **210/227-2020** for transit information or stop in at VIA's downtown center, 112 N. Soledad; it's open Monday through Friday from 7am to 6pm, Saturday 8am to 5pm.

BY STREETCAR   In addition to its bus lines, VIA offers four convenient downtown streetcar routes that cover all the most popular tourist stops. Designed to look like the turn-of-the-century trolleys used in San Antonio until 1933, the streetcars cost 50¢.

DISCOUNT PASSES   A $4 day-tripper pass, good for an entire day of travel on all VIA transportation except express buses, can be purchased at VIA's downtown Information Center. Seniors (62 and over) can get a discount card at this office or at two other VIA offices: 800 W. Myrtle (☎ **210/227-5371**) and the Crossroads Park and Ride in the Crossroads Mall parking lot (☎ **210/735-3317**). It's necessary to go in person with proof of age and a Social Security card; the picture ID that you'll receive on the spot will entitle you to half off all VIA fares, except the day-tripper pass.

BY CAR

One bit of advice about driving downtown: Unless you're familiar with the pattern of one-way streets and with the locations of the area's limited public parking—don't. It's not that the streets in downtown San Antonio are narrower or more crowded than those in most city centers; it's just that there's no need to bother when public transportation is so convenient.

As for highway driving, because of the many convergences of major freeways here—described in the "Main Arteries & Streets" section, above—if you're not constantly vigilant, you'll find yourself in the express lane to somewhere you really don't want to go. Don't let your mind wander; watch the signs carefully and be prepared to make lots of quick lane changes.

Rush hour lasts from about 7:45am to 9am and 4:30pm to 6pm Monday through Friday. It's best to avoid the I-10/Loop 410 interchange on the northwest side of town during this time, and all parts of I-35 and U.S. 281 north of downtown. (A good alternative route for U.S. 281 north is San Pedro.) San Antonio's rush hour may not be bad compared with those of Houston or Dallas, but it's getting worse all the time. Because of San Antonio's rapid growth, you can also expect to find major highway construction or repairs going on somewhere in the city at any given time.

RENTALS   **Advantage** (☎ 800/777-5500), **Alamo** (☎ 800/327-9633), **Avis** (☎ 800/831-2847), **Budget** (☎ 800/527-0700), **Dollar** (☎ 800/800-4000), **Enterprise** (☎ 800/325-8007), **Hertz** (☎ 800/654-3131), and **National** (☎ 800/ 227-7368) all have desks at both of the airport terminals. Hertz is also represented downtown at the Marriott Rivercenter at Bowie and Commerce (☎ 210/225-3676).

Almost all of the major car-rental companies have their own discount programs. Your rate will often depend on the organizations to which you belong, the dates of travel, and the length of your stay. Some companies give discounts to AAA members, for example, and some have special deals in conjunction with various airlines or telephone companies. Off-season rates are likely to be lower, and prices are sometimes reduced on weekends (or midweek). Call as far in advance as possible to book a car, and always ask about specials.

In case you were wondering—yes, the Alamo car-rental company got its start in San Antonio.

PARKING   Parking meters are not plentiful in the heart of downtown, though you can find some on the streets near the River Walk and on Broadway. The cost is 25¢ every half hour and the time limit is 1 hour; some meters also accept smaller change— a dime for every 12 minutes or a nickel for 6 minutes. There are some very inexpensive (1¹/₂ hours for a quarter) meters at the outskirts of town; the trick is to find one. Though too few signs inform you of this, parking next to meters is free after 6pm on Monday through Saturday and all day Sunday, except during Alamodome events, at which time meters are enforced. If you don't observe the laws, you'll be ticketed pretty quickly.

Except during Fiesta or other major events, you shouldn't have a problem finding a parking lot or garage for your car; rates run from $3 to $6 per day—the closer you get to the Alamo and the River Walk, the more expensive they become. Prices tend to go up during special events and summer weekends; a parking lot that ordinarily charges $3.50 a day is likely to charge $5. If you're only staying for a short time, consider leaving your car in the Rivercenter Mall garage and getting your ticket validated at one of the shops; you don't have to buy anything and you'll have 2 hours of free parking. This is only a good idea, however, if you're allergic to shopping or have an iron will; otherwise, this could end up costing you a lot more in the long run than a pay parking garage.

DRIVING RULES   Right turns on red are permitted after a full stop. Left turns on red are also allowed, but only if you're going from a one-way street onto another one-way street.

BY TAXI

Cabs are available outside the airport, near the Greyhound and Amtrak terminals, and at most major downtown hotels, but they're next to impossible to hail on the street; most of the time, you'll need to phone for one in advance. The best of the major taxi companies in town is **Checker Cab** (☎ 210/222-2151), which has an excellent record of turning up when promised. **Yellow Cab** (☎ 210/226-4242) is a reasonable alternative. See "By Plane" in the "Getting There" section of chapter 2 for rates. Most cabbies impose a minimum of $6 for trips from the airport, $3 for rides downtown.

ON FOOT

Downtown San Antonio is a treat for walkers, who can perambulate from one tourist attraction to another, or stroll along a beautifully landscaped river. Traffic lights even stay green long enough for pedestrians to cross without putting their lives in peril. Jaywalking is a ticketable offense, but one that's rarely enforced.

FAST FACTS: San Antonio

Airport   See "Getting There," in chapter 2.

American Express   8103 Broadway (☎ 210/828-4809).

Area Code   The telephone area code in San Antonio is **210.**

Baby-sitters   Your hotel should be able to recommend a reliable service.

Business Hours   Banks are usually open Monday through Friday from 9am to 6pm; most also have hours on Saturday from 9am to 1pm. Office hours are generally weekdays from 9am to 5pm. Shops tend to be open from 9 or 10am until 5:30 or 6pm on Monday through Saturday, with shorter hours on Sunday, but many downtown stores don't close their doors until dark or later in summer. Most malls are open Monday through Saturday from 10am to 9pm, Sunday from noon to 6pm. The majority of bars and clubs boot their last customers out at 2am.

Camera Repair   Havel Camera Service, 1102 Basse Rd. (☎ 210/735-7412), a reputable camera dealer and repair shop, is about 15 minutes north of downtown.

Car Rentals   See "Getting Around," earlier in this chapter.

Climate   See "When to Go," in chapter 2.

Dentist   To find a dentist near you in town, contact the San Antonio District Dental Society, 202 W. French Place (☎ 210/732-1264).

Doctor   For a referral, contact the Béxar County Medical Society at 202 W. French Place (☎ 210/734-6691).

Driving Rules   See "Getting Around," earlier in this chapter.

Drugstores   See "Pharmacies," below.

Embassies/Consulates   See "Fast Facts: For the Foreign Traveler," in the Appendix.

Emergencies   For police, fire, or medical emergencies, dial **911**. The Sheriff's Department number is 210/270-6000, and Texas Highway Patrol can be reached at 210/533-9171.

Eyeglass Repair   Downtown, Texas State Optical (TSO), 327 W. Commerce St. (☎ **210/227-4229**), is a trusted name for glasses. Near the airport, Eye Mart, 13417 San Pedro Ave. (☎ **210/496-6549**), offers quick and friendly service.

Hospitals   The main downtown hospital is Baptist Medical Center, 111 Dallas St. (☎ **210/222-8431**); Work Plus River Walk Clinic, 408 Navaro (☎ **210/ 271-1841**), and Santa Rosa Health Care Corp., 509 W. Houston (☎ **210/ 704-2011**), are also downtown. Contact the San Antonio Medical Foundation (☎ **210/614-3724**) for information on other facilities.

Hot Lines   A complete menu for the IT Network (☎ **210/ 524-4600**), an automated information hot line, can be found in the front of the local telephone directory and in various newspapers.

Information   See "Visitor Information," earlier in this chapter.

Libraries   In 1995, San Antonio opened its magnificent new main library at 600 Soledad Plaza (☎ **210/207-2500**); see "More Attractions" in chapter 6 for details.

Liquor Laws   The legal drinking age in Texas is 21. Underage drinkers can legally imbibe as long as they stay within sight of their legal-age spouses or parents; they need to be prepared to show proof of the relationship, however. Open containers are prohibited in public and in vehicles. Liquor laws are strictly enforced.

Lost Property   Airport (☎ **210/821-3527**); bus station (☎ **210/270-5826**).

Luggage Storage/Lockers   There are lockers at both airport terminals as well as at the Greyhound Bus Station and the Amtrak station.

Maps   See "City Layout," earlier in this chapter.

Newspapers/Magazines   Since 1993, when the Hearst Corporation, owner of the *San Antonio Express-News,* bought the competing *San Antonio Light* and shut it down, the *Express* has been the only mainstream source of news in town. See "Visitor Information," above, for magazine recommendations.

Pharmacies (Late-Night)   Most branches of Eckerd and Walgreens, the major chain pharmacies in San Antonio, are open late Monday through Saturday. There's an Eckerd downtown at 211 Losoya/River Walk (☎ **210/224-9293**). Call **800/ 925-4733** to find the Walgreens nearest you.

Police   The Sheriff's Department can be reached at **210/270-6000;** the Texas Highway Patrol at **210/533-9171**. Call **911** in an emergency.

Post Office   The main post office is at the far northeast part of town at 10410 Perrin-Beitel (☎ **210/650-1630**), but the most convenient location is downtown at 615 E. Houston St., just across from the Alamo (☎ **210/227-3399**).

Radio   You should be able to find something to suit your radio tastes in San Antonio. KISS at 99.5 FM plays heavy rock; KZEP at 104.5 FM, classic rock; KJ97 at 97.1 FM, country; KSMG at 105.3 FM, oldies. KSYM at 90.1 FM is the only college alternative station in south Texas. For Tejano music, tune in to KXTN at 107.1 FM. You'll find National Public Radio and some jazz and classical music on KSTX at 89.1 FM; KTSA 550 on the AM dial is a news/talk radio station.

Restrooms   You can use the restrooms downtown at the Rivercenter Mall or you can duck into any of the free tourist attractions (yes, you can go to the bathroom at the Alamo, gratis). Most restaurants don't mind quick visits, either—they never know, you might come back for a meal later on.

Safety   There are frequent police patrols downtown at night; as a result, there are not a lot of muggings, pickpocketings, or purse snatchings in the area. But use common sense, as you would anywhere else: Walk only in well-lit, well-populated streets. It's not a good idea to stroll south of Durango after dark.

Taxes   Sales tax is 7.75%; the city surcharge on hotel rooms comes to a whopping 15%.

Taxis   See "Getting Around," earlier in this chapter.

Television   The local television affiliates are as follows: KMOL on Channel 4, NBC; KENS on Channel 5, CBS; KSAT on Channel 12, ABC; KLRN on Channel 9, PBS. FOX 35 on Channel 35 is the Fox network.

Time Zone   San Antonio is on central daylight time and observes daylight saving time.

Transit Information   ☎ 210/227-2020.

Weather   ☎ 210/609-2029.

4 San Antonio Accommodations

You don't have to leave your lodgings to sightsee in San Antonio: The city has the highest concentration of historic hotels in Texas. Most of these, as well as other, more recently built luxury accommodations, are in the downtown area, which is where you'll likely want to be whether you're here on pleasure or convention business. Prices in this prime location can be high, especially for hotels on the river, but you'll generally get your money's worth. You'll also economize by eliminating the need to rent a car: Most of the tourist attractions are within walking distance or easily accessible by public transportation, and many of the best restaurants are only an inexpensive cab ride from downtown.

In recent years, a number of the old mansions in the King William and Monte Vista Historic Districts have been converted into bed-and-breakfasts; some are reviewed in this chapter. Assume that your room will have a private bath unless we say otherwise. For information about additional bed-and-breakfasts in these areas and in other neighborhoods around the city, contact **Bed & Breakfast Hosts of San Antonio,** P.O. Box 831203, San Antonio, TX 78283 (☎ **800/356-1605** or 210/824-8036 for reservations; fax 210/824-9926), or the **San Antonio Bed & Breakfast Association,** P.O. Box 830101, San Antonio, TX 78283 (☎ **800/210-8422** or 210/212-8422).

Spurred by the success of the Hyatt Regency Hill Country Resort, new destination resorts are being planned for the far northwest side of town. The luxurious 500-room Westin hotel will be part of the 1,600-acre, multiuse La Cantera community, which opened a popular new golf club in 1995; it's scheduled for completion in 1998.

Areas around town where moderately priced and inexpensive chain lodgings are concentrated are included in the listings that follow; the pricier or more distinctive properties in these sections are reviewed fully, while the more familiar standardized hotels or motels are noted in brief.

Wherever you decide to stay, but especially if it's downtown, try to book as far in advance as possible. And don't even think about coming to town during Fiesta (the third week in April) if you haven't reserved a room 6 months in advance.

The annual SAVE (San Antonio Vacation Experience) promotion, sponsored by local businesses, the San Antonio Convention and Visitors Bureau, and American Express, includes discounts on hotel rooms as well as on dining and entertainment; call **800/447-3372** to request a packet. Some bed-and-breakfasts and hotels offer better rates to those who book for at least 4 days, but generally a week is the minimum. Although most leisure travelers visit in summer, rooms are generally less expensive then; rates are highest from November through April, when the conventions come to town. Even in peak season, ask the hotel you're interested in when they have their lowest rates—some hotels in San Antonio do most of their business with conventions during the week, whereas others cater to tourists who come on the weekend.

Hotels included in the **Very Expensive** price category officially list their rooms for more than $170 per night for a double room during high season; **Expensive** hotels range from $120 to $170 for a double; **Moderate** hotels go from $80 to $120; and **Inexpensive** rooms cost less than $80. Don't be put off from a place because of these rough price categories, though; even in prime season, many hotels offer much lower prices when they're not fully booked. Unless otherwise specified, rates do not include the 15% room tax.

1 Best Bets

- **Best Historic Hotel:** Who can resist a place that's right across the street from the Alamo and still has the bar where Teddy Roosevelt recruited his Rough Riders? A 19th-century gem, the **Menger** (☎ **800/345-9285** or 210/223-4361) sparkles now as it did 100 years ago.
- **Best for Business Travelers:** The **Airport Hilton** (☎ **800-HILTONS** or 210/340-6060) offers a convenient location, data ports, a lubricate-those-business-deals sports bar, and an extremely helpful business center staff.
- **Best for Families:** If you can afford it, the **Hyatt Regency Hill Country Resort** (☎ **800/233-1234** or 210/647-1234), just down the road from Sea World, is ideal for a family getaway. Kids get to splash in their own shallow pool and go tubing on a little river; there are plenty of sophisticated play spots for grown-ups, too.
- **Best Moderately Priced Hotel:** The **Ramada Emily Morgan** (☎ **800/824-6674** or 210/225-8486) is a boon to those who want to stay downtown without paying downtown prices. Its location and amenities match those of far more expensive lodgings, and it's even in a historic building.
- **Best Budget Lodging:** If you don't mind sharing a bath, you can't beat the rates at **Bullis House Inn** (☎ **210/223-9426**), a bed-and-breakfast in a historic home near Fort Sam Houston. Two rooms with private baths are also available, and the possibility of seeing Geronimo's ghost is an added bonus.
- **Best B&B:** The King William area abounds with B&Bs, but the **Ogé House** (☎ **800/242-2770** or 210/223-2353) stands out as much for its professionalism as for its gorgeous mansion and lovely rooms. You don't have to sacrifice service for warmth here.
- **Best Health Club:** Not only does the health club at the **Marriott Rivercenter** (☎ **800/228-9290** or 210/223-1000) have the best weight machines and cardiovascular equipment of all the downtown luxury properties, but it's on the same floor as free washers and dryers. You can hop on the treadmill while your clothes are in the spin cycle.
- **Best Place to Soak in Some History While Sweating:** While not as extensive as that at the Marriott, the health club in the **Plaza San Antonio** (☎ **800/421-1172** or 210/229-1000), located in a stone building dating back to the 19th century, may be the most historic setting for StairMasters anywhere in the city.

- **Best Place to Spot Celebrities:** Everyone from Barbara Bush to ZZ Top has stayed at **La Mansión del Rio** (☎ **800/292-7300** or 210/225-2581); discretion, a willingness to cater to special requests, and a location that's just slightly away from the action may explain why.

- **Best Chance of Seeing the River from Your Room:** As their names attest, La Mansión del Rio, the Hyatt Regency on the River Walk, the Marriott Rivercenter, and the Holiday Inn Riverwalk all have rooms that look out on the water, but the **Hilton Palacio del Rio** (☎ **800/HILTONS** or 210/222-1400) offers the highest number of accommodations with river views. Stay here and you can people-watch one of the most bustling sections of the promenade without bumping into anyone.

2 Downtown

VERY EXPENSIVE

✪ Fairmount Hotel

401 S. Alamo St., San Antonio, TX 78205. ☎ **800/642-3363** or 210/224-8800. Fax 210/224-2767. 20 rms, 17 suites. A/C TV/VCR TEL. $165–$200 double; $225–$475 suite. Corporate rates, packages available. AE, DC, MC, V. Valet parking $8.

This lovely boutique hotel, built in an ornate Italianate-Victorian style in 1906, is across the street from HemisFair Park, adjacent to La Villita, and within walking distance of the King William Historic District—but it wasn't always. In 1985, it was hoisted six blocks across town, earning it a place in the Guinness Book of World Records as the heaviest building ever moved. Excavations of the site on which it now sits uncovered artifacts from the battle at the Alamo; some are showcased in the building's lobby.

The Fairmount once lodged railway travelers, but today's clientele is more likely to jet in; the hotel is sought out by film stars and other celebrities looking for low-key but luxurious digs. The hotel's intimate size, along with richly carpeted corridors and small parlors, makes it seem like the home of a rich—and very attentive—friend. The suites are naturally the largest rooms—some have hardwood floors, wet bars, skylights, Jacuzzi tubs, or combinations thereof—but even the so-called standard rooms are outstanding. All are individually decorated in muted southwestern tones, with rich wood furniture (some in Craftsman style), TVs with VCRs, live plants, and original artwork, and all have balconies overlooking the city or a small central courtyard. Italian marble and brass gleam in the bathrooms, which boast toney Lord & Mayfair toiletries along with makeup mirrors, hair dryers, and monogrammed terry robes.

Dining/Entertainment: You can enjoy the soft strains of a jazz piano at the Polo bar, a cushy, dimly lit room where deals are closed over single-malt scotches and romantic liaisons are celebrated with champagne (see chapter 8 for a full listing). Warm smells wafting from the pizza oven may lure folks next door to the elegant Polo's restaurant, which serves some of the most beautifully presented contemporary American food in town (see chapter 5 for details).

Services: 24-hour room service, twice-daily maid service, laundry, dry cleaning, complimentary newspaper, shoe shine service, concierge, film library (free movie rentals).

Hilton Palacio del Rio

200 S. Alamo, San Antonio, TX 78205. ☎ **800/HILTONS** or 210/222-1400. Fax 210/270-0761. 481 rms, 10 suites. A/C TV TEL. $215–$240 double; $375–$525 suite. AE, CB, DC, DISC, MC, V. Self-parking $8; valet parking $18.

Downtown San Antonio Accommodations

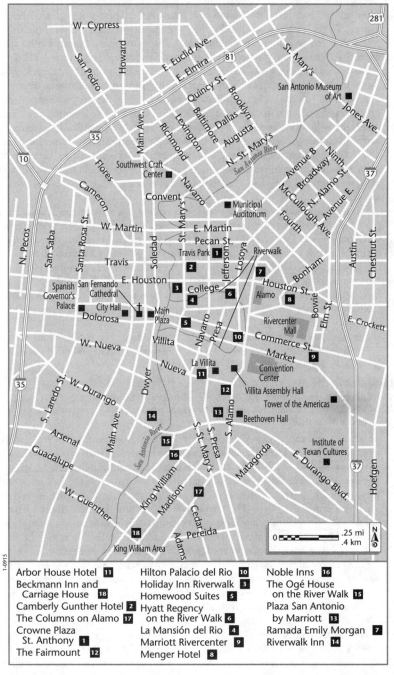

Arbor House Hotel **11**
Beckmann Inn and
  Carriage House **18**
Camberly Gunther Hotel **2**
The Columns on Alamo **17**
Crowne Plaza
  St. Anthony **1**
The Fairmount **12**

Hilton Palacio del Rio **10**
Holiday Inn Riverwalk **3**
Homewood Suites **5**
Hyatt Regency
  on the River Walk **6**
La Mansión del Rio **4**
Marriott Rivercenter **9**
Menger Hotel **8**

Noble Inns **16**
The Ogé House
  on the River Walk **15**
Plaza San Antonio
  by Marriott **13**
Ramada Emily Morgan **7**
Riverwalk Inn **14**

Although relatively new, the Hilton has already earned a footnote in San Antonio history. To get it finished in time for the 1968 HemisFair, the hotel was built using precast concrete modules: 500 fully furnished, 35-ton rooms were hoisted into a steel frame. The whole thing was designed, completed, and occupied in a record 202 days.

Inside this miracle of modern construction, the decor is European elegant, with more-than-passing nods to the Southwest: Polished parquet floors, oriental rugs, and a grand piano rub elbows in the hotel lobby with Mexican tile, sink-into-me leather couches, and a beautiful hand-tooled saddle. Guest rooms are done in traditional rich tones and dark woods, with lovely tapestry chairs and foot rests. All have balconies—half with city views, half with river views—and impressive standard amenities: hair dryers, coffeemakers, and irons and ironing boards. In addition, Tower Level guests get newspapers, mineral water, bathroom scales, and bathrobes in their rooms, and enjoy a continental breakfast, afternoon tea, and evening hors d'oeuvres in a private lounge.

Dining/Entertainment: All of the Hilton's dining and entertainment areas have plum locations either on or overlooking the river. The Rincón Alegre is your standard lobby piano lounge with a twist—the gleaming rosewood instrument plays itself. Ibiza, with its colorful Matisse-style cutouts, has a snazzy Mediterranean menu that matches its decor. Tex's sports bar, with its multiple TV and local team memorabilia, was so successful at the airport Hilton that a River Walk version was opened here. Most fun of all is Durty Nelly's Irish Pub, where you can throw your peanut shells on the floor and join in some seriously soppy sing-alongs (see chapter 8 for details).

Services: Room service, valet laundry and dry cleaning, free coffee in lobby.

Facilities: Outdoor heated pool, hot tub, fitness room, airline and car-rental desks, complimentary washer/dryer.

La Mansión del Rio

112 College St., San Antonio, TX 78205. ☎ **800/292-7300** or 210/225-2581. Fax 210/226-0389. 327 rms, 10 suites. A/C TV TEL. $190–$260 double; $430–$1,500 suite. AE, CB, DC, DISC, MC, V. Valet parking $12.

This lushly landscaped Spanish hacienda–style hotel, converted from a 19th-century seminary in 1968 to meet the city's room needs for the HemisFair exposition, fronts the Paseo del Rio and is down the block from the beautifully restored Majestic Theater. Moorish arches, Mexican tile, a central patio, wrought-iron balconies, and antique pieces in every nook and cranny combine to create a low-glitz, high-tone Mediterranean atmosphere. The layout is maze-like and the place doesn't have a health club, but discretion, a willingness to cater to special requests—say, a room just for shoes booked by a Middle Eastern sheik—and a location that's just slightly away from the action make this the hotel of choice for visiting high-profiles.

Guest rooms all have rough-hewn beamed ceilings, brick walls, and soothing earth-tone furnishings; luxurious touches include cotton robes and complimentary newspapers. The more expensive quarters boast balconies overlooking the River Walk, but the interior courtyard views are fine, too. Standard rooms have minibars, while suites offer wet bars and dining areas.

Dining/Entertainment: The hotel's upscale dining room, Las Canarias, serves up a terrific river view with its excellent American regional cuisine; cocktails can be enjoyed in an adjoining garden courtyard. The restaurant offers entertainment nightly and a romantic Champagne Sunday Brunch. Capistrano, which looks out on the pool and courtyard, is for those seeking more casual Mexican and American fare. The El Colegio piano bar, located in the lobby, boasts a cozy fireplace.

Services: 24-hour room service, express checkout, concierge.
Facilities: Outdoor pool, gift shop.

Marriott Rivercenter

101 Bowie St., San Antonio, TX 78205. ☎ **800/228-9290** or 210/223-1000. Fax 210/223-4092. 1,000 rms, 86 suites. A/C TV TEL. $205 double; $229–$900 suite. AE, DC, DISC, MC, V. Self-parking $9; valet parking $12.

Serious retail hounds will find heaven in this glitzy high-rise; they can shop more than 100 Rivercenter emporiums until they're ready to drop and then collapse back into their hotel rooms without ever leaving the mall. Sightseers will be happy here, too; a cruise along the River Walk departs from the mall's downstairs "dock," and the Alamo and HemisFair Park are just a few blocks away.

Convenience is definitely the goal here—facilities include transportation desks, a good range of dining-and-drinking areas, a large indoor/outdoor pool, and an extremely well-equipped exercise center with free weights, weight machines, stair climbers, bicycles, and treadmills. Free washers and dryers on the same floor as the health club and pool let you work out while you're waiting for the rinse cycle to finish. Well-appointed guest rooms are contemporary but elegant in muted pastel tones; many afford spectacular River Walk or city views. Those staying on the concierge level receive upgraded amenities, a free continental breakfast, and afternoon hors d'oeuvres in a concierge lounge. If you find all this convenience a bit overwhelming, an option is to stay at the smaller Marriott River Walk across the street. This slightly older and slightly less expensive sister hotel has equally comfortable rooms, and its guests have access to all the facilities of the Rivercenter.

Dining/Entertainment: The casual, plant-filled Garden Cafe is open for breakfast (including a buffet), lunch, and dinner; it's adjacent to J. W. Steakhouse, the hotel's fine dining room, where surf and turf rule. The Lobby Bar and the multilevel Atrium Lounge serve drinks and light fare. Guests at the Rivercenter can also charge any meals and drinks they have at the five restaurants and lounges in the Marriott River Walk to their rooms.

Services: 24-hour room service, valet laundry service, secretarial services, baby-sitting, doctor (24-hour call).

Facilities: Gift shops, airline-reservation desk, car-rental desk, separate men's and women's saunas, Jacuzzi.

EXPENSIVE

Camberly Gunther Hotel

205 E. Houston St., San Antonio, TX 78205. ☎ **800/325-3535** or 210/227-3241. Fax 210/227-3241. 322 rms, 10 suites. A/C TV TEL. $145 double; $200–$800 suite. AE, CB, DC, DISC, MC, V. Valet parking $9.

Western stars Will Rogers, John Wayne, and Tom Mix all trod the polished marble halls of this opulent hotel—in dusty, beat-up cowboy boots, one likes to imagine. The first steel structure in San Antonio when it was built in 1909, the Gunther had its posh tone restored in the early 1980s with crystal chandeliers, potted palms, ornate plaster ceiling casts, and rich mahogany fittings. Resting on the site of an even earlier series of hotels and military headquarters, the first one established in 1837 (ask at the front desk for a historical pamphlet), the hotel is a stone's throw from the Majestic Theater and close to the River Walk.

A $5 million renovation by new owners (this was a Sheraton for many years), started in November 1996, spiffed up the lobby and restyled all the guest rooms in a "cattleman" motif, with bold southwestern reds and golds. Standard amenities include data-port phones with voice mail, in-room coffeemakers, and irons. For guests staying on the Executive Level, rooms come wtih hair dryers, concierge service is provided, and two executive lounges serve a continental breakfast buffet spread in the morning and complimentary hors d'oeuvres and drinks in the evening.

Dining/Entertainment: Lots of local business folk come to the bilevel, glass-and-brass Upper Muldoon's to take advantage of the lunch buffet. Breakfast, lunch, and dinner are served at the turn-of-the-century-style Cafe, which also includes a deli and wonderful European bakery.

Services: Room service, valet laundry and dry cleaning.

Facilities: Outdoor pool, sundeck, exercise room, gift shop, barber shop, video arcade.

Crowne Plaza St. Anthony

300 E. Travis, San Antonio, TX 78204. ☎ **800/227-6963** or 210/227-4392. Fax 210/227-0915. 308 rms, 42 suites. A/C TV TEL. $140–$152 double; $250–$275 suite. Lower rates/breakfast packages on weekends. Self-parking $8; valet parking $11.

The place to stay when it opened in 1909, the St. Anthony's retains much of its old polish: The lobby is resplendent with crystal chandeliers, thick area rugs set on gleaming marble floors, and ornate French Provincial–style furnishings. The hotel also has a nice—if no longer quite central—location, just across from pretty Travis Park and only a few blocks from the River Walk. Fully carpeted guest rooms, done in rose or beige tones with floral prints and European dark-wood furnishings, have an old-world appeal.

Although the hotel tends to cater more to conventioneers than socialites these days, and the original 1909 tiles in the upstairs hall areas look a little tired (historic landmark status means no changes are allowed), service remains top-notch.

Dining/Entertainment: The informal first-floor Cafe serves breakfast, lunch, and dinner; at a lunchtime pasta bar, you can get noodles topped with a variety of cooked-to-order ingredients such as fresh vegetables. Pete's Pub is dark and Victorian style; drinks are also available at the Loggia, a lighter lobby area looking out on Travis Park.

Services: Room service, valet service, laundry service.

Facilities: Pool, sundeck, exercise room, gift shop.

Holiday Inn Riverwalk

217 N. St. Mary's St., San Antonio, TX 78205. ☎ **800/465-4329** or 210/224-2500. Fax 210/226-0154. 303 rms, 10 suites. A/C TV TEL. $125–$139 double; $175–$275 suite. AE, CB, DC, DISC, MC, V. Self-parking $5; valet parking $7.

This luxurious link in the Holiday Inn chain may not have the name-drop cachet of some of the historical hotels nearby, but it does offer a River Walk location and many of the same amenities for a much lower price. The hotel looks out on a quiet stretch of the river, but it's just a few minutes' walk from all the action.

Fairly standard and boxy from the outside, this high-rise opens into a plush lobby with lots of plants, comfortable chairs, and polished tile. Guest rooms are done in attractive contemporary style, and almost all of them have balconies; those looking out onto the river are slightly more expensive than those that overlook the city, although the urban vistas can be stunning at night, especially from the higher floors. Suites offer hair dryers, coffeemakers, and minirefrigerators.

Dining/Entertainment: The three-level Fandangos Restaurant serves up a spectacular view of the river with its fairly standard American cuisine; it's open for three meals daily and offers breakfast-and-lunch buffets during the week. Live music—everything from country to classical to pop—fills the Ripples Lounge every evening. A few of the tables peek over onto the river.

Services: Room service, nonsmoking rooms, wheelchair-accessible rooms.
Facilities: Outdoor heated pool, whirlpool, exercise room, gift shop.

Homewood Suites

432 Market St., San Antonio, TX 78205. ☎ **800/CALL-HOME** or 210/222-1515. Fax 210/222-1575; e-mail 73041.1111@compuserve.com. 146 suites. A/C TV TEL. $119–$159 suite. Rates lower during the week. AE, CB, DC, DISC, MC, V. Valet parking $10.

Opened in 1996 in the former San Antonio Drug Company building (1919), this all-suites hotel is a nice addition to downtown's accommodations. Located on a quiet stretch of the river, it's convenient to west side attractions such as Market Square and only a few extra blocks from the Alamo. In-room amenities such as microwave ovens, refrigerators with icemakers, dishwashers, and coffeemakers appeal to business travelers and families alike; the dining area can double as a workspace, and there's a sleeper sofa in each suite as well as two TVs equipped with VCRs. The decor is a cut above that of most chains, with Lone Star–design headboards, light wood desks and bureaus, and attractive southwestern bedspreads and drapes. Two suites feature river views.

Services: Free continental breakfast, complimentary downtown transportation via Trans Trolley passes.

Facilities: Heated rooftop pool and whirlpool, exercise room, guest laundry, business center.

Hyatt Regency on the River Walk

123 Losoya St., San Antonio, TX 78205. ☎ **800/233-1234** or 210/222-1234. Fax 210/227-4925. 604 rms, 27 suites. A/C MINIBAR TV TEL. $135–$229 double; $265–$725 suite. AE, CB, DC, DISC, MC, V. Self-parking $8; valet parking $13.

There's something stimulating about all that glass and steel rising from this hotel's lobby, where the Hyatt's signature cage elevators ascend and descend the skylit atrium. Maybe the quality of openness determines the difference between a hotel that's bustling—and this one is, both with business travelers and families who enjoy its convenience to all the downtown attractions—and one that just feels overcrowded. Having an extension of the river running through the lobby adds to the dramatic effect.

Guest rooms, refurbished in 1996, are unusually attractive: They offer light-wood furniture, earth-tone drapes and bedspreads, and live plants. All have excellent standard amenities including hair dryers, ironing boards, and servibars (the latter rather rare in this city). The key to the Gold Passport Floor will get you a slightly larger room with a coffeemaker and a newspaper delivered to your door.

Dining/Entertainment: You won't have a problem satisfying an oral urge in this hotel. On the river level are Dolce Dolce Ice Cream & Espresso Bar; Tropical Drink Co., where the libations come with names like Jamaica Me Crazy; The Landing, long-time home to the Dixieland jazz of Jim Callum and his band (see chapter 8); and Mad Dogs and Englishmen, a British-style pub (if you're wondering why there's Tuesday night Sumo wrestling, it's because the place has a sister restaurant in Hong Kong). On the lobby level, the casual Chaps Restaurant, which serves breakfast, lunch, and dinner, has recently added "cuisine naturelle" selections to its menu, which otherwise offers fairly standard continental fare. Just below it is the multilevel River Terrace lounge.

Services: Room service, valet dry cleaning and laundry service (Mon–Sat), 24-hour currency exchange, express checkout, concierge.

Facilities: Rooftop pool, Jacuzzi, and sundeck; health club; river-level shopping arcade.

✪ Menger Hotel

204 Alamo Plaza, San Antonio, TX 78205. ☎ **800/345-9285** or 210/223-4361. Fax 210/
228-0022. 320 rms, 25 suites. A/C TV TEL. $132 double; $182–$546 suite. Honeymoon packages available. AE, CB, DC, DISC, MC, V. Self-parking $6.95; valet parking $11.

Its location, smack between the Alamo and the Rivercenter Mall and a block from
the River Walk, is perfect. Its history is fascinating. Its public areas, particularly the
Victorian Lobby, are gorgeous. Its guest rooms are charming. And its rates are quite
reasonable. Why would anyone visiting San Antonio want to stay anywhere else but
the Menger?

Indeed, in the late 19th century, no one who was anyone would consider it. A self-guided tour pamphlet of the hotel will take you through halls, ballrooms, and gardens that Ulysses S. Grant, Sarah Bernhardt, and Oscar Wilde walked through.
Robert E. Lee even rode a horse through the hotel. Established in 1859, the Menger
is the only hotel west of the Mississippi that's never closed its doors. It successfully
combined the original, restored building with myriad additions (it now takes up an
entire city block).

Decor in the guest rooms ranges from ornate 19th-century style to modern, but
still characterful—some of the newer rooms have oriental touches, others tasteful
western motifs. Those in the rather plain central section built in 1944 offer kitchenettes and balconies. All have modern amenities. If you want to stay in one of the
antique-filled Victorian rooms, specifically request it when you book.

Dining/Entertainment: The Menger Bar is one of San Antonio's great historic
taverns (see chapter 8 for details). You can also enjoy cocktails in the lobby or at
poolside. The pretty Colonial Room Restaurant offers breakfast-and-lunch buffets
and a southwestern-style menu that includes a number of game specials for dinner.
Be sure to try the mango ice cream: President Clinton liked it so much that he had
hundreds of gallons shipped in for his inauguration. If you don't want a formal breakfast in the morning, nip down the block to the hotel's Blum Street Bake Shop and
pick up some coffee and a buttery pecan roll.

Services: 24-hour room service, valet-laundry and dry-cleaning service, limousine
service.

Facilities: Heated outdoor pool, hot tub, exercise room, Alamo Plaza Spa (facials,
wraps, massage), shopping arcade, tourist information center, game room, gift shop.

Plaza San Antonio by Marriott

555 S. Alamo St., San Antonio, TX 78205. ☎ **800/421-1172** or 210/229-1000. Fax 210/
223-6650. 242 rms, 10 suites. A/C TV TEL. $140–$240 double; suites from $370. AE, CB, DC,
DISC, MC, V. Self-parking $7; valet parking $9.

Pheasants stroll the beautifully landscaped grounds of this gracious hotel, located
across from HemisFair Park, close to La Villita, and just north of the King William
district. Four 19th-century buildings that were saved from HemisFair's bulldozer in
1968 were later incorporated into the Plaza complex. Three are used for intimate conference centers—President Bush, Canadian prime minister Mulrooney, and Mexican
president Salinas held the initialing ceremony for the North American Free Trade
Agreement in one of them—and the fourth houses the hotel's health club.

Service is excellent at this top-notch property; this is a place to come and feel pampered. And carpeted corridors lead to rooms as elegant as you might expect; they're
decorated in muted colors and floral patterns, with antique-style furnishings that include gleaming cherry headboards. Each accommodation offers a plush terry robe,
full-length mirror, snack drawer, and hair dryer. Bottled water and filled ice buckets are left at evening turndown service, and complimentary newspapers are available

in the morning. This is one of the few hotels in town that has tennis courts—not to mention a croquet lawn.

Dining/Entertainment: You can order drinks or snacks at the pool, or enjoy afternoon tea at the Palm Terrace, overlooking the hotel's lovely gardens (light meals are available here during the entire day). The adjacent Lobby Bar offers cappuccino and espresso in addition to cocktails. The full-service Anaqua restaurant is known for its innovative southwestern cuisine and its international Sunday brunch buffet (see Chapter 5 for details).

Services: Twice-daily maid service, 24-hour room service, complimentary shoe shine, complimentary use of bicycles, complimentary limousine to downtown business district Monday through Friday 7:30 to 9:30am, concierge.

Facilities: Health club with men's and women's saunas, swimming pool, Jacuzzi, two night-lit tennis courts, croquet lawn.

MODERATE

Arbor House Hotel

339 South Presa St., San Antonio, TX 78205. ☎ **210/472-2005.** Fax 210/472-2007. 11 suites. A/C TV TEL. $110–$195. Rates include continental breakfast. AE, DISC, MC, V. Free parking.

It's not exactly your standard hotel: Eleven suites with leopard rugs and repainted furniture from Las Vegas's MGM Grand Hotel occupy four adjacent cottages that share a restful backyard with a grape arbor. (The restoration of these homes garnered an award from the San Antonio Conservation Society.) But it's not a bed-and-breakfast either, although a repast of croissants, muffins, and juice arrives outside your door each morning. The personable owners clearly had fun designing the rooms, which include colorful work by a local artist and lots of interesting antiques that they collected over the years; all rooms have refrigerators and coffeemakers. Leisure travelers will like the proximity to the River Walk and La Villita, while business travelers who aren't overly buttoned down will appreciate the closeness to the Convention Center.

Ⓢ Ramada Emily Morgan

705 E. Houston St., San Antonio, TX 78205. ☎ **800/824-6674** or 210/225-8486. Fax 210/225-7227. 154 rms, 11 Executive rms, 12 Plaza rms. A/C TV TEL. $99 double during the week, $115 on weekends; $129 Executive rms; $149 Plaza rms. AE, CB, DC, DISC, MC, V. Self-parking $7.

Remodeled and converted to a hotel to the tune of $17.5 million in 1985, the Ramada Emily Morgan is one of downtown's great bargains. Centrally located directly across Alamo Plaza, it's set in a beautiful 1926 gothic revival building, the first documented skyscraper built west of the Mississippi. It was originally designed as a medical arts center; be sure to look up at the gargoyles, said to have been placed there to help the doctors ward off disease.

Guest rooms are modern, bright, and immaculate; each has a remote-control TV with HBO and pay-per-view movies as well as a hair dryer, coffeemaker, and iron—amenities frequently missing from far more expensive accommodations. In addition, pricier Executive and Plaza rooms offer minirefrigerators and double or single Jacuzzi tubs. Services and facilities include an outdoor pool and whirlpool, exercise room, his-and-her saunas, room service, free coffee in lobby, and concierge.

The lobby hosts the cheerful Yellow Rose Cafe, which features a breakfast-and-lunch buffet and Emily's Oasis Cocktail Lounge, where dinner is served and complimentary hors d'oeuvres are offered during happy hour. In case you were wondering—Emily Morgan, called the "Yellow Rose of Texas," was the mulatto slave mistress of Mexican general Santa Anna; she was reputed to have spied on him for the Texas independence fighters.

A BED & BREAKFAST

Riverwalk Inn

329 Old Guilbeau, San Antonio, TX 78204. ☎ **800/254-4440** or 210/212-8300. Fax 210/229-9422. 10 rms, 1 suite. A/C TV TEL. $89–$145 double; $160 suite. Rates include breakfast. AE, DISC, MC, V.

If you've ever had a hankering to stay in an old log cabin but don't really care to go rustic, consider this unusual bed-and-breakfast. Native Texans Jan and Tracy Hammer had eight 1840s Tennessee cabins taken apart log by log and put back together again near the banks of the San Antonio River, a few blocks south of HemisFair Park and north of the King William area.

Except for a few details—indoor plumbing, individual air-conditioning and heating units, refrigerators, TVs, phones with voice mail, coffeemakers, and digital alarm clocks—everything is in keeping with the original era of the cabins: Each room has a fireplace, quilt, braided rug, and many fascinating primitive antiques. Most rooms also have balconies or porches fronting the river. Fresh-made desserts are served in the parlor every evening, and storytellers come around most weekends to give historical presentations. The wooden plank breakfast table can get a bit crowded on weekend mornings, but that's in keeping with the inn's pioneer spirit—and at least guests don't all have to sleep together in one room.

3 King William Historic District

BED & BREAKFASTS

Beckmann Inn and Carriage House

222 E. Guenther St., San Antonio, TX 78204. ☎ **800/945-1449** or 210/229-1449. Fax 210/229-1061. 3 rms, 2 suites. A/C TV. $90–$110 double; $115–$130 suite. Rates include breakfast. AE, DC, DISC, MC, V. Free parking off street.

Sitting on the lovely wraparound porch of this 1886 Queen Anne home, surrounded by quiet, tree-lined streets on an uncommercialized stretch of the San Antonio River, you can easily imagine yourself in a kinder, gentler era. In fact, you can still see the flour mill on whose property the Beckmann Inn was originally built. Nor will the illusion of time travel be dispelled when you step through the rare Texas red-pine door into the high-ceilinged parlor.

Innkeepers Betty Jo and Don Schwartz filled the house with antique pieces that do justice to the setting, such as the ornately carved Victorian beds in each of the guest rooms. Two of the rooms have private entrances, as does the separate Carriage House, which is decorated in a somewhat lighter fashion. A full breakfast—perhaps stuffed cinnamon french toast with light cream cheese and pecans—is served in the formal dining room, but you can enjoy your coffee on a flower-filled sunporch.

The Columns on Alamo

1037 South Alamo, San Antonio, TX 78210. ☎ **800/233-3364** or 210/271-3245. 10 rms, 1 cottage. A/C TV TEL. $89–120 double; $148 cottage. Extended-stay discounts. Rates include breakfast. AE, MC, V. Free parking.

Guests at this B&B can stay in either the 1892 Greek revival mansion from which the inn derives its name or the adjacent guesthouse, built 9 years later. The former, where the innkeepers live, is slightly more opulent and offers unusual walk-through windows leading to a veranda, but the latter, where most of the rooms are located,

---

🏨 Family-Friendly Hotels

Hyatt Regency Hill Country Resort *(p. 42)*   In addition to its many great places for kids to play (including a beach with a shallow swimming area), this hotel has Camp Hyatt, a special program of excursions, sports, and social activities for children 3 to 12. Rates are $28 for the morning program ($39 with lunch), $28 for the afternoon program (1 to 5pm), and $32 (including dinner) for the evening program (6 to 10pm).

Homewood Suites *(p. 31)*   Downtown's addition of a reasonably priced all-suites hotel, with in-room kitchen facilities and two TVs (each with its own VCR), not to mention a guest laundry, is welcome news for families.

Camberly Gunther Hotel *(p. 29)*   You'd never expect it from the staid old boy, but this hotel has a fairly sizable video arcade tucked away on the downstairs level.

---

affords more privacy to those uncomfortable with the idea of staying in someone else's home. Rooms in both are light, airy, and very pretty, although this is not the place for those allergic to pastels and frills; pink dominates in many of the accommodations and even the darker-toned Imari Room has lace curtains. The inn straddles the boundary between King William and the livelier Southtown. Hosts Ellenor and Arthur Link are extremely helpful, and breakfasts are all you could ask for in morning indulgence. For lunch or dinner, Rosario's, one of the best Mexican restaurants in San Antonio, is right across the street.

✪ Noble Inns

102 Turner St., San Antonio, TX 78204. ☎ **800/221-4045** or 210/225-4045. Fax 210/225-4045. 6 rms, 3 suites. A/C TV TEL. $105–$135 double in the Jackson House; $110–$130 suite in the Pancoast Carriage House. Rates include breakfast. AE, DISC, MC, V. Free parking.

It's hard to imagine that Donald and Liesl Noble, both descended from King William founding families, grew up in the neighborhood when it was run-down; the area has undergone an amazing metamorphosis in the short span of the young couple's life. Indeed their lodgings—the 1894 Jackson House, a traditional-style B&B and, a few blocks away, the 1896 Pancoast Carriage House, offering three self-catering suites—are a tribute to just how far it has come.

The decor in both houses hearkens back to the period in which they were built, but manages to do so without being fussy. Rooms are individually decorated with fine antiques and striking wall coverings; all have gas fireplaces and three in the Jackson House feature two-person Jacuzzi tubs. Guests at the Jackson House gather together around a gleaming dining room table for a full breakfast, while those at the Pancoast Carriage House enjoy continental fare at leisure in their private dining areas. Both houses have gardens. There is a swimming pool and heated spa in Pancoast House; Jackson House features an excercise room and conservatory with a 14-foot swimmable spa.

✪ Ogé House on the River Walk

209 Washington St., San Antonio, TX 78204. ☎ **800/242-2770** or 210/223-2353. Fax 210/226-5812. 5 rms, 4 suites. A/C TV TEL. $135 double; $165–$195 suite. Rates include continental breakfast. AE, CB, DC, DISC, MC, V. Free parking.

One of the most glorious of the mansions that grace the King William district, the Greek revival–style Ogé House is more boutique inn than folksy bed-and-breakfast. You'll still get the personalized attention you would expect from a host home, but it's combined here with the luxury of a sophisticated small hotel. For example, a bountiful continental breakfast is served on individual white-clothed tables set with the finest of crystal and china. Single travelers who don't take to talking to strangers in the morning can bury themselves in one of the daily newspapers laid out on the bureau just beyond the dining room.

More social-minded folks might be seen lounging on the downstairs porch in the late afternoon, perhaps enjoying a drink with hosts Patrick and Sharrie Magatagan; they know all the best places to eat in town and can help you get a reservation. Impeccably decorated in high Victorian style, all the accommodations offer private telephone lines, cable TV, and refrigerators; many have fireplaces and views of the manicured, pecan-shaded grounds, and one looks out on the river from its own wrought-iron balcony. The painstakingly restored home now looks much as it did when it was built in 1867, but if you want to see the carriage house that was originally on the estate, you'll have to visit the Yturri-Edmunds House and Mill (see the "Historic Buildings/Complexes" section of chapter 6).

4 Monte Vista Historic District

A BED & BREAKFAST

Bonner Garden

145 E. Agarita, San Antonio, TX 78212. ☎ **800/396-4222** or 210/733-4222. Fax 210/733-6129. 5 rms. A/C TV TEL. $85–$125 double. Rates include breakfast. Weekly and corporate rates available. AE, CB, DISC, MC, V.

Those who like the intimacy of the bed-and-breakfast experience but aren't keen on Victorian froufrou should consider the Bonner Garden, located in the Monte Vista Historic District, about a mile north of downtown. Built for Louisiana artist Mary Bonner in 1910, this large, Italianate villa has a beautiful, classical simplicity *and* lots of gorgeous antiques. Not to mention a 50-foot sunken swimming pool.

The Portico Room, with a private poolside entrance, is the most opulent. Guests can gaze up at a painted blue sky with billowing clouds or look down at an intricate Italian mosaic-tile floor. Most of the rooms have European-type decor, but Mary Bonner's former studio, separate from the main house, is done in tasteful Santa Fe style. In addition to phones and TVs, all the rooms have VCRs—the better to take advantage of the excellent film library the hosts are compiling—and two have Jacuzzi tubs. A rooftop deck with a wet bar affords a sparkling nighttime view of downtown.

5 Fort Sam Houston / Northeast I-35

A couple of chain hotels along the section of I-35 just northeast of downtown and south of Fort Sam Houston offer rooms in the "Inexpensive" price category: **Holiday Inn Northeast,** 3855 I-35 north, 78219 (☎ 800/465-4329 or 210/226-4361), and **Super 8 Motel,** 3617 I-35 north, 78219 (☎ 210/227-8888); the nearby **Quality Inn & Suites,** 3817 I-35 north, 78219 (☎ 800/942-8913 or 210/224-3030), is in the moderate category. All offer swimming pools, and the Holiday Inn and Super 8 have restaurants and room service in addition. Scenic this area isn't, but it's convenient if you have a car.

BED & BREAKFASTS

Ⓢ **Bullis House Inn**

621 Pierce St., San Antonio, TX 78208. ☎ **210/223-9426.** Fax 210/299-1479. 7 rms (1 with bath, 6 share 3¹/₂ baths). A/C TV. $49–$59 double (shared bath); $69 double (private bath).

Weekly rates available; rates include continental breakfast. AE, DISC, MC, V. Free off-street parking.

For those who don't mind sharing a bath, this graceful neoclassical mansion is the best bed-and-breakfast bargain in town. Just down the street from the Fort Sam Houston quadrangle, it was built between 1906 and 1909 for General John Lapham Bullis, a frontier Indian fighter who played a key role in capturing Geronimo (some claim the Apache chief's spirit still roams the mansion). More concerned with creature comforts when he retired, the general had oak paneling, parquet floors, crystal chandeliers, and marble fireplaces installed in his home. Beautifully restored in the 1980s, it's often used for wedding receptions these days.

Guest rooms, all with 14-foot ceilings, are furnished with some period antiques along with good reproductions; three of them feature fireplaces. The family room, which sleeps up to six, has a refrigerator. Near I-35 and Hwy. 281, this bed-and-breakfast is easily accessible to the airport and downtown by car; it's also a short drive from the restaurants and nightlife of the North St. Mary's area. There is a swimming pool, movies are shown three nights a week, and VCR/video rental is available.

Terrell Castle

950 E. Grayson St., San Antonio, TX 78208. ☎ **210/271-9145.** For reservations, ☎ **800/356-1605** or 210/824-8036. 4 rms, 4 suites. A/C TV. $85 double; $100 suite. AE, DISC, MC, V.

Unless a trip to Scotland is in the cards, this could be your best chance to spend a night in a castle. Built in 1894 by English-born architect Alfred Giles, this massive limestone structure was commissioned by Edwin Terrell, a statesman who fell in love with the European grand style while serving as U.S. ambassador to Belgium. Converted into a bed-and-breakfast in 1986, it's an anomaly in the working-class area near the Fort Sam Houston quadrangle. As we went to press, the castle was up for sale; in the last couple of years it had gotten rather run-down. Still, if you're interested in trying something completely different, it's worth checking into when you're in town. New owners might have done some refurbishing.

A YOUTH HOSTEL

Hostelling International, San Antonio International Hostel

621 Pierce St., San Antonio, TX 78208. ☎ **210/223-9426.** Fax 210/299-1479. 40 beds. $12.85 for members; $15.85 for nonmembers. AE, DISC, MC, V.

Right next door to the Bullis House Inn (see above), this youth hostel has a reading room, small kitchen, dining area, lockers, and picnic tables, in addition to male and female dorms; hostelers are welcome at the Bullis House Inn on film nights, and the two lodgings share a pool. There's an evening cookout twice a week, and a continental breakfast is available for an additional $4. This pleasant facility is fairly close to downtown, but not especially convenient to it if you're using public transportation.

6 Near the Airport

EXPENSIVE

Red Lion Fiesta San Antonio

37 NE Loop 410, San Antonio, TX 78216. ☎ **800/535-1980** or 210/366-2424. Fax 210/341-0410. 284 rms, 7 suites. A/C TV TEL. $130–$160 double; $225–$295 suite. Various packages available. AE, CB, DC, DISC, MC, V. Free parking.

For an airport hotel in the busy Loop 410 business district, the Red Lion (long owned by Sheraton) is surprisingly serene. Developer Patrick J. Kennedy, who converted

Greater San Antonio Accommodations & Dining

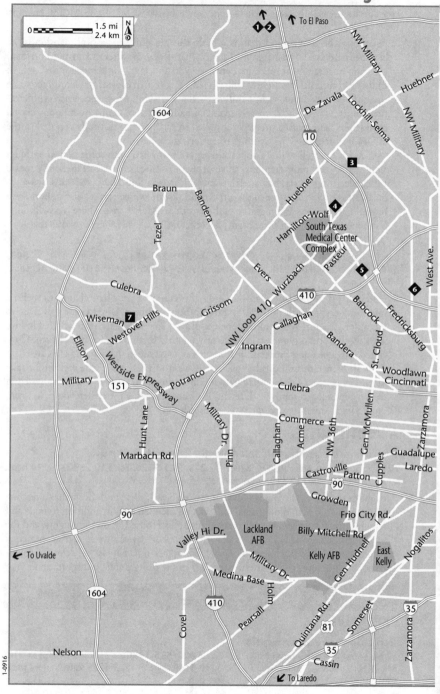

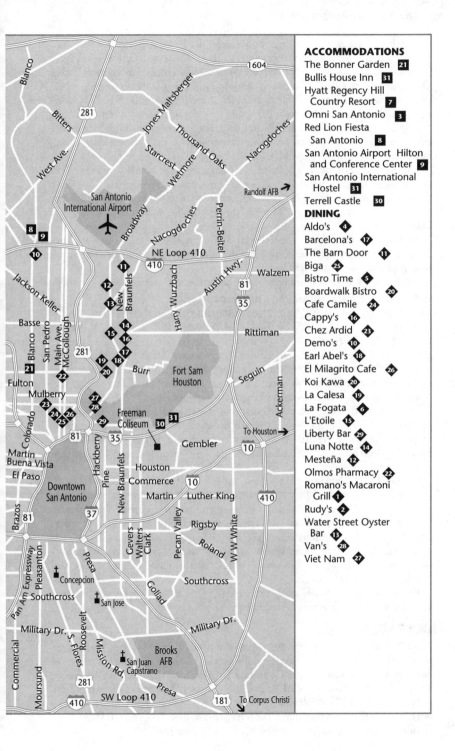

ACCOMMODATIONS

The Bonner Garden **21**
Bullis House Inn **31**
Hyatt Regency Hill
  Country Resort **7**
Omni San Antonio **3**
Red Lion Fiesta
  San Antonio **8**
San Antonio Airport Hilton
  and Conference Center **9**
San Antonio International
  Hostel **31**
Terrell Castle **30**

DINING

Aldo's **4**
Barcelona's **17**
The Barn Door **11**
Biga **25**
Bistro Time **5**
Boardwalk Bistro **20**
Cafe Camile **24**
Cappy's **16**
Chez Ardid **23**
Demo's **10**
Earl Abel's **18**
El Milagrito Cafe **26**
Koi Kawa **20**
La Calesa **19**
La Fogata **6**
L'Etoile **15**
Liberty Bar **29**
Luna Notte **14**
Mesteña **12**
Olmos Pharmacy **22**
Romano's Macaroni
  Grill **1**
Rudy's **2**
Water Street Oyster
  Bar **13**
Van's **28**
Viet Nam **27**

a downtown seminary into the posh Mansión del Río hotel (see "Downtown," above), was also responsible for this hotel's design. Moorish arches, potted plants, stone fountains, and colorful Mexican tile create a Mediterranean mood in the public areas; intricate wrought-iron elevators descend from the guest floors to the pool patio, eliminating the need to tromp through the lobby in a swimsuit. Guest rooms are equally appealing, with brick walls painted in peach or beige, wood-beamed ceilings, draped French doors, and colorful contemporary art. In-room irons, hair dryers, coffeemakers, and fax/modem hookups remind you that the hotel has a large business clientele, much of it from Mexico.

Dining/Entertainment: The hotel's contemporary-style fine dining room, Cascabel, lost its famous chef recently; it's okay now, but nothing special. Next door, you can sink down into one of the plush leather chairs of the Spanish colonial-style Cascabel Bar. From 5 to 9pm Monday through Friday there's live music at the Lobby Bar.

Services: Room service, complimentary newspaper delivered to your door, concierge level, fax service, laundry/valet, safe-deposit boxes, complimentary van service to airport and North Star and Central Malls.

Facilities: Outdoor swimming pool and Jacuzzi, sauna, exercise room, gift shop.

San Antonio Airport Hilton and Conference Center

611 NW Loop 410, San Antonio, TX 78216. ☎ **800/HILTONS** or 210/340-6060. Fax 210/377-4646. 376 rms, 11 suites. A/C TV TEL. $119–175 double; $425–550 suite. AE, CB, DC, DISC, MC, V. Free covered parking.

A recent $6 million renovation gave this Hilton's restaurants and downstairs public areas a spiffy new look. In the lobby, a copper-sheeted ceiling, polished Kentucky sandstone floors, and a marble-topped reception desk resembling a saloon bar successfully blend Old West themes with contemporary design.

The revamp didn't extend to the guest rooms—which are perfectly comfortable, just not as brand-spanking new and stylish as one might have expected after seeing the lobby; furnishings are dark wood, with a Victorian tone. Guests on the 14th-floor Executive Level get bathrobes, coffeemakers, daily newspaper delivery, and free continental breakfast.

Dining/Entertainment: Jocks will like the Hilton's sports bar, with Texas sports memorabilia and enough TVs to let patrons tune in to their favorite home games (see chapter 8 for details). The wood-burning grill and rotisserie of Tex's, serving three meals a day, turns out updated ranch-style food to match its updated ranch-style decor; prices are reasonable and preparations sophisticated.

Services: Room service, valet laundry service (Monday to Friday), complimentary shuttle to airport and nearby businesses, 24-hour security guards, in-room voice mail and data ports for modems.

Facilities: Outdoor heated pool, men's and women's saunas, Jacuzzi, exercise room with free weights, video-game room, full-service business center.

MODERATE

A number of chain properties in the airport area fall into the "Moderate" price range. Almost all offer courtesy van service to the airport; the ones that give you the most facilities for the money include **Courtyard by Marriott/Airport,** 8615 Broadway, 78717 (☎ **800/321-2211** or 210/828-7200); **Holiday Inn Select Airport,** 77 NE Loop 410, 78216 (☎ **800/HOLIDAY** or 210/349-9900); and **Ramada Inn Airport,** 1111 NE Loop 410, 78209 (☎ **800/228-2828** or 210/828-9031). All three feature an exercise room, pool, restaurant, and room service.

INEXPENSIVE

The only lodgings near the airport that fall into the "Inexpensive" price range are the **Best Western Town House Motel,** 942 NE Loop 410, 78209 (☎ **800/528-1234** or 210/826-6311), and the **Pear Tree Inn by Drury,** 143 NE Loop 410, 78216 (☎ **800/AT-A-TREE** or 210/366-9300). Both have pools.

7 Medical Center / Northwest

EXPENSIVE

Omni San Antonio

9821 Colonnade Blvd., San Antonio, TX 78230. ☎ **800/460-8881,** 800/843-6664, or 210/691-8888. Fax 210/691-1128. 323 rms, 3 suites. A/C TV TEL. $160 double; $275–$575 suite. AE, CB, DC, DISC, MC, V. Free self-parking; valet parking $3.

This polished granite high-rise off I-10 west is convenient to Sea World, Six Flags Fiesta Texas, the airport, and the Hill Country. In addition, a number of the shops and restaurants in the 66-acre Colonnade complex are within easy walking distance. At the back of the soaring, luxurious lobby, a health complex offers indoor-and-outdoor pools (the latter large enough for laps) and two Jacuzzis, along with a well-equipped exercise room and sauna; racquetball facilities are adjacent to the hotel. Guest rooms are well appointed in a contemporary European style, with rich blues and burgundies and floral patterns. Although the hotel sees a lot of tourist and Medical Center traffic, service here is prompt and courteous.

Dining/Entertainment: At a clubby lobby lounge, you can settle into plush leather chairs and listen to live piano music nightly. The hotel's full service eatery is the cheerful, light-filled Park Restaurant. Breakfasts there are fine, but if you're here on Sunday, don't miss the 19th-floor brunch, where wonderful views of the Hill Country accompany a copious spread.

Services: Room service, valet laundry/dry cleaning, complimentary airport shuttle.

Facilities: Gift shop, concierge, safe-deposit boxes.

MODERATE

A number of lower-end properties are concentrated around the area where NW Loop 410 meets I-10 west. This northwest section of San Antonio, home to the huge South Texas Medical Center, is one of the newest parts of town to be developed. It doesn't have much character, but it affords easy access to Six Flags Fiesta Texas and Sea World. Moderately priced places that offer the most extras for your money include **Courtyard by Marriott/Medical Center,** 8585 Marriott Dr., 78229 (☎ **800/321-2211** or 210/614-7100), which features an exercise room, restaurant, and pool; **Hawthorn Suites,** 4041 Bluemel Rd., 78240 (☎ **800/527-1133** or 210/561-9660), with an exercise room, pool, and tennis courts; and **Holiday Inn Northwest,** 3233 NW Loop 410, 78213 (☎ **800/HOLIDAY** or 210/377-3900), offering an exercise room, pool, restaurant, and room service.

INEXPENSIVE

The lodgings in the area that fall into the "Inexpensive" category include the **Hampton Inn–Sea World,** 4803 Manitou, 78228 (☎ **800/HAMPTON** or 210/684-9966); **Holiday Inn Express/Northwest,** 9411 Wurzbach, 78240 (☎ **800/HOLIDAY** or 210/561-9300); **La Quinta Wurzbach,** 9452 I-10 west, 78230 (☎ **800/531-5900** or 210/593-0338); **Motel 6,** 9400 Wurzbach 78219 (☎ **210/333-1850**); **Ramada Limited/Northwest,** 9447 I-10 west, 78230 (☎ **800/**

757-7407 or 210/558-9070); and **Rodeway Inn Crossroads,** 6804 I-10 west, 78201 (☎ **800/228-2000** or 210/734-7111). All offer a pool but no other facilities.

8 West

VERY EXPENSIVE

✪ Hyatt Regency Hill Country Resort
9800 Hyatt Resort Dr., San Antonio, TX 78251. ☎ **800/233-1234** or 210/647-1234. Fax 210/681-9681. 443 rms, 57 suites, 1 guesthouse. A/C TV TEL. $240 double; $320 Regency Club; $435–$1,560 suite. AE, CB, DC, DISC, MC, V. Free self-parking; valet parking $8.

There's only one problem with this cushy resort on the far west side of town: You might never want to leave it. The setting, on 200 acres of former ranchland, is idyllic. The on-site activities, ranging from golf to tubing on a man-made river, are endless, and Sea World of Texas sits at your doorstep. The restaurants are excellent, the rooms beautifully appointed, and there are even free laundry facilities and a country store for supplies. In short, you'll find something at the Hyatt to fulfill your every need—except the one to make money to pay for all this.

The best of Texas design is showcased here. The resort's low-slung buildings, made of native limestone, are inspired by the architecture of the nearby Hill Country. The light-filled lobby is rustic elegant—sort of Ralph Lauren with antlers—and the guest quarters are done in updated country style: Carved maple beds are topped with quilt-style covers and walls have stenciled borders, but the lines are clean and unfussy. Most rooms feature French doors that open out onto wood-trimmed porches, and all have in-room refrigerators.

The recreation facilities are top-notch. Along with an 18-hole championship golf course, the Hyatt boasts tennis courts; a well-equipped health club (with a Jacuzzi, aerobic and weight machines, free weights, and a massage room); two swimming pools (one for adults only); volleyball and basketball courts; and jogging and bike paths. Above all, there's the 950-foot-long Ramblin' River, a lushly landscaped 4-acre park where you can grab an inner tube and float your cares away.

Dining/Entertainment: Sit out on Aunt Mary's Porch and down a good local brew, or stop into Charlie's to see the 56-foot, carved-wood and copper bar; you might be inspired to shoot a few rounds of pool. Golfers tend to guzzle at the Cactus Oak Tavern, the clubhouse bar and grill with a great view of the course. The Springhouse Cafe, serving three meals a day in the hotel's main building, is country casual, offering both an à la carte menu and buffet service. One way or another, you'll want to drop by the hotel's fine dining room, featuring upscale southwestern cuisine: It boasts the world's largest antler chandelier, 9 feet high and made of 506 naturally shed horns.

Services: Room service, shuttle service to airport and to downtown ($10), concierge service, valet-laundry and dry-cleaning service.

Facilities: Gift shop, golf pro shop, car-rental agency, Regency Club lounge, business center, game room, Camp Hyatt (see the "Family-Friendly Hotels" feature in this chapter for details).

San Antonio Dining   5

It's easy to eat well in San Antonio, especially if you enjoy Mexican food—or are willing to give it a try in a city where it might surprise you with its variety. You can get great Tex-Mex standards here, but you'll find less familiar, often sophisticated, dishes from the interior of Mexico, too. Southwestern cuisine, emphasizing fresh regional ingredients and spices combined in exciting ways, is served in some of the most chic dining rooms in town as well as in some unlikely dives. Then there's great chicken-fried steak, burgers, barbecue . . . in short, something to satisfy every taste and wallet.

The downtown dining scene is burgeoning. Recently opened entertainment complexes around the River Walk include South Bank, which hosts a Hard Rock Cafe, Starbucks outlet, and other trendy refueling spots, and Presidio Plaza, anchored by Planet Hollywood. But although dining on the river is a unique, not-to-be-missed experience, many of the restaurants that overlook the water are overpriced and overcrowded. In general, even if you're willing to pass up a river view, downtown is not the best place for fine dining (though a number of hotel restaurants have excellent, if sometimes pricey, menus).

Most locals chow down a bit north of downtown. The two closest concentrations of places to eat are the San Antonio College/Monte Vista area, north of I-35 and west of Hwy. 281, and the section around North St. Mary's (the Strip), where you can get live entertainment dished up with your food on the weekends. There are also some good restaurants in Beacon Hill, a working-class neighborhood just northwest of downtown off I-10; and a dining scene at Southtown, the aptly named area just below downtown, is beginning to evolve. But by far the best eating area in San Antonio is still on and around Broadway, starting a few blocks south of Hildebrand, extending north to Loop 410, and comprising much of the posh area known as Alamo Heights. Brackenridge Park, the zoo, the botanical gardens, and the Witte and McNay museums are in this part of town, so you can combine your sightseeing with some serious eating.

If you're budget conscious, consider eating early, when some restaurants have early-bird specials, or hit the expensive restaurants at lunch; some of the most upscale eateries in town have good lunch specials. A number of popular places don't take reservations; if you arrive around 8pm when everyone else does, you can expect to wait up to an hour for a table. Make reservations wherever you can; watching those who didn't bother to wait in line or spend too much money at the bar is always a cheering accompaniment to a meal.

The price categories into which the restaurants have been divided are only rough approximations; by ordering carefully or by splurging, you can eat more or less expensively at almost any place you choose. In general, **Expensive** restaurants will cost you more than $25 per person for dinner with dessert, not including drinks, tax (7.75%), and tip (generally at least 15%). Meals at **Moderate** restaurants are likely to run $25 or less, and you can get by at **Inexpensive** places for under $12.

1 Best Bets

- **Best Spot for a Romantic Dinner:** The River Walk restaurants are swell for watching the water and other people, but their decibel level doesn't allow you to hear those sweet nothings your companion is trying to whisper in your ear. The nod for most romantic therefore goes to **Polo's,** in the Fairmount Hotel, 401 S. Alamo St. (☎ 210/224-8800), with its candlelight, superb service, and soothing relative silence.

- **Best Floating Feast:** It used to be that you could only dine on the river if you were with a group, but **Boudro's,** 421 E. Commerce St./River Walk (☎ 210/224-8484), now offers reservations on its dinner barges to individuals and couples. How sweet it is to drift downstream while enjoying one of the restaurant's excellent meals.

- **Best American Cuisine:** When we give the nod to **Restaurant Biga,** 206 E. Locust St. (☎ 210/225-0722), as tops in American cuisine, we're not talking meatloaf and mashed potatoes (although versions of both dishes may turn up on the menu). Biga's New American recipes, which rely on fresh seasonal ingredients from the area, will dazzle those willing to expand their culinary horizons.

- **Best Continental Cuisine:** Get out those elastic-waist clothes for **Bistro Time,** 5137 Fredericksburg Rd. (☎ 210/344-6626), where wonderfully rich sauces hearken back to the days before the word *cholesterol* became part of the national vocabulary.

- **Best French Cuisine:** It doesn't get more classically Gallic than at **Chez Ardid,** 1919 San Pedro Ave. (☎ 210/732-3203), a longtime San Antonio favorite for getting transported to Paris.

- **Best Italian Cuisine:** Whether you go for the more traditional fare of the original **Paesano's,** now in Lincoln Heights at 550 Basse Rd., Suite 100 (☎ 210/226-9541), or the somewhat lighter menu at the River Walk location, 111 Crockett, Suite 101 (☎ 210/22-PASTA), you'll enjoy the fresh, home-style cooking of this San Antonio favorite.

- **Best Mexican Cuisine:** This is a tough one to call in a city that has so many worthy contenders, but **Rosario's,** 1014 S. Alamo (☎ 210/223-1806), offers great atmosphere along with great food, especially on the weekends when you can eat to a live salsa beat. It doesn't hurt that the place also has the best margaritas in town.

- **Best New Restaurant:** It's not always possible to predict whether a dining room will succeed, but the augurs are excellent for **Mesteña,** 7959 Broadway (☎ 210/822-7733), which has a celebrity chef, a location in the city's poshest shopping complex, and a menu that goes where few in San Antonio have gone before.

- **Best Seafood:** For superb fish with a French accent, **L'Etoile,** 6106 Broadway (☎ 210/826-4551), swims to the fore. Fresh lobster, lots of garlic butter . . . ooh la la.

- **Best Ribs on the River Walk:** Okay, so **County Line,** 111 W. Crockett St., Suite 104 (☎ **210/229-1941**), is the only barbecue restaurant on the River Walk. What matters is that it's one of the places that has started to draw locals downtown in droves for their favorite meat platters, previously a long drive away.
- **Best Brunch:** At the Plaza San Antonio's **Anaqua Grill,** 555 S. Alamo (☎ **210/ 229-1000**), a copious buffet ($17.95 adults, $11.95 for children) gives diners the chance to try different dishes from a single country or region; food from Russia might be featured one week and the cuisine of the Yucatán another week. Prices include champagne.
- **Best Fast Food:** Bright-pink roofs and green neon palm trees have long signaled good fast food to San Antonians: The original **Taco Cabana,** opened in 1973 on 3310 San Pedro Ave., rapidly became a Hill Country chain as word spread of great grilled chicken, freshly made tacos, and other authentic Mexican specialties—not the Taco Bell type. There are now 26 Taco Cabanas in San Antonio; the most convenient locations are 101 Alamo Plaza (☎ **210/224-6158**), 2908 Broadway (☎ **210/829-1616**), and the original one on San Pedro Avenue (☎ **210/733-9332**).

2 Restaurants by Cuisine

AMERICAN

Barn Door (Broadway/Alamo Heights, *M*)

Cappy's (Broadway/Alamo Heights, *M*)

Earl Abel's (Broadway/Alamo Heights, *I*)

Guenther House (Southtown, *I*)

Liberty Bar (North St. Mary's, *M*)

Little Rhein Steak House (The River Walk & Downtown, *E*)

Olmos Pharmacy (San Antonio College/Monte Vista/Olmos Park, *I*)

Polo's (The River Walk & Downtown, *E*)

BARBECUE

Rudy's (Leon Springs, *M*)

County Line (The River Walk & Downtown, *M*)

CHINESE

Van's (Broadway/Alamo Heights, *M*)

CONTINENTAL

Bistro Time (Northwest/ Medical Center, *M*)

DELI

Pecan Street Market (The River Walk & Downtown, *I*)

Schilo's (The River Walk & Downtown, *I*)

ECLECTIC

Boardwalk Bistro and Brewery (Broadway/Alamo Heights, *M*)

Cafe Camile (North St. Mary's, *M*)

Carranza's Grocery & Market (The River Walk & Downtown, *M*)

FRENCH

Chez Ardid (San Antonio College/ Monte Vista/Olmos Park, *E*)

L'Etoile (Broadway/Alamo Heights, *E*)

GERMAN

Schilo's (The River Walk & Downtown, *I*)

GREEK

Demo's (The Airport Area, *I*)

ITALIAN

Aldo's (Northwest/Medical Center, *M*)

La Focaccia (Southtown, *M*)

Key to abbreviations: *I*=Inexpensive; *M*=Moderate; *E*=Expensive; *VE*=Very Expensive

Luna Notte (Broadway/Alamo
Heights, *M*)
Paesano's Riverwalk
(The River Walk &
Downtown, *M*)
Romano's Macaroni Grill
(Leon Springs, *M*)

JAPANESE

Koi Kawa (Broadway/Alamo
Heights, *M*)
Van's (Broadway/Alamo
Heights, *M*)

MEDITERRANEAN

Babylon Grill (Southtown, *M*)
Barcelona's Café (Broadway/
Alamo Heights, *M*)

MEXICAN

El Milagrito Cafe (North
St. Mary's, *I*)
El Mirador (Southtown, *M*)
La Calesa (Broadway/Alamo
Heights, *M*)
La Fogata (Balcones
Heights, *M*)
La Margarita (The River Walk
& Downtown, *M*)
Mi Tierra (The River Walk
& Downtown, *I*)
Rosario's (Southtown, *M*)

NEW AMERICAN

Restaurant Biga (San Antonio College/
Monte Vista/Olmos Park, *E*)

SEAFOOD

Water Street Oyster Bar (Broadway/
Alamo Heights, *M*)

SOUTHWESTERN

Anaqua Grill (The River Walk
& Downtown, *E*)
Boudro's (The River Walk
& Downtown, *E*)
Mestña (Broadway/Alamo
Heights, *E*)
Zuni Grill (The River Walk
& Downtown, *M*)

STEAKS

Barn Door (Broadway/Alamo
Heights, *M*)
Little Rhein Steak House (The River
Walk & Downtown, *E*)

THAI

Viet Nam (Broadway/Alamo
Heights, *M*)

VIETNAMESE

Van's (Broadway/Alamo Heights, *M*)
Viet Nam (Broadway/Alamo
Heights, *M*)

3 The River Walk & Downtown

EXPENSIVE

Anaqua Grill

Plaza San Antonio Hotel, 555 S. Alamo. ☎ **210/229-1000.** Reservations recommended. Main courses $13.75–$21, Sun brunch $17.95. AE, CB, DC, DISC, MC, V. Mon–Sat 7:30–10:30am, Sun 7–10am; Mon–Sat 11:30am–2pm, Sun brunch 10am–2pm; Sun–Thurs 6–10pm, Fri–Sat 6–11pm. SOUTHWESTERN.

The lobby restaurant of the Plaza San Antonio, looking out onto the hotel's beautifully landscaped grounds, dishes up some of the most interesting southwestern cooking in town. The adventurous combinations of local spices and ingredients that characterize this type of cuisine are generally successful here, and the menu is designed to invite diners to try lots of different things.

A selection from the tapas (appetizer) menu might include crayfish and boudin cannelloni in a tomato-fennel salsa or tandoori chicken skewers with plum ketchup; sampler dishes of both hot and cold tapas are available. Among the entrees, the charred ahi tuna with rice noodles and vegetables in black bean sauce and the oak-smoked medaillons of pork with Shiner Bock sauce are especially good. Service is not always as reliable as the cooking—it's sometimes attentive and sometimes nonexistent.

Downtown San Antonio Dining

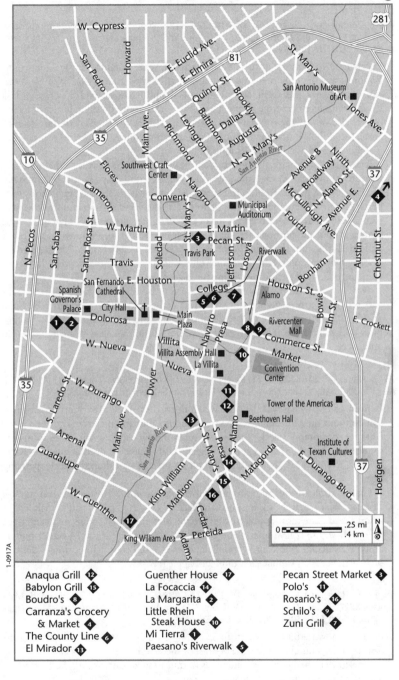

Anaqua Grill 12
Babylon Grill 15
Boudro's 8
Carranza's Grocery & Market 4
The County Line 6
El Mirador 13

Guenther House 17
La Focaccia 14
La Margarita 2
Little Rhein Steak House 10
Mi Tierra 1
Paesano's Riverwalk 5

Pecan Street Market 3
Polo's 11
Rosario's 16
Schilo's 9
Zuni Grill 7

47

✪ Boudro's

421 E. Commerce St./River Walk. ☎ **210/224-8484.** Reservations strongly recommended. Main courses $12.50–$24.50. AE, DC, DISC, MC, V. Sun–Thurs 11am–11pm, Fri–Sat 11am– midnight. SOUTHWESTERN.

Locals tend to look down their noses on River Walk restaurants; for a long time, Boudro's was the only one on which almost all heaped kudos. And with good reason. The kitchen uses fresh local ingredients—Gulf Coast seafood, Texas beef, Hill Country produce—and the preparations and presentations do them justice. The setting is also out of the ordinary: If you've entered from the river, be sure to turn around and look inside the turn-of-the-century limestone building to see its hardwood floors and handmade mesquite bar.

You might start with the guacamole, prepared in front of you at the table and served with tostadas; or the crab quesadillas topped with papaya salsa. The prime rib, blackened on a pecan-wood grill, is deservedly popular, as are the lamb chops with peach chutney and garlic mashed potatoes. The skewered shrimp and scallops with mango sauce and tomatillo cream make a good lighter alternative (the food may be innovative but the portions are not *nouvelle*). For dessert, the whisky-soaked bread pudding is fine, but the lime chess pie with a butter pecan crust . . . divine. Service is very good, especially considering the volume of business and the fact that the servers spend a good bit of their time mixing up guacamole.

Note: By the time you read this, the owners of Boudro's will have opened a culinary school, gourmet kitchen store, and restaurant called Firewheel at 205 N. Presa St. (☎ 225-1500) (some will remember this as the former home of Boccacio). Firewheel will feature an exciting Mediterranean fusion menu with strong Mexican influences.

Little Rhein Steak House

231 S. Alamo. ☎ **210/225-2111.** Reservations recommended. Main courses $13.75–$29.95. AE, DC, DISC, MC, V. Sun–Thurs 5–10pm, Fri and Sat 5–11pm. STEAKS/AMERICAN.

Built in 1847 in what was then the Rhein district, the oldest two-story structure in San Antonio now houses an elegant steakhouse abutting the river and La Villita. Antique memorabilia decks the indoor main dining room; a miniature train surrounded by historic replicas runs overhead. Leafy branches overhanging the River Walk patio—elevated slightly and railed off for privacy—are draped in little sparkling lights.

Choice steaks from the restaurant's own plant come with salad, baked potato, "Texas Caviar" (deliciously seasoned and baked black-eyed peas), and a small loaf of wheat bread. The most popular plates are the filet mignon, T-bone, and center-cut rib eye. If you're *really* hungry, you might call ahead to see if the 24-ounce porterhouse is available, but keep in mind the homey—and reasonably priced—desserts such as cheesecake, vanilla ice cream, and apple pie.

Polo's

Fairmount Hotel, 401 S. Alamo St. ☎ **210/224-8800.** Reservations recommended. Main courses $22–$38. AE, CB, DC, MC, V. Daily 7–10am; Mon–Fri 11:30am–2pm; Mon–Thurs 6–10pm, Fri–Sat 6–10:30pm. REGIONAL AMERICAN.

Polo's is known around town as the spawning ground for some of the best chefs in San Antonio; a number have gone on to start successful restaurants of their own. This has meant that the kitchen is sometimes in transition; at this writing the Fairmount restaurant's star is on the rise again.

A lovely setting for a special-occasion dinner, the dining rooms are done in muted tones of beige, with etched glass-and-brass partitions and tables adorned with fresh flowers and delicate liquid candles. As you enter, an open wood-burning pizza oven imported from Italy imparts the impression—and the aroma—that some serious cooking is going on.

That oven turns out some very creative pizzas, topped with seafood and bacon, for example, or Brie and apples. Combined with a salad, a 12-inch pie makes a nice, light meal. In fact, you could probably get by on just the generous spicy quail salad if you eat enough of the hard-to-resist sourdough rolls that come out hot from the pizza oven. But you're likely to want to try such substantial dishes as the rack of New Zealand lamb or grilled Norwegian salmon. The presentations are astounding; it's an effort to refrain from asking your fellow diners what they ordered when you see the artistic mounds of food emerging from the kitchen. Service is impeccable, but friendly enough for you to ask your server instead.

MODERATE

Carranza's Grocery & Market
701 Austin St. ☎ **210/223-0903.** Reservations only accepted for large parties. Main courses $7.50–$28.50. AE. Lunch Mon–Fri 11am–2pm; dinner Mon–Thurs 5–10pm, Fri–Sat 5–11pm. Closed Sun. ECLECTIC.

If you and your dining companion can't agree on the type of food you'd like or the amount of money you want to spend, you could reconsider the relationship—or come to Carranza. The combined lunch-and-dinner menu is broken down into categories for sandwiches, Italian, Mexican, seafood, and meats: You can get a hearty brisket sandwich on a Mexican roll for $5.50 or a delicious seafood platter, including red snapper, scallops, shrimp, and a soft-shell crab cake, for $28.50. But most people order the succulent mesquite-smoked meats: brisket, chicken, sausage, pork ribs, or chopped barbecue. They're available in reasonably priced combination plates if you don't want to decide between them.

You can also order your barbecue by the pound to go; Carranza has been around as a grocery and market since 1920 and still has a deli counter downstairs. From the upstairs dining room of the restored limestone building, you can watch trains go by during the day or view the city lights at night. Consider combining a meal here with a visit to the nearby San Antonio Museum of Art.

County Line
111 W. Crockett St., Suite 104. ☎ **210/229-1941.** Reservations not accepted. Platters $8.95–$13.95. AE, CB, DC, DISC, MC, V. Daily 11am–11pm. BARBECUE.

A roadhouse on the river? Why not? The County Line has transplanted the menu and the signature 1940s Texas decor of this popular Austin-based restaurant to the River Walk, where they're thriving. Even locals come downtown to dig into the fall-off-the-bone beef ribs or the tender pork; the restaurant's claim to fame is that it smokes all its meat for more than 18 hours. Barbecued chicken, turkey, and even some salads are also available. For a more countrified County Line experience, visit the older branch on 607 W. Afton Oaks, off Hwy. 1604 (☎ 210/496-0011); the wait can be long, especially on weekend nights, but there's a nice deck with a full-service bar.

La Margarita
120 Produce Row (Market Square). ☎ **210/227-7140.** Reservations not accepted. Main courses $5.25–$10.95. AE, CB, DC, DISC, MC, V. Sun–Thurs 11am–10pm, Fri–Sat 11am–midnight. MEXICAN.

Worked up an appetite with all that Market Square shopping? There's no better place to satisfy it than La Margarita. This lively restaurant is renowned for its fajitas and for its *parilla* platters: huge mounds of charbroiled sausage, chicken, and beef accompanied by *queso flameado* (melted cheese), fried potatoes, beans, guacamole, *pico de gallo,* and lots of hot flour tortillas. If you're not quite up to the task, there are many smaller if not exactly lighter dishes to consider—the enchiladas Acapulco filled with seafood stew and topped with shrimp, scallops, and cheese, for example. Or you can just sit outdoors with an order of nachos and sip a margarita; they do credit to the restaurant's name. The people-watching is great and who knows? After a margarita magnifica, you might be inspired to invite over one of the strolling mariachis (just don't forget that they expect to be paid).

Paesano's Riverwalk

111 Crockett, Suite 101. ☎ **210/22-PASTA.** Reservations accepted for lunch only. First courses (pasta) $7.95–$13.95; main courses $15.95–$21.95. AE, DC, MC, V. Sun–Thurs 11am–11pm, Fri–Sat 11am–midnight. ITALIAN.

When it opened a branch on the river, this longtime San Antonio favorite underwent a change: The old Italian Chianti bottle–kitsch decor gave way to a soaring ceiling and lots of inscrutable contemporary art. But the locals who ventured downtown were most surprised about the metamorphosis the menu had undergone: Almost none of the heavier staples of the old Monte Vista restaurant (which no longer exists) turned up here. But, by popular demand, the crispy shrimp Paesano's remained, and it's as good as its devotees claim; if you want to save money, order it as an appetizer and then get a reasonably priced pasta—say the cheese tortellini with artichokes, spinach, and tomato pesto cream. Portions are huge. Not that you have to worry about losing weight here, but those who want to try the more traditional menu should head for the latest incarnation of Paesano's, across from the Quarry Golf Club at 550 Basse Rd., Suite 100 (☎ 210/226-9541). Only the decor has been modernized at that toney new location.

Zuni Grill

511 River Walk/223 Losoya St. ☎ **210/227-0864.** Reservations accepted only for parties of six or more. Main courses $10.95–$18.95. AE, DC, DISC, MC, V. Sun–Thurs 8am–11pm, Fri–Sat 8am–midnight. SOUTHWESTERN.

With its stylized cactuses, metallic hump-backed flute players, and chic southwestern menu, this popular River Walk cafe is a little bit of Santa Fe-on-the-San Antonio. If you've never had a prickly pear margarita (and who has?), this is the place to try one: Puréed cactus fruit, marinated overnight in tequila and cactus-juice schnapps, turns the potent—and delicious—drink a shade ranging from pink to startling purple, depending on the ripeness of the fruit.

The grilled chicken salad with goat cheese and spicy roasted pecans makes a nice, light meal, and vegetarians will appreciate the gardener and gatherer platter (grilled vegetables accompanied by roasted garlic mashed potates and tortilla lasagna). For something more substantial, try the honey coriander pork loin with adobo sauce or snapper with achiote rice. You might want to finish with another culinary first, a bourbon pecan crème brûlée that tastes every bit as good as it sounds.

INEXPENSIVE

Mi Tierra

218 Produce Row. ☎ **210/225-1262.** Reservations accepted for large groups only. Main courses $6.95–$14.95. AE, MC, V. Open 24 hours. MEXICAN.

Almost anyone who's ever been within striking distance of San Antonio has heard of this Market Square restaurant, open since 1946. Much expanded and gussied up since then, it still draws a faithful clientele of Latino families and businesspeople along with busloads of tourists. Where else could you come at 2am and order anything from chorizo and eggs to an 8-ounce charbroiled rib eye—and be serenaded by mariachis? A full menu is available all night, but you needn't have anything heavy. Mi Tierra is justly renowned for its *panadería* (bakery), and you can get all kinds of delicious *pan dulces* to go along with a cup of coffee or Mexican hot chocolate.

Pecan Street Market

152 E. Pecan St., No. 102. ☎ **210/227-3226.** Reservations not accepted. Sandwiches $3.75–$4.99. Mon–Fri 7:30am–6pm, Sat 10am–4pm; closed Sun. AE, DC, DISC, MC, V. DELI.

Choosing a sandwich can be difficult at this downtown deli and gourmet minimarket on the ground floor of the historic Exchange Building across from the Greyhound Station. Picking the condiment alone is a challenge—will it be chipotle mayonnaise, cranberry dijon, or sun-dried tomato spread? Area businesses, long stuck with the same old, same old, have welcomed this little industrial chic spot and its fresh soups, salads, specialty sandwiches (say pâté with truffles on a baguette), and tempting desserts. If you want to hole up in your hotel room during lunch and don't like what room service has, you can order in from here.

Schilo's

424 E. Commerce St. ☎ **210/223-6692.** Reservations not accepted. Sandwiches $2.50–$4.95; hot or cold plates $3.95–$4.90; main dishes (served after 5pm) $6.95–$8.95. AE, CB, DC, DISC, MC, V. Mon–Sat 7am–8:30pm. Closed Sun. GERMAN DELI.

You can't leave town without stopping into this San Antonio institution, if only for a hearty bowl of split-pea soup or a piece of the signature cherry cheesecake. The large, open room with its worn wooden booths gives a glimpse into the city's German past; the waitresses—definitely *not* "servers"—wear dirndl-type outfits and an oompah band plays on Saturday from 5 to 8pm. It's a great place to come for refueling when you're sightseeing near Alamo Plaza; for under $5, a good, greasy reuben or a bratwurst plate should keep you going for the rest of the day.

4 Southtown

MODERATE

Babylon Grill

910 S. Alamo. ☎ **210/229-9335.** Reservations accepted. Main courses $7.95–$18. AE, DISC, MC, V. Mon–Thurs 11am–11pm, Fri–Sat 11am–midnight, Sunday 11am–10pm. MEDITERRANEAN.

With its floor-to-ceiling windows and giant prints and murals set against stark white walls, the Babylon Grill is more art space than dining room. True to its decor, this chic restaurant in Southtown draws local artists and aspiring writers; it's a great place to linger over coffee and come up with that new idea for a film script. It's also fine for a light lunch—a salad of artichoke hearts, tomato, and basil, say, or a warm spinach salad with grilled tuna, herbed potatoes, and roasted peppers—or an after-theater brandy; this is one of the few restaurants in town that stays open until midnight. But the entrees are uneven. The roast pork loin with spicy potatoes or roast chicken with rosemary are usually reliable choices for dinner.

El Mirador

722 S. St. Mary's St. ☎ **210/225-9444.** Reservations required for five or more only. Main courses $7–$19. MC, V. Mon–Sat 6:30am–3pm; Wed–Sat 5:30–10pm; Sun brunch 9am–3pm. MEXICAN.

It's not the decor that draws locals of all stripes to this family-owned restaurant near the King William area, though Saltillo tile floors and a few art prints give a bit of character to two otherwise nondscript rooms. At breakfast, it's the huge plates of eggs scrambled with spicy *machacado* (dried beef) or cooked ranchero style. At lunchtime, it's such specials as enchiladas with chili con carne, rice, refried beans, salad, and two tortillas for $3.95. And at dinner, when the menu ranges over different tastes and regions in Mexico, well, everyone has their favorite. . . . The Monterrey-style cabrito (grilled goat) and grilled chicken with roasted poblano sauce are among mine, and it's hard to go wrong with the shrimp diablo—not quite as devilishly hot as its name suggests, but wonderfully redolent with garlic. The fresh catch of the day is also usually a winner. Save some room for the fruit tacos, served with an array of sorbets and fresh berries, and topped with chocolate sauce.

La Focaccia

800 S. Alamo. ☎ **210/223-5353.** Reservations required for six or more only. Pizzas $4.95–$8.95, pastas $4.95–$6.95, main courses $7.95–$14.95. AE, CB, DC, DISC, MC, V. Mon–Thurs 11am–2:30pm and 5–10pm; Fri–Sat 11am–midnight. ITALIAN.

In spite of its trendy name, its fast-becoming-trendy Southtown location, and its funky former gas-station setting, this restaurant is about as traditional as they come. Owner/chef Luigi Ciccarelli was born and raised in Rome; his recipes were handed down from his grandfather, who used to be a chef for the royal house. It's the type of place where an elderly waiter might tease you about finishing your food, but would never think of introducing himself. The same large menu appears for both lunch and dinner. You can opt for a well-prepared version of standards such as lasagna or spaghetti and meatballs; the seafood preparations are especially good. Portions are large, so try to resist scarfing down the basket of focaccia, made in the wood-burning pizza oven, that'll turn up on your table.

✪ Rosario's

1014 S. Alamo. ☎ **210/223-1806.** Reservations not accepted. $5.95–$12.95. AE, DC, DISC, MC, V. Mon–Sat 10:45am–3pm; Tues–Thurs 3–10pm, Fri–Sat 3pm–12:30am. MEXICAN.

No serapes or piñatas for this hip Mexican hangout. Housed in a green-brick building with a pink neon sign, Rosario's is dimly lit, done in turquoise and terracotta, and hung with folk art and paintings by local artists. Killer margaritas and huge schooners of beer emerge continuously from a large bar.

You might start with the grilled marinated shrimp, served with a cilantro dipping sauce, or tortilla soup laced with melting mild cheese. But consider the large helpings of such entrees as pork *carnitas* in cascabel pepper sauce or the excellent mole enchiladas, which come with rice, refried beans, and tortillas. The bargain weekday lunch specials—perhaps three chicken flautas with mole sauce for $4.25—draw a sizable local crowd, but it's on weekend nights, when a live tropical band plays, that the place really sizzles. A new covered patio invites lounging.

INEXPENSIVE

Guenther House

205 E. Guenther St. ☎ **210/227-1061.** Reservations not accepted. Breakfast $2.95–$6.25; lunch $4.75–$6.75. AE, DISC, MC, V. Mon–Sat 7am–3pm, Sun 8am–2pm (the house and mill store are open Mon–Sat 9am–5pm, Sun 8am–2pm). AMERICAN.

Not only is the food good at the Guenther House, but dining here is a great way to spend some time inside one of King William's historic homes. Hearty breakfasts and light lunches are served indoors in a pretty art nouveau–style dining room added on to the Guenther family residence (built in 1860) or outdoors on a trellised patio. The biscuits and gravy are a morning specialty and the pasta salad at lunch is excellent, but you can't go wrong with anything that involves the wonderful baked goods made on the premises. Adjoining the restaurant are a small museum, a Victorian parlor, and a mill store featuring baking-related items. The house fronts a lovely stretch of the San Antonio River; in the back, you can still see the Pioneer Flour Mill that earned the family its fortune.

5 North St. Mary's

MODERATE

Cafe Camile

517 E. Woodlawn. ☎ **210/735-2307.** Reservations recommended, especially on weekends. Main courses $9.95–$18.95. CB, DISC, DC, MC, V. Sun and Tues–Fri 11am–2pm and 5–10pm, Sat 5–11pm. ECLECTIC.

Just off North St. Mary's is an unusual, very appealing cafe. Expanded recently to encompass a former coffeehouse that fronts the road, it's no longer as difficult as it used to be to find. The back wall of the original dining room—formerly a furniture refinishing shop—is covered with an enticing mural; it's dominated by a well-known Manet bar scene, but other French Impressionists also put in an appearance.

The menu is as hard to pin down as the mural, including Mediterranean, continental, Italian, and southwestern dishes. No matter; all the dishes are freshly prepared with great attention to detail. The duck confit crêpe with apple and red onion chutney makes a fine starter, to be followed, perhaps, by the linguine with scallops, shrimp, mussels, tomatoes, and garlic; or the chicken breast rolled in pecans and baked crisp, then topped with a creamy Dijon mustard sauce. The restaurant has some of the best live jazz in town on Friday and Saturday nights, and there's a great Sunday brunch menu.

Liberty Bar

328 E. Josephine St. ☎ **210/227-1187.** Reservations recommended. Main courses $5.95–$18.95. AE, DISC, MC, V. Sun–Thurs 11:30am–10:30pm, Fri–Sat 11:30am–midnight; bar open until midnight Sun–Thurs, until 2am Fri–Sat. AMERICAN.

You'd be hard-pressed to guess from the outside that this ramshackle former brothel hosts one of the most chic haunts in San Antonio; the area looks unlikely, and the restaurant's name is nowhere to be found (look for the word *Boehlers* on a green-roofed building near the Hwy. 281 underpass).

Don't be put off; it's bright and inviting inside, and you'll find everything here from comfort food (pot roast, say, or a ham-and-swiss sandwich) to cutting-edge cuisine (maybe mesquite-grilled chicken breast with achiote). The toasted French bread with roast garlic spread or eggplant puree goes great with many of the fine—and generally affordable—wines available by the glass; there's a good beer selection, too. And don't worry, even if you've had a few too many, you're not imagining it: The house really *is* leaning.

INEXPENSIVE

El Milagrito Cafe

521 E. Woodlawn (at North St. Mary's). ☎ **210/734-8964.** Reservations not accepted. Tacos 85¢–$1.25; main courses $2.95–$4.25. No credit cards accepted. Mon–Sat 6am–6pm, Sun 6am–3pm. MEXICAN.

After you've spent the night before overindulging on the Strip, come back to this friendly, family-owned restaurant in the morning for a home-style Mexican breakfast; the steaming bowls of *menudo* are reputed to cure even the worst hangovers (just don't think about the ingredients). Sure, the mariachis that play every Saturday and Sunday morning might not do much for a headache—but everyone else should

---

🏛 Family-Friendly Restaurants

La Calesa *(p. 58)* Here you'll find an inexpensive "chiquitos" menu ($3 to $3.95) and a staff that loves youngsters. It's a great place to introduce your kids to Mexican food.

Olmos Pharmacy *(p. 55)* Kids entertain themselves by swiveling the seats at this classic soda fountain, where the food is as reasonable as it comes. They won't even mind too much when you go on and on about how this is ice cream the way it's supposed be.

Schilo's *(p. 51)* A high noise level, a convenient location near the River Walk (but with prices far lower than anything you'll find there), as well as a wide selection of familiar food make this German deli a good choice.

---

enjoy the musical accompaniment to tacos loco (filled with potato, eggs, beans, and sausage) or huevos rancheros. Owned by the same couple for the last 25 years, El Milagrito is decked with posters and photos of Mexican revolutionary Emiliano Zapata. Much of the one-page photocopied menu is in Spanish only, but the staff is happy to explain anything you don't understand.

6 San Antonio College / Monte Vista / Olmos Park

EXPENSIVE

Chez Ardid

1919 San Pedro Ave. ☎ **210/732-3203.** Reservations recommended. Main courses $12.50–$25. AE, CB, DC, MC, V. Mon–Fri 11:30am–2pm; Mon–Sat 6–10pm. Closed Sun. FRENCH.

Wedding classic French cuisine with regional ingredients, Chef Miguel Ardid presides over one of the most enduring favorites in town (he took over the toque from his late father, Guillermo). It's hard to choose among the dining rooms in this lovely 1902 home, restored by the Ardid family in the late 1970s; the former central atrium, with its high ceilings and classical columns, has an appealing simplicity, but the Versailles Room behind it retains much of the house's original detail, with a lovely carved oak mantel, oak-and-mahogany parquet floors, and a tinwork ceiling. (Smokers don't have to wrack their brains; they get a smaller but still attractive dining room off to the side.)

You might start your meal with crevettes à la texanne (shrimp sautéed with cactus pads, sun-dried tomatoes, chèvre, and white wine) or a more classic escargot bourguigons. The deboned pheasant stuffed with wild boar sausage is an excellent entree selection, as is the tenderloin medaillon in green peppercorn sauce. This is one of the few places around that still serves, well, innards: tasty sweetbreads in a Madeira wine sauce, say, or tender veal kidneys with port wine and mushrooms. Along with the expected French labels, the wine list includes some good local bottles.

✪ Restaurant Biga

206 E. Locust St. ☎ **210/225-0722.** Reservations accepted for five or more only. Main courses $14–$26. AE, CB, DC, DISC, MC, V. Mon–Thurs 5:30–10:30pm, Fri–Sat 5:30–11pm; closed Sun. NEW AMERICAN.

Giving the lie to the maxim "Never trust a thin chef," lanky Bruce Auden turns out some of the finest food in San Antonio—and anywhere else for that matter. But while Auden's attention to menu detail is serious and the restaurant is set in a 100-year-old house, Biga is no hushed temple of haute cuisine.

For one thing, the dining rooms are not overly formal: One is bright with pale yellow walls and lots of windows; the other is masculine cozy, with dark wood and a fireplace. And the menu has a sense of humor. Among the appetizers is one called simply "expensive mushrooms." These—they're shiitakes—are very good, but the flavorful radicchio game packets are even better. Those who want to pace themselves might consider the mildly spicy Thai vegetable salad. (Much of the food—especially the habanero ketchup—has a definite kick; if you tend to walk on the mild side, inquire about the heat of the dishes.) Although the menu changes regularly, you can depend on seeing quail or pheasant and oak-roasted Nilgai antelope; the Texas-bred game imported from Africa is remarkably tender. Among the "Desserts to Cheat For" is a spectacular crème brûlée.

The wonderful peasant breads accompanying each meal come from next door's LocuStreet Bakery, the brainchild of Auden's wife, Debra (Biga is Italian slang for a sourdough starter). In addition to an extensive wine list, which thoughtfully groups together the "expensive red wines" and "expensive white wines," Biga also has the best beer selection in town.

INEXPENSIVE

Olmos Pharmacy

3902 McCullough. ☎ **210/822-3361.** Mon–Fri 7am–7:30pm, Sat 8am–5:30pm, Sun 9am–1:30pm. $1.45–$3.25. AMERICAN.

When was the last time you had a rich chocolate malt served in a large metal container with a glass of whipped cream on the side? Never mind, don't think about it—just grab a stool at the fountain's Formica counter and enjoy. Olmos Pharmacy, opened in 1938 (one of the waitresses has been around since the early '60s), also scoops up old-fashioned ice-cream sodas, Coke or rootbeer floats, sundaes, banana splits . . . if it's cold, sweet, and nostalgia inducing, they've got it. This is also the place to come for a filling breakfast, be it American or Mexican; for a vast array of tacos; and for classic burgers and sandwiches, all at seriously retro prices.

7 Broadway / Alamo Heights

EXPENSIVE

L'Etoile

6106 Broadway. ☎ **210/826-4551.** Reservations recommended. Main courses $9.95–$23.95 (lobster may be higher); early-bird menu (daily 5:30–6:30pm) $11.95. AE, DC, MC, V. Mon–Sat 11:30am–2:30pm; Sun–Thurs 5:30–10pm, Fri–Sat 5:30–11pm. FRENCH.

Knowing some attitude adjustment might be required, the three French owners of this appealing bistro set out to convince a kicked-back Texas town that French dining need not be overly formal. They've managed to combine top-notch service and excellent food with a relaxed atmosphere, and to offer a sufficient number of specials—especially at lunch—to show that you need not spend half the plane fare to France to eat like a Parisian.

Moorish archways, dun-colored brick walls, and an enclosed patio create a Mediterranean mood; upstairs there's an intimate skylit dining nook. The menus change daily, but the focus is always on seafood, as the live-lobster tank attests; you can order your favorite crustacean poached, flamed in cognac, or stuffed with crabmeat. Or, if it's available, consider the fresh red snapper in a potato crust. For dessert, the black-and-white chocolate mousse on a raspberry coulis looks almost too gorgeous to eat. Almost. Portions are large, French bread rolls are hot and crusty, and a good wine list has some affordable bottles.

It's easy to miss this restaurant, located in a small shopping complex on Albany that turns up suddenly as you round a bend heading north from downtown on Broadway. There's free valet parking once you find it.

✪ Mesteña

7959 Broadway. ☎ **210/822-7733.** Reservations recommended on weekends. $14–$24. AE, MC, V. Mon–Thurs 11:30am–2:30pm and 5:30–10pm, Fri–Sat 11:30am–2:30pm and 5:30–10:30, Sun 11am–3pm (brunch) and 5–9:30pm. SOUTHWESTERN.

San Antonio is not known for the type of creative cuisine that proliferates in Texas cities such as Austin and Dallas—which is why the 1996 arrival of Mesteña and chef Chris Swinyard, formerly of Washington D.C.'s famed Red Sage Restaurant, was such big news. The wild horses for which the restaurant is named apply more to the exciting menu than to the stark, high-ceilinged room, which only hints at the West with its faux exposed adobe walls and pictures by two western photographers.

Presentations are gorgeous: The roasted corn soup was swirled with smoked shrimp salsa, while the salmon and ahi tuna tartar appetizer was piled in a column flanked by horseradish lavash crackers. A seared rabbit loin entree arrived in round cuts with cheddar cheese grits (I had to wonder where they found such a large rabbit—but then, this is Texas), while the pecan-crusted rack of lamb came with goat cheese dumplings. With a few unimportant exceptions, the flavors complemented each other wonderfully. The impressive wine list is far longer than the menu; it tends toward the high end, but you can find some reasonable bottles.

MODERATE

Barcelona's Café

4901 Broadway. ☎ **210/822-6129.** Reservations accepted only for parties of six or more. Tapas $2–$6; main courses $8–$16. AE, DC, DISC, MC, V. Daily 11am–11pm. MEDITERRANEAN.

Stark white walls, wood beam ceilings, Saltillo tile floors, colorful art prints, and opaque blue glassware give Barcelona's an updated Mediterranean look—the perfect setting for its updated Mediterranean menu. The tapas are not the often-heavy appetizers served in Spain but, rather, small portions of such lighter fare as warm Brie, green apples, and raspberry sauce or red pepper hummus with pita toast. For an entree, try the terrific paella, with seafood, spicy sausage, ham, and saffron rice; or the Moorish lamb chops with yogurt feta sauce.

The adjoining patio bar offers a small tapas, dessert, and coffee menu; live flamenco music on Saturday night helps pass the time during the sometimes-long waits on the weekends, as does the delicious frozen sangría. In addition to a chic young crowd, you'll see lots of dark-haired men in business suits who look like they're cutting important NAFTA-related deals.

Barn Door

8400 N. New Braunfels Ave. ☎ **210/824-0116.** Reservations recommended for dinner. Main courses $7.95–$28.95. AE, DISC, MC, V. Mon–Fri 11am–2pm; Mon–Thurs 5–10pm, Fri–Sat 5–10:30pm; Sun noon–9pm. AMERICAN.

Photographs on the walls of this sprawling, down-home Texas steakhouse show a San Antonio of 1955, when the restaurant first opened its doors. Hundreds of business cards attached to every possible space attest to the number of folks who continue to come here from all around to enjoy good cuts of charcoal-broiled beef.

Not all of them scarf down steaks the size of the 24-ounce T-bone in the display case at the entryway; most opt for the 6-, 8-, or 12-ounce filets. However, if you've been feeling overly underindulgent, consider the chopped sirloin topped with spicy cheese and sliced avocado, or the chicken-fried steak: The usual versions of the latter dish use pounded thin, tenderized beef, but here a regular rib eye gets the Kentucky colonel treatment.

Call ahead if you're dining here to celebrate an anniversary or a birthday; the event will be announced on a billboard above the front door.

Boardwalk Bistro and Brewery

4011 Broadway. ☎ **210/824-0100.** Reservations required for five or more only. Main courses $7.95–$15.95. AE, DC, DISC, MC, V. Mon–Thurs 11am–10:30pm, Fri–Sat 11am–11:30pm. Closed Sun. ECLECTIC.

Alamo Heights residents seeking almost anything you can think of to eat head slightly south to this upscale local bistro. Many are drawn by the large vegetarian selection, hard to come by in this beef-oriented town. Among the standouts are the grilled tofu Caesar salad and the paella Gardinera, an all-vegetable version of the Spanish rice dish. An excellent Mediterranean sampler, including hummus, tabbouleh, Greek olives, and dolmas (grape leaves stuffed with herb rice and veggies), is served with warm pita bread.

But between the fine homemade soups and fresh-baked desserts, you'll also find everything from curried chicken salad to filet mignon on the huge menu. The cappuccino and espresso are as strong as they should be, as are some of the excellent beers produced by San Antonio's first microbrewery, opened next door in 1994. Live music on the weekends ranges from Celtic to jazz.

Cappy's

5011 Broadway. ☎ **210/828-9669.** Reservations recommended. Main courses $8.50–$17. AE, MC, V. Mon–Thurs 11am–10pm, Fri–Sat 11am–11pm, Sun 10:30am–10pm. REGIONAL AMERICAN.

One of the earliest businesses to open up in the now-burgeoning Alamo Heights neighborhood, Cappy's is set in an unusual broken-brick structure dating back to the late 1930s. But there's nothing outdated about this cheerful, light-filled place, with its high, wood-beam ceilings, hanging plants, and colorful work by local artists; there's also a romantic, tree-shaded outdoor patio.

As you enter, the enticing smell of the wood-burning grill (no, not mesquite, but the somewhat milder live oak) gives a hint of some of the house specialties: the prime rib eye or Mustang Chicken in a fresh horseradish crust. Lighter fare includes cappellini with artichoke hearts and grilled shrimp. Daily heart-healthy specials are offered and, after 5pm, you can order from a market menu that coordinates entrees with wines. When you're trying to find Cappy's, keep an eye out for the Twig Book Store; the restaurant is tucked away behind it. The recently opened Cappyccino's, just next door, is ideal for quick lunches, light dinners, or after-theater drinks.

✪ Koi Kawa

4051 Broadway. ☎ **210/521-7421.** Reservations recommended on the weekends. Main courses $10–$22. AE, DISC, DC, MC, V. Mon–Thurs 11:30am–2pm and 5:30–10pm, Fri and Sat 5:30–11pm. JAPANESE.

David Mukai is the sushi dude. At least that's what some of his devoted fans, who sit around Koi Kawa's sushi bar and watch him perform magic with raw fish, call him. Among the secrets of his success is the use of high-quality ingredients such as real crabmeat and hothouse-grown cucumbers. But if you don't want to put yourself in the amicable Mukai's hands, there are plenty of other options. The crispy tempuras, vegetable, seafood, or shrimp, get a lot of attention, as do the various udon (wheat noodle) and soba (cold buckwheat noodle) soups, meals in themselves. The unassuming Koi Kawa is in the back of the Boardwalk complex, with a view of the tree-shaded banks of the San Antonio River (admittedly, a generally stagnant section). It's a bit hard to locate, but by all means persevere.

⑤ La Calesa

2103 E. Hildebrand. ☎ **210/822-4475.** Reservations not accepted. Main courses $5.95–$16.50. AE, CB, DC, DISC, MC, V. Mon–Thurs 11am–9:30pm, Fri 11am–10pm, Sat 9am–10pm, Sun 9am–9pm. MEXICAN.

Tucked away in an old house just off Broadway—look for Earl Abel's large sign across the street—this family-run restaurant features dishes from the southern Yucatán region, rather than from the northern areas that tend to influence the Tex-Mex style. The difference is mainly in the sauces, and they're done to perfection here. The mole, for example, strikes a fine balance between its rich chocolate base and the picante spices. The conchinita pibil, a classic Yucatecan pork dish—the meat is marinated and served in an achiote sauce—also has a marvelous texture and taste. Rice and black beans (to my mind richer than the usual pintos) accompany many of the meals. Everything is cooked up fresh, including the tortilla chips; even the coffee is good. You can eat indoors in one of three cozy dining rooms, decorated with Diego Rivera prints and Mexican tile work, or outside on the wooden porch.

Luna Notte

6402 N. New Braunfels Ave. ☎ **210/822-4242.** Reservations recommended on weekends. Pasta $8.50–$12.95; main courses $14.95–$17.95. AE, CB, DC, DISC, MC, V. Mon–Thurs 5:30–10:30pm, Fri–Sat 5:30–11pm, Sun 5:30–10pm. ITALIAN.

The high-tech moon hanging above the door of this Sunset Mall restaurant hints at the stylish room inside. An open wood-burning oven imparts some warmth to the industrial-style dining space (not literally—the air-conditioning works just fine), which is all stark grays and blacks and designed down to the last candle holder. The kitchen turns out some mighty tasty pizzas, pastas, and breads. Ingredients are as chic as the setting, but the sauces and portion sizes are nowhere near as pared down.

The cappellini alla napoletana, topped with fresh tomatoes, basil, and olive oil, will leave you very satisfied, as will the linguini alla pescatore; you get a choice of a marinara or alfredo sauce for this seafood-heaped pasta. The smoked pork loin with sun-dried cherries and the hazelnut-roasted chicken breast stuffed with proscuitto, spinach, ricotta, and eggplant are also excellent.

Van's

3214 Broadway. ☎ **210/828-8449.** Reservations for large parties only. Main courses $6.95–$12.95. AE, DC, DISC, MC, V. Daily 11am–10pm. CHINESE/JAPANESE/VIETNAMESE.

The sign outside announces that Van's is a "Chinese Seafood Restaurant and Sushi Bar" and the menu also has a Vietnamese component. Viet Nam (see below), right next door, offers Thai dishes, so between the two, this little stretch of Broadway has got most of the favorite cuisines of Asia covered. The dining room at Van's is appealing with green and white tablecloths, and the menu is huge; if you like seafood, go for the restaurant's touted specialty—fresh lobster or crab with black-bean sauce (market prices)—or crispy jumbo shrimp, deep-fried and covered with peppercorns. You can also consider one of the meal-size soups—shredded pork with rice noodles, say, or a vegetarian clay pot preparation—or tasty versions of such Szechuan standards as the spicy kung pao chicken with carrots and peanuts.

Viet Nam

3244 Broadway. ☎ **210/822-7461.** Reservations required for five or more only. Main courses $5.50–$11. AE, MC, V. Daily 11am–10pm. VIETNAMESE/THAI.

This family-owned restaurant, just south of Alamo Heights, doesn't look like much from the outside—or from the inside, for that matter: It's dimly lit, with fairly standard Asian decor, though a large smiling Buddha greets you in the entryway. What draws the locals in is not the ambience, but a wide-ranging menu that includes everything from well-known Thai favorites such as the crispy noodle and vegetable *pad thai* to more exotic fare like *banh xeo,* a Vietnamese crêpe stuffed with pork. The delicate snow rolls with peanut sauce make a fine starter; heartier appetites might consider the pound of crab claws in a spicy butter and lemon sauce. The very reasonably priced chicken with lemongrass combination plate comes with crunchy spring rolls. All the dishes are well complemented by the Vietnamese "fish sauce" found on each table and by supersweet lemon ice tea.

Water Street Oyster Bar
7500 Broadway. ☎ **210/829-4853.** Reservations not accepted (but call-ahead is available). Main courses $7.95–$15.95. AE, DISC, MC, V. Sun–Thurs 11am–11pm, Fri–Sat 11am–midnight. SEAFOOD.

For seafood with a Cajun and south-of-the-border flair, come to this open, modern dining room in Alamo Heights' toney Lincoln Heights shopping center. Light meals or reasonably priced full-course plates are available throughout the day. The spicy seafood gumbo is always reliable, as are the New Orleans–style fried oyster sandwiches, but your best bet is the fresh-catch board; whatever comes in that day can be prepared for you blackened or—particularly recommended—*nueces* style (topped with shrimp and crabmeat in a browned butter sauce). Oysters are 25¢ each at happy hour (5 to 7pm every day).

A large mural of a fisherman, along with canvas rigging material on the side of the staircase leading to the upstairs dining area, lends this place an appropriately nautical look. And they run a tight ship here: Service is efficient, even when the room is crowded.

INEXPENSIVE

Earl Abel's
4200 Broadway. ☎ **210/822-3358.** Reservations accepted for parties of eight or more only. Sandwiches $4.25–$6.25; main courses $4.75–$12.95. AE, CB, DC, DISC, MC, V. Daily 6:30am–1am. AMERICAN.

Earl Abel opened his first restaurant on Main Street in 1933; an organist for silent-film theaters in the 1920s, he had to find something else to do when the talkies took over. But his old Hollywood pals didn't forget him; Bing Crosby and Gloria Swanson always dropped in to Earl's place when they blew through San Antone.

His granddaughter now runs the restaurant, which moved to Broadway in 1940, and the menu is much like it was more than 50 years ago, when what's now called comfort food was simply chow. The restaurant is no longer open 24 hours, but you can still come in after midnight for a cup of coffee and a thick slice of lemon-meringue pie. Fried chicken remains the all-time favorite, but lots of folks come around for a hearty breakfast of eggs and biscuits, gravy, and grits.

8 Balcones Heights

MODERATE

La Fogata
2427 Vance Jackson. ☎ **210/340-0636.** Reservations recommended on weekends. Main courses $6–$11. AE, CB, DC, DISC, MC, V. Mon–Thurs 11am–10:30pm, Fri 11am–midnight, Sat 7:30am–midnight, Sun 7:30am–11am. MEXICAN.

A massive carved wooden door opens into the fountain-splashed courtyard of this northside Mexican restaurant, reminiscent of a sprawling Spanish villa. (If you get lost, as I did, you can also enter through one of the many parking lots.) This place is huge: It started out in 1978 as a single dining room and then, like Topsy, just grew. Plant-draped trellises divide a number of smaller outdoor eating areas, all with Mexican tile floors, wrought-iron tables, and lots of greenery. The newest indoor dining room, done in light wood and hung with Frida Kahlo prints, is the best place to beat the heat.

Many of the dishes served here are from recipes of the owner's mother-in-law, who grew up in Cuernavaca. Along with the more familiar tacos and tamales, you'll find such dishes as *queso flameado* (Mexican sausage mixed with melted Oaxaca cheese and served with tortillas) or *chile poblano al carbon* (pepper stuffed with chicken and cheese and charcoal flamed). The menu is as large as the restaurant and often confusing—some items first listed among the appetizers and soups turn up again among the entrees—but the friendly servers will gladly help you sort it all out. Don't leave without checking out the celebrity photo wall; everyone from Bill Clinton to Shaquille O'Neal has eaten here.

9 Northwest / Medical Center

MODERATE

Aldo's

8539 Fredericksburg Rd. ☎ **210/696-2536.** Reservations recommended, especially on weekends. Main courses $11.50–$24. AE, CB, DC, DISC, MC, V. Mon–Thurs 11am–10pm, Fri 11am–11pm, Sat 5–11pm, Sun 5–10pm. ITALIAN.

A northwest San Antonio favorite, Aldo's offers good, old-fashioned Italian food in a pretty, old-fashioned setting. You can enjoy your meal outside on a tree-shaded patio or inside a 100-year-old former ranch house in one of a series of Victorian-style dining rooms.

The scampi Valentino, sautéed shrimp with a basil cream sauce, is a nice starter, as is the lighter steamed mussels in marinara sauce (available seasonally). For an Italian comfort food combo, try the *piatto del capo cuoco:* lasagna, cannelloni, veal parmigiana, and spaghetti. A house specialty, the sautéed snapper di Aldo comes topped with fresh lump crabmeat, artichoke hearts, mushrooms, and tomatoes in a lemon-butter white-wine sauce.

Bistro Time

5137 Fredericksburg Rd. ☎ **210/344-6626.** Reservations recommended. Main courses $9–$24. AE, CB, DC, MC, V. Mon–Thurs 5–9pm, Fri–Sat 5–10pm. Closed Sun. CONTINENTAL.

In a nondescript mall in a nondescript northwest neighborhood, a gem of a restaurant hides. This elegant place, with a central fountain and candlelit tables, features classic continental cuisine. The executive chef/owner is from Holland, but the only menu hint is the Matjes herring tucked away among the appetizers.

The menu changes twice weekly, but you can depend on seeing such standards as steak Diane, sautéed with brandy, mushrooms, green onions, and garlic in cream sauce. This is not a place to watch your weight; portions are huge and rich sauces are a specialty (it's easy to catch people surreptitiously mopping their plates with their rolls). And the desserts are especially hard to resist; if you're lucky, a supremely chocolatey Sacher torte might be in your stars. The early-bird specials (Mon–Thurs 5–6pm) are a good value.

10 The Airport Area

INEXPENSIVE

Demo's
7115 Blanco Rd. ☎ **210/342-2772.** No reservations. Main courses $3.25–$6.95. AE, DISC, MC, V. Mon–Thurs 11am–9pm, Fri–Sat 11am–10pm, Sun noon–8pm. GREEK.

The area around Loop 410 across from Central Park Mall is pretty soulless, which makes this little bit of Greece doubly welcome. In a two-tiered dining room with a trompe l'oeil painting of a white stucco fishing village, you can enjoy gyros, Greek burgers, dolmas, spanikopita, and other Mediterreanean specialties; if you go for the Dieter's Special, a Greek salad with your choice of gyros or souvlaki (chicken or beef), you might be able to justify the baklava. In addition to this original location, opened in 1979, there's another Demo's on St. Mary's strip at 2501 N. St. Mary's St. (☎ 210/732-7777), across from a Greek Orthodox church. A belly dancer gyrates at the Blanco location on Monday night, at St. Mary's on Wednesday.

11 Leon Springs

MODERATE

Romano's Macaroni Grill
24116 I-10 west (Leon Springs/Boerne Stage Rd. exit). ☎ **210/698-0003.** Reservations only accepted weeknights for parties of 15 or more. Main courses $5.95–$15.95. AE, CB, DC, DISC, MC, V. Sun–Thurs 11am–10pm, Fri–Sat 11am–11pm. ITALIAN.

Some Saturday nights it seems like everyone's abandoned San Antonio for tiny Leon Springs—a former stagecoach stop some 20 miles northwest of town—that's how crowded Macaroni's gets. Don't come here for a quiet, romantic evening; just grab everyone you can gather for a raucous Italian dinner.

The restaurant tries to hire opera-singing servers, so strains of Puccini might break out in the room anytime. Most revelry inspiring, however, are the open gallon jugs of wine from which diners help themselves; at the end of the meal, they simply report how many glasses they've had—if they can remember. The menu focuses on northern Italian dishes, particularly grilled seafood and meat; you'll see the mesquite rotisserie as you enter the large, wood-and-stone dining room, originally a dance hall. Such standards as chicken scaloppine are well prepared, and all the pastas and bread are baked fresh on the premises.

Rudy's
24152 I-10 west (Leon Springs/Boerne Stage Rd. exit). ☎ **210/698-0418.** Reservations not accepted. $4.99/lb for barbecue, $10.95 rack of ribs. Sun–Thurs 10am–9pm, Fri–Sat 10am–11pm. BARBECUE.

You've got to know the drill at Rudy's. Wait in one line (just follow the crowd) for the meat—pork ribs, beef short ribs, brisket, sausage, huge turkey legs, you name it; it'll come wrapped up in butcher paper, with lots and lots of white bread. Then, if you want a side dish—beans, creamed corn, potato salad, coleslaw—or some peach cobbler, go next door to the country store. Now plunk it all down on one of the red-and-white checked vinyl tablecloths or bring it back outside to the wooden picnic tables; there's barbecue sauce in both places. Enjoy. You'll be rubbing elbows here with cowboys, bicyclists, and other city folk who come from miles around for what they insist is the best barbecue in town.

It's Always Chili in San Antonio

It ranks up there with apple pie in the American culinary pantheon, but nobody's mom originated chili: The stew, which contains peppers, onions, and a variety of spices, was likely conceived around the 1840s by Texas cowboys who needed to make tough meat palatable and to cover up its taste when it began to go bad. The name is a Texas bowdlerization of the Spanish "chile" ("chill-ay"), the peppers most conventionally used.

The appellation *chili con carne* is really redundant in Texas, where chili without meat isn't considered chili at all; indeed, most Texans think that adding beans is only for wusses. Beef is the most commonly used base, but everything from armadillo to venison is acceptable.

No one really knows exactly where chili originated, but San Antonio is the prime candidate for that distinction: In the mid-19th century, accounts were widespread of the town's "chili queens," women who ladled steaming bowls of the concoction in open-air markets and street corners. It wasn't until the 1940s that they stopped dishing out chili in front of the Alamo.

William Gebhardt helped strengthen San Antonio's claim to chili fame when he began producing chili powder in the city in 1896. His Original Mexican Dinner package, which came out around 20 years later, included a can each of chili con carne, beans, and tamales, among other things; it fed five and cost $1. This precursor of the TV dinner proved so popular that it earned San Antonio the nickname "Tamaleville."

Oddly enough, chili isn't generally found on San Antonio restaurant menus. But modern-day chili queens come out in force for special events at Market Square, as well as for Nights in Old San Antonio, one of the most popular bashes of the city's huge Fiesta celebration. And there's not a weekend that goes by without a chili cookoff somewhere in the city. For the king of all chili competitions, however, you need to go to Terlingua, Texas, where the World Championship Chili Cookoff is held each November.

12 Only in San Antonio

Some of the best and most popular places to eat Mexican have been reviewed above, but you can be sure you'll run into San Antonians who are passionate about their personal favorite *tacquerias.* Many swear by **Blanco Cafe,** 5525 Blanco Rd. (☎ **210/ 344-0531**), and 419 N. St. Mary's (☎ **210/271-3300**); unless you like paintings on velvet, don't come here for atmosphere, but for good, greasy Tex-Mex at seriously low prices.

You'll also find emotions rising when the talk runs to barbecue, with many locals insisting that the place they go to is the best and most authentic—because the meat has been smoked the longest, because the place uses the best smoking technique, because the sauce is the tangiest . . . the criteria are endless and often completely arcane to outsiders. San Antonio has more than 90 places to sample barbecue. Rudy's in Leon Springs and the County Line in North Central are reviewed above; a few other possibilities in town for a smoked-meat fix include **Bob's Smokehouse** at 5145 Fredericksburg Rd. (☎ **210/344-8401**), 3306 Roland Ave. (☎ **210/ 333-9338**), and 1219 S. St. Mary's St. (☎ **210/224-4717**); **Texas Pride,** 2980 E.

Loop 1604 S at LaVernia Rd. (☎ **210/649-3730**); and **Tommy Wilson's,** U.S. 281 between Loop 1604 and Hwy. 46 (☎ 210/980-3052).

Bun 'N' Barrel, 1150 Austin Hwy. (☎ **210/828-2829**), stands out less for its cooking than for its classic cars; San Antonians have been coming here for 50 years to check out each other's cool Chevys. Hang around on Friday night and you might even see the occasional drag race down Austin Highway. The winner gets the other guy's car.

6

What to See & Do
in San Antonio

San Antonio's dogged preservation of its past and avid development of its future guarantee that there's something in town to suit every visitor's taste. The biggest problem with sightseeing here is figuring out how to get it all in; you can spend days in the downtown area alone and still not cover everything (the itineraries below give some suggestions on how to organize your time). Walkers will love being able to hoof it from one downtown attraction to another, but the sedentary needn't despair—or drive. One of the most visitor-friendly cities imaginable, San Antonio has excellent and inexpensive tourist transportation lines, extending to such far-flung sights as Sea World and Six Flags Fiesta Texas.

Before you visit any of the paid attractions, stop in at the San Antonio Visitor Information Center, 317 Alamo Plaza (☎ **210/ 270-8748**), across the street from the Alamo, and ask for their SAVE San Antonio discount book, including everything from the large theme parks to some city tours and museums. Many hotels also have a stash of discount coupons for their guests.

SUGGESTED ITINERARIES

If You Have 1 Day

If your time is very limited, it makes sense to stay downtown, where many of the prime attractions are concentrated. Start your day at the Alamo, which tends to get more crowded as the day goes on. When you finish touring the complex, take a streetcar from Alamo Square to HemisFair Park; from the observation deck at the Tower of the Americas you can literally see everything there is to see in town. Then board the streetcar again and head to the nearby King William Historic District, where you can pick up a self-guided walking tour at the office of the San Antonio Conservation Society. If you're really hungry by now, have lunch at the historic Guenther House; if you can hold out and have a hankering for Mexican food, wait until you get to Market Square (another streetcar will get you there) and eat at Mi Tierra or La Margarita, both owned by the same family. Spend the afternoon poking around the two square blocks of shops and stalls and then head over to the River Walk, where you might catch a riverboat tour before eating at one of the riverside restaurants (I'd vote for Boudro's). Or, if you can manage to get tickets to anything at either the Majestic or the Arneson River theaters, eat early (again, you'll have beaten the crowds) and enjoy the show.

If You Have 2 Days

Day 1   Follow the same itinerary outlined above.

Day 2   See the San Antonio missions in the morning (at the least, Mission San José). In the afternoon, go to the McNay, Lone Star, or Witte Museums, all on the same bus route as the missions. If you're traveling with kids, you might want to visit the Children's Museum first thing in the morning, and then go to Sea World or Six Flags Fiesta Texas in the afternoon (although the Witte is terrific for kids, too).

If You Have 3 Days

Day 1   Start at the Alamo and then tour the rest of the missions; that way you'll see the military shrine in its historic context. Spend the late afternoon at one of the theme parks or at one of the museums (the San Antonio Art Museum, the McNay, or the Witte).

Day 2   Go to HemisFair Park and visit the Tower of the Americas and the Institute of Texan Cultures; then stroll around nearby La Villita. Afterward, head down to the King William district and take the tour of the Steves Homestead. In the afternoon, enjoy a riverboat tour and/or visit the Southwest Craft Center.

Day 3   See the Spanish Governor's Palace and the Navarro Cathedral, and then shop and have lunch at Market Square. In the afternoon, go to one of the museums you haven't yet visited.

If You Have 4 Days

Days 1–3   Follow the itinerary outlined in "If You Have 3 Days," but eliminate the attractions in the Brackenridge Park area (the Witte and the McNay Museums), substituting another downtown sight or a theme park.

Day 4   Visit the attractions in the Brackenridge Park area, including the Japanese Tea Garden, the Witte Museum, the McNay Museum, the zoo, and the San Antonio Botanical Gardens. Some of the best restaurants in San Antonio are in this part of town.

If You Have 5 Days or More

Days 1–4   Follow the above 4-day itinerary, but break it up with:

Day 5   A day trip to Bandera, in scenic ranch country; this sleepy cowboy town will remind you that you're in the Wild West. An afternoon trail ride is great, but if you have more time, book a room at one of Bandera's many dude ranches; a 2-night minimum stay is usually required.

1 The Top Attractions

✪ The Alamo

300 Alamo Plaza. ☎ **210/225-1391.** Free admission (donations welcome). Mon–Sat 9am–5:30pm, Sun 10am–5:30pm, until 6:30pm Memorial Day–Labor Day. Closed Christmas Eve and Christmas. All streetcar lines.

Expecting something more dramatic and remote, many are surprised to find the Alamo, Texas's most visited site, sitting smack in the heart of downtown San Antonio. But you'll immediately recognize the graceful mission church, a ubiquitous symbol of the state. It was here that 188 Texas volunteers defied the much larger army—the size ranges with the Texas chauvinism of the teller—of Mexican dictator Santa Anna for 13 days in March 1836. Although all the men, including pioneers

Davy Crockett and Jim Bowie, were killed, their deaths were used by Sam Houston in the cry "Remember the Alamo" to rally his troops into defeating the Mexican army at the Battle of San Jacinto one month later, securing Texas's independence.

The Daughters of the Republic of Texas, who saved the crumbling complex from being turned into a hotel by a New York syndicate in 1905, maintain it as a shrine to these fighters. But there are some who would like to see more emphasis placed on the Alamo's other historic roles—including that of being a burial ground for the Native Americans for whom it was founded on a nearby site in 1718 as the Mission San Antonio de Valero. The complex was secularized by the end of the 18th century and leased out to a Spanish cavalry unit; by the time the famous battle took place, it had been abandoned.

Little remains of the original mission today; only the Long Barrack (formerly the *convento*, or living quarters for the missionaries) and the mission church are still here. The former houses a museum detailing the history of Texas in general and the battle in particular; the latter includes artifacts of the Alamo fighters, along with an information desk and small gift shop. A larger museum and gift shop are at the back of the complex; there's also a peaceful garden and an excellent research library (closed Sunday) on the grounds.

Six Flags Fiesta Texas

17000 I-10 west (corner of I-10 west and Loop 1604). ☎ **210/697-5050.** Admission $31 adults (48 inches and taller), children (under 48 inches) and seniors $21, children 2 and under free. Parking $5 per day. The schedule varies greatly with the season; the park is generally open weekends or Fri–Sun from Sept–Nov and Mar–May, open daily from late May–late Aug. Park opening hours are 10am; closing 9 or 10pm, depending on the season. Call ahead for current information. Closed Dec–Jan. Bus: 94. Take exit 555 on I-10 west.

Prices for this theme park were raised dramatically when Six Flags acquired it in 1996, and its signature live shows were cut back quite a bit. Still, this $100 million theme park is a good way to get a taste of the attractions of the entire state—literally as well as figuratively. A vast variety of food booths share the 200-acre amusement arena with rides, games, and craft demonstrations galore. Dramatic 100-foot cliffs surround the park, which is set in an abandoned limestone quarry on the north end of town.

The attractions are organized around four themes: Mexican fiesta, German village, country and western, and vintage rock and roll (remember, Buddy Holly was from Texas). Because Six Flags is a Time Warner company, such cartoon characters as Bugs Bunny have taken up residence. There's also a water park—bring your suit—and a simulated seaside boardwalk with a Ferris wheel, roller-skating rink, and nine-hole miniature golf course. Park highlights include the Rattler, the highest and fastest wooden roller coaster in the world; the Gully Washer, a soak-you-to-the-bone river-rapids ride; and the new Joker's Revenge roller coaster—with a funhouse entryway and a reverse start, it's the first of its kind in North America. The high-tech Atomic Adventure area includes laser games and virtual reality simulators. In summer, be sure to stay around for the laser-light show put on each evening before the park closes.

La Villita National Historic District

Bounded by Durango, Navarro, and Alamo Sts. and the River Walk. ☎ **210/207-8610.** Free admission. Daily; shop hours 10am–6pm. Closed Thanksgiving, Christmas, New Year's Day. Bus: 40. Streetcar: HemisFair Park/La Villita/Cattleman Square.

Developed by European settlers along the higher east bank of the San Antonio River in the late 18th and early 19th centuries, La Villita (the Little Village) was on the proverbial wrong side of the tracks until flooding of the west bank settlements made it the fashionable place to live. It fell back into poverty by the beginning of the 20th

Downtown San Antonio Attractions & Shopping

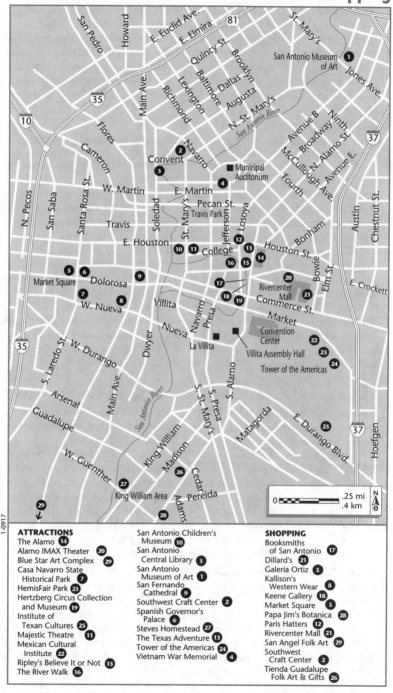

ATTRACTIONS
The Alamo ⑭
Alamo IMAX Theater ⑳
Blue Star Art Complex ㉙
Casa Navarro State
   Historical Park ⑦
HemisFair Park ㉓
Hertzberg Circus Collection
   and Museum ⑲
Institute of
   Texan Cultures ㉕
Majestic Theatre ⑪
Mexican Cultural
   Institute ㉒
Ripley's Believe It or Not ⑮
The River Walk ⑯

San Antonio Children's
   Museum ⑩
San Antonio
   Central Library ③
San Antonio
   Museum of Art ①
San Fernando
   Cathedral ⑨
Southwest Craft Center ②
Spanish Governor's
   Palace ⑥
Steves Homestead ㉗
The Texas Adventure ⑬
Tower of the Americas ㉔
Vietnam War Memorial ④

SHOPPING
Booksmiths
   of San Antonio ⑰
Dillard's ㉑
Galeria Ortiz ⑤
Kallison's
   Western Wear ⑧
Keene Gallery ⑱
Market Square ⑤
Papa Jim's Botanica ㉘
Paris Hatters ⑫
Rivercenter Mall ㉑
San Angel Folk Art ㉙
Southwest
   Craft Center ②
Tienda Guadalupe
   Folk Art & Gifts ㉖

1-0917

century, only to be revitalized in the late 1930s by artists and craftspeople and by the San Antonio Conservation Society. Now boutiques, craft shops, and restaurants occupy this historic district, which resembles a Spanish/Mexican village, replete with shaded patios, plazas, brick-and-tile streets, and some of the settlement's original adobe structures. You can see (but not enter) the house of General Cós, the Mexican military leader who surrendered to the Texas revolutionary army in 1835, or attend a performance at the Arneson River Theatre (see "The Performing Arts" in chapter 8).

Market Square

Between Dolorosa and Commerce Sts. ☎ **210/207-8600.** Free admission. El Mercado and Farmer's Market Plaza open daily June–Aug 10am–8pm, Sept–May 10am–6pm; restaurants and some of the shops open later. Closed Thanksgiving, Christmas, New Year's Day, Easter. Streetcar: St. Paul Square/Market Square; Alamo Plaza/Market Square.

It may not be quite as colorful as it was when live chickens squawked around overflowing, makeshift vegetable stands, but Market Square will still transport you south of the border. Stalls in the indoor El Mercado sell everything from onyx chess sets and cheap serapes to beautifully made crafts from the interior of Mexico. More formal shops, some rather pricey, line the outside of the structure. Across the street, the Farmer's Market, which formerly housed the produce market, has carts with more modern goods. If you can tear yourself away from the merchandise, take a look around at the buildings in the complex; some date back to the late 1800s.

Bring your appetite along with your wallet: In addition to two good Mexican restaurants (one open 24 hours a day), almost every weekend sees the emergence of food stalls selling specialties such as *gorditas* (chubby corn cakes topped with a variety of goodies) or funnel cakes (fried dough sprinkled with powdered sugar). Most of the city's Hispanic festivals are held here, and mariachis usually stroll the square.

King William Historic District

East bank of the river just south of downtown. Streetcar: Via Romana/King William route.

San Antonio's first suburb, King William was settled in the late 19th century by prosperous German merchants who displayed their wealth through extravagant homes. They named the 25-block area after Kaiser Wilhelm of Prussia.

The neighborhood fell into disrepair for a few decades, but you'd never know it from the pristine condition of most of the houses here today. Before you stroll up and down along tree-shaded King William Street, gawking at the beautifully landscaped, magnificent mansions, stop at the headquarters of the San Antonio Conservation Society, 107 King William St. (☎ **210/224-6163**), and pick up a self-guided walking tour booklet outside the gate. Only the Steves Homestead (see "More Attractions," below) and the Guenther House (see chapter 5) are open to the public. The neighborhood is within walking distance of the Convention Center.

✪ Paseo Del Rio/The River Walk

Downtown from the Municipal Auditorium on the north end to the King William Historic District on the south end. All streetcar lines.

Just a few steps below the streets of downtown San Antonio lies another world, alternately soothing and exhilarating, depending on where you venture. The quieter areas of the 2^{1}/$_{2}$ paved miles of winding riverbank, shaded by cypresses, oaks, and willows, exude a tropical, exotic aura; the Big Bend section, filled with sidewalk cafes, toney restaurants, bustling bars, high-rise hotels, and even a huge shopping mall, has a festive, sometimes frenetic feel. Tour boats, water taxis, and floating picnic barges regularly ply the river, and local parades and festivals fill its banks with revelers.

Although plans to cement over the river, inspired by a disastrous flood in 1921, were stymied, it wasn't until the late 1930s that the federal Works Project Administration (WPA) carried out architect Robert Hugman's designs for the waterway, installing cobblestone walks, arched bridges, and entrance steps from various street-level locations. And it wasn't until the late 1960s, when the River Walk proved to be one of the most popular attractions of the HemisFair exposition, that its commercial development began in earnest.

There's a real danger of the River Walk becoming overdeveloped—new restaurants and entertainment complexes are opening at an alarming pace, and the crush of bodies along the busiest sections can be claustrophobic in the summer heat—but plenty of quieter spots still exist. And if you're caught up in the sparkling lights reflected on the water on a breeze-swept night, you might forget there was ever anyone else around.

✪ San Antonio Missions National Historic Park

2202 Roosevelt Ave. ☎ **210/229-5701**. Free admission, donations accepted. All the missions are open daily 9am–5pm. Closed Christmas, New Year's Day. Call ahead to inquire about National Park Ranger tours. Bus: 40.

It's impossible *not* to remember the Alamo when you're in San Antonio; more difficult to recall is that it was originally just the first of five missions established by the Franciscans along the San Antonio River to Christianize the native population. The four missions that now fall under the aegis of the National Parks Department are still active parishes, run in cooperation with the Archdiocese of San Antonio. In 1996, a new $9.5 million visitor center opened just outside Mission San José, at 6701 San José Drive. The handsome building, made of Texas Hill Country sandstone to match the mission walls, offers an excellent introduction to the park via a variety of technically exciting displays, including a touchscreen itinerary planner, a three-dimensional fiber-optic map, an interactive slide show, and a theater with an advanced audio system. There's also a good bookstore.

The missions were complex communities, not only churches, and the Parks Department has assigned each of the four an interpretive theme to educate visitors about the roles they played in early San Antonio society. They may be visited separately, but if you have the time, see all of them—they were built uncharacteristically close to each other and the cumulative experience is hard to match. Signs direct visitors from the Alamo to the 5¹/₂-mile mission trail that begins at Mission Concepción and winds its way south through the city streets to Mission Espada. A more cohesive connecting trail is in the works, but for the time being pay close attention to the brown directional signs or to the National Parks map. Or take the bus, which runs frequently and stops at each of the missions.

Concepción, 807 Mission Rd. at Felisa (☎ 210/229-5732), was built in 1731. The oldest unrestored Texas mission, Concepción looks much as it did 200 years ago. Many of us tend to think of religious sites as somber and austere, but traces of color on the facade and restored wall paintings inside show how cheerful this one originally was.

San José, 6539 San José Dr. at Mission Road (☎ **210/229-4770** or 210/229-4771), established in 1720, was the largest, best-known, and most beautiful of the Texas missions. It was reconstructed to give visitors a complete picture of life in a mission community—right down to the granary, mill, and Indian pueblo. Popular mariachi masses are held here every Sunday at noon (come early if you want a seat), and pageants and plays are put on at an outdoor arena.

Moved from an earlier site in east Texas to its present location in 1731, **San Juan Capistrano,** 9102 Graf at Ashley (☎ **210/229-5734**), doesn't have the grandeur of the missions to the north—the larger church intended for it was never completed—but the original simple chapel and the wilder setting give it a peaceful, spiritual aura. A short (three-tenths of a mile) interpretive trail, with a number of overlook platforms, winds through the woods to the banks of the old river channel.

The southernmost mission in the San Antonio chain, **San Francisco de la Espada,** 10040 Espada Rd. (☎ **210/627-2021**), also has an ancient, isolated feel, although the beautifully kept-up church shows just how vital it still is to the local community. Be sure to visit the **Espada Aqueduct,** part of the mission's original *acequia* (irrigation ditch) system, about 1 mile to the north of the mission; dating from 1740, it's one of the oldest Spanish aqueducts in the United States.

Sea World of Texas

10500 Sea World Dr., 16 miles northwest of downtown San Antonio at Ellison Dr. and Westover Hills Blvd. ☎ **210/523-3611.** Admission, 1-day pass $29.95 adults, seniors (55 and over) 10% discount, $19.95 children 3–11, children 2 and under free. Parking $5 per day. The schedule varies greatly with the season; the park is generally open weekends and some holidays in spring and fall, daily during summer. Opening 10am, closing hours 6, 8, or 10pm, depending on the season. Call ahead for current information. Closed Nov to mid-March. Bus: 63. From Loop 410 or from Hwy. 90 west, exit Hwy. 151 west to the park.

Leave it to Texas to provide Shamu, the performing killer whale, with his most spacious digs: At 250 acres, this $140 million Sea World is the largest of the Anheuser Busch–owned parks, which also makes it the largest marine theme park in the world. The walk-through habitats where you can watch penguins, sea lions, sharks, tropical fish, and flamingos do their thing are endlessly fascinating, but the aquatic acrobatics at the stadium shows might be even more fun. The humans hold their own with an impressive water-skiing exhibition on a $12^1/_2$-acre lake.

One needn't get frustrated by just looking at all that water: There are lots of places here to get wet. The Lost Lagoon has a huge wave pool and water slides aplenty, and the Texas Splashdown flume ride and the Rio Loco river rapids ride also offer splashy fun; younger children can cavort in Shamu's Happy Harbor. Sea World's latest addition is a multimillion-dollar roller coaster called Big White, the Southwest's only inverted coaster—which means riders will go head-over-heels during 2,500 feet of loops (don't eat before this one). Whatever you do during the day, stick around for the Mermaids, Myths and Monsters summer-night multimedia laser shows or one of the special high-season concerts. In 1996 these featured such big names as Alabama and Alan Jackson; there was also a nostalgia night with the Turtles and the Monkees.

2 More Attractions

A CHURCH

San Fernando Cathedral

115 Main Plaza. ☎ **210/227-1297.** Free admission. Daily 6am–5pm; gift shop open daily 9am–5pm. Streetcar: Alamo Plaza/Market Square; Romana Plaza/King William.

Construction of a church on this site, overlooking what was once the town's central plaza, was begun in 1738 by San Antonio's original Canary Island settlers and completed in 1749. Part of the early structure—the oldest cathedral sanctuary in the United States and the oldest parish church in Texas—is incorporated into the magnificent gothic revival–style cathedral built in 1868. Jim Bowie got married here and General Santa Anna raised the flag of "no quarter" from the roof during the siege of the Alamo in 1836. A bronze plaque outside directs visitors to the chapel where, it says, the bones of the Alamo heroes are entombed, but that claim is widely disputed.

HISTORIC BUILDINGS/COMPLEXES

Fort Sam Houston

Grayson St. and New Braunfels Ave., about 2^1/$_2$ miles northeast of downtown. Bus: 15, Fort Sam Houston.

Since 1718, when the armed Presidio de Béxar was established to defend the Spanish missions, the military has played a key role in San Antonio's development; it remains the number one employer in town today. The 3,434-acre Fort Sam Houston affords visitors an unusual opportunity to view the city's military past in the context of its military present. Most of its historic buildings are still in use and thus off limits, but three are open to the public. The **Fort Sam Houston Museum** (☎ 210/221-1886; open Wednesday to Sunday from 10am to 4pm, free admission) details the history of the armed forces in Texas, with a focus on San Antonio, while the **U.S. Army Medical Department Museum** (☎ 210/221-6358; open Tuesday to Saturday from 10am to 4pm, free admission) includes displays of army medical equipment and American prisoner-of-war memorabilia. Free self-guided tour maps of the historic sites are available at the gift shop in the **Quadrangle** (New Braunfels Avenue, between Grayson Street and Wilson Road; gift shop open daily 8am to 4pm). This impressive 1876 limestone structure, the oldest on the post, is centered by a brick clock tower and encloses a grassy square where peacocks, deer, and rabbits roam freely; the Apache chief Geronimo was held captive here for 40 days in 1886.

Casa Navarro State Historical Park

228 S. Laredo St. ☎ **210/226-4801**. Admission $2 adults, $1 children 6–12. Open Wed–Sun 10–4pm; closed Mon and Tues. Streetcar: HemisFair Park/Cattleman Square; Romano Plaza/Blue Star Arts Complex.

A key player in the transition of Texas from Spanish territory to American state, José Antonio Navarro was a Mexican mayor of San Antonio in 1821; a signer of the 1836 declaration of Texas independence; and the only native Texan to take part in the convention that ratified the annexation of Texas to the United States in 1845. His former living quarters, built around 1850, are an interesting amalgam of the architectural fashions of his time: A restored office, house, and separate kitchen, constructed of adobe and limestone, blend elements from Mexican, French, German, and pioneer styles. Guided tours and demonstrations are available; call ahead to inquire.

Majestic Theatre

230 E. Houston St. ☎ **210/226-3333** (box office) or 210/226-5700 (administration). Streetcar: Alamo Plaza/Market Square, St. Paul Square/Market Square, or HemisFair Park/Cattleman Square.

Everyone from Jack Benny to Mae West played this opulent vaudeville and film palace, designed in baroque Moorish/Spanish Revival style by John Eberson in 1929 and magnificently restored in 1989. One of the last "atmospheric" theaters to be built— the stock market crashed 4 months after it opened and no one could afford such elaborate showplaces again—it's also one of the few such theaters remaining in the United States, and has been designated a National Historic Landmark. The Majestic is not generally open to the public during the day, but you may be able to get on a group guided tour (these, offered Tuesday through Friday for 10 people or more, cost $5 per person and must be arranged 2 weeks in advance); call Las Casas (☎ **210/223-4343**) to find out. If not, book a seat for whatever's on at the theater at night (see "The Performing Arts" in chapter 8 for details); a glimpse at the fabulous overhead dome, with its simulated stars and clouds, is alone worth the price of admission.

Greater San Antonio Attractions & Shopping

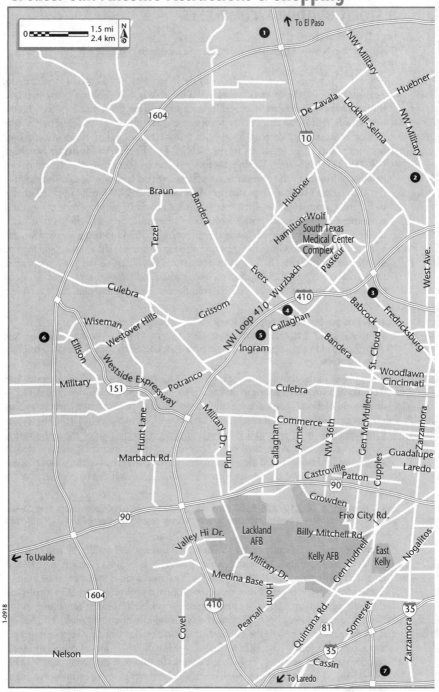

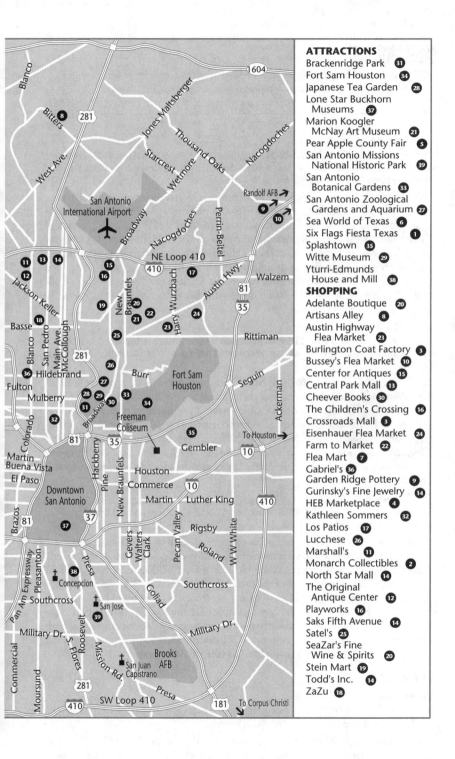

ATTRACTIONS

Brackenridge Park ③①
Fort Sam Houston ③④
Japanese Tea Garden ②⑧
Lone Star Buckhorn
  Museums ③⑦
Marion Koogler
  McNay Art Museum ②①
Pear Apple County Fair ⑤
San Antonio Missions
  National Historic Park ③⑨
San Antonio
  Botanical Gardens ③③
San Antonio Zoological
  Gardens and Aquarium ②⑦
Sea World of Texas ⑥
Six Flags Fiesta Texas ①
Splashtown ③⑤
Witte Museum ②⑨
Yturri-Edmunds
  House and Mill ③⑧

SHOPPING

Adelante Boutique ②⓪
Artisans Alley ⑧
Austin Highway
  Flea Market ②③
Burlington Coat Factory ③
Bussey's Flea Market ①⓪
Center for Antiques ①⑤
Central Park Mall ①③
Cheever Books ③⓪
The Children's Crossing ①⑥
Crossroads Mall ③
Eisenhauer Flea Market ②④
Farm to Market ②②
Flea Mart ⑦
Gabriel's ③⑥
Garden Ridge Pottery ⑨
Gurinsky's Fine Jewelry ①④
HEB Marketplace ④
Kathleen Sommers ③②
Los Patios ①⑦
Lucchese ②⑥
Marshall's ①①
Monarch Collectibles ②
North Star Mall ①④
The Original
  Antique Center ①②
Playworks ①⑥
Saks Fifth Avenue ①④
Satel's ②⑤
SeaZar's Fine
  Wine & Spirits ②⓪
Stein Mart ①⑨
Todd's Inc. ①④
ZaZu ①⑧

Impressions

We have no city, except, perhaps, New Orleans, that can vie, in point of picturesque
interest that attaches to odd and antiquated foreignness, with San Antonio.
—Frederick Law Olmsted, *A Journey Through Texas* (1853)

Spanish Governor's Palace

105 Plaza de Armas. ☎ **210/224-0601.** Admission $1 adults, 50¢ children 7–13, children 6 and under free. Mon–Sat 9am–5pm, Sun 10am–5pm. Closed Christmas, New Year's Day, and Fiesta week. Streetcar: Romana Plaza/King William.

Never actually a palace, this 1749 adobe structure formerly served as the residence and headquarters for the captain of the Spanish presidio. It became the seat of Texas government in 1772 when San Antonio was made capital of the Spanish province of Texas and, by the time it was purchased by the city in 1928, had served as a tailor's shop, barroom, and schoolhouse. The building, with high ceilings crossed by protruding *viga* beams, is beautiful in its simplicity, and the 10 rooms crowded with period furnishings paint a vivid portrait of upper-class life in a rough-hewn society. Consider taking a picnic lunch to eat on the tree-shaded, cobblestoned patio, overlooking a flowing stone fountain.

Steves Homestead

509 King William St. ☎ **210/225-5924.** Admission $2. Daily 10am–4:15pm (hours subject to change); tours, lasting 30 to 45 minutes, given every half hour. Streetcar: Romana Plaza/King William.

Built in 1876 for lumber magnate Edward Steves by prominent San Antonio architect Alfred Giles, this Victorian mansion was restored by the San Antonio Conservation Society, to whom it was willed by Steves's granddaughter. One of the only houses in the King William Historic District open to the public, it gives a fascinating glimpse into the lifestyle of the rich and locally famous of the late 19th century. You can't enter without taking a docent-led tour, which is fine: You wouldn't want to miss the great gossip about the Steves family that the society's very knowledgeable volunteers pass along.

Yturri-Edmunds House and Mill

257 Yellowstone. ☎ **210/534-8237.** Admission $2 adults, children under 12 free. Mon–Sat 10am–4pm, Sun noon–4pm. Bus: 40.

More than 150 years of the city's architecture are spanned by the exhibits on this site. Acquired in 1824 by Manuel Yturri-Castillo, a native of Spain, the property formerly belonged to Mission Concepción and included a gristmill that may have been built as early as 1720, as well as one of the mission's irrigation ditches. A six-room adobe house, one of the few that still exists in San Antonio, was constructed between 1840 and 1860. Also here are an 1881 carriage house from the King William Historic District and an 1855 block-and-rubble house that was originally located downtown; both were moved here by the San Antonio Conservation Society, which now owns the property. A tour guide is always on hand to take visitors around.

A LIBRARY

San Antonio Central Library

600 Soledad. ☎ **210/207-2500**. Free admission. Mon–Thurs 9am–9pm, Fri–Sat 9am–5pm, Sun 11am–5pm. Streetcar: Romana Plaza/King William.

San Antonio's new main library, opened in May 1995 at a cost of $38 million, has a number of important collections, but it is most notable for its architecture: Ricardo

Legorreta, renowned for his buildings throughout Mexico, has designed a wildly colorful and whimsical public space that people apparently love to enter—by the second month after the library opened, circulation had gone up 95%. The boxy building, painted what has been called "enchilada red," is designed like an hacienda around an internal courtyard; via a variety of skylights, windows, and wall colors (including bright purples and yellows), you get a different perpective from each of the six floors.

MUSEUMS & GALLERIES

Blue Stars Arts Complex

Bordered by Probandt, Blue Star, and South Alamo Sts., and the San Antonio River. ☎ **210/227-6960.** Free admission. Hours vary from gallery to gallery; most are open Wed–Sun noon–6pm. Streetcar: Romano Plaza/Blue Star.

This huge former warehouse in Southtown hosts a collection of working studios and galleries, along with a performance space for the Jump-Start theater company; the artist-run, 11,000-square-foot Contemporary Art Museum is its anchor. The style of work varies from gallery to gallery—you'll see everything from primitive-style folk art to feminist photography—but the level of professionalism is generally high. A number of spaces are devoted to (or have sections purveying) arty gift items such as jewelry, picture frames, and crafts.

Hertzberg Circus Collection and Museum

210 W. Market St. ☎ **210/207-7810.** Admission $2.50 adults, $2 seniors, $1 children 3–12. Mon–Sat 10am–5pm and (June–Aug only) Sun and holidays 1–5pm. Near all four streetcar lines.

They're not as large as the ones in the circus, but colorful elephants posted as sentries beside the front steps of this nostalgia-inducing museum hint at what's inside. Displays chosen from the massive collection of "circusana" that Harry Hertzberg bequeathed to the San Antonio Public Library (of which this is a branch) include Tom Thumb's carriage, a flea circus, and photographs of Buffalo Bill's Wild West show. On weekends, kids are entertained by jugglers, mimes, face-painting workshops, and the like, but when there are no such special shows on, adults will probably get the most out of this history-oriented place.

Institute of Texan Cultures

801 S. Bowie St., in HemisFair Park. ☎ **210/558-2300.** Admission $4 adults, $2 seniors and children 3–12. Tues–Sun 9am–5pm. Dome shows presented at 10:15am, noon, 2 and 3:30pm. Closed Mon, Thanksgiving, and Christmas. Streetcar: HemisFair Park/La Villita/Cattleman Square.

It's the rare visitor who won't discover here that his or her ethnic group has contributed to the history of Texas: 28 different cultures are represented in the imaginative, hands-on displays of this educational center, part of the University of Texas at San Antonio. Outbuildings include a one-room schoolhouse and a windmill, and the multimedia Dome Theater presents images of Texas on 36 screens. Volunteer docents frequently put on puppet shows; call ahead to see if one is scheduled for the day you plan to visit.

Lone Star Buckhorn Museums

600 Lone Star Blvd. ☎ **210/270-9469.** Admission $5 adults, $4 senior citizens, $1.75 children 6–11, children under 6 free. Daily 9:30am–5pm. Bus: 40.

If you like your educational experiences accompanied by a cold one, this is the place to come. With its huge stuffed animals, mounted fish, and Lone Star "memorabeeria," this complex on the grounds of an active brewery fulfills every out-of-stater's stereotype of what a Texas museum might be like. In addition to the Hall of Horns, Hall of Feathers, Hall of Fins, and Texas History Wax Museum, there's a small office that was once occupied by the short-story writer O. Henry; outside are a lake and picnic grounds. Regardless of what you might think of great white hunters, it's hard to resist pictures made out of beer-can tabs or designed from rattlesnake rattles. A free beer or soft drink is included in the price of admission.

Mexican Cultural Institute

600 HemisFair Plaza Way, HemisFair Park. ☎ **210/227-0123.** Free admission, donations accepted. Tues–Fri 9:30am–5:30pm, Sat–Sun 11am–5pm. Streetcar: HemisFair Park/Cattleman Square.

Sponsored by the Mexican Ministry of Foreign Affairs, the institute hosts shifting displays of art and artifacts relating to Mexican history and culture, from pre-Colombian to contemporary. Latin American film series, conferences, performances, contests, and workshops—including ones on language, literature, and folklore as well as art—are also held here. Every Saturday at 7pm there's a free concert, featuring jazz with a Latino flavor.

✪ Marion Koogler McNay Art Museum

6000 N. New Braunfels Ave. ☎ **210/824-5368.** Free admission. Fee for special exhibits. Tues–Sat 10am–5pm, Sun noon–5pm. Docent tours given Sun at 2pm from Oct–May. Closed Mon, New Years Day, Fourth of July, Thanksgiving, Christmas. Bus: 7.

Set on a hill north of Brackenridge Park with a striking view of downtown, the sprawling Spanish Mediterranean–style mansion of oil heiress and artist Marion Koogler McNay has been an art museum since 1954. Its main strength is French post-Impressionist and early 20th-century European painting, but there's also a fine collection of theater arts (costumes, set designs, etc.) and some excellent special exhibits (the opening of Red Grooms' amusing *Ruckus Rodeo* in 1997 coincides with the opening of San Antonio's Stock Show and Rodeo). A well-stocked gift shop adjoins a shaded central patio. The graciousness of the setting, used for numerous weddings and photo shoots, combined with the intimacy of the collection, make this a most appealing place to view art.

San Antonio Museum of Art

200 W. Jones Ave. ☎ **210/978-8100.** Admission $4 adults, $2 senior citizens and students with ID, $1.75 children 4–11, children 3 and under free. Free on Tues from 3–9pm. Mon and Wed–Sat 10am–5pm, Tues 10am–9pm, Sun noon–5pm. Bus: 7.

A number of the castlelike buildings of the 1904 Lone Star Brewery were gutted, connected, and turned into a visually exciting exhibition space in 1981. The spare and, in some sections, skylit interiors of the structures contrast strikingly with the more intricately detailed brick exterior; the multiwindowed crosswalk between the two buildings affords fine views of downtown. The Latin American folk art collection is outstanding. The other collections range from early Egyptian, Greek, and Asian to 19th- and 20th-century American.

Southwest Craft Center

300 Augusta. ☎ **210/224-1848.** Free admission. Galleries, Mon–Sat 10am–5pm. Streetcar: Romana Plaza/King William.

A stroll along the River Walk to the northern corner of downtown will bring you to another world—or two: a rare French-designed cloister where contemporary crafts are now being created. Two exhibition galleries and artist studios-cum-classrooms occupy the garden-filled grounds of the first girl's school in San Antonio, established by the Ursuline order in the mid-19th century. Take a look around—note the First Academy Building, made by an unusual rammed-earth process, and the wood-and-native limestone gothic church—and then relax in one of many oak-shaded nooks.

The Ursuline Gallery's gift shop carries unique craft items, and you can enjoy a nice, light lunch in the Copper Kitchen Restaurant (open Monday through Friday from 11:30am to 2pm).

✪ Witte Museum

3810 Broadway, at the edge of Brackenridge Park. ☎ **210/820-2111.** Admission $4 adults, $2 senior citizens and students with ID, $1.75 children 4–11, children 3 and under free. Free on Tues from 3–9pm. Mon and Wed–Sat 10am–5pm (until 6pm Jun–Aug), Tues 10am–9pm, Sun noon–5pm (until 6pm Jun–Aug). Closed Thanksgiving, Christmas. Bus: 7.

A family museum that adults will enjoy as much as children, the Witte focuses on Texas history, natural science, and anthropology, but often ranges far afield—to the Berlin Wall, say, or the history of bridal gowns in the U.S. Your senses will be engaged along with your intellect: You might hear animal cries as you crouch through south Texas thorn brush, or feel rough-hewn stone carved with Native American pictographs under your feet. An EcoLab is home to live Texas critters ranging from tarantulas to tortoises. Outside the museum are a butterfly and hummingbird garden and three restored historic homes. March 1997 saw the opening of the HEB Science Treehouse, a four-level, 15,000-square-foot science center with hands-on activities for all ages, on the bank of the San Antonio River behind the museum. Excellent film, concert, and performing arts series draw folks back here on weekend afternoons and weekday evenings.

OUTDOOR ART

Vietnam War Memorial

Veterans Memorial Plaza, one block north of Travis Park at East Martin and Jefferson Sts. Bus: 3, 4, 84, 86, 87, 90, or 92.

"Hill 881 S," a moving bronze monument created by combat artist Austin Deuel and dedicated to the Vietnam War veterans, depicts a marine holding a wounded comrade while looking skyward for an Evac helicopter.

PARKS & GARDENS

Brackenridge Park

Main entrance 2800 block of North Broadway. ☎ **210/207-8480.** Ride ticket office at 3910 N. St. Mary's St. ☎ 210/736-9534. Admission to the sky ride, railway, and carousel each cost $2.17 adults, $1.62 children 1–11. The park is open daily from 8am–dusk. The sky ride, railway, and carousel operate Mon–Fri 9:30am–5pm, Sat–Sun 9:30am–5:30pm. Bus: 7.

With its rustic stone bridges and winding walkways, the city's main park, opened in 1899, has a charming, old-fashioned quality; it also serves as a popular center for recreational activities including golf, polo, biking, picnicking, horseback riding, and paddleboating. Just opposite the zoo entrance are a cable-car sky ride, offering a panoramic view of the San Antonio skyline; a miniature railway that replicates an 1863 steam locomotive and runs 3$^{1}/_{2}$ miles through the park; and a carousel that features 60 antique horses. See also entries for the San Antonio Zoo and the Japanese Tea Garden in this section, and for "Horseback Riding" and "Paddleboats" in "Staying Active," below.

HemisFair Park

200 S. Alamo. ☎ **210/207-8572.** Bus: 40. Streetcar: HemisFair Park/Cattleman Square.

Built for the 1968 HemisFair, an exposition celebrating the 250th anniversary of the founding of San Antonio, this urban oasis boasts water gardens and a wood-and-sand playground constructed by children. Among its indoor diversions are the Institute of Texan Cultures, the Tower of the Americas, and the Mexican Cultural Institute (all described above). Be sure to walk over to the Henry B. Gonzales Convention Center—currently being expanded—and take a look at the striking mosaic mural by Mexican artist Juan O'Gorman.

Japanese Tea Garden

3800 N. St. Mary's St., Brackenridge Park, next to the zoo. ☎ **210/821-3120.** Free admission. Daily 8am–dusk. Bus: 7.

In 1917, the Japanese Tea Garden—also called the Japanese Sunken Garden—was created by prison labor to beautify an abandoned cement quarry, one of the largest in the world in the 1880s and 1890s; cement rock taken from it helped create the state capitol in Austin. You can still glimpse a brick smokestack and a number of the old lime kilns among the beautiful flower arrangements, which are less austere than those in many Japanese gardens. After Pearl Harbor, the site was officially renamed the Chinese Sunken Garden and a Chinese-style entryway added on; not until 1983 was the original name restored. Just to the southwest, a bowl of limestone cliffs found to have natural acoustic properties was turned into the Sunken Garden Theater (see "The Performing Arts" in chapter 8 for details).

San Antonio Botanical Gardens

555 Funston. ☎ **210/821-5115.** Admission $3 adults, $2 seniors, $1 children 3–13, children under 3 free. Daily 9am–6pm. Closed Christmas, New Year's Day. Bus: 7.

Take a horticultural tour of Texas at this gracious 38-acre garden, encompassing everything from south Texas scrub to Hill Country wildflowers and east Texas formal rose gardens. Fountains, pools, paved paths, and examples of Texas architecture provide visual contrast. There's also a garden for the blind, an herb garden, and a children's garden. Perhaps most outstanding is the $6.5 million Lucile Halsell Conservatory complex, a bermed, below-ground greenhouse replicating a variety of tropical and desert environments. In 1995, the 1896 Sullivan Carriage House, built by Alfred Giles and moved stone-by-stone from its original downtown site, became the new entryway to the gardens. It hosts a gift shop and restaurant, which offers salads, quiches, and sandwiches (open Tuesday through Sunday from 11am to 3pm).

A VIEW

Tower of the Americas

600 HemisFair Park. ☎ **210/207-8616.** Admission $3 adults, $2 senior citizens 55 and over, $1 children 4–11, children under 4 free. Daily 8am–11pm. Streetcar: HemisFair Park/Cattleman Square.

If you want to get the lay of the land, circle the eight panoramic panels on the observation level of the Tower of the Americas. The 750-foot-high tower was built for the HemisFair in 1968; the deck sits at the equivalent of 59 stories and is lit for spectacular night viewing. The tower also hosts a revolving restaurant and a cocktail lounge that sits still.

A ZOO

San Antonio Zoological Gardens and Aquarium

3903 N. St. Mary's St. in Brackenridge Park. ☎ **210/734-7183.** Admission $6 adults, $4 children 3–11 and seniors 62 and over, children 2 and under free. Boat rides $1.25. Summer, daily 9am–6:30pm; winter, daily 9am–5pm. Bus: 7 or 8.

Home to more than 700 different species, this zoo in Brackenridge Park hosts one of the largest animal collections in the U.S. It's also considered one of the top facilities in the country because of its conservation efforts and its excellent success in

❷ Did You Know?

- The world's largest bowling-ball manufacturer, Columbia 300 Inc., is in San Antonio.
- Elmer Doolin, manufacturer of Fritos corn chips, bought the original recipe for $100 from a San Antonio restaurant in 1932. He sold the first batch from the back of his model-T Ford.
- The first military flight by an American took place at Fort Sam Houston in 1910; in 1915, the entire U.S. Air Force—six reconnaissance planes—resided at the fort.
- *Wings,* a silent World War I epic that won the first Academy Award for best picture in 1927, was filmed in San Antonio. The film also marked the debut of Gary Cooper, who was on screen for a total of 102 seconds.
- Barbed wire was first demonstrated in San Antonio's Military Plaza.
- Lyndon and Lady Bird Johnson were married in San Antonio's St. Mark's Episcopal Church.

breeding programs—it produced the first white rhino in the U.S. A children's zoo features a Tropical Tour boat ride that visits miniature exhibits of animals from many countries. The zoo has expanded and upgraded its exhibits since it opened in 1914, but it may still strike those who are familiar with newer zoos as a bit old-fashioned.

3 Especially for Kids

Without a doubt, the prime spots for kids are **Sea World** and **Six Flags Fiesta Texas.** They'll also like the hands-on, interactive **Witte Museum** and the miniature train ride and carousel at **Brackenridge Park.** There's a children's area in the **zoo,** which vends food packets throughout so people of all ages can feed the animals. Youngsters will also get a kick out of petting the critters roaming around the **Quadrangle at Fort Sam Houston.** The third floor of the new main branch of the **San Antonio Public Library** is devoted to children, who get to use their own catalogs and search tools. Puppet shows are held on a regular basis, and there are story hours three times a week. In addition to these sights, detailed in "The Top Attractions" and "More Attractions" sections, above, the following should also appeal to the sandbox set and up.

Alamo Imax Theater

849 E. Commerce St., in the Rivercenter Mall. ☎ **210/225-4629** (recording schedule information). Admission $6.40 adults, $4.25 children 3–11. Daily 9am–10pm. All four streetcar lines.

Having them view *Alamo: Price of Freedom* on a six-story-high screen with a stereo sound system is a good way to get kids psyched for the historical battle site (which, though it's across the street, can't be reached without wending your way past lots and lots of Rivercenter shops). The theater also shows nature movies produced especially for the large screen, and, occasionally, commercial films such as *Jurassic Park.*

Pear Apple County Fair

5820 NW Loop 410. ☎ **210/521-9500.** Free admission; prices on individual games and attractions vary (ride packages available for $6.45 or $15); Lazer Runner is $3 for 5 minutes, $5 for 10 minutes. Memorial Day until start of school, Mon–Thurs 3–10pm, Fri–Sat 11am–midnight; rest of the year open Mon–Thurs 4–10pm, Fri–Sat 11am–11pm, Sun 1–10pm. Exit Loop 410 on Bandera Rd. and drive south on access road.

Miniature golf, an indoor Ferris wheel, bumper cars, and go-carts are among the at-tractions at this completely kid-oriented amusement park. Some of these might even lure your children away from the fair's huge video arcade. The newest feature is the state-of-the-art (but, one hopes, not the art of spelling) Lazer Runner Battle Cruiser.

Ripley's Believe It or Not & Plaza Theater of Wax

301 Alamo Plaza. ☎ 210/224-9299. Plaza Theater of Wax $6.95 adults, $4.95 children 4–12; Ripley's Believe It or Not $7.95 adults, $4.95 children 4–12; both attractions ticket $10.95 adults, $7.95 children 4–12. Memorial Day to Labor Day, daily 9am–10pm; remainder of the year, Sun–Thurs 9am–7pm, Fri–Sun 9am–10pm (ticket office closes an hour before listed closing times). All four streetcar lines.

Adults may get the bigger charge out of the waxy stars—Denzel Washington and Jessica Tandy are among the latest to be added to an impressive array—and some of the oddities collected by the globe-trotting Mr. Ripley, but there's plenty for kids to enjoy at this twofer attraction. Although tame compared to Jason's *Friday the Thir-teenth* adventures, the walk-through wax Theater of Horrors should elicit some pleas-ant shudders. At Believe It or Not, children will enjoy learning about people around the world whose habits—such as sticking nails through their noses—are even weirder than their own.

✪ San Antonio Children's Museum

305 E. Houston St. ☎ 210/21-CHILD. Admission $3.50 adults, $1.50 children. Tues–Sat 9am–6pm, Sun noon–5pm. Bus: 7 or 40. All four streetcar lines.

Opened in 1995, San Antonio's new children's museum offers a wonderful introduc-tion to the city for the pint-sized and grown-up alike. Local history, population, and geography are all explored through such features as a miniature River Walk, a multicultural grocery store, and a bird-watching platform. Activities range from high tech to low, with everything from crawl spaces and corn-grinding rocks to a weather station and radar room. Kids can be left for up to 3 hours at a variety of educational drop-in activities during the summer—they might put together a newsletter, say, or make their own stamps. If you're traveling with children, don't miss this place.

Splashtown

3600 North Pan Am Expressway. ☎ 210/227-1100. Admission $15.99 adults, $10.99 chil-dren under 4 feet tall, seniors over 65 and children under 2 free. Most weekends in May, daily late May to late Aug, weekends in early Sept (call ahead for exact schedule). Open Sun–Tues 11am–9pm, Wed–Thurs 11am–10pm, Fri–Sat 11am–11pm. Closed mid-Sept to Apr. Get off I-35 at exit 160 (Splashtown Drive).

Cool off at this 15-acre water recreation park, which includes the largest wave pool in Texas, hydro tubes nearly 300 feet long, more than a dozen water slides, and a two-story playhouse for the smaller children. A variety of concerts, contests, and special events are held here.

The Texas Adventure

307 Alamo Plaza. ☎ 210/227-0388. Admission $6.25 adults, $4.25 children 3–11. Winter, daily 9am–6pm; summer, daily 9am–10pm. All four streetcar lines.

San Antonio's latest foray into the high-tech history field, the world's first Encoun-tarium F·X Theatre retells the story of the battle for the Alamo with special effects that include life-size holographic images of the Alamo heroes and cannon fire roar-ing through a sophisticated stereo sound system. The depiction of events is more ac-curate than in most such displays, but a bit of noise and smoke aside, this isn't terribly exciting. The holograms, which are rather ghostly looking, do little more than hold forth who they are.

4 Special-Interest Sightseeing

FOR GHOST LOVERS

If you enjoy things that go bump in the night, the **Spirits of San Antonio Tour** (☎ 210/493-2454) is right up your dark alley. Docia Williams, author of two historical guides to haunts around Texas, will take you to hotels, homes, and other spook-ridden spots in town. Your guide can't guarantee a ghost—apparently they're not big on command performances—but she will guarantee a good time. Tours (conducted at night, naturally) last around 3 hours and include dinner at a haunted restaurant. A minimum of 20 is required for each outing; if you can't get that number of specter lovers together, you might be able to squeeze in on another group's tour (they're especially popular around Halloween). The tour costs $36 per person, and dinner is included.

FOR MILITARY HISTORY BUFFS

San Antonio's military installations are crucial to the city's economy, and testaments to their past abound. Those who aren't satisfied with touring Fort Sam Houston (see "More Attractions," above) can also visit the **Hangar 9/Edward H. White Museum at Brooks Airforce Base,** Southeast Military Drive at the junction of I-37 (☎ 210/536-3234; free; open Moday through Friday from 8am to 4pm). The history of flight medicine, among other things, is detailed via exhibits in the oldest aircraft hangar in the Air Force. Lackland Air Force Base (12 miles southwest of downtown off U.S. 90 at S.W. Military Drive exit) is home to the **Air Force History and Traditions Museum,** Orville Wright Drive (☎ 210/671-3055; free; open Tuesday through Saturday from 8am to 4:45pm), which hosts a collection of rare aircraft and components dating back to World War II. Although Randolph Air Force Base (17 miles northeast of downtown off I-35) doesn't have any museums, the Taj Mahal (Bldg. #100) is on the National Register of Historic Places. Call **210/652-4407** for tour information. In all cases, phone ahead before you go; the bases are sometimes restricted.

FOR JOCKS

Alamodome

100 Montana St. ☎ **210/207-3652.** Tues–Sat 10am, 1pm, 3pm (disabled guests can call to arrange private tours by appointment). Admission $3 adults, $1.50 senior citizens over 55 and children 12 and under. Parking is free in the south (Durango Blvd.) lot on days that no events are scheduled. Streetcar: St. Paul Square/Market Square.

You don't have to be a sports nut to want to tour San Antonio's new, $186 million athletic arena, even when there's no team playing here, but it helps. It also helps to be in good shape, because the 1-hour tour involves lots of walking and some stair climbing (consider that each of the two locker rooms alone measures nearly 5,000 square feet). The Alamodome has the world's largest retractable seating system, and its roof encompasses 9 acres. Call ahead; tours are sometimes canceled because of special events.

FOR THOSE INTERESTED IN HISPANIC HERITAGE

A Hispanic heritage tour is almost redundant in San Antonio, which is a living testament to the role that Hispanics have played in shaping the city. Casa Navarro State Historical Park, La Villita, Market Square, San Antonio Missions Historical Park, and the Spanish Governor's Palace, all detailed above, give visitors a feel for the city's Spanish Colonial past, while the Guadalupe Cultural Arts Center (see chapter 8) and the Mexican Cultural Institute (see above) bring you up to the present state of Mexican and Mexican-American history and art. The sixth floor of the new main branch of the San Antonio Public Library (see above) hosts an excellent noncirculating Latino collection, featuring books about the Mexican-American experience in Texas and the rest of the Southwest. It's also the place to come to do genealogical research into your family's roots.

5 Walking Tour—Downtown

One of downtown San Antonio's great gifts to visitors on foot is its wonderfully meandering early pathways—not laid out by drunken cattle drivers as has been wryly suggested, but formed by the course of the San Antonio River and the various settlements that grew up around it. Turn any corner in this area and you'll come across some fascinating testament to the city's historically rich past.

Note: Stops 1, 5, 6, 7, 9, 11, 13, and 14 are described earlier in this chapter; entrance hours and admission fees (if applicable) are listed there. See chapter 4 for additional information on stop no. 2.

Start: The Alamo.

Finish: Market Square.

Time: Approximately 1½ hours, not including stops at shops, eateries, or attractions.

Best Times: Early morning during the week, when the streets and attractions are less crowded. If you're willing to tour the Alamo museums and shrine another time, consider starting out before they open (9am).

Worst Times: Weekend afternoons, especially in summer, when the crowds and the heat render this long stroll rather uncomfortable (if you do get tired, you can always pick up a streetcar within a block or two of most parts of this route).

Built to be within easy reach of each other, San Antonio's earliest military, religious, and civil settlements are concentrated in the downtown area. The city spread out quite a bit in the next two-and-a-half centuries, but downtown still functions as the seat of the municipal and county government, as well as the hub of tourist activities.

Start your tour at Alamo Plaza (bounded by East Houston Street on the north); at the plaza's northeast corner you'll come to the entrance for:

1. **The Alamo,** originally established in 1718 as the Mission San Antonio de Valero; the first of the city's five missions, it was moved twice before settling into this site. The heavy limestone walls of the church and its adjacent compound were later discovered to make an excellent fortress; in 1836, the fighters for Texas's independence from Mexico took a heroic, if ultimately unsuccessful, stand against Mexican general Santa Anna here.

   When you leave the walled complex, walk south along the plaza to reach:

2. **The Menger Hotel,** built by German immigrant William Menger in 1859 on the site of Texas's first brewery, which he had opened with partner Charles Deegan in 1855; legend has it that Menger wanted a place to lodge hard-drinking friends who used to spend the night sleeping on his long bar. Far more prestigious guests—presidents, Civil War generals, writers, stage actors, you name it—stayed here over the years; the hotel turns up in several short stories by frequent guest William Sidney Porter (O. Henry). The Menger has been much expanded since it first opened, but retains its gorgeous, three-tiered Victorian lobby.

   ☕ **TAKE A BREAK** Fortify yourself for the rest of this walk with coffee and a pecan roll at the **Blum Street Bake Shop** (on the Dillard's side of the Menger Hotel); at 7am, when it opens, you'll see the local businesspeople lining up.

Walking Tour—Downtown San Antonio

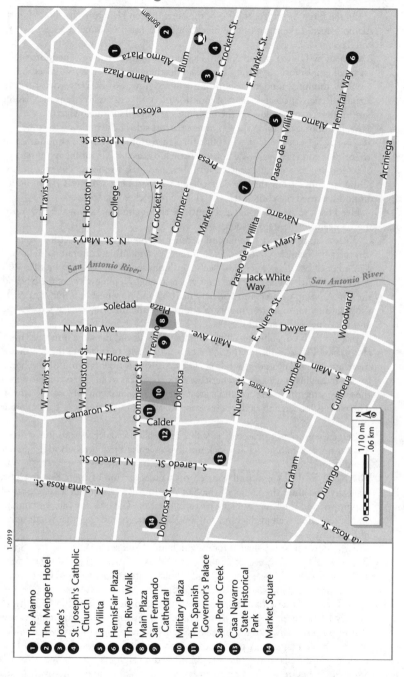

1-0919

1. The Alamo
2. The Menger Hotel
3. Joske's
4. St. Joseph's Catholic Church
5. La Villita
6. HemisFair Plaza
7. The River Walk
8. Main Plaza
9. San Fernando Cathedral
10. Military Plaza
11. The Spanish Governor's Palace
12. San Pedro Creek
13. Casa Navarro State Historical Park
14. Market Square

On the Blum Street (south) side of the hotel, Alamo Plaza turns back into North Alamo Street. Take it south one block until you reach Commerce Street, where you'll see:

3. **Joske's** (now Dillard's), San Antonio's oldest department store. The more modest retail emporium opened by the Joske Brothers in 1889 was swallowed up in 1939 by the huge modernist building you see now, distinctive for its intricate Spanish Renaissance–style details; look for the miniaturized versions of Mission San José's sacristy window on the building's ground-floor shadowboxes.

Walk a short way along the Commerce Street side of the building to come to:

4. **St. Joseph's Catholic Church,** built for San Antonio's German community in 1876. This gothic revival–style house of worship is as notable for the intransigence of its congregation as it is for its beautiful stained-glass windows. The worshipers' refusal to move from the site when Joske's department store was rising up all around it earned the church the affectionate monicker "St. Joske's."

Head back to Alamo Street and continue south two blocks past the San Antonio Convention Center to reach:

5. **La Villita,** once the site of a Coahuiltecan Indian village. It was settled over the centuries by Spanish, Germans, and, in the '30s and '40s, a community of artists; a number of buildings here have been continuously occupied for more than 200 years. The "Little Village" on the river was restored by a joint effort of the city and the San Antonio Conservation Society in 1939 and now hosts a number of crafts shops and two upscale restaurants in addition to the historic General Cós House and the Arneson River Theatre.

Just south of La Villita you'll see HemisFair Way and the large iron gates of:

6. **HemisFair Plaza,** built for the 1968 exposition held to celebrate the 250th anniversary of San Antonio's founding. The expansive former fairgrounds are home to two museums and a German heritage park, as well as to an observation tower—the tallest structure in the city and a great reference point if you get lost downtown. The plaza is too large to explore even superficially on this tour; come back another time.

Retrace your steps to Paseo de la Villita and walk one block west to Presa Street. Take it north for about half a block until you see the Presa Street Bridge and descend from it to:

7. **The River Walk.** You'll find yourself on a quiet section of the 2.8-mile paved walkway that lines the banks of the San Antonio River through a large part of downtown and the King William Historic District. The bustling cafe, restaurant, and hotel action is all just behind you, on the stretch of the river that winds north of La Villita.

Stroll down this tree-shaded thoroughfare until you reach the St. Mary's Street Bridge (you'll pass only one other bridge, the Navarro Street Bridge, along the way) and ascend here. Then walk north half a block until you come to Market Street. Take it west one long block, where you'll find:

8. **Main Plaza** (Plaza de Las Islas), the heart of the town established in 1731 by 15 Canary Island families sent by King Philip V of Spain to settle his remote New World outpost. Much of the history of San Antonio—and of Texas—unfolded on this modest square. A peace treaty with the Apaches was signed (and later broken) on the plaza in 1749; in 1835, freedom fighters battled Santa Anna's troops here before barricading themselves in the Alamo across the river. Much calmer these days, the plaza still sees some action as home to the Romanesque-style Béxar County Courthouse, built out of native Texas granite and sandstone in 1892.

Walk along the south side of Main Plaza to the corner of Main Avenue. Across the street and just to the north you'll see:

9. **San Fernando Cathedral,** the oldest parish church building in Texas and site of the earliest marked graves in San Antonio. Three walls of the original church started by the Canary Island settlers in 1738 can still be seen in the rear of the 1868 gothic revival cathedral. Among those buried within the sanctuary walls are Eugenio Navarro, brother of José Antonio Navarro (see below), and Don Manuel Muñoz, first governor of Texas when it was a province of a newly independent Mexico.

On the north side of the cathedral is Trevino Street; take it west to the next corner and cross the street to reach:

10. **Military Plaza** (Plaza de Armas), once the drill ground for the Presidio San Antonio de Béxar; the garrison, established in 1718 to protect the Mission San Antonio de Valero, was moved to this nearby site 4 years later. Military Plaza was one of the liveliest spots in Texas for the 50 years after Texas won its independence. In the 1860s, it was the site of vigilante lynchings, and after the Civil War it hosted a bustling outdoor market; at night the townsfolk would come to its open-air booths to buy chili con carne from their favorite chili queen. The plaza remained completely open until 1889, when the ornate City Hall was built at its center.

The one-story white building you'll see directly across the street from the west side of the plaza is:

11. **The Spanish Governor's Palace,** former residence and headquarters of the captain of the Presidio de Béxar (but not of any Spanish governors); from here, the commander could watch his troops going through their drills across the street. The source of the house's misnomer is not entirely clear; as the home of the highest local authority and thus the nicest digs in the area, the "palace" probably hosted important Spanish officials who came through town.

From the front of the Governor's Palace, walk south until you come to the crosswalk; just west across Dolorosa Street you'll see a drainage ditch, the sad remains of:

12. **San Pedro Creek.** The west bank of this body of water, once lovely and full flowing, was the original site of both the Mission San Antonio de Valero and the Presidio de Béxar. At the creek's former headwaters, approximately 2 miles north of here, San Pedro Park was established in 1729 by a grant from the king of Spain; it's the second-oldest municipal park in the United States (the oldest is the Boston Common).

Continue west along Dolorosa Street to Laredo Street and take it south about three-quarters of a block until you come to:

13. **Casa Navarro State Historical Park.** The life of José Antonio Navarro, for whom the park is named, traces the history of Texas itself: He was born in Spanish territory, fought for Mexico's independence from Spain, then worked to achieve Texas's freedom from Mexico (he was one of only two native-born Texans to sign the 1836 Declaration of Independence). In 1845, he voted for Texas's annexation to the United States, and a year later became a senator in the new Texas State Legislature. Navarro died here in 1871 at the age of 76.

Trace your steps back to Laredo and Dolorosa, and go west on Dolorosa Street; when you reach Santa Rosa you'll be facing:

14. **Market Square,** home to the city's Market House at the turn of the century; when the low, arcaded structure was converted to El Mercado in 1973, it switched from selling household goods and personal items to crafts, clothing, and other more tourist-oriented Mexican wares. Directly behind and west of this lively square, the

former Haymarket Plaza has become the Farmer's Market, and now sells souvenirs instead of produce.

6 Organized Tours

BUS TOURS

Gray Line
217 Alamo Plaza. ☎ **800/472-9546** or 210/226-1706. Tours range from $20 adults and $10 children under 12 (3½ hours) to $39 adults and $19.50 children (full day). Children under 5 ride free. Lunch is not included in tour prices. Earliest tours depart at 8:30am, latest return at 6:30pm; tours run daily except Thanksgiving, Christmas, New Year's Day, Easter, and Battle of Flowers Parade.

Gray Line serves up a large menu of guided bus tours, covering everything from the Spanish missions, military bases, and museums to forays south of the border or to the Hill Country. Call for details.

TROLLEY TOURS

Lone Star Trolley
301 Alamo Plaza (Ripley's Believe It or Not and Plaza Theater of Wax). ☎ **210/224-9299.** Tickets $7.50 adults, $4 children 4–12. Daily 10am–6:15pm.

Lots of people confuse the red-and-green Lone Star Trolleys with the plain green (and unguided) city-run streetcars. Boarding these will cost you a bit more—but you'll also be learning a lot about what you're looking at. Hour-long tours touch on all the downtown highlights, taking you to the King William Historic District, Market Square, and more. Lone Stars are the only handicapped-accessible trolleys in town.

RIVER CRUISES

Yanaguana Cruises
Ticket offices: Holiday Inn Riverwalk on St. Mary's; Rivercenter Mall; River Walk, across the street from the Hilton Hotel, ☎ **210/244-5700.** Tickets $4 ages 5–64, $3 seniors 65 and older, $1 children under 5. In summer, tickets sold daily 9am–11pm (at the Holiday Inn Riverwalk until 8pm), off season daily 9am–10pm.

Maybe you've sat in a River Walk cafe looking out at people riding back and forth in open, flat-bottom barges. Go ahead, give in, join 'em. An amusing, informative tour, lasting from 35 to 40 minutes, will take you more than 2 miles down the most built-up sections of the Paseo del Rio, pointing out interesting sights along the way. You'll learn a lot about the river—and find out what all those folks you watched were laughing about.

7 Staying Active

Most San Antonians head to the hills—that is, nearby Hill Country—for outdoor recreation. Some suggestions of sports in or around town follow; see chapter 17 for more.

BICYCLING   There aren't many scenic cycling trails within San Antonio itself—locals tend to ride in Brackenridge Park; in McAllister Park on the city's north side, 13102 Jones-Maltsberger (☎ 210/821-3120); and around the area near Sea World of Texas—but there are a number of appealing places to bike in the vicinity. Phone **San Antonio Wheelmen** (☎ 210/826-5015 [recorded ride information hot line]) for details on organized rides in the area.

FISHING   Closest to town for good angling are Braunig Lake, a 1,350-acre, city-owned reservoir, a few miles southeast of San Antonio off I-37, and Calaveras Lake, one of Texas's great bass lakes, a few miles southeast of San Antonio off U.S. 181 south and Loop 1604. A bit farther afield (astream?) but still easy to reach from San Antonio are Canyon Lake, about 20 miles north of New Braunfels, and Medina Lake, some 23 miles southeast of Bandera. Fishing licenses, sold at most sporting goods and tackle stores, county courthouses, and Parks and Wildlife Department offices, are required for all nonresidents; for current information, call **800/792-1112** or 512/389-4800 (in Texas only).

GOLF   Golf has become a big deal in San Antonio, with more and more duffers coming to town expressly to tee-off. Of the city's eight municipal golf courses, one of the most notable is **Brackenridge,** 2315 Ave. B (☎ **210/226-5612**), the oldest public course in Texas, opened in 1916. Oaks and pecans shade its fairways and greens fees are very reasonable. The $4.3 million **Cedar Creek,** 8250 Vista Colina (☎ **210/695-5050**), in northwest San Antonio, offers three-tiered greens and scenic Hill Country views; it's repeatedly ranked as South Texas's best municipal course in golfing surveys. Getting rave reviews, too, is the high-end **Quarry,** 444 E. Basse Rd. (☎ **210/824-4500**), one of San Antonio's newest 18-hole public golf courses; as its name suggests, it's located on the site of a former quarry (about 10 minutes from downtown). **La Cantera,** 16401 La Cantera Parkway (☎ **210/558-4653**), the latest addition to the greens scene, also has a limestone quarry as its setting; designed by Jay Morish and Tom Weiskopf, it's both difficult and dramatic (*Golf Digest* named it "The Best New Public Golf Course of 1995"). Unaffiliated golfers can also play at the 200-acre **Pecan Valley,** 4700 Pecan Valley Dr. (☎ **210/333-9018**), site of the 50th PGA Championship; it crosses the Salado Creek seven times and has an 800-year-old oak near its 13th hole. To get a copy of the free *San Antonio Golfing Guide,* call 800/447-3372.

HIKING   **Friedrich Wilderness Park,** 21395 Milsa (☎ **210/698-1057**), operated by the city of San Antonio as a nature preserve, is crisscrossed by 5¹/₂ miles of trails that attract bird watchers as well as hikers; a recently opened 2-mile stretch is handicapped accessible. The park offers free guided hikes the first Saturday of every month at 9am. Enchanted Rock State Park near Fredericksburg is the most popular spot for trekking out of town.

HORSEBACK RIDING   In town, **Brackenridge Stables,** 840 E. Mulberry Ave. (☎ **210/732-8881**), offers year-round rides through wooded trails in Brackenridge Park; rates are $23 per hour for riding on your own, $15 for a 20- to 30-minute guided trail ride, and $20 for a 45-minute ride. Hours change seasonally; call ahead to check the schedule.

PADDLEBOATS   To paddle around the lake at Brackenridge Park ($8 an hour, $5 for a half hour), go to the boat-rental office at 3910 N. St. Mary's St. (☎ **210/734-5401**), across the street from the main entrance to the San Antonio Zoo.

RIVER SPORTS   For tubing, rafting, or canoeing along a cypress-lined river, San Antonio river rats head 35 miles northwest of downtown to the 2,000-acre **Guadalupe River State Park,** 3350 Park Rd. 31 (☎ **210/438-2656**). On Hwy. 46, just outside the park, you can rent tubes, rafts, and canoes at the **Bergheim Campground,** F.M. 3351 in Bergheim (☎ **210/336-2235**); standard tubes run $6 per person (but the ones with a bottom for your cooler, at $7, are better), rafts are $15 per person (children 12 and under half-price), and canoes go for $25. The section of the Guadalupe River near Gruene is also extremely popular; see the New Braunfels section of chapter 17 for details.

SWIMMING/WATER PARKS   Most hotels have swimming pools, but if yours doesn't, call the Parks and Recreation Department (☎ 210/207-8480) to find the nearest municipal one. Splashtown water recreation park is described in the "Especially for Kids" section, above. Many San Antonians head out to New Braunfels to get wet at the **Schlitterbahn,** the largest water park in Texas; see the New Braunfels section of chapter 17 for additional information.

TENNIS   You can play at the lighted courts at the **Fairchild Tennis Center,** 1214 E. Crockett (☎ 210/226-6912), and **McFarlin Tennis Center,** 1503 San Pedro Ave. (☎ 210/732-1223), both municipal facilities, for $1.50 per hour per person ($1 for students and seniors), $2.50 after 5pm.

8 Spectator Sports

AUTO RACING   The best local drag-race action is at the **River City Raceway,** 14901 S. Hwy. 16, 4 miles south of Loop 410 ☎ 210/628-1499. Another good option is the **Alamo Dragway,** 15030 Watson Rd. (☎ 210/628-1371).

BASEBALL   From mid-April through the end of August, the minor league **San Antonio Missions** play at the new Municipal Stadium, 5757 Hwy 90 west. All home games start at 7:05pm except Sunday games, which start at 6:05pm. Tickets range from $4 for adult general admission to $7 for seats in the Executive Box. Call **210/675-7275** for schedules and tickets.

BASKETBALL   Spur madness hits San Antonio every year from mid-October through May, when the city's only major-league franchise, the **San Antonio Spurs,** shoots hoops at the huge new Alamodome (see "Special-Interest Sightseeing" above). For most games, tickets are sold only for the dome's lower level, where prices range from $15 for seats behind the basket end zones to $47 for seats on the corners of the court. Nosebleed-level seats, running from $5 to $8, open up for the most popular games. Tickets are available at the Spurs Ticket Office (south end of the Alamodome) or by phoning Rainbow Ticketmaster (☎ 210/224-9600).

GOLF   The **Dominion Senior PGA Tournament** is held each May at the Dominion Country Club, 1 Dominion Dr. (☎ 210/698-1146). The **Texas Open,** one of the oldest professional golf tournaments, moved in fall 1995 to the newest golf course in San Antonio, La Cantera, 16401 La Cantera Parkway (☎ 201/558-4653). Call the San Antonio Golf Association (☎ 800/TEX-OPEN or 210/341-0823) for additional information.

HORSE RACING   Opened in 1995, the $79 million **Retama Park,** some 15 minutes north of San Antonio in Selma (☎ 210/651-7000), is now the hottest place to play the ponies; take exit 174-A from I-35, or the Lookout Road exit from Loop 1604. The five-level Spanish-style grandstand is impressive, and the variety of food courts, restaurants, and lounges is almost as diverting as the horses (ask about the Saturday Sunrise programs, which allow visitors to watch training sessions and tour the barn area). The thoroughbreds run from Wednesday through Saturday, June 8 through September 28, and the quarter horses are scheduled the same days of the week from October 11 through November 30. Gates open at 5:30pm and the first race post time is 7pm; if you just want to see the simulcasts, you can come every day as early as 10:30am. General admission is $2.50 adults, $1.50 seniors; clubhouse, $3.50 adults, $2.50 seniors; simulcast, $1. Kids 15 and under and active military don't have to pay. A bit farther away, **Bandera Downs** is also popular with racing enthusiasts; see the Bandera section in chapter 17.

ICE HOCKEY   The first hockey team in city history, the Central Hockey League's **San Antonio Iguanas** dropped their first puck at the Freeman Coliseum (3201 E. Houston St.) in 1994. CHL adult tickets cost $8, $10, or $12 (☎ **210/227-4449**).

RODEO   If you're in town in early February, don't miss the chance to see 2 weeks of Wild West events like calf roping, steer wrestling, and bull riding at the annual **San Antonio Stock Show and Rodeo.** (You'll also enjoy live country and western bands, and you're likely to find something to add to your luggage at an exposition hall packed with Texas handcrafts.) Write San Antonio Livestock Exposition Inc. (P.O. Box 200230, San Antonio, TX 78220) for additional information in advance, or call **210/225-5851. Smaller rodeos** are held throughout the year in nearby Bandera County, the self-proclaimed "Cowboy Capital of the World"; call the Bandera County Convention and Visitors Bureau (☎ **800/364-3833** or 210/ 796-3045) for more information.

SOCCER   The **San Antonio Pumas,** members of the U.S. Interregional Soccer League, have tried to reach their goals at a variety of fields around town. They generally play from mid-April through the end of July. Call **210/223-KICK** for the current game locations, as well as for ticket prices and schedules.

7

San Antonio Shopping

San Antonio offers the retail-bound a nice balance of large malls and little enclaves of specialized shops. You'll find everything here from the utilitarian to the unusual: huge Sears and Kmart department stores, along with a Saks Fifth Avenue fronted by a 40-foot pair of cowboy boots, a mall with a river running through it, and some of the best Mexican markets north of the border.

You can count on most shops around town being open from 9 or 10am until 5:30 or 6pm on Monday through Saturday, with shorter hours on Sunday. In the downtown area, many shops don't close their doors until dark (or later) during the busy summer tourist season. Malls are generally open on Monday through Saturday from 10am to 9pm and on Sunday from noon to 6pm.

1 The Shopping Scene

Most out-of-town shoppers will find all they need downtown. In this area are concentrated the large **Rivercenter Mall;** the boutiques and craft shops of **La Villita;** the colorful Mexican wares of **Market Square;** the **Southwest Craft Center;** and assorted retailers and galleries on and around Alamo Plaza.

San Antonians tend to shop the **Loop 410 malls,** especially North Star and Central Park near the airport, and cruise the upscale **strip centers along Broadway** in Alamo Heights (the posh Collection and Lincoln Heights are particularly noteworthy). Weekends might see locals poking around a number of terrific **flea markets.** For serious bargains on brand labels, they head out to New Braunfels and San Marcos, home to three large **factory outlet malls** (see chapter 17 for details).

2 Shopping A to Z

ANTIQUES

In addition to the places that follow, a number of antique shops line Hildebrand between Blanco and San Pedro.

The Original Antique Center
5525 Blanco. ☎ **210/344-4131.**

In this air-conditioned antique mall, the focus is on hand-selected American furniture and accessories. But you can find fun and funky items here, too: jukeboxes, Coke machines, old advertising signs, toys, vintage jewelry, and more.

Center for Antiques

8505 Broadway. ☎ **210/804-6300.**

About 25 different vendors ply their goods at this huge, open warehouse near the airport, making the Center for Antiques an eclectic and interesting place to shop. There are booths specializing in knickknacks; others in old records, jewelry, or clothes; and still others in good-quality furniture for serious collectors. Some contemporary southwestern crafts are sold here, too.

ART GALLERIES

In the Southtown section near King William, the **Blue Star Arts Complex,** 1400 S. Alamo (☎ 210/227-6960), is the up-and-coming place to buy art; see the "More Attractions" section in chapter 6 for details. Downtown is also beginning to hold its own in the art world, as more and more galleries enter the area. For a copy of the *San Antonio Gallery Guide,* write or phone the San Antonio Art Gallery Association, 11451 Jones Maltsberger, 78216 (☎ 210/490-7599).

Galeria Ortiz

102 Concho (in Market Square). ☎ **210/225-0731.**

If a big-name artist is represented or temporarily shown in town, it'll be at Galeria Ortiz (formerly DagenBela), San Antonio's premier southwestern gallery. In addition to Native American and New Mexican painters, local San Antonio artists are represented. A new branch, which focuses on contemporary Latino work, recently opened at 248 Losoya (☎ 210/225-8489).

Keene Gallery

242 Losoya St. ☎ **210/299-1999.**

Just off Alamo Plaza, this gallery has 7,500 square feet of work by contemporary local and regional artists: pottery, sculpture, paintings, jewelry, even furniture, much of it lots of fun. Don't miss the recently added contemporary neon art gallery. Prices are relatively reasonable for art of this quality, especially for downtown where they're often jacked up for tourists; consider investing in some of the lesser-known artists who show here.

BOOKS

Booksmiths of San Antonio

209 Alamo Plaza. ☎ **210/271-9177.**

You'll find a wide-ranging selection at this friendly downtown bookstore; it's particularly strong on Texas and regional volumes, carrying everything from southwestern cookbooks to San Antonio ghost guides. It sometimes hosts book signings by local authors. Kiddie lit is the focus of the adjoining **Red Balloon** (☎ 210/271-9461), owned by the same family. Both stores deliver free to any of the downtown hotels.

Cheever Books

140 Carnahan. ☎ **210/824-2665.**

Come to Cheever's, across the street from the Witte Museum, for good-quality used books; there are more than 50,000 of them in stock. You'll find lots of rare volumes, as well as many recent history and art books.

CRAFTS

See also Tienda Guadalupe in "Gifts/Souvenirs," below.

Southwest Craft Center

300 Augusta. ☎ **210/224-1848.**

The gift shop at the restored Ursuline Academy for girls (see "More Attractions" in chapter 6 for details) sells handcrafted pottery, jewelry, clothing, and carryalls, most made by local artisans, and none of it run-of-the mill.

DO-IT-YOURSELF

Garden Ridge Pottery

17975 I-35 north. ☎ **210/599-5700.**

As its name suggests, this huge store once sold only unglazed outdoor pottery, from teacup size to practically large enough to fill half a yard. Now San Antonio crafters of every kind drive out to Schertz (about half an hour north of downtown) every weekend to buy embroidery kits, appliqués, beads, candles, baskets, and dried flowers, along with paving stones and other garden decorations: If an indoor or outdoor artisan needs it, they've got it here.

DEPARTMENT STORES

Dillard's

102 Alamo Plaza/Rivercenter Mall. ☎ **210/227-4343.**

You'll find links in this Arkansas-based chain in many Southwest cities and in a number of San Antonio malls; they all offer nice mid- to upper-range clothing and housewares, but the Dillard's in the Rivercenter Mall also has a section specializing in stylish western fashions. Enter or exit on Alamo Plaza so you can get a look at the historic building's ornate facade (see stop 3 under "Walking Tour—Downtown" in chapter 6 for details).

Saks Fifth Avenue

650 North Star Mall. ☎ **210/341-4111.**

Forget low-key and unobtrusive; this is Texas. Sure this department store has the high-quality, upscale wares and attentive service one would expect from a Saks Fifth Avenue, but it also has something more: a 40-foot-high pair of cowboy boots in front.

DISCOUNT SHOPPING

Burlington Coat Factory

4522 Fredericksburg Rd., Crossroads Mall. ☎ **210/735-9595.**

As anyone who's ever shopped at—or listened to a TV ad for—one of these outlets knows, Burlington Coat Factory sells much more than just coats, and almost all at significant discounts. Like most bargain stores, this one is hit-and-miss; some days you'll find terrific styles in just your size, and other days it'll seem like there's nothing but schlock—usually in just your size, too.

Marshall's

8505 Blanco. ☎ **210/340-9576.**

You can also catch Marshall's on a bad day (or two), but usually this is a good bet for fashionable, up-to-date clothing at cut-rate prices. Nice, inexpensive jewelry, especially silver, is also available here.

Stein Mart

999 E. Basse (in Lincoln Heights). ☎ **210/829-7198.**

Although the Lincoln Heights shopping center can go head-to-head with the Collection for pricey items, this clothing store offers bargains galore: Stein Mart carries high-quality goods at prices 25% to 50% lower than those in the department stores. Children as well as adults can be stylishly outfitted here for less. There's another Stein Mart in the Crossroads Mall (☎ **210/732-7012**).

FASHIONS

The following stores offer clothing in a variety of styles; if you're keen on the cowpuncher look, see "Western Wear," below.

CHILDREN'S FASHION

Children's Crossing
7959 Broadway (in the Collection). ☎ **210/828-1388.**

The well-dressed child—or the dresser thereof—will find out-of-the-ordinary items here for anything from slumber parties to special occasions. Smaller manufacturers from California are featured. As parents are all too aware, pint-sized clothing doesn't mean pint-sized prices; stores in the upscale Collection retail center tend toward the expensive, and this one is no exception.

MEN'S FASHION

Satel's
5100 Broadway. ☎ **210/822-3376.**

This family-run Alamo Heights store has been *the* place to shop for menswear in San Antonio since 1950; classic, high-quality clothing and personal service make it a standout. There have been sightings here of the neighborhood's most famous resident, Tommy Lee Jones.

Todd's Inc.
722 North Star Mall. ☎ **210/349-6464.**

Mexico's elite come to Todd's to buy their suits, casual wear, and accessories. Fine style doesn't come cheap, however; shop here only if you're prepared to part with some big bucks.

WOMEN'S FASHION

Adelante Boutique
6414 N. Braunfels Ave. (in Sunset Ridge). ☎ **210/826-6770.**

The focus here is on the ethnic and the handmade, with lots of colorful, natural fabrics and free-flowing lines. The store also offers a nice selection of leather belts and whimsical jewelry and gifts.

Kathleen Sommers
2417 N. Main. ☎ **210/732-8437.**

This small shop on the corner of Main and Woodlawn has been setting trends for San Antonio women for years. Kathleen Sommers, who works mainly in linen and other natural fabrics, designs all the clothes herself and they bear her label. The store also carries great jewelry, bath items, books, and a selection of unusual gifts.

FOOD

Farm to Market
1133 Austin Hwy. ☎ **210/822-4450.**

Consider bringing back jars of salsa, *nopalitos* (tender marinated cactus strips), and other southwestern treats from this small Alamo Heights market, also a good place to shop for fruits and vegetables, pâtés, fresh pasta, homemade sausage, and other gourmet goodies. The ready-to-eat entrees are excellent, too. Saturday is samples day; keep coming back for tastes of the cilantro bread or other delicious baked goods and you might not have to buy lunch.

HEB Marketplace
5601 Bandera Rd. at Loop 410. ☎ **210/657-2700.**

The HEB grocery chain, headquartered in San Antonio, runs this huge marketplace; it's a bit out of the way (about 20 to 25 minutes from downtown), but an impressive array of edibles makes it worth the trip. Along with packaged grocery items—among them many Mexican, Asian, and Middle Eastern foods—are fresh goods from a bakery, deli, butcher shop (pick up your rattlesnake and buffalo steaks here), tortilla factory, and ice creamery. There's also a terrific flower section. Shipping is available.

GIFTS/SOUVENIRS

See also Artisans Alley under "Malls/Shopping Complexes," below.

San Angel Folk Art
110 Blue Star St. ☎ **210/226-6688.**

Combing the crafts markets of Mexico might be more fun, but exploring this large store in the Blue Star Arts Complex is a pretty good substitute. Painted animals from Oaxaca, elaborate masks from the state of Guerrero—if it's colorful, whimsical, and well-made, you'll find it here. Of course prices are better south of the border, but hey, you're saving yourself plane fare.

Tienda Guadalupe Folk Art & Gifts
1001 S. Alamo. ☎ **210/226-5873.**

This incense-scented shop in the Southtown/King William area, just across the street from Rosario's restaurant, is also chock-full of things Hispanic: painting and handicrafts from Latin America, Mexican antiques and religious items, and more. Come here to pick up a Day of the Dead T-shirt and anything else you can think of relating to the early November holiday celebrated with great fanfare in San Antonio.

ZaZu
555 E. Basse Rd. ☎ **210/828-9838.**

How many picture frames, clocks, and coffee cups does a person need? The superb and unusual designs at this chic sundries boutique, recently moved from the Collection shopping center to Village on the Green, across from the Quarry golf course, make you want to acquire more than you could ever use—or afford. Which makes ZaZu an ideal gift shop, the perfect place to pick up something wonderful and nonutilitarian for someone you really like. The artful, airy space makes browsing here even more appealing.

JEWELRY

For more casual jewelry, see also "Crafts" and "Gifts/Souvenirs."

Gurinsky's Fine Jewelry
North Star Mall, ☎ **210/524-9999;** Central Park Mall, ☎ 210/349-2446; 7900 I-35 north, ☎ 210/599-0116; 6301 NW Loop 410, ☎ 210/647-0073.

The Gurinsky family has decked San Antonio in diamonds for years—also in pearls, gold, and other precious stones and metals. This is a trusted name in high-quality jewelry.

Love Potion No. 9

Ask a proprietor of a *botanica*, "What kind of store is this?" and you'll hear anything from "a drugstore" to "a religious bookstore." But along with Christian artifacts (including glow-in-the-dark rosaries and dashboard icons), botanicas carry magic floor washes; candles designed to keep the law off your back; wolf skulls; amulets; herbal remedies; and, of course, love potions. The common theme is happiness enhancement, whether by self-improvement, prayer, or luck.

Many of San Antonio's countless small botanicas specialize in articles used in the practice of *curandera,* a Latin American version of voodoo, though the owners are loath to admit it. Books directing laypersons in the use of medicinal herbs sit next to volumes that retell the lives of the saints. It's easy enough to figure out the use of the *santos* (saint), candles in tall glass jars to which are affixed such labels as "Peaceful Home," "Find Work," and "Bingo." *Milagros* (miracles) are small charms that represent parts of the body—or mind—that a person wishes to have healed. Don't worry that many of the labels are in Spanish; the person behind the counter will be happy to translate. He or she is likely to be an herbalist and will often offer common-sense diet advice, gratis.

Papa Jim's, 5630 S. Flores (☎ 210/922-6665), is the best known of all the botanicas; for a bit extra, Papa Jim will bless almost anything you buy. And in case of an emergency down the road, Papa Jim can supply you with the remedy through his mail-order business. For some magic closer to downtown, try **Botanica Hildebrand,** 735 West Hildebrand (☎ 210/737-2171).

MALLS/SHOPPING COMPLEXES

Artisans Alley
555 Bitters Rd. ☎ 210/494-3226.

This place packs a lot of charm under one large, wooden roof: It offers folk art, jewelry, antiques, ethnic clothing, pottery and sculpture studios, even a tearoom.

Central Park Mall
Loop 410 and Blanco. ☎ 210/344-2236.

Lots of shoppers start out by ogling the goods at North Star Mall and then head next door to Central Park, where they can actually afford to buy something. Anchored by Bealls, Dillard's, and Sears department stores, this mall has lots of popular chains among its 90-plus stores, and many reasonably priced places to eat in its food court.

Crossroads Mall
4522 Fredericksburg Rd. (off Loop 410 and I-10). ☎ 210/735-9137.

Located near the South Texas Medical Center, this is San Antonio's bargain mall, featuring Burlington Coat Factory, Montgomery Ward, and Woolworth department stores along with smaller discount shops.

Los Patios
2015 NE Loop 410 at the Starcrest exit. ☎ 210/655-6171.

The self-proclaimed "other River Walk" features 11 upscale specialty shops—selling, among other things, imported clothing, crafts, jewelry, and antique furniture—in an 18-acre wooded setting. Although the food at Los Patios's three restaurants isn't especially exciting, the setting is hard to beat; the Brazier is the only eatery that actually looks out over Salado Creek, but all have outdoor decks or patios shaded by spreading oaks.

North Star Mall

Loop 410 at McCullough. ☎ **210/342-2325.**

Starring Saks Fifth Avenue and upscale boutiques like Abercrombie & Fitch, Pappagallo, Crabtree & Evelyn, Laura Ashley, and Williams-Sonoma, this is the crème de la crème of the San Antonio malls. But there are many sensible shops here, too, including a Mervyn's department store. Food choices also climb up and down the class scale, ranging from a Godiva Chocolatier to a Luby's Cafeteria.

Rivercenter Mall

849 E. Commerce, between Alamo Plaza and Bowie, Crockett, and Commerce. ☎ **210/ 225-0000.**

There's a festive atmosphere at this bustling, light-filled mall, created, among other things, by its location on an extension of the San Antonio River: You can pick up a ferry from a downstairs dock or listen to bands play on a stage surrounded by water. Other entertainment options include the IMAX theater, the multiple-screen AMC, and the Rivercenter Comedy Club. The shops—more than 135 of them—run the price gamut, but tend toward the upscale casual; Dillard's and Foleys are the anchors. For food, you'll find everything from Dairy Queen and A&W Hot Dogs to Morton's of Chicago, as well as the restaurants at the huge Rivercenter Marriott.

MARKETS

Market Square

514 W. Commerce St., near Dolorosa. ☎ **210/207-8600.**

Two large indoor markets, El Mercado and the Farmer's Market, occupy adjacent blocks on Market Square, sharing the space with other shops, restaurants, and food stalls; the whole complex is often just called the Mexican market. Come here for local Hispanic handcrafts and south-of-the-border imports, as well as for a good time; you'll often find yourself buying to the beat of a mariachi band.

FLEA MARKETS

Austin Highway Flea Market

1428 Austin Hwy. ☎ **210/828-1488.**

This open-air flea market sells used and vintage clothing (the line between these categories is drawn according to one's age), plants, toys, jewelry, and coins, among other things. You can find some real furniture bargains here.

Bussey's Flea Market

18738 I-35 north. ☎ **210/651-6830.**

Unless you're heading to New Braunfels or Austin, Bussey's is a bit out of the way. But these 20 acres of indoor-and-outdoor vendors selling goods from as far afield as Asia and Africa are definitely worth the drive (about a half-hour north of downtown). Crafts, jewelry, antiques, incense, fruits and vegetables—it's hard to imagine what you *couldn't* find in this market. There's even a botanica (see the "Love Potion No. 9" box, above) here.

Eisenhauer Road Flea Market

3903 Eisenhauer Rd. ☎ **210/653-7592.**

The all-indoors, all–air-conditioned Eisenhower, replete with snack bar and Old West–style saloon, is a good flea market to hit in the height of summer. You'll see lots of new stuff here—purses, jewelry, furniture, toys, shoes—and everything from house plants to kinky leatherwear; you can even get a tattoo to go along with the latter.

Flea Mart
12280 Hwy. 16 south (about 1 mile south of Loop 410). ☎ **210/624-2666.**

For a bit of Mexico that hasn't been gussied up for the tourists, this is the place to come. On weekends, Mexican-American families make a day of this huge market, bringing the entire family to exchange gossip, listen to live bands, and eat freshly made tamales and tacos. There are always fruits and vegetables, electronics, crafts, and new and used clothing—and you never know what else you might find.

TOYS

The following stores carry unusual but often pricey toys. If your child is especially hard on playthings or your cash supply is running low, consider buying used toys at **Kids Junction Resale Station,** 2267 NW Military Hwy. (☎ **210/340-5532**), or **Too Good to Be Threw,** 7115 Blanco (☎ **210/340-2422**).

Monarch Collectibles
2012 NW Military Hwy. ☎ **210/341-3655.**

Welcome to doll heaven. Many of the models that fill Monarch's four rooms—about 3,000 dolls in all—are collectible and made from delicate materials like porcelain and baked clay, but others are cute and cuddly; some come with real hair and eyelashes, and some, like a 3-foot-high Lillie Langtry, are literally one of a kind. Doll furniture is also sold here, along with plates and a few stuffed animals.

Playworks
7959 Broadway (in the Collection). ☎ **210/828-3400.**

It's a toss-up who's going to spend more time oohing and aahing their way through this store, children or their parents. Along with the detailed Playmobil universe, imported from Germany, Playworks carries all kinds of life-science projects: ant farms, Grow-A-Frog, butterfly gardens . . . you'd be amazed at the creatures that are sent through the mail. Adults will have trouble staying away from the nostalgia toys: pogo sticks, stilts, and puppet theaters. A second Playworks store is located at 1931 NW Military Hwy. (☎ **210/340-2328**).

WESTERN WEAR
GENERAL

Kallison's Western Wear
123 S. Flores. ☎ **210/222-1364.**

When this place opened down the road from the county courthouse in 1899, the idea of anyone wearing blue jeans who wasn't prepared to handle a horse would have been considered plum loco. Real ranch hands still shop at Kallison's, but these days urban cowboys and cowgirls also get outfitted here, from their Stetson hats down to their Justin boots. There's a newer Kallison's across from Sears in Shopper City Mall, 616A SW Military Dr. (☎ **210/924-9441**).

BOOTS

Lucchese Gallery
4025 Broadway (in the Boardwalk). ☎ **210/828-9419.**

The name says it all: Footwear is raised to the level of art at Lucchese. If it once crawled, ran, hopped, or swam, these folks can probably put it on your feet: The store has got boots made of alligator, anteater, ostrich, kangaroo, stingray, lizard, and snake. Come here for everything from executive to special-occasion boots, all handmade and expensive—the catalog alone costs $12 if you don't buy anything—and all serious Texas status symbols. Lucchese also carries jackets, belts, and sterling silver belt buckles.

HATS

✪ Paris Hatters
119 Broadway. ☎ **210/223-3453.**

What do Pope John Paul II, Prince Charles, and Dwight Yoakam have in common? They all have had headgear made for them by Paris Hatters, in business since 1917 and still owned by the same family. About half of the sales are special order, but the shelves are stocked with high-quality ready-to-wear hats, including Kangol caps from Britain, Panama hats from Ecuador, and, of course, Stetson, Resistol, Dobbs, and other western brands. A lot of them can be adjusted to your liking while you wait. If you want to see which other famous heads have been covered here, check out the pictures and newspaper articles in the back.

WINES

Gabriel's
837 Hildebrand. ☎ **210/735-8329.**

A large, warehouse-style store, Gabriel's combines a good selection with good prices. A recorded specials hot line (☎ **210/599-7700**) will clue you in to the bargains of the day for whatever spirits you're seeking. The Hildebrand store is slightly north of downtown; there's also another location near the airport at 7233 Blanco (☎ **210/349-7472**).

SeaZar's Fine Wine & Spirits
6422 N. New Braunfels, in the Sunset Ridge Shopping Center. ☎ **210/822-6094.**

A temperature-controlled wine cellar, a large selection of beer and spirits, a cigar humidor, and a knowledgeable staff all make this a good choice for aficionados of the various legal vices.

8

San Antonio After Dark

San Antonio has its symphony and its Broadway shows, and you can see both at one of the most beautiful old movie palaces in the country. This is also a town where you can sit on one side of a river and watch colorful dance troupes like Ballet Folklórico perform on the other. But much of what the city has to offer is less mainstream. A Latin flavor lends spice to some of the best local nightlife: San Antonio is America's capital for Tejano music, a unique blend of German polka and northern Mexico ranchero sounds, with a touch of pop for good measure; and a Latino Laugh Festival, first held in the summer of 1996, now promises to be an annual event.

Keep in mind, too, that the Fiesta City throws big public parties year-round: These include Fiestas Navidenas and Las Posadas around Christmastime; Fiesta San Antonio and Cinco de Mayo events in spring; the Texas Folklife Festival in summer; and the Day of the Dead celebration in fall (see also "San Antonio Calendar of Events" in chapter 2). And Southtown, which has lots of Hispanic-oriented shops and galleries, celebrates its art scene with the monthly First Friday, an extended block party of sorts; a free trolley runs up and down the artist-rich South Alamo Street.

For the most complete listings of what's on while you're visiting, pick up a free copy of the weekly alternative newspaper, the *Current,* or the Friday "Weekender" section of the *San Antonio Express-News.* You can also call the new **San Antonio Arts Hotline** at **800/ 894-3819** or 210/207-2166. There is no central office in town for tickets, discounted or otherwise. You'll need to reserve seats directly through the theaters or clubs, or, in the case of large events, through **TicketMaster** (☎ **210/224-9600**).

1 The Performing Arts

The San Antonio Symphony is the city's only resident performing arts company of national stature, but smaller, less professional groups keep the local arts scene lively, and cultural organizations draw world-renowned artists. The city provides them with some unique venues for their work—everything from standout historic stuctures like the Majestic, Arneson, and Sunken Garden theaters to the brand-new, high-tech Alamodome. Because, in some cases, the theater is the show and, in others, a single venue offers an eclectic array of performances, we've included a category called Major Arts Venues, below.

CLASSICAL MUSIC

San Antonio Symphony
222 E. Houston St. ☎ **210/554-1010.**

Winner of the Award for Programming of Contemporary Music by the American Society of Composers, Authors, and Publishers (ASCAP) in 1995, San Antonio's symphony is one of the finest in the United States. Founded in 1939, the orchestra celebrated its 50th anniversary by being installed in the stunning Majestic Theatre, the reopening of which was planned to coincide with the event. The symphony offers two annual series: a standard classical one and a pops. The former showcases the talents of music director Christopher Wilkens and resident conductor David Mairs; for the latter, the orchestra plays second fiddle to such artists as Dave Brubeck, Larry Gatlin, and Tito Puente.

THEATER

Actors Theater of San Antonio
1608 N. Main. ☎ **210/227-2872.**

Established in the early 1980s, the Actors Theater uses local talent for its productions, which tend to be in the off-Broadway tradition. Dramatic performances have included *Suddenly Last Summer, Bent,* and *Someone to Watch Over Me; The Fantasticks* and *Chicago* were among the musicals. The company divides its time between the small (80-seat) Main Avenue Studio and the upstairs stage of the Alamo Street Theater & Restaurant (see below).

Josephine Theater
339 W. Josephine St. ☎ **210/734-4646.**

This community-based company puts on an average of five productions a year at the art deco–style Josephine Street Theater, built in 1945. The award-winning group does mostly musicals—*My Fair Lady, Dreamgirls,* and *Crazy for You* among them—but it also performs dramatic classics such as *Of Mice and Men* and *Desire Under the Elms.* The Josephine Street Theater is only 5 minutes from downtown and around the corner from several restaurants and nightclubs.

Jump-Start Performance Company
108 Blue Star Arts Complex (1400 S. Alamo). ☎ **210/227-JUMP.**

Whether it's an original piece by a member of the company or a work by a guest artist, anything you see at Jump-Start is bound to be unconventional. Works here tend to push the social and political envelope. This is the place to find the big-name performance artists like Karen Finley or Holly Hughes who tour San Antonio, and also to discover what's happening on the cutting edge in town.

San Pedro Playhouse
800 W. Ashby (at San Pedro Avenue). ☎ **210/733-7258.**

This local troupe presents a wide range of plays in a neoclassical-style performance hall built in 1930. Recently renovated, it was the first public theater to open in San Antonio. SALT's season might open with a blockbuster musical like *George M!,* include a family show such as *Cinderella* at Christmas, and move on to something a bit more offbeat—say, *Nunsense*—later in the year. Original works by San Antonio playwrights are performed at the smaller Cellar Theatre downstairs.

MAJOR ARTS VENUES

✪ Arneson River Theatre
La Villita. ☎ 210/927-3389.

If you're visiting San Antonio in the summer, be sure to see something at the Arneson. Built by the Works Project Administration in 1939 as part of architect Robert Hugman's design for the River Walk, this unique theater stages shows on one side of the river while the audience watches from an amphitheater on the other. Most of the year performance schedules are erratic and include everything from opera to Tejano, but June through August run on a strict calendar: The Fiesta Flamenca on Sunday, Monday, and Tuesday; the Fandango folkloric troupe every Wednesday; and the Fiesta Rio del Noche on Thursday, Friday, and Saturday. All offer lively music and dance with a south-of-the-border flair.

Beethoven Hall
422 Pereida. ☎ 210/222-1521.

San Antonio's German heritage is celebrated at Beethoven Hall, a converted 1894 Victorian mansion in the King William area. The season starts in April with music and dance performances for the citywide Fiesta. After that, monthly concerts with a choir and brass band are held in a lovely pecan-shaded garden. The Beethoven folk dancers entertain here, too. Traditional German food, drink, and revelry make Oktoberfest an autumn high point. The hall closes down after November, when a Kristkindle Markt welcomes the holiday season with an old country–style arts-and-crafts fair.

Carver Community Cultural Center
226 N. Hackberry. ☎ 210/225-6516.

Located near the Alamodome on the east edge of downtown, the Carver's theater was built for the city's African-American community in 1928 and continues to serve that group while providing a widely popular venue for an international array of performers. Roughly 20 seasonal events include drama, music, and dance. The 1996–1997 season saw performances as diverse as *La Boheme;* the Alvin Ailey American Dance Company; and *Jam on the Groove,* featuring a hip-hop ensemble.

Guadalupe Cultural Arts Center
1300 Guadalupe. ☎ 210/271-3151.

There's always something happening at the Guadalupe Center, the main locus for Latino cultural activity in San Antonio: Visiting or local directors put on six or seven plays a year; the resident Guadalupe Dance Company might collaborate with the city's symphony or invite modern masters up from Mexico City; the Xicano Music Program celebrates the popular local conjunto and Tejano sounds; an annual book fair brings in Spanish-language literature from around the world; and the CineFestival, running since 1977, is one of the town's major film events. And then there are always the parties thrown to celebrate new installations at the theater's art gallery and its annex.

Laurie Auditorium
Trinity University, 715 Stadium Dr. ☎ 210/736-8117 (taped box office information line) or 210/736-8119.

Some pretty high-powered people turn up at the Laurie Auditorium, on the Trinity University campus in the north-central part of town. Everyone from Margaret Thatcher to Colin Powell has taken part in the university's Distinguished Lecture

Series, subsidized by grants and open to the public for free. The 2,700-seat hall also hosts major players in the performing arts: Lyle Lovett, Marcel Marceau, and Carol Burnett all took the stage in the 1996–1997 season. Dance recitals, jazz concerts, and plays, many including internationally renowned artists, are held here, too.

✪ Majestic Theatre
230 E. Houston. ☎ **210/226-3333.**

The Majestic hosts much of the best entertainment in town—the symphony, major Broadway productions, big-name solo performers—but it's also a show unto itself. John Eberson, the prolific architect who built it, introduced the concept of the "atmospheric" theater to the United States. While you wait for the feature to begin, a three-dimensional Moorish-Italian village, replete with cypresses, palm trees, trailing vines, peacocks, and fountains, slowly darkens as stars begin to twinkle and clouds drift in shifting patterns overhead. Because the Majestic brought air-conditioning to San Antonio for the first time—the hall was billed beforehand as "an acre of cool, comfortable seats"—society women wore fur coats to its opening, held on a warm June night in 1929. Thanks to a wonderful restoration of this fabulous showplace, coming here is still a major event.

Sunken Garden Theater
Brackenridge Park, North St. Mary's St./Mulberry Ave. entrance. ☎ **210/735-0663.**

Built by the WPA in 1936 in a natural acoustic bowl in Brackenridge Park, the Sunken Garden Theater boasts an open-air stage set against a wooded hillside; cut-limestone buildings in Greek revival style hold the wings and the dressing rooms. This appealing outdoor arena offers a little bit of everything—rock, country, hip-hop, rap, jazz, Tejano, Cajun, sometimes even the San Antonio Symphony. Bob Dylan, Kenny G., and Merle Haggard have all performed here, and the bard has been coming around almost every summer since 1990 for a week and a half of Shakespeare in the Park.

A DINNER THEATER

Alamo Street Theatre & Restaurant
1150 S. Alamo. ☎ **210/271-7791.**

You're bound to have a good time at the King William district's Alamo Street Theatre, no matter which of its two shows you decide to attend. Interactive comedies and murder mysteries take place in the dining room, where meals are buffet style; entrees change depending on the accompanying comedy or thriller, but there are always soups, salads, veggies, and desserts to die for (as it were). Upstairs it's straight comedy—everything from local Texas plays like *Quaint It Ain't* to Neil Simon's *California Suite*. The church, now occupied by the Alamo Street Theater, was built in 1912 and is on the National Register of Historic Places; the interactive plays take place in what were once choir rooms, the comedies in the old sanctuary.

2 The Club & Music Scene

The closest San Antonio comes to having a club district is the stretch of North St. Mary's between Josephine and Magnolia—just north of downtown and south of Brackenridge Park—known as the Strip. This area was hotter—or is that cooler?— 5 or 6 years ago, but it still draws locals to its restaurants and lounges on the weekend.

COUNTRY & WESTERN

Cibolo Creek Country Club

8640 Evans Rd. (1 mile north of 1604). ☎ **210/651-6652.**

For a taste of down-home Texas, come to this friendly honky-tonk in the northeastern part of town; folks have been doing just that for about 100 years. There's always a couple of dogs running around the large outdoor patio and a couple of people hanging out on the porch swing. Inside, you can flop down on one of the old couches next to the bar, sit at a table that has legs wearing blue jeans and boots, or stand around and shoot pool. Live bands play alternative Texas music, from rockabilly and updated country and western to rock, zydeco, and blues.

✪ Floore Country Store

14664 Bandera Rd./Hwy. 16, Helotes (2 miles north of Loop 1604). ☎ **210/695-8827.**

The first manager of the Majestic Theatre and an unsuccessful candidate for mayor of San Antonio, John P. Floore opened up his country store in 1942. A couple of years later, he added a cafe and a dance floor—at half an acre, the largest in south Texas. The cafe is only open now when it's not functioning as a dance hall—Monday through Friday from 11am to 2pm—but otherwise nothingmuch else has changed. Boots, hats, and antique farm equipment hang from the ceiling of this typical Texas roadhouse; pictures of Willie Nelson, Hank Williams, Sr., Conway Twitty, Ernest Tubb, and other country greats who have played here line the walls. There's always live music on weekends—Willie still performs now and then, as does his friend Jerry Jeff Walker. The cafe still serves homemade bread, homemade tamales, and old-fashioned sausage.

Leon Springs Dancehall

24135 I-10 (Boerne Stage Road exit). ☎ **210/698-7072.**

This lively 1880s-style dance hall can pack about 1,200 people into its 7,000 square feet—and often does. Don't fret if you can't two-step: There are free dance lessons Thursday night. Lots of people come with their kids when the place opens at 6pm, though the crowd turns older (but not that much) as the evening wears on. Some of the best local country and western talent is showcased here on Thursday, Friday, and Saturday nights. It's closed Sunday through Wednesday.

ROCK

Borracho's

320 Beauregard. ☎ **210/226-2106.**

Formerly Beauregard's, this Southtown club serves up live rock from mainstream to alternative, along with some reggae, jazz, and rhythm and blues. If you don't like the band, you can always look at the artwork behind the stage, a Guernica-like mural by artist Robert Tatum. Crawfish etouffee is a house specialty.

Sneakers

11431 Perrin Beitel. ☎ **210/653-9176.**

Fans of Foghat and Blue Oyster Cult turn out for these bands in droves when they play Sneakers, in the far northeast part of town. Heavy rock and metal dominate at this huge club, but you can also find some blues and alternative rock here.

Taco Land

103 W. Grayson St. ☎ **210/223-8406.**

Loud and not much to look at—low ceilings, red vinyl booths, garage pin-up calendars stapled to the ceiling—tiny Taco Land is the hottest alternative music club in San Antonio, showcasing everything from mainstream rock to surf punk. Some of the bands that turn up may seem less than impressive, but, hey, you never know; Nirvana played here before they hit the big time. College kids mingle at this club with the crew from the nearby Pearl Brewery. Name notwithstanding, Taco Land only recently began selling tacos.

JAZZ & BLUES

In addition to the clubs listed below, you might also try Camille's and Rosario's, both listed in chapter 5.

✪ The Landing

Hyatt Regency Hotel, River Walk. ☎ **210/223-7266.**

You might have heard cornetist Jim Cullum on the airwaves: His American Public Radio program, *Riverwalk, Live from the Landing,* is broadcast on more than 150 stations nationwide. The Landing is one of the best traditional jazz clubs in the country; if you like big bands and Dixieland, there's no better place to listen to music downtown. Jim Cullum and his band have backed some of the finest jazz artists of our time. A recently added kitchen features a New Orleans–style menu.

Tycoon Flats

2926 N. St. Mary's St. ☎ **210/737-1929.**

A friendly music garden, Tycoon Flats is a fun place to kick back and listen to some blues, rock, acoustic, or jazz; the burgers are good, too. Bring the kids; an outdoor sandbox is larger than the dance floor. There's never any cover for the almost-nightly live music.

A COMEDY CLUB

Rivercenter Comedy Club

849 E. Commerce St./Rivercenter Mall, third level. ☎ **210/229-1420.**

This club books the big names in stand-up like Dennis Miller and Garry Shandling, but it also takes advantage of local talent. Every other Monday, two ComedySportz teams improvise on athletic themes suggested by the audience. It's open-mike night every Friday in the Ha!Lapeno Lounge, and you can watch the Local Comedians Invitational Comedy Showcase for free on Saturday afternoon at 3:30.

GAY CLUBS

Bonham Exchange

411 Bonham. ☎ **210/271-3811.**

Tina Turner, Deborah Harry, and La Toya Jackson have all played this high-tech dance club near the Alamo—the real stars, not drag impersonators. While you may find an occasional cross-dressing show here, the mixed crowd of gays and straights, young and old, come mainly to move to the beat under wildly flashing lights. All the action takes place in a restored German-style building dating back to the 1880s. Roll over, Beethoven.

Nexus

8021 Pine Brook Dr. (near I-10 and Callahan). ☎ **210/341-2818.**

If you don't find your friend out on the floor dancing to a country-and-western or Top 40 beat, she might be out back playing volleyball or, on Thursday night,

Conjunto: An American Classic

Cruise a San Antonio radio dial or go to any major city festival and you'll most likely hear the happy, boisterous sound of *conjunto*. Never heard of it? Don't worry. Although conjunto is one of our country's original contributions to world music, for a long time few Americans outside of Texas knew much about it.

Conjunto evolved at the end of the 19th century when South Texas was swept by a wave of German immigrants who brought with them popular polkas and waltzes. These sounds were easily incorporated into—and transformed by— Mexican folk music; the newcomer accordian, which could mimic several instruments at a low cost, was happily adopted, too. With the addition of the bajo sexto (a 12-string guitarlike instrument) for rhythmic bass accompaniment at the turn of the century, conjunto was born.

Tejano (Spanish for Texas) is the 20th-century offspring of conjunto. The two most prominent instruments in Tejano remain the accordion and the bajo sexto, but the music incorporates more modern forms, including pop, jazz, and country and western, into the traditional conjunto repertoire. At clubs not exclusively devoted to Latino sounds, what you're likely to hear is Tejano.

Although the mainstream had long ignored conjunto and Tejano, the shooting of Hispanic superstar Selena brought her music into America's consciousness. Before she was killed, Selena had already been slotted for crossover success—she had done the title song and put in a cameo appearance in the film *Don Juan de Marco* with Johnny Depp—and the movie based on her life will no doubt boost awareness of her music even further.

San Antonio is to conjunto music what Nashville is to country. Many of the bajo sextos used nationally and in Mexico are made in San Antonio by the Macías family. The undisputed king of conjunto, Flaco Jimenez, lives in the city; the mild-mannered triple-Grammy winner has recorded with the Rolling Stones, Bob Dylan, and Willie Nelson, among others, and put in appearances on David Letterman. And San Antonio's Tejano Conjunto Festival, held every May (see "San Antonio Calendar of Events" in chapter 2), is the largest of its kind, drawing international aficionados; there's even a Japanese conjunto band.

Note: I haven't listed any places for visitors to listen to conjunto/Tejano because all of them are pretty sleazy and not especially visitor friendly. The best place to hear the music is at one of San Antonio's many festivals—most of them feature the lively music.

enjoying a barbecue; bring your own meat, and the owner will cook it for you and supply the trimmings. This clean, friendly club in the northwest attracts mostly professional women, who tend to get dressed up on Friday and Saturday nights.

3 The Bar Scene

Blue Star Brewing Company Restaurant & Bar
1414 S. Alamo, No. 105 (Blue Star Arts Complex). ☎ 210/212-5506.

Since 1994, when brew pubs became legal in Texas, a number of these combination breweries and restaurants have been turning up throughout the state; the Blue Star, opened in 1996, is one of the newest. Preppie and gallery types don't often mingle, but the popularity of this brew pub in the Blue Star Art Complex with a collegiate crowd demonstrates the transcendent power of good beer. And if a few folks who wouldn't know a Picasso from a piccolo wander in to see some art after dinner, the owners will have performed a public service.

If you want to sample other local brews, check out the Boardwalk Bistro and Brewery (see chapter 5).

Cadillac Bar & Restaurant
212 S. Flores. ☎ **210/223-5533.**

During the week, lawyers and judges come to unwind at the Cadillac Bar, set in a historic stucco building near the Béxar County Courthouse and City Hall; on the weekends, singles take the stand. On Wednesday, Friday, and Saturday nights a deejay spins. Full dinners are served on a patio out back.

Durty Nellie's Irish Pub
715 River Walk (Hilton Palacio del Rio Hotel). ☎ **210/222-1400.**

Chug a lager and lime, toss your peanut shells on the floor, and sing along with the piano player at this wonderfully corny version of an Irish pub. You've forgotten the words to "Danny Boy"? Not to worry—18 old-time favorite songs are printed on the back of the menu. After a couple of Guinnesses, you'll be bellowing "H-A-, double R-I, G-A-N spells Harrigan," loud as the rest of 'em.

Houston Street Alehouse
420 E. Houston. ☎ **210/354-4694.**

A hundred bottles of beer on the wall, and all of them different brands—not to mention the 48 brews on tap. Add a large selection of martinis, some expensive cigars, and lots of glass, wood, and brass, and you've got your basic yuppie bar, only a few blocks from the River Walk.

Howl at the Moon Saloon
111 W. Crockett St. ☎ **210/212-4695.**

It's hard to avoid having a good time at this rowdy River Walk bar next to the Hard Rock Cafe; if you're disposed to be shy, one of the dueling piano players will inevitably embarrass you into joining the crowd belting out off-key oldies from the '60s, '70s, and '80s. But hey, don't worry; you're not likely to see most of these people ever again.

La Tuna
100 Probant. ☎ **210/224-8862.**

Gallery groupies tend to gather at this bar in Southtown's Blue Star Arts district—look for the brightly colored sign on a tiny concrete-and-corrugated aluminum building—but lots of nonartsy types drop by for a beer, too. You can sit on the patio and watch the trains roll slowly by a block away; after downtown parades, the floats cruise past on their way back to the warehouses. There's music on Saturday night, weather permitting, year-round; in winter, a bonfire blazes from a pit built into the patio.

Menger Bar
Menger Hotel, 204 Alamo Plaza. ☎ **210/223-4361.**

More than 100 years ago, Teddy Roosevelt recruited men for his Rough Riders unit at this dark, wooded bar; they were outfitted for the Spanish-American War at nearby Fort Sam Houston. William Menger built his landmark hotel in 1859 on the site of his earlier, successful brewery and saloon, and it's still a good spot to toss back a few.

Polo's
Fairmount Hotel, 40 S. Alamo St. ☎ **210/224-8800.**

For piano music in a high-tone atmosphere, come to Polo's Thursday through Saturday night; you can sink into a plush green leather couch or perch on a stool at the marble bar and enjoy some jazz or Broadway sounds. This romantic spot tends to draw an older crowd, who can afford the price of the drinks.

Tex's
San Antonio Airport Hilton and Conference Center, 611 NW Loop 410. ☎ **210/340-6060.**

If you want to hang with the Spurs, come to Tex's, voted San Antonio's best sports bar in the last two *Current* reader's polls. Three satellite dishes, two large-screen TVs and 17 smaller sets, along with killer margaritas and giant burgers, keep the bleachers happy. Among Tex's major array of exclusively Texas sports memorabilia are a signed Nolan Ryan jersey; a football used by the champion Dallas Cowboys in the 1977 Super Bowl; and one of George Gervin's basketball shoes (the other is at the new Tex's on the River, at the Hilton Palacio del Rio).

Tower of the Americas
600 HemisFair Park. ☎ **210/223-3101.**

No matter what, or how much, you have to drink, you'll get higher here than anywhere else in San Antonio—more than 700 feet high, in fact. Just below the observation-deck level, the bar at the Tower of the Americas Restaurant affords dazzling views of the city at night.

4 Movies

There's not much of a cinema scene in San Antonio—art-and-foreign movies turn up primarily at the **Crossroads Mall Theater,** Crossroads Mall, No. 14 Loop 410 at Frederickburg Road (☎ 210/737-0291)—but the **Guadalupe Cultural Arts Center** and the **McNay** and **Witte Museums** often have interesting film series. In addition to *Alamo, the Price of Freedom,* **IMAX,** Rivercenter Mall, 849 E. Crockett (☎ **210/225-4629**), shows nature films designed for the theater's huge screen.

9

Introducing Austin

Aaah, Austin, that laid-back city in the lake-laced hills, home to cyberpunks and environmentalists, high culture and haute cuisine. A leafy intellectual enclave lying well outside the realm of Lone Star stereotypes, Austin has been compared to Berkeley and Seattle, but it is at once its own place and entirely of Texas.

Many Texans who live in faster-paced places like Dallas or Houston dream of someday escaping to Austin, which, though it's passed the half-million population mark, still has a leisurely, small-town feel. Meanwhile, they smile upon the city as they would on a beloved but eccentric younger sister; whenever an especially contrary story about her is told, they shrug and shake their heads and fondly say, "Well, that's Austin."

1 Frommer's Favorite Austin Experiences

- **Accelerating Along the Hike & Bike Trail.** Head over to the shores of Town Lake to see why *Walking* magazine chose Austin as America's "Most Fit" city; speed walkers, joggers, and in-line skaters share the turf with bicyclists and hikers on one of the many trails set up by the city for its urban athletes.
- **Swimming at Barton Springs Pool.** The bracing waters of this natural pool have been drawing Austinites to its banks for more than 100 years; if there's anything that everyone in town can agree on, it's that there's no better plunge on a hot day.
- **Bat Watching.** From late March through November, thousands of bats emerge in smoky clouds from under the Congress Avenue Bridge, heading west for dinner; it's a thrilling sight, and you can thank each of the little mammals for keeping the air pest-free—a single bat can eat as many as 600 mosquitoes per hour.
- **Listening to the Blues at Antone's.** Antone's is proof that much of Austin's best music lies beyond its famed Sixth Street. Major blues stars who come through town always end up doing a few sets here.
- **Playing in the Water at Lake Travis.** The longest of the chain of seven Highland Lakes, Travis offers the most opportunities for cavorting in the wet stuff. Whether your thing is jet skiing, snorkeling, or angling, you'll have plenty of choices here.
- **Touring the Newly Refurbished Capitol.** The country's largest state capitol was pretty impressive even in its run-down state, but

after a massive face-lift visitors can really see that it's a legislative center fit for Texas.

- **Seeing What's Blooming at the National Wildflower Research Center.** Spring is prime viewing time for the flowers, but Austin's mild winters assure that there'll always be bursts of color at Lady Bird Johnson's pet project.
- **Laughing over the Political Cartoons at the LBJ Library.** At the largest and most visited of this country's presidential libraries, an entire room is devoted to LBJ's collection of satirical drawings, many of them directed against himself.
- **Paying Your Respects to Barbara Jordan at the State Cemetery.** One of the most beloved of Texas politicians, Jordan is the first African-American to be laid to rest in this historic boneyard, where many of Texas's other best and brightest are permanently retired.
- **Ascending Mt. Bonnell.** Sure the 100-odd steps are steep, but climbing them is far more rewarding than getting on a StairMaster: When you reach the top, the view of the city will take away whatever breath you have left.
- **Taking One of the Visitors Center's Walking Tours.** We wouldn't ordinarily suggest herding activities, but the historic excursions provided free by the city are superb.
- **Having Coffee at Mozart's.** Caffeine and conversation on a deck overlooking Lake Austin—it's hard to get much more stimulating.
- **Following the Dinosaur Tracks in Zilker Botanical Garden.** When you've agreed to take them to see the 100-million-year-old dinosaur tracks, most kids won't mind if you linger a little over the lovely flowers nearby.
- **Visiting O. Henry's Former Office.** The short-story writer used to work as a draftsman at the General Land Office, Texas's oldest surviving office building. Displays and a life-size cutout photo at what is now the visitors center for the Capitol Complex show how O. Henry spent his days.
- **Drink in Some History at Scholtz's.** The oldest biergarten in Texas has been spiffed up with a new sound system. Just don't come here after the Longhorns have won (or lost) a game; the place will be filled with singing (or sulking) U.T. fans.
- **Saying Hi to Stevie Ray Vaughan at Town Lake.** The late country rock star looks uncharacteristically stiff in his bronze incarnation, but he has a great view of Austin across the lake, and it's fun to see what kind of stuff his fans have left him.

2 Austin Today

Born on the frontier out of the grandiose dreams of a man whose middle name was Buonaparte, Austin spent its formative years fighting to maintain its status as capital. Texan hubris and feistiness remain key to Austin's character today—from state legislators who descend, squabbling, on the town every other year, to the locals fighting to save the golden-cheeked warbler from the developer's bulldozer.

Arguably the state's intellectual center—and undeniably its techie mecca—Austin indulges the good life with pure Texas excess. It has the largest travel store in the state, gigantic health food emporiums, and supermarket-size bookstores—not to mention the most movie screens and restaurants per capita in the U.S.

Much of Austin's success is attributable to the country's huge digital boom (in 1996, the *Austin Chronicle*'s "Best of" reader poll added a high-tech section). Austin's many high-paying computer-related jobs have drawn out-of-staters, quite a few of them Californians with lots of disposable cash. And although the majority of Austin's new residents are moving to the suburbs, the current economic expansion, which shows little sign of abating, has also aided a resurgence in downtown's growth. The restoration of the capitol and the construction of the new Austin Museum of Art are part of this process, as is the opening of a number of new theater venues.

But there are many signs that Austin is becoming a victim of its growth. Locals complain that the people moving in from California drive like they're still in LA; overcrowding and the death of a bicyclist caused the city to enact a helmet law in 1996, which has gotten two-wheelers up in arms. The low-key, libertarian atmosphere of the city is no longer a given; there's a new gated residential complex right down the street from the famed Continental Club. In 1995, with thefts in microchips and circuit boards rising, the Austin Police Department introduced a high-tech crime unit, one of only two such units in the country (the other is in Silicon Valley's San Jose, California).

And, as is usually the case, gentrification is resulting in the displacement of the poor and older people on fixed incomes. This is likely to happen increasingly in the predominantly black and Hispanic East Austin. And while newer arts venues move into downtown, older ones like the Capitol Theater, which long occupied a historic venue in the warehouse district, are being pushed out by high rents. Many of the restaurants in that newly burgeoning arts area are owned by groups of California investors rather than locals, and some funky midtown original restaurants like Kerbey Lane are spinning off characterless counterparts in the city's northwest industrial section.

3 A Look at the Past

A vast territory that threw off foreign rule to become an independent nation—remember the Alamo?— Texas has always played a starring role in the romance of the American West. So it is only fitting that Texas's capital should spring, full-blown, from the imagination of a man on a buffalo hunt.

A CAPITAL DILEMMA

The man was Mirabeau Buonaparte Lamar, who had earned a reputation for bravery in Texas's struggle for independence from Mexico. In 1838, when our story begins, Lamar was vice president of the 2-year-old Republic of Texas; Sam Houston, the even more renowned hero of the Battle of San Jacinto, was president. Though they had a strong will in common, the two men had very different ideas about the future of the nation whose reins they held: Houston tended to look eastward, toward union with the United States, while Lamar saw independence as the first step to establishing an empire that would stretch to the Pacific.

That year, an adventurer named Jacob Harrell set up a camp called Waterloo at the western edge of the frontier; lying on the northern banks of Texas's Colorado River (not to be confused with the larger waterway up north), it was nestled against a series of gentle hills. Some 100 years earlier, the Franciscans had established a temporary mission here; in the

Dateline

- **1730** Franciscans build a mission at Barton Springs, but abandon it within a year.
- **1836** Texas wins independence from Mexico; Republic of Texas established.
- **1838** Jacob Harrell sets up camp on the Colorado River, calling the settlement Waterloo; Mirabeau B. Lamar succeeds Sam Houston as president of Texas.
- **1839** Congressional commission recommends Waterloo as site for new capital of the republic. Waterloo's name changes to Austin.
- **1842** Sam Houston succeeds Lamar as president, reestablishes Houston as Texas's capital, and orders nation's archives moved there. Austinites resist.
- **1844** Anson Jones succeeds Houston as president, returns capital to Austin.

continues

- **1845** Constitutional convention in Austin approves annexation of Texas by the United States.
- **1850s** Austin undergoes a building boom; construction includes limestone capitol (1853), Governor's Mansion (1856), and General Land Office (1857).
- **1861** At Austin convention, Texas votes to secede from the Union (Travis County, which includes Austin, votes against secession).
- **1865** General Custer is among those who come to restore order in Austin during Reconstruction.
- **1871** First rail line to Austin completed.
- **1883** University of Texas opens.
- **1923** Santa Rita No. 1, an oil well on University of Texas land, strikes a gusher.
- **1937** Lyndon Johnson elected U.S. representative from Tenth Congressional District, which includes Austin.
- **Late 1930s to early 1950s** Six dams built on the Colorado River by the Lower Colorado River Authority, resulting in formation of the Highland Lakes chain.
- **1960s** High-tech firms, including IBM, move to Austin.
- **1972** Willie Nelson moves to Austin from Nashville, helps spur live-music scene on Sixth Street.
- **1980s** Booming real-estate market goes bust.
- **1995** Capitol, including new annex, reopens after massive refurbishing.

1820s, Stephen F. Austin, Texas's earliest and greatest land developer, had the area surveyed for the smaller of the two colonies he was to establish on Mexican territory.

But the place had otherwise seen few Anglos before Harrell arrived; for thousands of years it had been visited mainly by nomadic Indian tribes, including the Comanches, Lipan Apaches, and Tonkawas. Thus it was to a rather pristine spot that, in the autumn of 1838, Harrell invited his friend Mirabeau Lamar to take part in a shooting expedition. The buffalo hunt proved extremely successful, and when Lamar gazed at the rolling, wooded land surrounding Waterloo, he saw that it was good.

In December of the same year, Lamar became president. He ordered the congressional commission that had been charged with the task of selecting a site for a permanent capital, to be named after Stephen F. Austin, to check out Waterloo. Much to the horror of those who lived in Houston, home to the temporary capital, and in east Texas, which considered Waterloo a dangerous wilderness outpost, the commission recommended Lamar's pet site.

In early 1839, Lamar's friend Edwin Waller was dispatched to plan a city—the only one in the United States besides Washington, D.C., designed to be an independent nation's capital. The first public lots went on sale on August 1, 1839; by November of that year, Austin was ready to host its first session of Congress.

Austin's position as capital was far from entrenched, however. Attacks on the republic by Mexico in 1842 gave Sam Houston, now president again, sufficient excuse to order the national archives relocated from remote Austin for security reasons. Resistant Austinites greeted with a cannon the 26 armed men who came to repossess the historic papers. After a struggle, the men returned empty-handed and Houston abandoned his plan, thus ceding Austin the victory in what came to be called the Archive War.

Although Austin won this skirmish, it was losing a larger battle for existence. Houston refused to convene Congress in Austin; by 1843, Austin's population had dropped down to 200 and its buildings lay in disrepair. Help came in the person of Anson Jones, who succeeded to the presidency in 1844. The constitutional convention that he called in 1845 not only approved Texas's annexation to the United States, but also named Austin capital until 1850, when voters of what was now the state of Texas would choose their governmental seat for the next 20 years. In 1850, Austin campaigned hard for the position, and won by a landslide.

*Like the ancient city of Rome, Austin is built upon seven hills, and it is impossible to
conceive of a more beautiful and lovely situation.*
—George W. Bonnell, Commissioner of Indian Affairs
of the Republic of Texas (1840)

A CAPITAL SOLUTION

Under the protection of the U.S. Army, Austin thrived. The first permanent buildings to go up during the 1850s construction boom following statehood included an
impressive limestone capitol; two of the buildings in its complex, the General Land
Office and the Governor's Mansion, are still in use today.

The boom was short-lived, however: Although Austin's Travis County voted
against secession, Texas decided to put in its lot with the Confederacy in 1861. By
1865, Union army units—including one led by General George Armstrong Custer—
were sent to restore order to a defeated and looted Austin after the Civil War.

But Austin once again rebounded: With the arrival of the railroad in 1871, the
city's recovery was sealed. By the following year, when Austin won the final general
election to choose the state's capital, it was delivered.

Still, there were more battles for status to be fought. Back in 1839, the Republic
of Texas had declared that a "university of the first class" was to be built; in 1876, a
new state constitution mandated its establishment. Through yet another bout of
heavy electioneering, Austin won the right to have the flagship of Texas's higher educational system on its soil. In 1883, their classrooms not yet completed, the first 221
members of what is now a student body of 50,000 met the eight instructors of the
University of Texas for the first time.

In that year, the university wasn't the only Austin institution without permanent
quarters: The old limestone capitol had burned in 1881, and a new, much larger
home for the legislature was being built. In 1888, after a series of mishaps—the need
to construct a railroad branch to transport the donated building materials, among
them—the current capitol was completed. The grand red-granite edifice looking
down upon the city proclaimed that Austin had arrived at last.

DAMS, OIL & MICROCHIPS

This symbol of prosperity notwithstanding, the city was once again in a slump. Although some believed that quality of life would be sacrificed to growth—a view still
strongly argued today—most townspeople embraced the idea of harnessing the fast-
flowing waters of the Colorado River as the solution to Austin's economic woes. A
dam, they thought, would not only provide a cheap source of electricity for residents,
but also supply power for irrigation and new factories. Dedicated in 1893, the Austin Dam did indeed fulfill these goals—but only temporarily. The energy source
proved to be limited, and when torrential rains pelted the city in April 1900, Austin's
dreams came crashing down with its dam.

Another dam, attempted in 1915, was never finished. It wasn't until the late 1930s
that a permanent solution to the water-power problem was found. The successful plea
of young Lyndon Johnson, the newly elected representative from Austin's Tenth
Congressional District, to President Roosevelt for federal funds was crucial to the
construction of six dams along the lower Colorado River. In conjunction with each
other, these dams not only afforded Austin and central Texas all the hydroelectric
power and drinking water they needed, but also created the seven Highland Lakes—
aesthetically appealing and a great source of recreational revenues.

Still, Austin might have remained a backwater capital seat abutting a beautiful lake had it not been for the discovery of oil on University of Texas (U.T.) land in 1923. The huge amounts of money that subsequently flowed into the Permanent University Fund—worth some $4 billion today—enabled Austin's campus to become truly first-class. While most of the country was cutting back during the Depression, U.T. went on a building binge and began hiring faculty as impressive as the new halls of academe in which they were to hold forth.

The indirect effects of the oil bonus reached far beyond College Hill. Tracor, the first of Austin's more than 250 high-tech companies, was founded by U.T. scientists and engineers in 1955. Lured by the city's natural attractions and its access to a growing bank of young brainpower, many outside companies soon arrived: IBM (1967), Texas Instruments (1968), and Motorola's Semiconductor Products Section (1974). In the 1980s, two huge computer consortiums, MCC and SEMATECH, opted to make Austin their home.

Willie Nelson's move to Austin from Nashville in 1972 didn't have quite as profound an effect on the economy, but it had one on the city's live-music scene. Hippies and country-and-western fans now found common ground at the many clubs that began to sprout up along downtown's Sixth Street, which had largely been abandoned. Combined with the construction that followed in the wake of the city's high-tech success, these music venues helped spur downtown's resurgence. True, the oil and savings-and-loan crashes of the mid-1980s left many of the new office towers partially empty, but—wouldn't you know it?—within a decade, the comeback kid of cities had already made a complete recovery. In late 1996, Austin had the lowest commercial vacancy rates in the state, with occupancy at 90.5%.

4 The Great Outdoors

If you look up as you pass along Austin's Balcones Drive, you can glimpse a portion of the Balcones Escarpment, a fault zone that marks the boundary between the rich Blacklands Prairie to the east and the hilly Edwards Plateau to the west. The limestone comprising the plateau, uplifted millions of years ago from the bottom of the shallow sea that covered most of Texas, renders the underground water that rises at such pools as Austin's Barton Springs remarkably clear. It also acts as a filter for the waters of the Highland Lakes, a sparkling, 150-mile-long chain, created by a series of dams, which spreads northwest from the city in an ever-widening pattern.

Austin has taken full advantage of its natural endowments, fighting to keep them intact and establishing myriad bicycle trails and hiking paths. Bird watchers find bliss here, and sailboard concessionaires do a brisk business. To witness Austin's cult of the outdoors, go down to the hike-and-bike trail at Town Lake, where, in the morning and late afternoon, worshippers at the shrine of fitness jostle each other for a place. You can't blame a visitor for wondering if, in this city that has so many ordinances, there's a law on the books that requires people to get out of their house and exercise.

5 The Austin Sound

When they're not exercising—and often even when they are—Austinites are listening to music. The city has gigantic record stores, a shop devoted solely to music art, and more than 50 live music venues. One of the most appealing aspects of the local scene is the wide range of good sounds to be found at unexpected, totally original places—barbecue joints, Mexican restaurants, converted gas stations. The atmosphere almost everywhere is assiduously laid-back—legends like Bob Dylan and Joan Baez still perform at intimate spots like the Backyard—and most covers are nice and low.

Some music aficionados may have heard about Austin in the mid-1960s as the locus for hootenannies at Threadgill's, where a young Janis Joplin used to put in frequent appearances, but the city only began to get a reputation for alternative country when Willie Nelson returned to town in the early 1970s. He, Waylon Jennings, and Jerry Jeff Walker were followed by a new generation of progressive country rockers, including Jimmie Dale Gilmore, Butch Hancock, Joe Ely, and Nanci Griffith. Not that country is all that Austin has to offer—this ain't just Texas, this is Austin, the self-proclaimed Live Music Capital of the World. Blues greats like Stevie Ray Vaughan and alternative bands like the Butthole Surfers have stitched their patch into the quilt of Austin music; the early punk rockers the Big Boys arose from the Austin scene.

On any given night, pretty much any type of music you could ever want to hear—from reggae to jazz, from funk to folk, from metal to hip-hop—is bound to be on stage somewhere in town. And the strength of this live scene, combined with Austin's livability, is beginning to attract musicians away from the established music cities of Los Angeles, New York, and Nashville—Sugar frontman Bob Mould now calls Austin home, as do roots rock favorites the Silos. But what's the next big sound to spring from this musical oasis? The many music promoters who attend the city's annual SXSW (South by Southwest) conference, the music industry's most influential confab (see box in chapter 16 for details), are banking on believing they can tell.

6 Recommended Books, Films & Recordings

BOOKS

The foibles of the Texas "lege"—along with those of Congress and the rest of Washington—are hilariously pilloried by Molly Ivins, Austin's resident scourge, in two collections of her syndicated newspaper columns: *Molly Ivins Can't Say That, Can She?* and *Nothing But Good Times Ahead*. For background into the city's unique music scene, try Jan Reid's *The Improbable Rise of Red Neck Rock*. It's been followed more recently by Barry Shank's scholarly tome, *Dissonant Identities: The Rock 'n' Roll Scene in Austin, Texas*. Serious history buffs might want to dip into Robert Caro's excellent multivolume biography of Lyndon Baines Johnson, the consummate Texas politician who had a profound effect on the Austin area.

William Syndey Porter, better known as O. Henry, published a satirical newspaper in Austin in the late 19th century. Among the many short tales he wrote about the area—collected in *O. Henry's Texas Stories*—are four inspired by his stint as a draftsman in the General Land Office. Set largely in Austin, Billy Lee Brammer's *The Gay Place*—the title adjective meant only "lively" when the book was published (1961)—is a fictional portrait of a political figure loosely based on LBJ. The more recent *Strange Sunlight* by Peter LaSalle details the corruption during the real estate boom years in Austin. The city is also the locus for *Zero at the Bone*, an acclaimed mystery by Austin resident Mary Willis Walker, and *The Boyfriend School*, a humorous novel by Sarah Bird. The city's most famous scribe, James Michener, placed his historical epic, *Texas*, in the frame of a governor's task force operating out of Austin.

It's only logical that the king of cyberpunk writers, Bruce Sterling, should live in Austin; he gets megabytes of fan mail each week for such books as *Islands in the Net,*

The Difference Engine (with William Gibson), and *Holy Fire*. His nonfiction work, *The Hacker Crackdown*, details a failed antihacker raid in Austin.

FILMS

If you don't recognize Austin in many of the Hollywood films that were shot here—more than 75 in the last two decades—it's because the area offers such a wide range of landscapes, filling in for locations as far afield as Vietnam. But Texas does feature prominently in a number of the following famous Austin area productions: *Texas Chainsaw Massacre* (1972); *Honeysuckle Rose* (1980, Willie Nelson and Dyann Cannon); *The Best Little Whorehouse in Texas* (1982, Burt Reynolds and Dolly Parton); the Coen brothers' *Blood Simple* (1984); *Songwriter* (1984, Willie Nelson and Kris Kristofferson); *Nadine* (1987, Jeff Bridges and Kim Basinger); *D.O.A.* (1988, Meg Ryan and Dennis Quaid); *The Ballad of the Sad Cafe* (1991, Vanessa Redgrave and Keith Carradine); *What's Eating Gilbert Grape* (1993, Johnny Depp and Juliette Lewis); *A Perfect World* (1993, Kevin Costner and Clint Eastwood); and *Courage Under Fire* (1996, Meg Ryan and Denzel Washington). Shot in 1996 but not yet released are *The War at Home* with Emilio Estevez; *Little Boy Blue*, featuring Nastasia Kinski, and director Steven Soderbergh's new film, *The Underneath*.

Independent films have also put Austin on the cinematic map. University of Texas graduate Richard Linklater captured some of the loopier members of his alma mater in *Slacker*, at the same time adding a word to the national vocabulary. His similarly acclaimed follow-up, *Dazed and Confused*, turned to high school for its satire of school days. His latest, *SubUrbia*, shot largely in a south Austin convenience store, has more of a structured plot than the earlier two, and his next film, to everyone's surprise, will be a historic drama. As a further sign of Austin's cinematic coming of age, the SXSW Music Conference recently added a film component. Past panelists have included Linklater and John Sayles, whose film *Lone Star* had its world premiere here.

Austin has also been showcased on the tube. *Lonesome Dove*, featuring Robert Duvall, Tommy Lee Jones, and Anjelica Houston, is the most famous of many miniseries shot in the area, but the more recent *True Women*, which traces three generations who lived in the Austin area, is the more historically accurate. And the Public Broadcasting Service has kept the city consistently on the small screen since 1975, when the network first began taping concerts by renowned country-and-western performers for *Austin City Limits*.

RECORDINGS

Janis Joplin, who attended U.T. for a time, played local gigs around town for years; many other famous musicians such as the late Stevie Ray Vaughan (enshrined in a statue overlooking Town Lake) also got their start in Austin clubs. Since 1980, the list of artists who signed on to major record labels while living in Austin includes Asleep at the Wheel, the Butthole Surfers, Timbuk 3, Lucinda Williams, Lee Roy Parnell, Joe Ely, Jerry Jeff Walker, Hal Ketchum, and Jimmie Dale Gilmore. Local hero Willie Nelson has his own recording studio on the outskirts of town, and it's not surprising that the offbeat Lyle Lovett is an Austin resident.

10 Planning a Trip to Austin

Planning a trip is not only half the fun of getting there, but helps to ensure your enjoyment when you arrive. If you're inclined to using your own sports gear, for example, you'll want to check out Austin's many outdoor options (see chapter 14) so you'll know just what to bring.

Because Austin doesn't have an overabundance of hotel rooms, it's always important to book ahead of time. Summer season is typically busy, but legislative sessions (the first half of odd-numbered years) and University of Texas events (graduation, say, or home-team games) can also help fill up the town's lodgings.

1 Visitor Information

Call the **Austin Convention and Visitors Bureau,** 201 E. Second St., 78701 (☎ **800/926-2282**), to receive a general information packet in the mail; the same toll-free number will connect you to a menu with recorded data on everything from the city's current events to its outdoor recreation and tour possibilities, or to a representative who can answer any of your specific questions. If you're connected to the Internet, you can also get information by logging in to www.visit.ci.austin.tx.us. The *Austin Chronicle,* the city's alternative newspaper, is also on-line: www.auschron.com.

See this same section in chapter 2 for suggestions on getting information about other parts of Texas.

2 When to Go

CLIMATE

May showers follow April flowers in the Austin/Texas Hill Country area; by the time the late spring rains set in, the bluebonnets and most of the other wildflowers have already peaked. Mother Nature thoughtfully arranges mild, generally dry weather in which to enjoy her glorious floral arrangements in early spring—an ideal and deservedly popular time to visit. Summers can be steamy, but Austin offers plenty of great places to cool off, among them the Highland Lakes and Barton Springs. Fall foliage in this leafy area is another treat, and it's hard to beat a Texas evening by a cozy fireplace—admittedly more for show than for warmth in Austin, which generally enjoys mild winters.

What Things Cost in Austin	U.S. $
Taxi from the airport to the city center	8.00–10.00
Bus ride between any two downtown points	Free
Local telephone call	.25
Double at the Four Seasons (very expensive)	170.00–240.00
Double at the Radisson Hotel on Town Lake (moderate)	115.00
Double at Days Inn North (inexpensive)	60.00
Lunch for one at the Shoreline Grill (expensive)	12.00
Lunch for one at Las Manitas (inexpensive)	6.00
Dinner for one, without wine, at Jeffrey's (expensive)	32.00
Dinner for one, without wine, at Manuel's (moderate)	17.00
Dinner for one, without beer, at Stubbs (inexpensive)	8.00
Pint of beer at brew pub	2.50
Coca-Cola	1.00
Cup of espresso	1.50
Admission to Austin Museum of Art, Laguna Gloria	2.00
Roll of ASA 100 Kodacolor film, 36 exposures	5.50
Movie ticket	1.50–6.50
Austin Symphony ticket	11.00–25.00

Austin's Average Monthly Temperature & Rainfall

	Jan	Feb	Mar	Apr	May	June	July	Aug	Sept	Oct	Nov	Dec
Avg. Temp. (°F)	52.0	54.5	60.8	68.2	75.3	81.9	84.0	83.8	79.3	70.5	59.7	53.2
Rainfall (in.)	1.66	2.06	1.54	2.54	3.07	2.79	1.69	2.41	3.71	2.84	1.77	1.46

AUSTIN CALENDAR OF EVENTS

A party for a fictional donkey and a tribute to canned meat? Austin wouldn't be Austin if some of its festivals weren't offbeat. Other events are more traditional; many capitalize on the great outdoors and the large community of local musicians. The major annual events are listed below; see also chapter 16 for information on the various free concerts and other cultural events held every summer.

January
- **Red Eye Regatta,** Austin Yacht Club, Lake Travis. The bracing lake air at this New Year's Day keelboat race should help cure what ails you from the night before. ☎ 512/266-1336.

February
- **Carnival Brasileiro,** City Coliseum. Conga lines, elaborate costumes, samba bands, and confetti are all part of this sizzling event, started by homesick Brazilian University of Texas students in 1975. ☎ 512/452-6832.

March
- **Austin/Travis County Livestock Show and Rodeo,** Travis County Exposition and Heritage Center. This 10-day Wild West extravaganza features rodeos, cattle auctions, a youth fair, and lots of live country music. ☎ 512/467-9811.

- **Kite Festival,** Zilker Park. Colorful handmade kites fill the sky during this popular annual contest, held the second Sunday in March. ☎ 512/478-0905.
- **Jerry Jeff Walker's Birthday Weekend,** various locations. Each year the legendary singer/songwriter performs at such places as the Broken Spoke and the Paramount Theatre, and takes part in a golf tournament with other musicians. The man knows how to throw a party. ☎ 512/477-0036.
- ✪ **South by Southwest (SXSW) Music & Media Conference.** The Austin Music Awards kick off this huge conference, which organizes hundreds of concerts at more than two dozen city venues. Aspiring music industry professionals sign up months in advance; keynote speakers have included Johnny Cash.

  Where: Austin Convention Center, all around town. **When:** 5 days in mid-March. **How:** ☎ 512/467-7979 for conference and concert schedules.

April
- **Capitol 10,000.** Texas's largest 10K race winds its way from the state capitol through West Austin, ending up at Town Lake. ☎ 512/445-3598.
- **Spamarama,** Auditorium Shores. The awards for creative cooking with Spam are the highlight of this hilarious event, judged by Texas celebrities; there's also a live music Spam Jam. ☎ 512/416-9307.
- **Texas Hill Country Wine and Food Festival** (most events at the Four Seasons Hotel). Book a month in advance for the cooking demonstrations, beer, wine, and food tastings, and celebrity chef dinners; for the food fair, just turn up with an appetite. ☎ 512/329-0770.
- **Eeyore's Birthday Party,** Pease Park. Costume contests, face painting, and live music celebrate A. A. Milne's donkey at this huge rites-of-spring fest. ☎ 512/912-5080.
- **Wildflower Days,** National Wildflower Research Center. Everything's coming up bluebonnets at this spring celebration, where Texas's native plants are the stars. Maybe you'll see Lady Bird Johnson, the center's founder. ☎ 512/292-4200.

May
- **Flora Rama,** Zilker Botanical Gardens. There's plenty of flower power at this huge gathering—sales booths, gardening demonstrations, and a variety of entertainment. ☎ 512/477-8672.
- **O. Henry Pun-Off,** O. Henry Museum. One of the punniest events around, this annual battle of the wits is for a wordy cause—the upkeep of the O. Henry Museum. ☎ 512/472-1903.
- **Old Pecan Street Spring Arts and Crafts Festival,** Sixth Street. Eat and shop your way along Austin's restored Victorian main street while bands play in the background. ☎ 512/448-1704.
- **Cinco de Mayo,** Fiesta Gardens. Mariachis, flamenco dancers, Tejano music, tacos, and tamales are all part of the traditional May 5 Mexican freedom celebration. ☎ 512/499-6720.
- **Fiesta Laguna Gloria,** Austin Museum of Art at Laguna Gloria Art Museum. Set on the shores of Lake Austin, the museum's major fundraiser features a juried art show, an auction, and lots of kids' activities. ☎ 512/458-6073.

June
- ✪ **Juneteenth Freedom Festival.** This huge celebration of African-American emancipation features parades, a jazz and blues festival, gospel singing, a rap competition, and a children's rodeo and carnival.

  Where: Travis County Exposition Center and east Austin. **When:** 5 days surrounding June 15. **How:** ☎ 512/472-6838 for details on tickets and events.

In case you want to be welcomed there.

We're here to see that you're always welcomed at establishments everywhere. That's why millions of people carry the American Express® Card – for peace of mind, confidence, and security, around the world or just around the corner.

do more

Cards

In case you're running low.

We're here to help with more than 118,000 Express Cash locations around the world. In order to enroll, just call American Express before you start your vacation.

do more

Express Cash

And just in case.

We're here with American Express® Travelers Cheques
and Cheques *for Two*.® They're the safest way to carry
money on your vacation and the surest way to get a
refund, practically anywhere, anytime.

Another way we help you…

do more ®

**Travelers
Cheques**

- **Hyde Park Historic Homes Tour.** The Victorian and early 20th-century homes of Austin's first residential suburb are open to the public every Father's Day weekend. ☎ 512/452-4139.

July

- **Freedom Festival and Fireworks,** Zilker Park. Top rock and country entertainers draw huge crowds for this outdoor event, which ends with the traditional pyrotechnics. ☎ 512/472-8180.
- **Austin Aqua Festival,** at Town Lake and throughout the city. Nine days of sporting events, feasting, and especially music are played out on the land as well as on the lake. ☎ 512/472-5664.
- **Fall Creek Vineyards Celebration & Grape Stomp,** Lake Buchanan. Grape squishing, footprint T-shirts, and wine tastings are all part of the fun on the last two Saturdays in August. ☎ 512/476-4477.
- **Hot Sauce Festival,** Travis County Farmer's Market. Fresh chile pepper month, which runs from August through September, peaks with the largest event of its kind in the world, featuring more than 400 entries judged by celebrity chefs and food editors. ☎ 512/454-1002.

September

○ **Fiestas Patrias.** Mariachis and folk dancers, Tex-Mex conjunto and Tejano music, as well as fajitas, piñatas, and clowns help celebrate Mexico's independence from Spain. The highlight: the crowning of the Fiestas Patrias Queen.
   Where: Fiesta Gardens. **When:** 4 days, around September 16. **How:** ☎ 512/476-3868 for information.

- **Fall Jazz Festival,** Zilker Hillside Theater. Zilker Park swings on the second weekend of September, when top local jazz acts turn out for 2 days of free concerts. ☎ 512/397-1468.
- **Pioneer Farm Fall Festival,** Jourdan-Bachman Pioneer Farm. Historic presentations, including spinning, fiddle-making, and quilting, are among the family-style attractions at the 1852 farm. ☎ 512/837-1215.

October

- **Pumpkin Festival,** Travis County Farmer's Market. Children's Halloween festivities near the end of the month include a costume parade, apple bobbing, and pumpkin painting. ☎ 512/454-1002.
- **Halloween,** Sixth Street. Seven blocks of historic Sixth Street are barricaded off for Texas's kookiest spook parade. ☎ 512/476-8876.

November

- **Dia de los Muertos** (Day of the Dead), Congress Avenue. Death is embraced as part of the life cycle in this Halloween-like Hispanic festival, involving Latino music, a parade, and, of course, food. ☎ 512/480-9373.
- **Victorian Christmas on Sixth Street.** Downtown's former main drag takes on a turn-of-the-century aura at the end of the month, with five blocks of crafts booths kicking off the holiday shopping season. ☎ 512/478-1704.

December

- **Zilker Park Tree Lighting.** The lighting of a magnificent 165-foot tree on the first Sunday in December is followed the week after by the Trail of Lights, a mile-long display of life-size holiday scenes. ☎ 512/499-6700.
- **Christmas Open House,** French Legation. Père Nöel (the French Santa Claus) and costumed guides help host this lively gift bazaar, held in an 1840 historic house. ☎ 512/472-8180.

- **Armadillo Christmas Bazaar,** Austin Opera House at the Terrace. Revel in Tex-Mex food, live music, and a full bar at this high-quality art, craft, and gift show, starting around 2 weeks before Christmas. ☎ **512/447-1605.**

3 Tips for Travelers with Special Needs

FOR TRAVELERS WITH DISABILITIES

See this section in chapter 2 for details on **Travelin' Talk,** an organization that can put you in touch with resources for travelers with disabilities in Austin.

FOR GAY & LESBIAN TRAVELERS

Book Woman, 918 W. 12th St., at Lamar (☎ **512/472-2785**) and **Lobo,** 3204-A Guadalupe St. (☎ **512/454-5406**), are the best places to find gay and lesbian books and magazines; the stores also carry the local gay newspapers, the weekly *Texas Triangle* and the bimonthly *Fag Rag,* as well as *This Week in Texas,* a resource for the whole state. The *Austin Gay-Friendly Resource Directory,* published by Austin Media Visions, has gone on-line and can be accessed at www.gayfriendly.com; it's also available in a free hardcopy edition, published every November, at Book Woman and Lobo. A number of gay bars and dance clubs are listed in chapter 16. Hippie Hollow, near Lake Travis, is a popular daytime gathering spot for gays.

FOR SENIORS

The Old Bakery and Emporium, 1006 Congress Ave. (☎ **512/477-5961**), not only sells crafts and baked goods made by senior citizens, but also serves as a volunteer center for people over 50. It's a good place to find out about any senior activities in town. Another excellent resource is the monthly *Senior Advocate* newspaper, P.O. Box 4806, 78765 (☎ **512/451-7433**), available for free at Food Land and Albertson's supermarkets, bingo halls, libraries, and many other places. You can also call or write in advance for a subscription.

For information about the **American Association of Retired Persons (AARP)** and about **Elderhostel,** see chapter 2. Among the Elderhostel classes offered in Austin in 1996 were "Birding in the Central Flyway at Lake Texoma" and "Texas Wines: Hear It Through the Grapevine."

FOR FAMILIES

See this section of chapter 2 for information about the *Family Travel Times* newsletter, "Travel with Your Children."

FOR STUDENTS

There are endless resources for students in this university town. Persons of the college persuasion need only go over to the **University of Texas Student Union Building** (see map in chapter 14) to find out what they need to know—or where they can go to find out. Austin's oldest institution of higher learning, **Huston Tillotson College,** 600 Chicon St. (☎ **512/505-3000**), in east Austin, is especially helpful for getting African-American students oriented. The AYH Hostel (see "A Youth Hostel," in chapter 12) is another great repository of information for students.

To find out about the discounts on airfares, rail fares, and lodgings offered by the **Council on International Educational Exchange (CIEE),** 205 E. 42nd St., New York, NY 10017 (☎ **212/822-2600**), send for the organization's *Student Travels* magazine. A Council travel office in Austin, 2000 Guadalupe St., 78705 (☎ **512/**

472-4932), can arrange tour bookings. See this section of chapter 2 for details on **Hostelling International–American Youth Hostels (HI-AYH).**

4 Getting There

BY PLANE

THE MAJOR AIRLINES   America West (☎ 800/235-9292), **American** (☎ 800/433-7300), **Continental** (☎ 800/525-0280), **Delta** (☎ 800/221-1212), **Northwest** (☎ 800/225-2525), **Southwest** (☎ 800/435-9792), **TWA** (☎ 800/221-2000), **United** (☎ 800/241-6522), and **USAir** (☎ 800/428-4322) all fly into Austin. **Conquest** (☎ 800/722-0860) is Austin's short-hop commuter airline. There is no direct international service to the city.

FINDING THE BEST AIRFARE   All the airlines run seasonal specials that can lower fares considerably. If your dates of travel don't coincide with these promotions, however, the least expensive way to travel is to purchase tickets 21 days in advance, stay over Saturday night, and travel during the week. Within these parameters, Continental had the best round-trip fare from **New York** to Austin (from $238, not including tax); on American, Delta, Northwest, TWA, United, and USAir, fares ranged from $396 to $436. Those flying from **Chicago** to Austin will get the lowest rates on Continental, Southwest, TWA, and United (around $140). From **Los Angeles,** the fare differences were not substantial; prices were lowest on Delta ($183) and highest on Northwest and TWA ($214 and $218), with America West, American, Continental, Southwest, and United all hovering around $200 round-trip.

AUSTIN'S AIRPORT   Small and easy to negotiate, **Robert Mueller Municipal Airport,** 3600 Manor Rd. (☎ 512/495-7550), is located about 2 miles north of downtown, near I-35. However, this single-terminal airport has been slated to be replaced by a larger one at the former Bergstrom Air Force Base on the south side; cargo services at Bergstrom are scheduled to start up in March 1997 and passenger operations should begin in May 1999.

A list of hotels that offer shuttle service from the airport is posted just outside the terminal. The service is complimentary in many cases, but some hotels tack on a charge to your bill after the fact. Inquire when you make reservations whether or not your hotel sends out a van—and whether or not it's free for guests.

Taxis from the major companies in town form a queue across the street from the terminal. The cab line sometimes thins at the busiest times (around 9am, 11:30am, 5pm, and 8:30pm); if you don't see a taxi or if you need special service, call one of the companies whose numbers are posted on the door leading to the ground transportation area. To ensure off-hour pickup in advance, phone Yellow-Checker American Cab (☎ **800/456-TAXI**) before you leave home. The ride between the airport and downtown generally costs between $8 and $10. The flag-drop charge is $1.50, and it's $1.50 for every mile after that.

It's approximately 20 minutes from the airport to downtown via bus no. 20 on Capital Metro Transit (☎ **512/474-1200,** TDD ☎ **512/385-5872**); detailed schedules are available inside the terminal. The fare is 50¢ for adults; see the "By Bus" section in "Getting Around" in chapter 11 for additional information.

Most of the major car-rental companies—Advantage, Alamo, Avis, Budget, Dollar, Hertz, National Interrent, and Thrifty—have outlets at the airport; see "Car Rentals" in the "Getting Around" section of chapter 11 for details. The trip from the airport to downtown by car or taxi isn't likely to take more than 15 minutes at any time of the day.

BY CAR

I-35 is the north–south approach to Austin; it intersects with Hwy. 290, a major east–west thoroughfare, and Hwy. 183, which also runs roughly north–south through town. If you're staying on the west side of Austin, hook up with Loop 1, almost always called Mo-Pac by locals.

Hwy. 290 leads east to Dallas/Forth Worth, about 4 hours away, and goes west via a scenic Hill Country route to I-10, the main east–west thoroughfare. I-10 can also be picked up by heading south to San Antonio, some 80 miles away on I-35.

In case you're planning a state capital tour, it's 896 miles from Austin to Atlanta; 1,911 miles to Boston; 921 miles to Springfield, Illinois; 671 miles to Santa Fe; 963 miles to Phoenix; and 1,745 miles to Sacramento, California.

BY TRAIN

To get to points east or west of Austin by **Amtrak,** 250 N. Lamar Blvd. (☎ **800/ 872-7245** or 512/476-5684), you'll have to go to San Antonio (see the "By Train" section of chapter 2); trains depart from Austin to San Antonio on Monday, Wednesday, and Saturday at night. The Texas Eagle departs from Austin to Chicago three times a week. The Amtrak station is in the southwest corner of downtown, at Lamar and West First Street near the Seton Medical Center. There are generally a few cabs around to meet the trains, but if you don't see one, a list of phone numbers of taxi companies is posted near the pay phones. Some of the downtown hotels offer courtesy pickup from the train station. A cab ride shouldn't run more than $4 or $5 (there's a $3 minimum charge).

BY BUS

You'll also be going through San Antonio if you're traveling from the east or west to Austin via **Greyhound,** 916 E. Koenig Lane (☎ **800/231-2222** or 512/ 458-3823); see chapter 2 for details. There are approximately 14 buses between the two cities each day, with one-way fares running around $15.

The bus terminal is near Highland Mall, about 10 minutes north of downtown and just south of the I-35 motel zone. Some places to sleep are within walking distance, and many others are a short cab ride away; a few taxis usually wait outside the station. If you want to go downtown, you can catch either bus no. 7 (Duval) or no. 15 (Red River) from the stop across the street. A cab ride downtown—about 10 minutes away on the freeway—should cost from $8 to $10.

Getting to Know Austin 11

Thousands of acres of parks, preserves, and lakes have been set aside for public enjoyment in Austin, making it an unusually people-friendly city. But if you spend a lot of time negotiating I-35 between the airport motels and the downtown business and historical district, it would be easy to get the wrong impression. Be sure to go just a few blocks past the office towers to the green shores of Town Lake, where you'll begin to see what Austin is all about.

Central Austin is, very roughly, bounded by Town Lake to the south, Hwy. 290 to the north, I-35 to the east, and Mo-Pac (Loop 1) to the west. South Austin, east of Mo-Pac, tends to be blue-collar residential, though the northern sections have been gentrified; the volume of high-tech companies moving into this area is likely to be turned up when the city's new international airport is completed. High-tech development is also proceeding apace in north Austin, which is seeing a good deal of residential growth, too. The flat former farmland of older east Austin is largely Hispanic and black, while the lakeshores and hills of west Austin host some of the most opulent mansions in town.

1 Orientation

VISITOR INFORMATION

The **Austin Convention and Visitors Bureau,** 201 E. Second St. (☎ **800/926-2282**), across the street from the Convention Center in the southeast section of downtown, is open Monday through Friday from 8:30am to 5pm, Saturday from 9am to 5pm, and Sunday from noon to 5pm (except Thanksgiving Day and Christmas). A branch of the ACVB is supposed to be open at the airport Monday through Friday from 9am to 8pm and Saturday from 1 to 5pm, but it is staffed solely by volunteers and is frequently left unattended. You can pick up tourist information pamphlets downtown at the **Old Bakery and Emporium,** 1006 Congress Ave. (☎ **512/477-5961**), which is open Monday through Friday from 9am to 4pm; it is also open the first three Saturdays in December from 10am to 3pm. **The Capitol Complex Visitors Center,** 112 E. 11th St. (☎ **512/305-8400**), dispenses information on the entire state of Texas. Those particularly interested in Austin's African-American community might contact the **Capital City Chamber of Commerce,** 5407 I-35 north, Suite 304 (☎ **512/459-1181**).

The free alternative newspaper, the *Chronicle,* distributed to stores, hotels, and restaurants around town every Thursday, used to be the best source of information about Austin events. It's now got a rival in *XLent,* the weekend entertainment guide put out by the *Austin-American Statesman,* which is also free and also turns up on Thursday at most of the same places that carry the *Chronicle.*

CITY LAYOUT

In 1839, Austin was laid out in a grid on the northern shore of the Colorado River, bounded by Shoal Creek to the west and Waller Creek to the east. The section of the river abutting the original settlement is now known as Town Lake, and the city has spread far beyond its original borders in all directions. The land to the east is flat Texas plain; the rolling Hill Country begins on the west side of town.

MAIN ARTERIES & STREETS   I-35, comprising the border between central and east Austin, is the main north–south thoroughfare; Loop 1, usually called Mo-Pac (it follows the course of the Missouri–Pacific railroad), is its west-side equivalent. Hwy. 290, which frequently changes its name on the north end of town (to 2222, Northland, and Koenig) runs east and west, as does 183, also called Research Boulevard. Ben White Boulevard, a major east–west road to the south of town, is another incarnation of Hwy. 290, connecting with Hwy. 71 east of I-35. Important north–south city streets include Lamar, Guadalupe, and Burnet; if you want to get across town north of the river, use First Street (officially Cesar Chavez); 12th Street (which turns into Enfield west of Lamar); Martin Luther King Jr. Blvd. (the equivalent of 19th Street); 38th Street; and 45th Street.

FINDING AN ADDRESS   Congress Avenue was the earliest dividing line between east and west, while the Colorado River marks the north and south border of the city. This system of determining addresses works reasonably well in the older sections of town, but breaks down where the neat street grid does (look at a street map to see where the right angles end). All the east–west streets were originally named after trees native to the city (for example, Sixth Street was once Pecan Street); many that run north and south, such as San Jacinto, Lavaca, and Guadalupe, retain their original Texas river monickers.

STREET MAPS   A number of the car-rental companies give out surprisingly detailed street maps of central Austin. If you're going farther afield, I'd recommend the Gousha city maps, available at most convenience stores, drugstores, newsstands, and bookstores.

NEIGHBORHOODS IN BRIEF

With a few exceptions, locals tend to speak in terms of landmarks (the University of Texas) or geographical sections (east Austin) rather than neighborhoods. In recent years, booming bedroom communities like Round Rock have grown up to the north of Austin; the west, in the direction of Hill Country, has seen such affluent residential developments as the separately incorporated Westlake Hills. Following are descriptions of some of the city's older and closer-knit areas.

Downtown   The original city, laid out by Edwin Waller in 1839, runs roughly north–south from the river (First Street) to the capitol (15th Street), and east–west between I-35 and Lamar. This prime sightseeing and hotel area has seen a resurgence in the last two decades, with more and more music clubs, restaurants, shops, and galleries moving onto and around Sixth Street. Businesses are also coming back to the beautiful old office buildings that line Sixth Street and Congress Avenue as well as to the newer towers that lay partially abandoned after the savings-and-loan and oil crashes of the 1980s.

Fairview Park & Travis Heights These adjoining neighborhoods between Congress and I-35 from Town Lake to Oltdorf Street were Austin's first settlements south of the river. At the end of the 19th century, the bluffs here became desirable as Austin residents realized they were not as likely to be flooded as the lower-ground residents north of the Colorado. Many mansions in what had become a working-class district have lately been reclaimed, and galleries and antique shops have begun springing up all over South Congress Street.

East Austin The section east of I-35 between First Street and Martin Luther King Jr. Boulevard is home to many of Austin's Latino and black residents. Mexican restaurants and markets dot the area, which also hosts a number of African-American heritage sites, including Huston Tillotson College, Metropolitan African Methodist Episcopal Church, and Madison Cabin. Hispanic festivals are often held at Parque Zaragosa.

French Place Austin's newest reclaimed neighborhood, this area just east of I-35 between Manor and $38^1/2$ Streets is being settled by middle-class people being pushed out of other areas by rising rents. It's a quiet, tree-lined section with some beautifully Xeriscaped homes, some shabby rental properties, and everything in between.

Old West Austin Of the neighborhoods that developed as downtown Austin expanded beyond Shoal Creek, Clarksville, just east of Mo-Pac, is among the most interesting: Founded by a former slave in 1871 as a utopian community for freed blacks, it's now an artists enclave that's fast becoming populated by wealthy California techies. Directly to the north, from about West 15th to West 24th Streets, Enfield boasts a number of beautiful homes and upscale restaurants. Larger mansions line the northern shores of Lake Austin, in the section known as Tarrytown; it's just south of Mt. Bonnell and a beautiful stretch of land where, some historians say, Stephen F. Austin himself planned to retire.

University of Texas The original 40 acres that were alloted to build an institution of higher education just north of the capitol have expanded to 357 since the 19th century, and Guadalupe Street, along the west side of the campus, is now the popular shopping strip known as the Drag. Many of the large old houses in the area had been converted to apartments, but the trend has turned toward restoring them to family residences. West Campus is still the hangout for students, poststudents, and young artists who will move to South Austin when they get older; there's a band in every garage.

Hyde Park North of the university between 38th and 45th Streets, Hyde Park got its start in 1891 as one of Austin's first planned suburbs; its Victorian and early Craftsman houses began to be renovated in the 1970s. There's a real neighborhood feel about this pretty area, where children ride tricycles and people walk their dogs along quiet, tree-lined streets.

2 Getting Around

BY CAR

It's not a good idea to fall into a driver's daze in Austin: Those unfamiliar with the local turf need to be vigilant on the city streets as well as the highways. The former are rife with signs that suddenly insist "Left lane must turn left" or "Right lane must turn right"—positioned so they're most noticeable when it's too late to switch. A number of major downtown streets are one-way only; many don't have visible street signs. Driving is particularly confusing in the university area, where streets like

"32¹/₂" suddenly turn up, and even more so at night, when it's difficult to read the ill-lit signs. I-35 is mined with tricky on-and-off ramps and, around downtown, a confusing complex of upper and lower levels; it's easy to miss your exit or to find yourself exiting where you don't want to. If you possibly can, avoid Hwy. 183, which connects I-35 with Mo-Pac and the Capital of Texas Hwy. to the west: Perpetually under construction, the road is rife with narrowing lane mergings and sudden, precipitous turnoffs. You can still see bumper stickers around town proclaiming, "Pray for me, I drive 183."

CAR RENTALS If you're planning to travel at a popular time, it's a good idea to book as far in advance as you can, both to secure the quoted rates and to ensure that you get a car. Some of the companies I phoned in early October to inquire about the winter holiday season were already filled up for Christmas.

Advantage (☎ 800/777-5500), **Alamo** (☎ 800/327-9633), **Avis** (☎ 800/831-2847), **Budget** (☎ 800/527-0700), **Dollar** (☎ 800/800-4000), **Hertz** (☎ 800/654-3131), **National Interrent** (☎ 800/227-7368), and **Thrifty** (☎ 800/367-2277) all have representatives at the airport.

Lower prices are often available for those who are flexible about dates of travel or who are members of frequent-flyer or frequent hotel stay programs or of organizations such as AAA or AARP. It can't hurt to mention every travel-related program you belong to when you're calling to reserve a car; you'd be surprised at the bargains you might turn up.

PARKING Unless you have congressional plates, you're likely to find the selection of parking spots downtown extremely limited during the week. Bring pocketfuls of quarters and prepare to feed the meter at intervals that can be as short as 15 minutes. There are a number of lots around the area, costing anywhere from $2.50 to $4, but the most convenient ones tend to fill up quickly. Although there's virtually no street parking available near the capitol during the week before 5pm, there is a free visitor lot on 15th and Congress (2-hour time limit). The university area is similarly congested during the week; trying to find a spot near the shopping strip known as the Drag can be just that. Cruise the side streets; you're eventually bound to find a lot that's not filled. The two on-campus parking garages are near San Jacinto and E. 26th Streets and off 25th Street between San Antonio and Nueces; there are also parking lots near the visitors centers at the LBJ Library and the Arno Nowotny Building.

DRIVING RULES Unless specifically forbidden, right turns are permitted on red after coming to a full stop. Seat belts and child-restraint seats are mandatory in Texas.

BY TAXI

Among the major cab companies in Austin are **Austin Cab** (☎ 512/478-2222), **Roy's Taxi** (☎ 512/482-0000), and **Yellow-Checker American Cab** (☎ 512/472-1111). Rates are regulated by the city: It's $1.50 for the first fifth of a mile, $1.50 for each additional mile.

BY BUS

Austin's public transportation system, **Capital Metropolitan Transportation Authority,** is excellent, including more than 50 bus lines and a variety of pay strata. The regular adult one-way fare on Metro routes is 50¢; express service from various Park & Ride lots costs $1; three 'Dillo routes—Congress, Lavaca, and Old Pecan Street—are free. You'll need exact change or fare tickets (see below) to board the bus; free transfers are good for 3 hours on weekdays, 4 hours on weekends. Call **800/474-1201** or 512/474-1200 from local pay phones (TDD **512/385-5872**) for point-to-point routing information; you can also pick up a schedule booklet at any HEB, Fiesta, and Albertson grocery store or at the Capital Metro Information Center, 106 E. 8th St., just off Congress, behind Hit or Miss.

DISCOUNT FARES With the exception of Special Transit Service and Public Event shuttles, passengers 65 and older or those with mobility impairments may ride all fixed bus routes for free upon presenting a Capital Metro ID card to the driver; these cards are available for a $3 charge from the Capital Metro Information Center (open Monday through Friday from 7:30am to 5:30pm). University of Texas students also ride for free upon presentation of a U.T. ID card; all other students who get a Capital Metro ID card pay half-price. If you buy a Ticket Book, available at the same place as schedule booklets (see above), you can get twenty 50¢ tickets for only $5—a 50% savings. Children 5 years or younger ride free when accompanied by adults.

BY BICYCLE

It would be hard to find a city more accommodating to two-wheelers than Austin. Many city streets have separate bicycle lanes, and lots of scenic areas have been set aside for hiking and biking or for biking alone; see the "Staying Active" section of chapter 14 for details. Austinites are up in arms about a new helmet law that was passed in 1996 (go figure; you'd think all those techies would want to keep their heads intact).

ON FOOT

Crossing wide avenues such as Congress is not as easy as it might be because lights tend to be geared toward motorists rather than pedestrians, but downtown Austin and the other older sections of the city are generally very walkable. And Austin is dotted with lovely, tree-shaded spots for everything from strolling to in-line skating. The jaywalking laws are not generally enforced, except downtown.

FAST FACTS: Austin

American Express   2943 W. Anderson Lane (☎ **512/452-8166**).

Area Code   The telephone area code in Austin is **512.**

Baby-sitters   Grandparents Unlimited (☎ **512/280-5108**) and Austin's Capital Grannies (☎ **512/371-3402**) are licensed and bonded child-care providers that use seniors or older reliable people. If it's boundless energy you're after, the Financial Aid Office at the University of Texas (☎ **512/495-6200**) can refer you to a college student.

Business Hours   Banks and office hours are generally Monday through Friday from 8 or 9am to 5pm. Some banks offer drive-through service on Saturday from 9am to noon or 1pm. Specialty shops and malls tend to open around 9 or 10am, Monday through Saturday; the former close at about 5 or 6pm, the latter at around 9 or 10pm. You can also shop at most malls and boutiques on Sunday from noon until 6pm. Bars and clubs don't tend to close until midnight during the week, 2am on weekends.

Camera Repair   Precision Camera & Video, 3810 N. Lamar Blvd. (☎ **512/467-7676**), is a reliable place to take a broken camera.

Car Rentals   See "Getting Around," earlier in this chapter.

Climate   See "When to Go," in chapter 2.

Dentist   Both the Dental Referral Service (☎ 800/917-6453) and the Medical Service Bureau (☎ 512/458-1121) can recommend local dentists.

Doctor   In addition to the Medical Service Bureau (see above), Brackenridge (☎ 512/480-1122) and Seton (☎ 800/542-1522 or 512/338-5065) hospitals have physician referral services.

Driving Rules   See "Getting Around," earlier in this chapter.

Drugstores   See "Pharmacies," below.

Embassies/Consulates   See "Fast Facts: For the Foreign Traveler," in the Appendix.

Emergencies   Call **911** if you need the police, fire department, or an ambulance.

Eyeglass Repair   TSO and Lenscrafters are two fast, dependable chains with many convenient locations around town.

Hospitals   Brackenridge, 601 E. 15th St. (☎ 512/476-6461), and St. David's, 919 E. 32nd St. at I-35 (☎ 512/397-4240), have good and convenient emergency-care facilities.

Hot Lines   Inside Line (☎ 512/416-5700) can clue you in on Austin information from the essential to the esoteric—everything from weather forecasts (ext. 7034) and restaurant reviews (ext. 3663) to comedy (ext. 5233) and bat viewing (ext. 1630). Other possibilities include nightclub updates (ext. 2582), movie reviews (ext. 3465), theater reviews (ext. 7439), traveler's forecasts (ext. 6849), world-news updates (ext. 6700), and current events (ext. 5463). Punch extension 6955 for instructions on how to use the system.

Information   See "Visitor Information," earlier in this chapter.

Libraries   The downtown Austin Public Library and adjoining Austin History Center, 810 Guadalupe St. (☎ 512/499-7480), are excellent information resources.

Liquor Laws   See chapter 3. You have to be 21 to drink in Texas. It's illegal to have an open container in your car, and liquor cannot be served before noon on Sunday except at brunches.

Lost Property   You can phone the police at **512/480-5028** to check if something you've lost has been turned in. If you leave something on a city bus, call **512/389-7454**; on a train heading for Austin or at the Amtrak station, call **512/476-5684**; on a Greyhound bus or at the station, call **512/458-4463**; at the airport terminal, call **512/495-7600**; at the airport parking lot, call **512/476-7200.**

Luggage Storage/Lockers   Coin-operated storage lockers in the airport cost from 75¢ to $1, depending on the size. At the Greyhound station, there's only one size locker; the price is $1 per 24 hours. You can check your luggage at the Amtrak station for $1.50 per bag per 24 hours.

Maps   See "City Layout," earlier in this chapter.

Newspapers/Magazines   The daily *Austin American-Statesman* is the only large-circulation, mainstream newspaper in town. The *Austin Chronicle,* a free alternative weekly, focuses on the arts, entertainment, and politics. Monday through Thursday, the University of Texas publishes the surprisingly sophisticated *Daily Texan* newspaper, covering everything from on-campus to international events.

Pharmacies   You'll find many Walgreens and Eckerd drugstores around the city; most HEB grocery stores also have pharmacies. The Walgreens at Capitol Plaza, I-35 and Cameron Road (☎ 512/452-9452), is open 24 hours.

Police The 24-hour nonemergency number for the Austin Police Department is **512/480-5000.**

Post Office The city's main post office is at 8225 Cross Park Dr. (☎ **512/ 342-1252**); more convenient to tourist sights are the Capitol Station, 111 E. 17th St., in the LBJ Building (☎ **512/477-3903**), and the Downtown Station, 510 Guadalupe St. (☎ **512/499-8183**).

Radio On the FM dial, turn to KMFA (89.5) for classical music; KUT (90.5) for National Public Radio; KASE (100.7) for country; KUTZ (98.9) for contemporary rock; KGSR (107.1) for folk, reggae, rock, blues, and jazz. AM stations include KVET (1300) for news and talk and KJCE (1300) for soul and Motown oldies.

Restrooms Good luck finding a restroom downtown on Sunday morning when most of the stores and restaurants are closed; the capitol complex and hotels are your best bet. Malls and parks are well provided with public bathrooms.

Safety Austin has the third-lowest crime rate of America's major cities, but that doesn't mean you should throw common sense to the winds. It's never a good idea to walk down dark streets alone at night, and major tourist areas always attract pickpockets; keep your purse or wallet in a safe place.

Taxes The tax on hotel rooms is 13%. Sales tax, added to restaurant bills as well as to other purchases, is 8.25%.

Taxis See "Getting Around," in this chapter.

Television If you want to tune into your favorite noncable TV shows, you'll find CBS (KEYE) on Channel 5; ABC (KVUE) on Channel 3; NBC (KXAN) on Channel 4; Fox (KTBC) on Channel 2; and PBS (KLRU) on Channel 9.

Time Zone Austin is on central daylight time and observes daylight saving time.

Transit Information Capital Metro Transit (☎ **800/474-1201** or 512/474-1200 from local pay phones, TDD **512/385-5872**).

Useful Telephone Numbers Time and temperature (☎ **512/973-3555**).

Weather ☎ **512/451-2424.**

12 | Austin Accommodations

Endless chain motels strung along I-35 north of the airport notwithstanding, Austin has a room shortage. Resistance to development, strict residential zoning laws, and uncertainty about the opening date—and, for a long time, the location—of a new airport have all added to the pinch. Sometimes it's a cinch to find a place to stay; other times those needing to attend an event in Austin can find themselves lodged almost as far away as San Antonio.

If you can't guess when major microchip conventions are going to come to town, you can make some sense out of what might seem like random runs on hotel space by keeping two things in mind: the state legislature and the University of Texas (enrollment nearly 50,000). Lawmakers and lobbyists converge on the capital for 140-day sessions at the start of odd-numbered years, so you can expect fewer free rooms in the first half of 1997 and 1999. And figure that the beginning of fall term, graduation week, and important home games of the Longhorns football team—U.T.'s Darrell K. Royal/ Memorial Stadium has nearly 80,000 seats—are going to draw parents and sports fans into town en masse. And during the third week in March, record label execs and aspiring artists attending the huge annual SXSW music conference take up all the town's rooms. It's always a good idea to book as far in advance as possible; it's essential if you're planning to come in around these times.

Along with airport proximity (for the time being—see the "By Plane" section in chapter 10), low cost and quick downtown freeway access help fill the I-35 motels. But you'll get a far better feel for what makes Austin special if you stay in the verdant Town Lake area; closer than any others to the major sights, the hotels here are also on or near a 10-mile hike-and-bike trail. Farther afield but convenient to various high-tech complexes are the accommodation clusters to the south (which will be convenient to the new airport when it opens) and northwest of town. Those with a penchant for playing on the water or putting should consider staying out near the lakes and golf courses to the west.

Austin offers some glitzy high-rises but only one historic hotel; if it's character you're after, you might opt for one of the bed-and-breakfasts increasingly cropping up around town. The recently formed Greater Austin Bed and Breakfast Association currently has 13 members; for information, call the **Woodburn House** (☎ **512/ 458-4335**). Some of the member inns also belong to the **Historic Hotel Association of Texas,** P.O. Box 1399, Fredericksburg, TX

78624 (☎ **800/428-8669** or 210/997-3980); write or phone for a pamphlet listing bed-and-breakfasts in the Austin area.

Most hotels offer substantially lower prices on the weekends, while some bed-and-breakfasts have reduced rates on Sunday through Thursday. If you don't mind changing rooms once, you can get the best of both discount worlds.

In the reviews that follow, the **Very Expensive** category covers hotels that charge more than $170 for a double room, not including tax (13%); **Expensive** means you'll pay from $120 to $170; **Moderate** rooms run from $75 to $120; and you'll sleep for under $75 if you stay in an **Inexpensive** place. Remember, these are only rough approximations based on published rates; you're likely to find lower prices if a hotel isn't full, or higher prices in the case of a special event.

1 Best Bets

- **Best Historic Hotel:** The delightful **Driskill** (☎ **800/252-9367** or 512/474-5911) is a hands-down winner in this category, since it's the only remaining remnant of Austin hospitality past. It had gotten a bit shabby over the years, but an ongoing $10 million restoration is smoothing all the rough edges.
- **Best for Business Travelers:** Located near a lot of high-tech companies in northwest Austin, the **Renaissance Austin** (☎ **800/HOTELS-1** or 512/343-2626) has top-notch meeting and shmoozing spaces, not to mention fine close-the-deal partying places.
- **Best for a Romantic Getaway:** Choose one of the beautifully decorated theme rooms at the **Inn at Pearl Street** (☎ **512/477-2233**) if you want to be transported to the French countryside, say, or to the Orient, without suffering from jet lag.
- **Best Hotel Lobby for Pretending that You're Rich:** Settle in at the lobby lounge at the posh **Four Seasons** (☎ **800/332-3442** or 512/478-4500), overlooking Town Lake, and for the price of a Dubonnet you can act like you stay here every time you fly in on your LearJet.
- **Best Budget Hotel:** Look for the classic neon sign for the **Austin Motel** (☎ **512/441-1157**) on South Congress Street, Austin's next growth area. It's being refurbished but promises to retain its 1950s character and lower-than-1990s prices.
- **Best B&B:** It's hard to beat the friendly **Brook House** (☎ **512/459-0534**) for attractive antique furnishings, good breakfasts, reasonable prices, and an affectionate pet—Labrador Ernie is a lap-dog wannabe.
- **Best View of Town Lake:** Lots of downtown properties have nice water views, but its location on the lake's south shore gives the **Hyatt Regency** (☎ **800/233-1234** or 512/477-1234) the edge because here the panoramic spread of the city and the capitol serves as a backdrop.
- **Best Health Club:** All those high-tech ways to sweat, and all those massage rooms to soothe sore muscles afterward—the **Barton Creek Resort** (☎ **800/336-6158** or 512/329-4000) raises exercise to an art form.
- **Best Menagerie:** No question. The **Citiview B&B** (☎ **800/BST-VIEW** or 512/441-2606) can provide more critters per guest than any other Austin accommodation. Birds, dogs, fish, even a llama entertain animal lovers.
- **Best Hotel Shopping:** Stay at the **Omni** (☎ **800/THE-OMNI** or 512/476-3700) and you can have a suit custom-made or rent a tuxedo without stepping outdoors: The hotel shares space with toney shops and offices at the ultramodern Austin Center complex, including a jeweler, art gallery, travel agent, and hairdresser.
- **Best for Forgetting Your Troubles:** Stress? That's a dirty word at the **Lake Austin Spa** (☎ **800/847-5637,** 800/338-6651, or 512/266-4362), and after a few days

at this lovely, ultrarelaxing spot, you'll be ready to face the world again (even if you don't especially want to).

2 Downtown

VERY EXPENSIVE

✪ Four Seasons Austin

98 San Jacinto Blvd., Austin, TX 78701. ☎ **800/332-3442** or 512/478-4500. Fax 512/478-3117. 251 rms, 28 suites. A/C TV TEL. $170–$240 double; $245–$1,200 suite. Packages available. AE, CB, DC, MC, V. Self-parking $7; valet parking $12.

Queen Elizabeth, Prince Charles, and King Philip of Spain have all bedded down—at different times—in this, the most luxe of the luxe hotels on Town Lake, but you don't have to be royalty to be treated that way at the Four Seasons. Can't be parted from your pooch? Bring him along; you can treat him to German Shepherds Pie from a special room service menu for pets and get a bellman to trot him around the grounds after dinner. Your taste in animals runs to the more exotic? Still no sweat. A group of Busch Gardens penguins were given their own room, its bathtub constantly replenished with ice.

But while you revel in posh European-type treatment, you won't forget you're in Texas: Polished sandstone floors, a cowhide sofa, horn lamps, and an elk head hanging over the fireplace lend the lobby a Hill Country ranch-house look. Elegant guest rooms also have southwestern touches, with Native American patterned bedspreads, leatherette headboards, and light-wood furnishings. Not all are as enormous as the Presidential Suite where the queen slept, but you'll have plenty of space to stretch out. The city views are fine, but the ones of the lake are prime.

Those inclined toward self-punishment can indulge at one of the best health clubs in town, gratis (you can't use the old "I-forgot-my-workout-clothes" excuse here; the hotel will lend guests shorts and T-shirts). More sybaritic types might depart the premises with that polished, pampered glow brought on by one of the myriad masks, massages, and wraps offered at the spa.

Dining/Entertainment: Order snacks and drinks by the pool or gaze out at the lake over cocktails in the Lobby Lounge, which serves hors d'oeuvres from midday until the wee hours. You'll get the same idyllic vista from the windows or patio of the excellent Café, serving continental fare with southwest influences; some of the best bat watching in the city draws diners to vie for seating at dusk.

Services: 24-hour room service and concierge service, 24-hour security rounds, valet laundry/dry cleaning, 1-hour pressing service, physician on call, complimentary morning newspaper, complimentary overnight shoe shine.

Facilities: Health club/spa, Jacuzzi, saunas, pool, running trails, gift shop, car-rental desk.

Hyatt Regency Austin on Town Lake

208 Barton Springs Rd., Austin TX 78704. ☎ **800/233-1234** or 512/477-1234. Fax 512/480-2069. 429 rms, 17 suites. A/C TV TEL. $175–$185 double; $250–$650 suite. Weekend specials, corporate and state-government rates available. AE, CB, DC, DISC, MC, V. Free self-parking; valet parking $8.

Austin's Hyatt Regency brings the outdoors in—its signature atrium lobby is anchored by a Hill Country–type tableau of a limestone-banked flowing stream, waterfalls, and oak trees. It's impressive all right, but the genuine item outside is more striking still: Because the hotel sits on Town Lake's south shore, its watery vistas have stunning city backdrops.

Although the Hyatt is just minutes from downtown, outdoor recreation makes the hotel tick. Bat tours depart from a private dock, which also rents paddleboats and canoes. Guests can borrow mountain bikes to ride on the hike-and-bike trail, right outside the door.

All the accommodations, decorated in western denims, plaids, and oak, have desks, hair dryers, ironing boards, and irons; special business plan rooms offer fax machines and two-line phones, along with access to computer printers, copy machines, and office supplies. Gold Passport Floors for frequent travelers provide coffee and tea areas and newspaper delivery to rooms.

Dining/Entertainment: Townies as well as hotel guests come to the casual La Vista restaurant for its great fajitas and tasty selection of low-fat items. The atrium's Branchwater Lounge is hooked up to La Vista's kitchen, so you can order from its menu or, in the evening, just enjoy a drink to the accompaniment of country-and-western music.

Services: Room service, laundry/valet, concierge, staff fluency in French, German, and Spanish.

Facilities: Fitness room, outdoor pool, whirlpool, newsstand, drugstore, gift shop.

Omni Austin

700 San Jacinto Blvd., Austin, TX 78701. ☎ **800/THE-OMNI** or 512/476-3700. Fax 512/ 320-5882. 304 rms, 26 suites. A/C TV TEL. $175 double; $180–$230 suite. Weekend and summer specials available. AE, CB, DC, DISC, MC, V. Self-parking $5; valet parking $8.

Part of the posh Austin Center office and retail complex, the hotel's spectacular 200-foot rise of sun-struck glass and steel makes one feel simultaneously dwarfed and exhilarated. In contrast to the ultramodern lobby are extra-large guest quarters with Louis XV– and empire-style furnishings and polished parquet floors; warm wine tones predominate. Each room has a sitting area, marble desk, and spacious bath with a full-length mirror as well as a hair dryer and ironing board. Omni Club rooms on the 13th and 14th floors offer such upgraded amenities as terry-cloth robes, scales, and makeup mirrors. The complimentary continental breakfast and afternoon hors d'oeuvres and cocktails are all par for an executive-level course, but you're also treated here to the ultimate bedtime comfort snack: fresh-baked cookies and milk.

It'd be tough to beat the views from the Omni's rooftop pool, perched 20 stories high. You can also bask on the adjoining sundeck or soak in the Jacuzzi while gazing out over the city.

Dining/Entertainment: An outdoor menu lets you order snacks upstairs by the pool, but the rest of the hotel's eating and entertainment are grounded on the lobby level. You can listen to piano music nightly at the Atrium Lounge, or throw darts in Billiards, which is part English pub, part American sports bar. New Texan cuisine and singing waiters are featured at the hotel's full-service restaurant, Anchos.

Services: Room service, valet/laundry service, business center services, massage therapists, complimentary airport van.

Facilities: Pool, sundeck, Jacuzzi, health club, sauna, shops, car-rental agency.

Sheraton Austin

I-35 and Sixth St., Austin TX 78701. ☎ **800/325-3535** or 512/480-8181. Fax 512/ 462-0660. 242 rms, 7 suites. A/C TV TEL. $199 double; $450 suite. Weekend specials, summer specials, holiday-saver rates available. AE, CB, DC, DISC, MC, V. Self-parking $7 in covered garage.

Austin's downtown Sheraton, although well located near the convention center and the Sixth Street entertainment district, suffers from multiple personalities. A marble-and-brass lobby, bustling with activity, is separated from a hushed skylit atrium rising from the 10th floor. The latter, done in Roman neoclassical style with a central fountain, is attractive, and the arrangement blocks entry-level noise from the guest rooms, but the soaring space doesn't invite lingering, so the area can be disconcertingly deserted during the day.

Then there are the English/European–style rooms, beautifully furnished with Queen Anne and Chippendale Drexel Heritage pieces and southwestern touches. Deluxe suites are similarly decked out, but enjoy an extra bedroom and a Jacuzzi in each bath. Windows look out onto the atrium or the exterior, which could mean the highway, unless you specify otherwise. It's back to ancient Rome at the health club, where a 25-person hot tub needs only toga-clad attendants to complete the hedonistic picture.

Dining/Entertainment: This aspect of the hotel is similarly schizophrenic: The lobby bar is appropriately cushy, but you'd expect an ITT Sheraton to have a fine-dining room, and this one doesn't. The romantic city views afforded by the 18th-floor Rooftop Cafe aren't as well served as they could be by the casual, collegiate-type fare.

Services: Room service, valet laundry/dry cleaning.

Facilities: Outdoor pool, exercise room, steam bath, sauna, massage room.

EXPENSIVE

Austin Marriott at the Capitol

701 E. 11th St., Austin, TX 78701. ☎ **800/228-9290** or 512/478-1111. Fax 512/478-3700. 365 rms, 4 suites. A/C TV TEL. $160 double; $450 suite. Weekend packages available. AE, CB, DC, DISC, MC, V. Self-parking $5; valet parking $8.

Austin's Marriot offers a convenient downtown location and lots of perks for business travelers, including guaranteed quick check-in and irons in all the rooms. Three-day advance booking and weekend deals lower the rates here considerably. The walls of windows on the atrium levels of the blocky high-rise lend the public areas an open, airy look. Rooms, done in light green and burgundy with standard hotel florals, also feel unconfined; the ones on the higher floors have terrific city views, and those on the west side all look out on the state capitol, four blocks away. Booking a room on the concierge floor will get you mineral water, plants, and an electric shoe-shine machine in your room, along with newspaper delivery and access to a lounge where a continental breakfast and afternoon hors d'oeuvres are on the house.

Dining/Entertainment: The Marriott's sports lounge, with a casual menu, boasts two pool tables and TVs that broadcast games from around the world. In the evening, you can also drink in the lobby lounge. The skylit Allie's American Grille is the hotel's main restaurant, serving somewhat southwestern American and continental fare.

Services: Room service, valet/laundry service.

Facilities: Indoor/outdoor pool, whirlpool, sauna, exercise room, gift shop, guest washer and dryer, video arcade.

Doubletree Guest Suites

303 W. 15th St., Austin, TX 78701. ☎ **800/222-TREE** or 512/478-7000. Fax 512/478-5103. 189 suites, including 14 two-bedroom suites. A/C TV TEL. $155 suite; $225 two-bedroom suite. Corporate rates, extended-stay rates available. AE, DC, DISC, MC, V. Self- or valet parking $7.

Lobbyists sock in for winter legislative sessions at this toney all-suites high-rise, a stone's throw from the state capitol; in summer, the Dallas Cowboys, in town for training camp at St. Edward's University, touch down in some of the rooms. It would be hard to find more comfortable temporary quarters: At 625 square feet, the standard one-bedroom suites are larger than many New York apartments.

Downtown Austin Accommodations

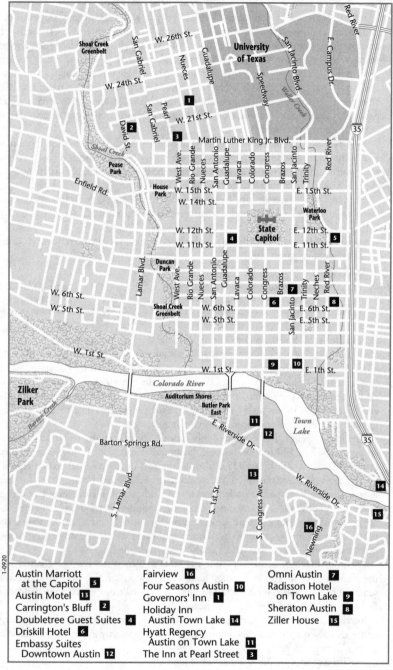

Austin Marriott
  at the Capitol **5**
Austin Motel **13**
Carrington's Bluff **2**
Doubletree Guest Suites **4**
Driskill Hotel **6**
Embassy Suites
  Downtown Austin **12**

Fairview **16**
Four Seasons Austin **10**
Governors' Inn **1**
Holiday Inn
  Austin Town Lake **14**
Hyatt Regency
  Austin on Town Lake **11**
The Inn at Pearl Street **3**

Omni Austin **7**
Radisson Hotel
  on Town Lake **9**
Sheraton Austin **8**
Ziller House **15**

All are decorated in tasteful contemporary style, with blue or gray carpets, floral bedspreads, rattan-style chairs, cushy sofas, and large mirrored closets; baths are spacious, too. Many rooms have balconies with capitol views. Full-sized refrigerators, toasters, stoves, coffeemakers, and cookware allow guests to prepare meals in comfort; unlike kitchens in many all-suite hotels, those here are separate, so you don't have to stare at dirty dishes—washed by the maid every day—after you eat. For folks who don't like to cook on vacation (or ever), there's also 24-hour room service. You'll get a fresh supply of coffee every day and, if you request it, a newspaper delivered to your door during the week.

Dining/Entertainment: For hearty seafood, Tex-Mex, or steak, dine indoors or out at the white tableclothed 15th Street Cafe, serving three meals a day. You can sink your teeth (and your diet) into a Texas reuben—the usual, plus jalepeños—at the more casual adjoining lounge.

Services: Valet laundry/dry cleaning, safe-deposit boxes, complimentary hotel shuttle within 2-mile radius, pets allowed in some suites, secretarial services and baby-sitting available.

Facilities: Heated outdoor pool, sundeck, whirlpool, saunas, exercise room, coin-operated laundry, guest library.

✪ Driskill Hotel

604 Brazos St., Austin TX 78701. ☎ **800/252-9367** or 512/474-5911. Fax 512/474-2214. 160 rms, 15 suites. A/C TV TEL. $105–$220 double; suites $200 and up. Corporate and weekend rates and various packages available. AE, CB, DC, DISC, MC, V. Self-parking $4; valet parking $9.

Lyndon Johnson holed up here during the final days of his presidential campaign, anxiously awaiting the election results. Ann Richards held her inaugural ball at the Driskill when she became governor, and the hotel hosted Tommy Lee Jones's wedding reception. This is where the Daughters of the Republic of Texas gathered to decide the fate of the Alamo, and Texas lawmen met to set an ambush for Bonnie and Clyde. Since 1886, cattle baron Jesse Driskill has perched on a column atop his grand hotel, literally stone-faced, surveying it all.

The magnificent halls of Austin's only historic hotel had gotten a tad shabby, but an ongoing $7 to $10 million renovation should restore their former sheen. Guest rooms—100 of them in a 1929 addition, the rest in the original structure—are being redone in luxurious style. Many will have the original 19th-century furnishings, including handmade wooden desks, while others will include excellent reproductions. All offer modern amenities, including phones with modem capability, and are conveniently arranged with sinks and mirrors outside the bathroom area; the refurbished rooms have minibars. The unrenovated rooms are considerably less expensive than the ones that have already been overhauled.

Dining/Entertainment: Adjoining the hotel's cushy piano bar (see chapter 16), the Driskill Grill looks like a ladies' tearoom; one would expect to find watercress sandwiches here, not southwestern fare such as smoked trout with nopalitos (cactus pads) or wild game with green chili chutney.

Services: 24-hour room service; valet dry cleaning/laundry service; complimentary coffee and newspaper in the morning, peanut butter and jelly in the evening; nearby Gold's Gym privileges.

Facilities: Shop, airline ticket office in lobby.

Embassy Suites Downtown Austin

300 S. Congress Ave., Austin, TX 78704. ☎ **800/EMBASSY** or 512/469-9000. Fax 512/480-9164. 261 suites. A/C TV TEL. $129–$169. Rates include full breakfast. AE, CB, DC, DISC, MC, V. Free parking.

Embassy Suites are generally a good deal for those traveling on business or with families, and this link in the national chain has a great location to boot. It's a straight shot north from the property to the state capitol, and only a few blocks west to the row of restaurants on Barton Springs Road. And when you step outside the hotel's door, you're only a few minutes on foot from the Town Lake hike-and-bike trail (you can rent a bike from the front desk).

All the attractive, modern accommodations have two TVs, two telephones, a microwave, refrigerator, wet bar, coffeemaker and coffee supplies, full-size ironing board and iron, and hair dryer; living rooms feature queen-size sleeper sofas along with well-lighted work areas. About a third of the suites look out on downtown, the lake, and the hills. The open atrium arrangement of the rooms is its own security system, but the hotel also offers 24-hour security escort service around the grounds. On top of all this, Embassy Suites has a hard-to-beat guarantee policy: You don't pay if you're not satisfied. Chances are they don't lose any money on the deal at this property.

Dining/Entertainment: The free full breakfast is one of the hotel's draws: Cooked-to-order eggs, pancakes, and other griddle fare go along with a fresh fruit, cereal, and baked-goods buffet in the morning. From 5:30 to 7:30pm, it's complimentary cocktails (a margarita machine was just added) with salty snacks and hot hors d'oeuvres. If you don't want to drink your dinner, drop in at the Capital City Bistro, where you can order from a limited Pizza Hut menu.

Services: Room service, complimentary transportation to the airport and the downtown business district, complimentary newspapers.

Facilities: Pool, whirlpool, sauna, exercise room, guest laundry, gift shop, video-game room.

Holiday Inn Austin Town Lake

200 N. I-35, Austin, TX 78701. ☎ **800/HOLIDAY** or 512/472-8211. Fax 512/472-4636. 319 rms. A/C TV TEL. $130–$140 double. Weekend and holiday rates available. AE, CB, DC, DISC, MC, V. Free parking.

The most upscale Holiday Inn in Austin, this high-rise is also the best situated: It's on the north shore of Town Lake, at the edge of downtown and just off I-35. Recently renovated guest rooms are stylish, with simulated brick walls, light-wood furniture, and southwestern patterns; the ones looking out on Town Lake are the most expensive. Fifty of the accommodations have additional sofa sleepers; since children under 18 stay free, that can translate into real family savings. Rooms on the executive level offer robes, hair dryers, and coffeemakers. A rooftop pool large enough for laps affords fine lake views.

Dining/Entertainment: Dabber's sports bar and lounge holds its happy-hour specials from 5 to 7pm; you can watch the games here or shoot some pool. Monday through Friday, breakfast and lunch at the Pecan Tree Restaurant are all-you-can-eat bargains; dinner is served here, too.

Services: Room service, valet dry cleaning during the week, complimentary airport transportation.

Facilities: Exercise room, outdoor heated pool, sundeck, sauna, whirlpool, gift shop, coin-operated guest laundry.

MODERATE

⑤ Radisson Hotel on Town Lake

11 E. First St., Austin, TX 78701. ☎ **800/333-3333** or 512/478-9611. Fax 512/473-8399. 260 rms, 20 suites. A/C TV TEL. $110–$120 double; $135 suite. Corporate, family, and weekend rates available. AE, CB, DC, DISC, MC, V. Self-parking $4; valet parking $7.

A lower-priced alternative to the downtown luxury high-rises, the Radisson offers its guests a prime Town Lake location along with many of the perks of the pricier properties (among them, free newspaper delivery on weekdays, as well as coffeemakers and irons in all rooms). Supersaver rates can bring prices down to as low as $79. From the airy, open lobby, with its potted palms and patterned rug, to pleasant rooms decorated in shades of turquoise or peach, the ambience is light and cheery. The lakeside views are the most sought after, but the ones of the capitol are not to be scoffed at.

One of Austin's favorite bat-watching venues, the on-site TGIF's upholds the tradition of the national chain for hearty collegiate food—chicken wings, burgers, pizza—and general rowdiness. Services and facilities offered include room service, valet laundry/dry cleaning (Monday through Saturday), complimentary airport transfers and transportation within 4-mile radius of hotel, an outdoor pool, exercise room, and gift shop.

INEXPENSIVE

Austin Motel

1220 S. Congress St., Austin, TX 78704. ☎ **512/441-1157.** Fax 512/444-2610. 41 rooms, including 4 suites (1 with kitchenette). A/C TV TEL. $46–$73 double; $99 suite. AE, DC, MC, V. Free parking.

It's not only nostalgia that draws repeat guests to this Austin institution, established in 1938 and in the current owner's family since the 1950s; a convenient (though not quiet) location, just south of downtown, and reasonable rates help, too. Other assets: a classic kidney-shaped pool, a great neon sign, and El Sol y Luna, a Latin restaurant that's popular with Town Lake athletes on weekend mornings. Unless you're on a rock-bottom budget, ask for one of the renovated pool rooms; they're much more cheerful.

BED & BREAKFASTS

Citiview

1405 E. Riverside Dr., Austin, TX 78741. ☎ **800/BST-VIEW** or 512/441-2606. Fax 512/441-2949; Internet www.hyperweb.com/citiview. 3 rooms, all with private bath. A/C TV TEL. $139–$159 weekdays, $189 weekends. Rates include breakfast. AE, MC, V.

With its smashing art deco furnishings, beautifully landscaped grounds, and huge menagerie of pets, this bed-and-breakfast is a bit of a hybrid. That is, with all the wildlife—including some 50 birds, a llama, a goat, and two Great Danes—one might expect something more low-key, but Citiview is rather formal. The light-filled rooms all have TVs, refrigerators, private phones with voice mail, and stereos; a full breakfast includes organic produce. Prices are rather steep, considering the city view for which the B&B is named takes in a lot of I-35, but the recent addition of a conservatory with a pool and yoga classes, as well as the novelty of this place, helps justify the rates.

Fairview

1304 Newning Ave., Austin, TX 78704. ☎ **800/310-4746** or 512/444-4746. Fax 512/444-3494. 3 rms, 1 suite, 2 suites with kitchen. A/C TV TEL. $89–$99 double; $109–$129 suite. Rates include breakfast and afternoon refreshments. Discounts for stays of 4 nights or longer available. AE, CB, DC, MC, V.

In 1886, Fairview Park was developed as a posh residential subdivision, its bluffs less susceptible to flooding than the lower ground north of the river. Such stately homes as Duke and Nancy Waggoner's colonial revival mansion, only minutes from downtown by car, attest to the area's cachet.

After buying it in 1991, the Waggoners spent a year refurbishing the place, and the results are impressive, indeed; the house received an award from the Austin Heritage Society for its impeccable preservation. The furnishings the couple brought into it are equally outstanding; serious antique freaks, the Waggoners can tell you the provenance of every item in their gracious guest accommodations—four of them in the main house, two in a carriage house set off from a rose arbor out back. Breakfast here is an elaborate affair that might include stuffed French toast garnished with fresh fruit. The imperious Sasha, a long-haired, domesticated alley cat, entertains guests throughout the day.

Ziller House

800 Edgecliff Terrace, Austin, TX 78704. ☎ **800/949-5446** or 512/462-0100. Fax 512/462-9166; e-mail ziller@realtime.net. 4 rms, 1 suite, carriage house. A/C TV TEL. $100 weekdays, $130 weekends. Rates include breakfast; corporate rates and extended-stay rates available. AE, MC, V.

Ziller House could bill itself as "Bed-and-Breakfast to the Stars," but it's far too discreet to do anything of the sort. Which is why this wooded retreat on a rise overlooking the south shore of Town Lake has hosted the likes of Lyle Lovett and Julia Roberts—yes, at the same time—Clint Eastwood, Walter Cronkite, and Al Gore. Although you might bump into them in the hallways or find yourself soaking with them in the Jacuzzi that looks out on Town Lake, don't expect to rub elbows with the celebs around a cozy breakfast table: quiches, frittatas, and other gourmet goodies cooked up in the afternoon are placed in an in-room refrigerator, to be heated in an accompanying microwave the next morning.

Originally the headquarters for Austin's Humane Society, which was founded by the somewhat eccentric Zillers, this 1928 Italianate mansion was built without doors so animals could roam through it freely. Now only Alexander Magnus, a lion-faced Shar Pei dog belonging to Sam Kindred and Wendy Sandberg, holds sway here, and the house has come under its owners' civilizing influence. A rustic stone-and-fossil fireplace in the living room is set off by a meltingly supple green leather sofa, jade miniature peach tree, and intricately carved emperor's chairs. Guest rooms, many with the original art deco fixtures, are individually decorated in the best of eclectic taste right down to the last detail without being overly fussy; original artwork from local galleries is rotated every 6 months. A carriage house that was recently converted into guest quarters offers a full kitchen.

A YOUTH HOSTEL

Hostelling International—Austin

2200 S. Lakeshore Blvd., Austin, TX 78741. ☎ **800/725-2333** or 512/444-2294. Fax 512/444-2309; e-mail austinayh@aol.com. 40 beds in 3 dorms and 1 private rm. $13 dorm for AYH members, $3 additional for nonmembers; $30 double private room for members, $3 additional for nonmembers. MC, V.

Youth- and nature-oriented Austin goes all out for its hostelers at this winning facility, located on the hike-and-bike trail, with a glass-fronted common room overlooking Town Lake. In addition to being an excellent all-around resource for visitors, the hostel organizes inexpensive day trips (one to New Braunfels for rafting, for example). Facilities include a TV room, laundry room, kitchen, and small store selling such things as sleep sacks and hosteling books. The building, which once served as a boathouse, is solar paneled and—shades of the 1960s—the dorms offer eight waterbeds along with their 32 solid mattresses.

3 University / Hyde Park

BED & BREAKFASTS

✪ Brook House

609 W. 33rd St., Austin, TX 78705. ☎ **512/459-0534.** 6 rms. A/C TV TEL. $69–$99. Rates include breakfast, lower weekday rates available Sun–Thurs. AE, CB, DC, DISC, MC, V.

Colorado-born Barbara Love has a smile as wide as the river that runs through her home state; she and her Labrador Ernie extend a warm welcome to guests at this immaculate but homey bed-and-breakfast. The 1922 colonial revival–style home near the university used to be a crash pad; chances are that Janis Joplin, who lived in the area in the 1960s, dropped in now and then. Although it's been a respectable bed-and-breakfast since 1985, the Brook House has still got good vibes.

You'd be hard-pressed to find better rates for such sunny, appealing quarters. The main house contains three lovely but unfussy rooms, two with their own screened porches and all with antique furnishings. A romantic private cottage has its own kitchen and sitting deck, as does the lower of the two bedrooms in the separate carriage house. On nice days, a full breakfast—lots of fresh-baked goods, fruit, juices, and a hot dish—is served outside on the peaceful covered patio.

Carrington's Bluff

1900 David St., Austin, TX 78705. ☎ **800/871-8908** or 512/479-0638. Fax 512/476-4769. 8 rms (6 with private baths, 2 with 1 shared bath). A/C TV TEL. $69–$99. Rates include breakfast. AE, CB, DC, DISC, MC, V.

The acreage of the lot on which this 1877 farmhouse stands may have dwindled from 22 down to 1 over the years, but Carrington's Bluff still has a bucolic atmosphere, with its manicured front lawn, shade trees, rambling 35-foot porch, and pretty gazebo. Owner Lisa Mugford, who worked for the Four Seasons Hotel for 10 years, wants to make the whole world more idyllic: She and her husband, Ed, are involved in a lot of social causes, including Greyhound rescue (as their dog, Madison, can attest). They're also members of the environmentally conscious Green Hotel association.

The house is decorated in a pleasing mix of contemporary country patterns and dark-wood antiques; florals predominate, but this place feels relaxed rather than precious. After breakfast—a spread of fresh fruit, low-fat yogurt, homemade granola, and an egg dish if desired—guests are welcome to use the kitchen anytime. Convenient to the university and the capitol, Carrington's Bluff draws a lot of satisfied repeat visitors, including the various wordsmiths who have had rooms in the separate Writer's Cottage named after them.

Governors' Inn

611 W. 22nd St., Austin, TX 78705. ☎ **800/871-8908** or 512/477-0711. Fax 512/476-4769. 10 rms (one a single). A/C TEL. $69–$99 double. Rates include breakfast. AE, CB, DC, DISC, MC, V.

Lisa Mugford, who owns Carrington's Bluff (see above), also runs the Governors' Inn. This 1897 neoclassical residence is more spacious but feels citified, in part because it's only two blocks from the busy U.T. campus. Guest rooms, named for long dead and thus noncontroversial governors of Texas, are a bit more formal, too, decorated in floral prints and boasting good antique pieces. Rooms vary quite a bit in size and layout; most are reasonably large, but this bed-and-breakfast also harbors that rarity, a real single ($55). It's little but not claustrophobic; in fact, all the accommodations are nice and light. Three rooms open directly onto a covered porch, and the rest have access to it. Breakfast, which includes a hot dish along with cereals and fruit, is served buffet style during the week, so guests can eat when they like. Desks and answering machines have recently been installed in rooms to better accommodate the business travelers that this place attracts.

✪ The Inn at Pearl Street

809 W. Martin Luther King Jr. Blvd. ☎ **512/477-2233.** Fax 512/477-4571. 3 rms, 1 suite. Weekdays: $100 rooms, $125 suite; weekends: $150 rooms, $175 suite. Rates include breakfast. AE, DC, DISC, MC, V.

One might not expect a place on one of Austin's busier streets to be especially serene, but the rise on which this 1896 Greek revival–style house sits manages to preserve the peace. And though Austin's newest B&B is unassuming on the outside, the home is an interior decorator's dream (it was chosen as the Symphony Designer Showcase in 1995). You'll be ogling all the public areas, with their silk wallpaper and oriental rugs, and asking other guests for a peek in their rooms (or at least wanting to). The gothic suite features a medieval-style draped canopy bed, as well as its own marble bath with a Jacuzzi tub; it adjoins a mint-green sunporch with a refrigerator and tape deck. The Far East room, resplendent in red, gold, and black, has a gorgeous inlaid chest and other Asian treasures. On nice days, you can enjoy breakfast on a tree-shaded, 1,600-foot deck. By the time you read this, five bedrooms in the three-story house next door should be ready for guests.

McCallum House

613 W. 32nd St., Austin, TX 78705. ☎ **512/451-6744.** Fax 512/451-4752. 3 rms, 2 suites. A/C TV TEL. Sun–Thurs: $89 double, $109 suite; Fri–Sat and holidays: $99 double, $119 suite. Rates include breakfast; extended-stay discounts available during the week. MC, V.

In 1907, Jane Y. McCallum took time out from tending five children and leading the Texas Women's Suffrage Movement to design this appealingly eclectic house—part Queen Anne, part early craftsman. Nancy and Roger Danley didn't have quite so much on their plates when they bought and refurbished the place, but they did make modest history by opening it up to the public in 1983 as the first bed-and-breakfast in Austin. They also achieved recognition for their fine restoration and were listed on the National Register for Historic Places in early 1997.

As befits a home intended for a large family, the McCallum House is comfortable and unpretentious, with wall-to-wall carpeting in the guest quarters. The accommodations seem more like intimate apartments than temporary lodgings: Each room has its own kitchen, telephone with answering machine, desk, clock radio, iron and ironing board, and color TV; rooms also have private porches that look out onto a front lawn graced by old pecans, oaks, and elms. These amenities, along with the peaceful residential setting and proximity to the university, make this inn especially popular with visiting academics.

Woodburn House

4401 Ave. D, Austin, TX 78751. ☎ **512/458-4335.** Fax 512/458-4319; e-mail woodburn@iamerica.net. 4 rms. A/C TEL. $79–$89 double. Rates include breakfast; corporate and monthly rates available. AE, MC, V.

Herb and Sandra Dickson's late Victorian home couldn't look more firmly rooted; one would be hard-pressed to guess that, in danger of being bulldozed in 1980, it was jacked up, loaded on a flatbed trailer, and shifted from its original location six blocks away. Now settled in as the only bed-and-breakfast in Hyde Park, the Woodburn House is not only a delightful place to stay, but also a prime source of information about the historic neighborhood.

The inn itself speaks volumes about the first decade of the 20th century, the era in which it was built: Lustrous moldings made of Louisiana long-leaf pine, hardwood floors, and a built-in corner cabinet recall an age of meticulous attention to detail.

Such original attributes are complemented throughout by American period antiques handed down over the years by the Dickson family. Breakfasts are designed to be heart healthy, though you'd never know it: Strawberry-filled crêpes topped with yogurt, apple-cinammon pancakes, or a Mexican casserole might turn up on any given morning, along with delicious home-baked bread.

4 The Airport Area

EXPENSIVE

Austin North Hilton and Towers

6000 Middle Fiskville Rd., Austin, TX 78752. ☎ **800/HILTONS** (reservations), 800/347-0330, or 512/451-5757. Fax 512/467-7644. 237 rms, 3 suites. A/C TV TEL. $146–$166 double; $275–$350 suite. Weekend and seasonal specials available. AE, CB, DC, DISC, MC, V. Free parking.

This airport-area property, Austin's first convention hotel, is a nice surprise: A blocky, nondescript exterior gives no hint of the gracious public areas inside. The lobby was recently redone in a rustic, elegant Hill Country style, including hardwood floors, leather chairs, an antler chandelier, and a native-limestone reception desk. The pool area is a tree-shaded oasis in a concrete desert—but one where you can drop a lot of dough. The Hilton adjoins the shops, restaurants, and movie theaters of the Highland Mall and is within walking distance of the tonier Lincoln Village.

Rooms are done with plush teal or mint rugs, delicately striped bedspreads, and tastefully contrasting floral drapes and chairs; all are large and some have vaulted ceilings. Designed for business travelers, they also have oversized desks and two telephones. A concierge-key level offers the usual amenities—continental breakfast, evening hors d'oeuvres, and an honor bar—in an unusually homey lounge.

Dining/Entertainment: Ma Ferguson's marks the last leg of the Hilton's renovation: Opened in September 1996, this restaurant and lounge features homey fare— chicken and dumplings, say, or a comforting brisket—in a spiffily redone room that takes up the lobby's Hill Country theme. Blue-plate specials and dishes on the copious buffets change every day.

Services: Room service, valet laundry/dry cleaning, complimentary airport transfers, World Gym privileges for $5.

Facilities: Exercise room, outdoor pool, gift shop.

Doubletree Hotel Austin

6505 N. I-35, Austin, TX 78752. ☎ **800/222-TREE** or 512/454-3737. Fax 512/454-6915. 330 rms, 20 suites. A/C TV TEL. $124 double; $139–$169 suite. Corporate, weekend rates; romance package available. AE, CB, DC, DISC, MC, V. Self-parking $4.35; valet parking $7.60.

Leisure travelers should take advantage of the fact that prices plummet on weekends at Austin's Doubletree, a toney business-oriented hotel near the airport. Once you step inside, you'll feel as though you're in a private luxury property rather than a chain lodging just off the freeway. The reception lobby has polished Mexican-tile floors and carved-wood ceiling beams; an adjoining colonnade boasts a massive cherry hutch and other antiques from Mexico, along with 19th-century English wall tapestries. A sophisticated new business center was recently added.

In keeping with the hacienda theme, rooms are arranged around a lushly landscaped courtyard, dotted with umbrella-shaded tables. Writing desks and separate sitting areas allow business to be conducted comfortably in the spacious guest quarters, which are decorated in earth tones and feature French doors, floral tapestry chairs, and stenciled borders. An upgrade to the concierge floor will get you extra room amenities, as well as free continental breakfast and afternoon hors d'oeuvres.

Wherever you stay, you needn't walk very far to reach your car; all the sleeping floors have direct access, via room key, to the parking garage.

Dining/Entertainment: Resembling the library of a large estate, the Courtyard Lounge sports a fireplace, large-screen TV, and billiards table. Breakfast, lunch, and dinner are served at the Courtyard Cafe, overlooking multilevel waterscapes and profuse greenery; the evening menu is continental with a Texas flair.

Services: 24-hour room service, same-day laundry and dry cleaning, complimentary shuttle within 2-mile radius, including airport and Highland Mall.

Facilities: Business center, outdoor pool, whirlpool, fitness center, sauna, gift shop/boutique.

Red Lion Hotel Austin Airport

6121 N. I-35, Austin, TX 78752. ☎ **800/RED-LION** or 512/323-5466. Fax 512/453-1945. 300 rms. A/C TV TEL. $129 double. Spring value specials available. AE, CB, DC, DISC, MC, V. Free parking.

The West Coast–based Red Lion chain is known for its high-tone properties, and this one is no exception. A low-lit, carpeted lobby is decked out with large chandeliers, potted plants, and classical columns (though the elegant mood is somewhat broken by the presence of a large-screen TV).

Red Lions are also known for their roomy rooms, and the Austin hotel doesn't disappoint in that area, either. They're decorated in deep greens, burgundies, and beiges, with dark-wood furniture and framed oriental prints on the walls; each has an executive-size desk and conference table. One caveat: Corridors are creepily dim, even during the day.

Dining/Entertainment: You'll be taken back to the 1970s at Club Max, a popular disco replete with dance floor and deejay booth. That decade give you the shudders? Just come in for happy hour; there's a copious complimentary hors d'oeuvres buffet for guests Monday to Friday. There are also buffets—though not free—at the lobby's Garden Terrace restaurant; if you don't feel like helping yourself, full à la carte menus are available for breakfast, lunch, and dinner.

Services: Room service, valet laundry/dry cleaning, complimentary airport and Highland Mall shuttle, World Gym privileges for $5.

Facilities: Exercise room, outdoor swimming pool, whirlpool, sauna, airline-ticket desk, gift shop.

MODERATE

A number of chain hotels along the freeway north of the airport fall into the low end of the moderate price range. These include **Drury Inn Highland Mall,** 919 Koenig Lane, 78751 (☎ **800/325-8300** or 512/454-1144); **Drury Inn North,** 6511 N. I-35, 78752 (☎ **800/325-8300** or 512/467-9500); **Hampton Inn North,** 7619 N. I-35, 78752 (☎ **512/452-3300**); and **Holiday Inn Express,** 7622 N. I-35, 78752 (☎ **800/HOLIDAY** or 512/467-1701). All of the above hotels offer a pool. The **Four Points Hotel by ITT Sheraton,** 7800 N. I-35, 78753 (☎ **800/325-3535** or 512/836-8520), and **Holiday Inn Airport,** 6911 N. I-35, 78752 (☎ **800/HOLIDAY** or 512/459-4251), run a little higher in price—though still in the moderate range—but offer more facilities. Both have a pool and on-premises restaurant; the Holiday Inn also has a cocktail lounge, while the Sheraton has an exercise room, Jacuzzi, and guest laundry.

Courtyard by Marriott

5660 N. I-35, Austin, TX 78751. ☎ **800/321-2211** or 512/458-2340. Fax 512/458-8535. 186 rms, 12 suites. A/C TV TEL. $119 double; $129 suite. Weekend and corporate rates available. AE, CB, DC, DISC, MC, V. Free parking.

This recently renovated hotel stands out from many of the drab chain hotels in this area; it has a fresh, clean look, evident as soon as you enter the cheery, plant-filled lobby. Guest rooms are also light and attractive, with dusty rose decor, silk-flower arrangements, and silk ivy twining along the walls. They're comfortable and utilitarian, too: Each has a coffeemaker, iron and ironing board, hair dryer, nice-sized desk, cushy chairs or couch, and phone with an extra-long cord. Refrigerators are available upon request. An outdoor heated pool in the courtyard is surprisingly quiet, considering the hotel's off-highway location. The hotel also offers an exercise room, complimentary guest laundry, and free airport transfers. There's a breakfast buffet and evening cocktails with complimentary snacks (Monday to Saturday), but no full-service restaurant. However, a large number of eateries in the area will deliver directly to your room; the hotel can provide you with their menus.

INEXPENSIVE

The following familiar names along I-35 offer rooms for under $70: **Best Western Chariot Inn,** 7300 N. I-35, 78752 (☎ **800/528-1234** or 512/452-9371; pool, restaurant); **Best Western Atrium North,** 7928 Gessner Dr., 78753 (☎ **800/528-1234** or 512/339-7311; pool); **Days Inn North,** 8210 N. I-35, 78753 (☎ **800/325-2525** or 512/835-2200; pool); **Econo Lodge-Airport,** 6201 Hwy. 290 east, 78723 (☎ **800/553-2666** or 512/458-4759; pool, restaurant); **La Quinta Inn Highland Mall,** 5812 N. I-35, 78751 (☎ **800/531-5900** or 512/459-4381; pool); **La Quinta Inn North,** 7100 N. I-35, 78752 (☎ **800/531-5900** or 512/452-9401; pool); **Motel 6 Airport,** 5330 N. I-35, 78751 (☎ **512/467-9111;** pool); **Motel 6 North,** 9420 N. I-35, 78753 (☎ **512/339-6161;** pool); **Quality Inn Airport,** 909 E. Koenig Lane, 78751 (☎ **800/228-5151** or 512/452-4200; pool, exercise room); **Ramada Inn Airport North,** 9121 N. I-35, 78753 (☎ **800/843-9077** or 512/836-0079; restaurant, cocktail lounge); **Ramada Limited Airport,** 5526 N. I-35, 78751 (☎ **800/880-0709** or 512/451-7001; pool, whirlpool); **Super 8 Motel,** 6000 Middle Fiskville Rd., 78752 (☎ **800/800-8000** or 512/467-8163); and **Travelodge Suites Austin North,** 8300 N. I-35 (☎ **800/255-3050** or 512/835-5050; pool, kitchens, guest laundry).

5 South Austin

EXPENSIVE

Omni Austin Hotel at Southpark

4140 Governor's Row, Austin, TX 78744. ☎ **800/433-2241** (U.S.), 800/631-4200 (Canada), or 512/448-2222. Fax 512/448-4744. 307 rms, 7 suites. A/C TV TEL. $139 double; $89 double on weekends; $239–$250 suite. AE, CB, DC, DISC, MC, V. Free parking.

Rising above the industrial sprawl south of Austin, the Omni Austin primarily attracts a high-tech business trade. But you never know what unbuttoned types might turn up at this executive-style hotel; actor Dennis Hopper, rocker Ted Nugent, *L.A. Law*'s Jill Eikenberry, and baseball's Nolan Ryan have all stayed here at one time or another. Whoever you are, you can expect friendly and efficient service from a staff who actually seem happy you're here.

Sleeping quarters are the picture of updated traditional taste, their dark-wood furnishings complemented by the deep blues, roses, and burgundies of the bedspreads and carpeting; all come with coffeemakers and desks and many offer comfortable ottomans. Open long hours, the Omni Austin's health club stands out in a town where many hotels have only minimal exercise facilities; it includes a lap-length pool

🔘 Family-Friendly Hotels

Four Seasons Austin *(p. 132)*   Tell the reservations clerk that you're traveling with kids when you book a room here and you'll be automatically enrolled in the free amenities program: Age-appropriate snacks—cookies and milk for children under 10, popcorn and soda for those older than 10—along with various toys and games will be waiting for you when you arrive.

Hyatt Regency Austin on Town Lake *(p. 132)*   This hotel no longer has a camp for kids, but there's a play area with toys in the hotel's La Vista restaurant as well as a playscape near the pool. Subject to availability, rooms for children 3 to 12, adjoining adult rooms, are half-price.

Embassy Suites Downtown Austin *(p. 136)*   Large quarters give children enough space to play at Embassy Suites, and the hotel's Town Lake location allows for lots of running around outside; there's also a video-game room on the first floor.

that's half in-, half out-of-doors, a whirlpool, a sauna, and an exercise room with a full array of aerobic equipment and weight machines.

Dining/Entertainment: Everyone looks like they're having fun sitting around the sunken bar in the lobby, chatting animatedly to the backdrop of an automatic piano; in the morning they're tanking up on espresso here. The skylit Onion Creek Grille, the hotel's full-service restaurant, serves breakfast and lunch (including a pasta bar) in a casual setting that turns more formal when the candles and white tablecloths come out at night. Next door, the Republic of Texas sports bar, with a peanut shell-strewn floor, serves burgers, sandwiches, and nachos from 11am until midnight or 1am.

Services: Room service, valet laundry/dry cleaning, complimentary shoe-shine service, complimentary area transportation.

Facilities: Indoor/outdoor pool, exercise room, whirlpool, sauna, basketball court, newsstand/gift shop.

MODERATE

Hawthorne Suites South

4020 I-35 south, Austin, TX 78704. ☎ **800/527-1133** or 512/440-7722. Fax 512/440-4815. 89 standard suites, 30 penthouse suites. A/C TV TEL. $119 standard studio suites. Weekend specials, corporate rates available. Free parking.

If you want to settle in for a spell and get someone else to do your grocery shopping, Hawthorne Suites is a good way to go. Accommodations are set up like small studio apartments, with separate kitchens; penthouse suites offer bedrooms on two levels. Done in your basic southwestern pastels—peaches, teals, and beiges—accommodations are fairly generic, but pleasant enough all the same; many have fireplaces. There are two additional properties in Austin, one near the airport, one in the northwest. Services and facilities include valet laundry/dry cleaning, airport shuttle, business services, free newspaper, pool, hot tub, sports court, and Laundromat. A complimentary continental breakfast buffet is laid out in the lobby every morning; the free drinks and light hors d'oeuvres are restricted to Monday through Thursday (5 to 7pm).

INEXPENSIVE

A number of low-end chains have properties on I-35 south in the vicinity of Ben White Boulevard; more are likely to join them as the date approaches for the opening of the new airport in this area. For the time being, the following are among the places where you can find cut-rate lodgings: **Best Western Seville Plaza Inn,** 4323 S. I-35, 78744 (☎ **800/528-1234** or 512/447-5511); **Exel Inn,** 2711 S. I-35, 78741 (☎ **512/462-9201**); **La Quinta Inn–Ben White,** 4200 S. I-35, 78745 (☎ **800/531-5900** or 512/443-1774); and **Motel 6 South,** 2704 S. I-35, 78741 (☎ **512/444-5882**). All offer a pool; the Best Western also offers a restaurant, cocktail lounge, and coin laundry.

6 Northwest Austin

VERY EXPENSIVE

Renaissance Austin Hotel

9721 Arboretum Blvd., Austin, TX 78759. ☎ **800/HOTELS-1** or 512/343-2626. Fax 512/346-7945. 478 rms, including 43 suites. A/C TV TEL. $175–$185 double; $230–$270 suite. Weekend packages available. AE, CB, DC, DISC, MC, V. Free self-parking; valet parking $8.

Anchoring the upscale Arboretum mall on Austin's northwest side, the luxurious Renaissance (formerly the Stouffer) caters to executives visiting the nearby computer firms. But on weekends, when rates are slashed, even underlings can afford to take advantage of the hotel's many amenities, including an excellent health club and direct access to the myriad allures of the mall (movie theaters among them). Guests buzz around the eateries, elevator banks, and lounges of a nine-story-high atrium lobby, but the space is sufficiently large to avoid any sense of crowding.

Silk wallpaper, lacquer chests, and Japanese-design draperies and bedspreads add an oriental flavor to the oversized guest rooms, all with comfortable sitting areas. Many of the suites offer refrigerators, wet bars, and electric shoe buffers. Rooms on the Club Floor include bathrobes and extended services such as express checkout, a concierge, and free continental breakfast and afternoon hors d'oeuvres. No matter where you stay, tell housekeeping what time you want to get up and a complimentary carafe of coffee and a newspaper will appear at your door immediately following your wake-up call.

Dining/Entertainment: Who knows what wheels of high-tech intrigue have been oiled in the hotel's clubby Lobby Bar, where cocktails are expertly mixed to the tunes of a live piano. Discussions can be fueled all night long at the nearby Pavilion, with a 24-hour menu of deli sandwiches, snacks, and desserts. Another place to chow down in the lobby is the Garden Cafe, offering a full breakfast-and-lunch menu. Upstairs, the northern Italian Trattoria Grande doubles as a power-lunch spot and a romantic evening retreat. Business and leisure travelers alike are drawn to the happy hour and complimentary buffet at Tangerine's nightclub; many linger on to dance to music that spans the decades.

Services: 24-hour room service, same-day laundry Monday to Saturday, valet dry cleaning, complimentary shoe shine.

Facilities: Indoor and outdoor pools, exercise room, whirlpool, sauna, game room, access to jogging-and-walking trail, gift shop.

7 West Austin

VERY EXPENSIVE

✪ Barton Creek Resort

8212 Barton Club Dr., Austin, TX 78735. ☎ **800/336-6158** or 512/329-4000. Fax 512/329-4597. 147 rms, 4 suites. A/C TV TEL. $210 double; $350–$715 suite. Spa and golf packages available. AE, CB, DC, MC, V. Free self- or valet parking.

Sure it's a conference resort, but with three 18-hole championship golf courses, 12 outdoor tennis courts, and a state-of-the-art spa and fitness center, just how much work do you suppose actually gets done here, anyway? If you don't happen to be employed by a company that plans to send you, go ahead and book a room on your own; Barton Creek has put together a variety of golf-and-spa packages designed to draw individual travelers.

This place is gorgeous. Spread out over 4,000 gently rolling and wooded acres in west Austin, the hotel complex includes two main buildings resembling European châteaus. Both host accommodations as large and as high-toned as one might expect, with 10-foot ceilings, custom-made Drexel Heritage pieces, marble-topped sinks and vanities, and—that rarity in Texas—minibars. Some have balconies; rooms in the back offer superb views of the Texas Hill Country.

The resort's three courses were designed by a trinity of golf greats—Tom Fazio, Ben Crenshaw, and Arnold Palmer. The first two greens are on the premises, the latter on the stunning Lakeside satellite facility. Don't worry if your drive is not up to par; a Golf Advantage School can help set it straight. And although aromatherapy is among the featured services, Barton Creek's spa is nothing to sneeze at. You can get buffed, pummeled, and wrapped to your heart's content, or indulge in a 1-hour pedicure.

Dining/Entertainment: Aside from the resort's two clubhouses, the Crenshaw Grille is the most relaxed place to replenish your fluids after a hard day of teeing off; it offers light meals, a large-screen TV, a billiard table, and a liquor list as long as a pool cue. Generous breakfast-and-lunch buffets are laid out on the light-wood Terrace. The Tejas Room, serving southwestern fare (including "smart cuisine" options), is the more informal of the two dinner restaurants; it's open for lunch, too. You'll dine to the dulcet tones of two harps at the ultraposh Palm Court, probably the only place in Austin that requires men to wear jackets; lots of tableside tossing and flambéing add drama to an otherwise staid atmosphere.

Services: Room service, same-day dry cleaning and pressing, complimentary newspaper delivery.

Facilities: Tennis clinic, indoor and outdoor pools, spa, hair salon, indoor track, steam room, Jacuzzi, weight room, aerobics, sauna, sporting clays, Ping-Pong, volleyball, jogging course.

✪ Lake Austin Spa Resort

1705 Quinlan Park Rd., Austin TX 78732. ☎ **800/847-5637**, 800/338-6651, or 512/266-4362. Fax 512/266-1572. 40 rms. AC, TV, TEL. $553.50 per person for 2 nights, double occupancy (2-night minimum). Rates include all meals, classes, and activities; 3-, 4-, and 7-night packages available. AE, MC, V. Free parking.

If you had to create the quintessential Austin spa, it would be laid-back, located on a serene body of water, offer lots of outdoor activities, and feature superhealthy food that lives up to the locals' high culinary standards. You'll sign off on every item of that wish list here. Some spas create their own stress by inspiring style competitions among guests; here single women are more likely than not to bond with each other.

The spa takes advantage of its proximity to the lovely Texas Hill Country by offering such activities as combination canoe/hiking trips or excursions to view the wildflowers. The aromatic ingredients for such soothing spa treatments as the honey mango scrub are grown in the resort's garden, which is also the source for the herbs used at mealtimes. Rooms, in lakeview cottages, are country French cheerful; comforts include soothing egg-crate mattresses.

Services: Spa with wide range of body treatments and massages; classes including cooking, personal care, stress management, fishing.

Greater Austin Accommodations & Dining

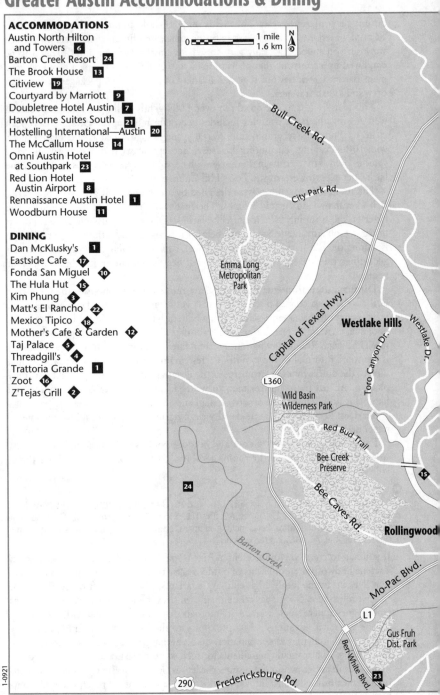

ACCOMMODATIONS
Austin North Hilton
 and Towers **6**
Barton Creek Resort **24**
The Brook House **13**
Citiview **19**
Courtyard by Marriott **9**
Doubletree Hotel Austin **7**
Hawthorne Suites South **21**
Hostelling International—Austin **20**
The McCallum House **14**
Omni Austin Hotel
 at Southpark **23**
Red Lion Hotel
 Austin Airport **8**
Rennaissance Austin Hotel **1**
Woodburn House **11**

DINING
Dan McKlusky's **1**
Eastside Cafe **17**
Fonda San Miguel **10**
The Hula Hut **15**
Kim Phung **3**
Matt's El Rancho **22**
Mexico Tipico **18**
Mother's Cafe & Garden **12**
Taj Palace **5**
Threadgill's **4**
Trattoria Grande **1**
Zoot **16**
Z'Tejas Grill **2**

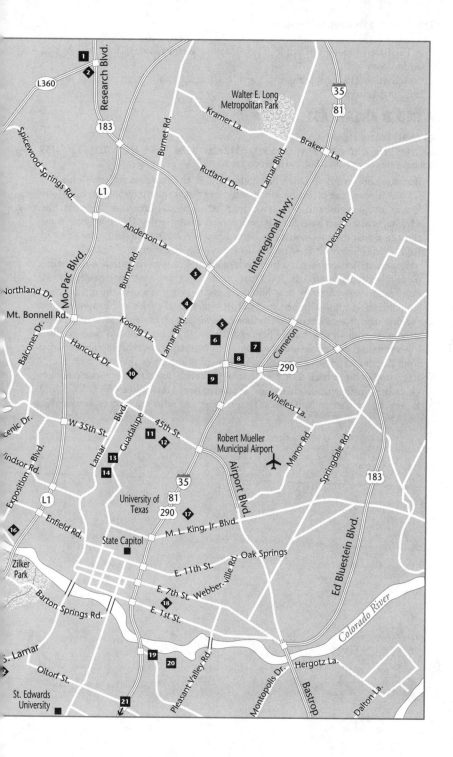

Facilities: Indoor and outdoor pools, sauna, steam room, Jacuzzi, weight and cardio room.

Activities: Hiking, biking, water aerobics, yoga, tai chi, circuit training, toning, canoeing, kayaking.

A BED & BREAKFAST

✪ Lake Travis B&B

4446 Eck Lane, Austin, TX 78734. ☎ and fax **512/266-3386.** 3 rms. A/C TV TEL. $135–$155 double. Rates include breakfast and afternoon snacks. AE, MC, V.

Best described as a destination bed-and-breakfast, this inn gives its guests only two reasons to leave the premises: lunch and dinner. A former travel agent, host Judy Dwyer and her husband, Vic, have designed a bed-and-breakfast that offers the advantages of a resort hotel in an intimate and dramatic setting. The limestone in the cliffs on which their seven-level property sits acts as a filter, rendering the water of Lake Travis directly off their private dock unusually transparent.

Rooms are incredibly romantic: Each has a private lake-view deck and contains plush robes, fluffy comforters, and a marble tub, along with a welcome basket of fruit, Perrier, and nuts. A teddy bear holding a poem—a slightly over-the-top touch—announces that a tray with breakfast will arrive outside the door in the morning. But the best part of a stay here lies outdoors. Guests can play board games on a raised table in the pool, or descend to a floating dock with a kitchen, bar, and sundeck. Fishing, swimming, and sailing are all options. Oh yes, there is one other incentive to stray from paradise: The Slaughter Leftwich Winery is just down the road, within easy staggering distance back after a wine tasting. Services and facilities include nightly chocolate-truffle turndown service, fireplace, pool table, library with VCR and movies, hot tub, steam bath, fitness area; massage and other spa services are available.

In addition, many restaurants, especially those in converted homes, have terrible acoustics; at the height of the dinner rush, you're likely to find yourself shouting to your companion. Make reservations whenever you can, and make them as far in advance as possible; dining out can be a competitive sport in Austin.

In the reviews that follow, dinner at a restaurant in the **Very Expensive** price category will run more than $40 per person, including dessert but not drinks, tax (8%), and tip (around 15%); an **Expensive** restaurant will cost you $25 to $40 per person; meals at **Moderate** restaurants are likely to run $12 to $25; and you can get by at **Inexpensive** places for under $12.

1 Best Bets

- **Best Spot for a Romantic Dinner:** We'll have to agree with the *Austin Chronicle* readers, who voted the wine cellar at **Bertram's,** 1601 Guadalupe St. (☎ 512/476-2743), as the best place to propose. It's got intimate tables for two in a quiet, dimly lit room—and a wine list that'll break down any last vestige of resistance.
- **Best View:** Oh, those multiple decks overlooking Lake Travis and the Texas Hill Country, oh yes, **The Oasis,** 6550 Comanche Trail, near Lake Travis (☎ 512/266-2441).
- **Best Wine List:** The wine list at **Jeffrey's,** 1204 W. Lynn (☎ 512/477-5584), repeatedly cited by *Wine Spectator* magazine as one of the most outstanding in the world, has more than 150 domestic and European items, 20 of which are available by the glass.
- **Best American Cuisine:** With its just-off-the-farm ingredients, gorgeous presentations, and smashing recipes—not to mention a backdrop of our indigenous music, jazz—**Zoot,** 509 Hearn (☎ 512/477-6535), gives American cooking a fresh new name.
- **Best French Cuisine:** Not only is the Gallic food at **Chez Nous,** 510 Neches St. (☎ 512/473-2413), excellent, but you don't have to pay an arm and a leg to enjoy it. Vive la not-so-cher France.
- **Best Italian Cuisine:** It's modern, it's cosmopolitan, it's **Mezzaluna,** 310 Colorado St. (☎ 512/472-6770), where the best of new Italian cooking trends and fine Italian wines find an enthusiastic Austin audience.
- **Best Steakhouse:** Sorry, we know it's a chain, but **Ruth's Chris,** 3010 Guadalupe St. (☎ 512/477-RUTH), has the most succulent meat in town, in part because it's cooked in butter. Of course, the high-cholesterol award might be due this eatery, too.
- **Best Vegetarian Cuisine:** The **West Lynn Cafe,** 1110 West Lynn (☎ 512/482-0950), has the largest selection of that green-good-for-you stuff prepared in the most innovative ways. Vegetarians of all stripes leave here well satisfied.
- **Best Place to Spot Celebrities:** You can expect to see the likes of Quentin Tarantino, Emilio Estevez, and Richard Linklater lounging in one of the back booths of ultrahip **Güero's,** 1412 S. Congress (☎ 512/447-7688), or hugging a bar stool up front; even President Clinton chowed down here in 1996.
- **Best Outdoor Dining:** Those decks overlooking Lake Austin make any fine Sunday afternoon at **Hula Hut,** 3826 Lake Austin Blvd. (☎ 512/476-4852), a supremely mellow experience.
- **Best Brunch:** It's a tie between the Sunday buffet at **Green Pastures,** 811 W. Live Oak Rd. (☎ 512/444-4747), where Austinites have been imbibing milk punch, liberally dosed with bourbon, rum, brandy, ice cream, and nutmeg, for years; and the one at **Fonda San Miguel,** 2330 W. North Loop (☎ 512/459-4121), where the spread runs a delicious Mexican geographical gamut. Both cost around $19.

Austin Dining

13

You might expect to eat well in a town where lawmakers schmooze power brokers, high-tech firms try to lure outside talent, and academics can be tough culinary graders. With more restaurants per capita than any other city in the United States, Austin doesn't disappoint. Chic industrial spaces vie for diners' dollars with gracious 100-year-old houses and plant-filled hippie shacks. Inside, the food ranges from the stylish but reasonably priced cuisine once dubbed "Nouveau Grub" by *Texas Monthly* magazine to tofu burgers, barbecue, and Mexican.

Downtown's West End/Warehouse district, near 4th and Colorado Streets, is the hot new area to eat, with hip new restaurants opening at a rapid rate. The other rapidly expanding restaurant area is the northwest, near the Arboretum, where many popular downtown restaurants are installing branches. This industrial area is not exactly scenic, but those doing business around here are glad for the trend.

At many of the more established downtown restaurants, you can enjoy a meal with a view of Town Lake. Fast-food and chain eateries are concentrated to the north off I-35, near the strip of airport hotels. Barton Springs Road, near Zilker Park; the Enfield area around Mo-Pac; Lake Austin, near the Tom Miller Dam; and the tiny town of Bee Cave to the far west are also popular dining enclaves, but there's good food to be found in almost every part of town. Wherever you eat, think casual. The Palm Court at the Barton Creek Resort aside, there isn't a restaurant in town that requires men to put on a tie and jacket.

Austin isn't as well known as San Antonio for its Mexican restaurants, but there are plenty of places to enjoy authentic Mexican fare on the city's east side. An ¡Olé México! promotion, which includes a Metro Capital bus map to the area and a **Salsa Hotline** (☎ **512/ 499-0611**), is designed to encourage visitors to head over to this undeservedly undervisited area.

It's a good idea to eat at off-hours, either early or late, if the restaurant you're interested in doesn't take reservations (quite a few don't). If you arrive at a popular place at prime time—around 8pm—you may find yourself waiting an hour or more for a table.

2 Restaurants by Cuisine

AMERICAN

Bitter End Bistro & Brewery (Downtown/Capitol, *M*)

Eastside Cafe (University/North Central, *M*)

The Oasis (Far West Side, *M*)

Ruth's Chris (University/North Central, *E*)

Shady Grove (Near West Side, *M*)

Shoreline Grill (Downtown/Capitol, *E*)

Threadgill's (University/North Central, *I*)

ASIAN

Mars (Downtown/Capitol, *M*)

Mongolian Barbecue (Downtown/Capitol, *I*)

BARBECUE

County Line on the Hill (Far West Side, *M*)

The Salt Lick (Far West Side, *M*)

Stubb's Bar-B-Q (Downtown/Capitol, *I*)

CARIBBEAN

Gilligan's (Downtown/Capitol, *M*)

CHINESE

Kim Phung (North/Airport, *I*)

CONTINENTAL

Green Pastures (South Austin, *E*)

DELI

Katz's (Downtown/Capitol, *I*)

FRENCH

Chez Nous (Downtown/Capitol, *M*)

INDIAN

Taj Palace (North/Airport, *M*)

ITALIAN

Basil's (Downtown/Capitol, *M*)

Mezzaluna (Downtown/Capitol, *M*)

JAPANESE

Kyoto (Downtown/Capitol, *E*)

MEDITERRANEAN

Louie's 106 (Downtown/Capitol, *M*)

Mars (Downtown/Capitol, *M*)

MEXICAN

Fonda San Miguel (North/Airport, *M*)

Güero's (South Austin, *I*)

Hula Hut (Near West Side, *M*)

Manuel's (Downtown/Capitol, *M*)

Mexico Tipico (East Austin, *M*)

NEW AMERICAN

Bertram's (Downtown/Capitol, *E*)

Zoot (Near West Side, *M*)

NEW TEXAN

Castle Hill Cafe (Near West Side, *M*)

POLYNESIAN

Hula Hut (Near West Side, *M*)

SEAFOOD

Shoreline Grill (Downtown/Capitol, *E*)

SOUTHERN

Threadgill's (University/North Central, *I*)

SOUTHWESTERN

Granite Cafe (University/North Central, *M*)

Hudson's on the Bend (Far West Side, *VE*)

Jeffrey's (Near West Side, *E*)

Z'Tejas Grill (North/Airport, *M*)

STEAKS

Dan McKlusky's (North/Airport, *E*)

Ruth's Chris (University/North Central, *E*)

Sullivan's (Downtown/Capitol, *E*)

TEX-MEX

Chuy's (Near West Side, *M*)

Las Manitas (Downtown/Capitol, *I*)

Matt's El Rancho (South Austin, *M*)

Rosie's Tamale House (Far West Side, *I*)

Key to abbreviations: *I*=Inexpensive; *M*=Moderate; *E*=Expensive; *VE*=Very Expensive

VEGETARIAN

Mother's Cafe & Garden (University/
  North Central, *I*)
West Lynn Cafe (Near West Side, *I*)

VIETNAMESE

Kim Phung
  (North/Airport, *I*)

3   Downtown / Capitol

EXPENSIVE

Bertram's

1601 Guadalupe St. ☎ **512/476-2743.** Reservations recommended. Main courses $13.95–
$19.95. AE, DC, DISC, MC, V. Sun–Thurs 5–10pm, Fri and Sat 5–11pm. NEW AMERICAN.

At Bertram's, you get a taste of Austin history to accompany your meal. When the
European-style building that housed Bertram's General Merchandise store was raised
in 1862, Apaches still roamed the area; this accounts, in part, for the double-thick
brick construction—and its noise insulation, so rare in Austin eateries. Moreover, one
of the proprietors, Buckner Hightower, is the great-great-great-grandson of Texas
hero Sam Houston. The credentials of the chef, Peter O'Brien, are also stellar: Before coming here, he cooked at Dallas's famed Mansion on Turtle Creek. O'Brien
brings a classical training to his New American menu; starters like vegetable polenta
tart and ostrich satay, and main courses such as sautéed Gulf red snapper or wood-
roasted boar chops, balance culinary excitement with a nice restraint. Only fresh local products are used, and all the pastries and breads are made in-house. A fine wine
list covers a good price range, with lots of domestic bottles.

Kyoto

315 Congress Ave., upstairs. ☎ **512/482-9010.** Reservations accepted for parties of more than
six. Sushi 50¢–$9.50; main courses $9–$26. AE, MC, V. Tues–Fri 11:30am–2pm; Mon–Thurs
6–10:30pm, Fri–Sat 6–11pm. JAPANESE.

Dine at the sushi bar or one of the two small dining rooms of this attractive Japanese restaurant, and you can keep your shoes on; opt for the cushioned and
bamboo-matted tatami room, and you'll have to remove them. Shod or unshod,
you'll enjoy Kyoto's well-prepared specialties, especially the sushi. Along with the
standard tuna, salmon, and mackerel, all flown in fresh, are rarer delicacies such as
fresh and saltwater eel, salmon skin, and sea urchin; the Texas rolls with jalapeños
are a tasty nod to local culture.

There are plenty of choices for those who prefer their food cooked—the soft, pork-
filled gyoza dumplings, for starters. The Seafood Delight platter lays on crab claws,
teriyaki salmon, and shrimp and scallop shish kebabs, among other delights; the beef
teriyaki and deep-fried chicken *karaage* are very satisfying, too. Sweet ginger or green-
tea ice cream make clean, light finishes to the meal.

Shoreline Grill

98 San Jacinto Blvd. ☎ **512/477-3300.** Reservations recommended for lunch and dinner
(patio is first-come, first-served). Main courses $11.95–$25.95. AE, CB, DC, DISC, MC, V. Mon–
Thurs 11am–10pm; Fri 11am–10:30pm; Sat 5–10:30pm, Sun 5–10pm. SEAFOOD/REGIONAL
AMERICAN.

Fish is the prime bait at this toney grill, which looks out over Town Lake and the
Congress Avenue Bridge, but in late spring through early fall, bats run a close second. During this period, when thousands of Mexican free-tailed bats emerge in uni-
son from under the bridge at dusk, patio tables for viewing the phenomenon are at
a premium.

Downtown Austin Dining

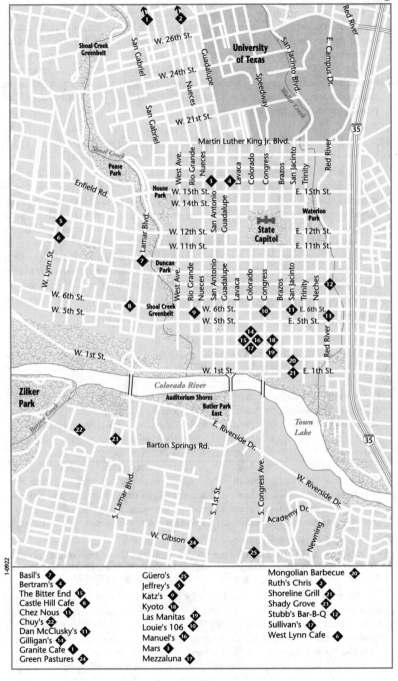

Basil's **7**
Bertram's **4**
The Bitter End **15**
Castle Hill Cafe **8**
Chez Nous **13**
Chuy's **22**
Dan McClusky's **11**
Gilligan's **14**
Granite Cafe **1**
Green Pastures **24**

Güero's **25**
Jeffrey's **5**
Katz's **9**
Kyoto **18**
Las Manitas **19**
Louie's 106 **10**
Manuel's **16**
Mars **3**
Mezzaluna **17**

Mongolian Barbecue **20**
Ruth's Chris **2**
Shoreline Grill **21**
Shady Grove **23**
Stubb's Bar-B-Q **12**
Sullivan's **17**
West Lynn Cafe **6**

When they're not going batty, diners focus on such starters as semolina-crusted oysters or crab cakes with roast pepper relish. Menus change seasonally; in summer, lots of entree-sized salads are offered. Drum, a moist, meaty fish from the Gulf, is worth trying, however it's prepared; the grilled salmon in a dill mustard sauce is excellent, too. Among the options for those who don't like food that has spent its life wet are medallions of pork with a cornmeal crust; grilled prime rib with a shallot and cabernet sauce; or any of the pasta dishes (a vegetarian one is always included). Service is prompt and cheerful.

Sullivan's
300 Colorado St., Suite 200. ☎ **512/495-6504.** Reservations suggested. Main courses $10.95–$23.95. AE, DC, DISC, MC, V. Mon–Sat 5:30–11pm (bar opens at 4:30pm). STEAKS.

Serious business suits rule at Sullivan's, which is rare in supercasual Austin. But, then, the setting and menu seem to demand that kind of attire. This is classic men's club territory, miles of dark cherry wood and cushy black booths and enough beef consumed at each sitting to keep Elsie busy producing offspring for years. (If it feels like Chicago, that could have something to do with the fact that the former president of Morton's Steakhouses is the head honcho here.) Midwestern grain-fed cattle are the stars, whether in bone-in cowboy rib-eye cuts (24 ounces) or diminutive (8-ounce) filet mignon. Accompaniments such as creamed spinach or horseradish mashed potatoes come à la carte, but they're low priced and large enough to serve two (unless you're the cowboy rib-eye type, of course).

MODERATE

Basil's
900 W. 10th St. ☎ **512/477-5576.** Reservations advised, especially on weekends. Main courses $8.25–$16.95. AE, CB, DC, DISC, MC, V. Sun–Thurs 6–10pm, Fri–Sat 6–10:30pm. ITALIAN.

Pretty in pink, with lace curtains, oak trim, and lazily swirling ceiling fans, Basil's dining room is a romantic backdrop for fine northern Italian cuisine. You'll find the traditional dishes here, but turned out with innovative touches. For example, the spaghetti primavera is heaped with vegetables served al dente, not soggy or overcooked, and many of the preparations include colorful carrot or spinach noodles.

Consider starting with a half order of the primavera instead of a salad; it's a delicious way to get your greens in for the day. You might follow it with one of the restaurant's specialty fish dishes: the Pesce Angelica, sautéed with crab and artichokes in a mustard cream sauce, or the scampi in white-wine and garlic sauce. Amy's ice cream, a popular local brand, makes a sweet successor to the meal.

✪ Bitter End Bistro & Brewery
311 Colorado St. ☎ **512/478-2337.** Reservations accepted for five or more only. Pizzas $5.50–$6.50; main courses $9.50–$18.50. AE, DC, DISC, MC, V. Mon–Thurs 11:30am–1am, Fri 11:30am–2am, Sat 2pm–2am, Sun 5pm–midnight. REGIONAL AMERICAN.

The food is as good as the beer at this brew pub—and the beer is very good indeed, especially the smooth, light E-Z Wheat and the toasty Uptown Brown. One of the earliest of the downtown warehouses to have been renovated, the Bitter End is all tall windows, brick walls, and galvanized metal light fixtures. But such touches as a rustic wood bar and large, comfy booths keep the atmosphere from being too austere.

Steamed mussels with pesto, semolina-fried calamari, or a refreshing salade niçoise are all auspicious ways to begin. Perfectly cooked entrees have included wood-roasted trout stuffed with shrimp; grilled beef tenderloin in red wine; and cappellini with summer vegetables in roasted corn sauce. Pizzas, topped with chicken, sweet peppers, and provolone, for example, are deliciously imaginative, too.

There used to be live music on the restaurant's covered patio, but the new B-Side Lounge & Tap Room has taken over that role. From Thursday through Saturday nights, happy-hour (5:30pm) and late-night (9:30pm) bands play swing, blues, and jazz. Additional draws: a cask-conditioned beer tap and a separate cigar room.

ⓢ Chez Nous

510 Neches St. ☎ **512/473-2413.** Reservations only accepted for five or more. Main courses $13.50–$19.50; menu du jour $16.50. AE, CB, DC, MC, V. Tues–Fri 11:45am–2pm; Tues–Sun 6–10:30pm. FRENCH.

Just around the corner from the Sixth Street action, this intimate little restaurant feels as far away as Paris; lace curtains, fresh flowers in anisette bottles, and Folies-Bergère posters create a casual Left-Bank atmosphere. Since the early 1980s, Chez Nous's friendly French owners have been offering Austin fine bistro fare.

Items on the à la carte dinner menu are reasonably priced, but the real bargain is the Menu du Jour: $16.50 gets you a choice of soup, salad, or pâté; one of three designated entrees; and crème caramel, chocolate mousse, or Brie for dessert. The main courses might include an excellent *poisson poivre vert* (fresh fish of the day with a green-peppercorn sauce) or a simple but delicious roast chicken. Lunch is even more of a steal, with its $7.50 daily special and crêpes that run no higher than $5.50. Everything from the pâtés to the profiteroles (puff pastry filled with ice cream and dripping with warm chocolate) is made on the premises.

Gilligan's

407 Colorado St. ☎ **512/474-7474.** Reservations recommended on weekends. Main courses $9.95–$19.95. AE, DC, DISC, MC, V. Mon–Fri 11:15am–2pm; Mon–Thurs 5–10pm, Fri–Sat 5–11pm, Sun 5:30–9:30pm. CARIBBEAN.

If you like your seafood with a kick, get yourself to Gilligan's, located in one of the converted buildings in the warehouse district. The building started out as a restaurant more than 100 years ago and spent time as a garage, telephone supply house, and disco—among other things. You might start with the crispy conch fritters or three-alarm seafood gumbo and move on from there to, say, the Jamaican grilled yellowfin or macademia-crusted mahimahi. There's also a selection of Caribbean-style nonfish dishes, including wild boar potstickers and Jamaican jerk chicken. Don't be misled by the name: This is no collegiate meet mart, but a skylit, sophisticated place, with colorful tropical murals and a nightly piano player—in fact, this may be the only restaurant in the area quiet enough to hear the music.

Louie's 106

106 E. Sixth St. ☎ **512/476-1997.** Reservations recommended for lunch, accepted only for six or more at dinner. Tapas $1.50–$5; main courses $9.75–$17.50. AE, CB, DC, DISC, MC, V. Mon–Fri 11:15am–5pm; Mon–Thurs 5–10:30pm, Fri–Sat 5–11pm, Sun 5:30–10pm. MEDITERRANEAN.

Looking for a place to cut a serious deal? Louie's has all the requisites: a location in the historic Littlefield office building, the toney atmosphere of a private club, even a separate cigar room for puffing expensive stogies. But this is not to suggest it doesn't double as a pleasure palace, especially on the weekends when a classical guitarist entertains waiting diners in the glossy outside corridor.

You can enjoy Louie's updated versions of the traditional Spanish tapas—for example, portabello mushroom potato blini or beef carpaccio with capers—at the bar of the large, high-ceilinged dining room, or at one of the downstairs or mezzanine-level tables; larger portions of similar appetizers are also available on the regular lunch and dinner menus. A classic paella Valenciana (saffron rice with seafood and sausage) makes a good, hearty entree, as does the veal chop with garlic mashed potatoes. Portions are more substantial than the prices.

Manuel's

310 Congress Ave. ☎ 512/472-7555. Reservations not accepted. Main courses $5.95–$14.50. AE, DC, MC, V. Daily 11am–10:30pm (half-price appetizers available Fri and Sat 10:30pm–midnight). MEXICAN.

The setting—black-leather booths, floor-to-ceiling mirrors, a neon-backed bar—says upscale, but the prices and the atmosphere both say have a good time. Downtown executives are among the many who come to relax during Manuel's happy hour (daily 4 to 7pm), animatedly downing half-price hors d'oeuvres to a salsa music backdrop.

The food, which includes dishes from the interior of Mexico, is a creative cut above many Tex-Mex places. You can get well-prepared versions of the standards, but Manuel's also offers unusual variations on the theme—blue-crab nachos, for example, or a chicken with cheese and piquant mole appetizer. The excellent *enchiladas banderas* come topped with the colors of the Mexican flag: a green tomatillo *verde* sauce; a white sour-creamy *suiza;* and a red *adobada,* made with ancho chiles. At a sizzling Sunday Jazz Brunch, eggs with venison chorizo or spicy *chili con queso* (cheese and peppers) are accompanied by live music.

✪ Mars

1610 San Antonio St. ☎ **512/472-3901.** Reservations advisable on weekends. Main courses $9.50–$16.95; bistro menu (noodle and rice dishes) $7.95–$10.25. AE, DISC, MC, V. Mon–Thurs 5:30–10:30pm, Fri–Sat 5:30–11pm, Sun 5:30–10pm. MEDITERRANEAN/ASIAN.

In Austin's growing constellation of interesting restaurants, Mars is shining increasingly bright. A new owner has retained the best of a proven menu and enhanced it with innovations from chef James Fischer, who picked up some interesting culinary influences when he lived in Cairo. An eclectic array of starters includes beautifully grilled portabello mushrooms with parmesan and balsamic vinegar; order the assortment and you'll get potstickers, ribs, a spring roll, hummus, and baba ganoush. The entree of tandoori lamb loin medallions with pomegranate sauce comes out tender and succulent, while the shrimp and green Thai curry is not blanded down too much for an American audience. A standout among the desserts is the chocolate pâté, not overly rich and topped with vanilla crème anglaise and raspberries. The dining room is a bit dark for some tastes, with deep reddish-rust walls that allude to you-know-what planet and a ceiling resembling the night sky, but the food more than compensates for any trouble you might have seeing the menu.

Mezzaluna

310 Colorado St. ☎ **512/472-6770.** No reservations. Pasta $9–$14.50; main courses $13–$18.50. AE, DC, DISC, MC, V. Mon–Fri 11:30–midnight, Sat 5pm–midnight, Sun 6–10pm. ITALIAN.

One of the first restaurants to open in the now chic warehouse district, Mezzaluna is still ahead of the pack with its contemporary Italian menu. Pizzas emerge from the wood-fired oven topped with such items as radicchio, calamata olives, and roasted squash; and the house lasagne is layered with smoked chicken and bell peppers along with the more conventional spinach, ricotta, and mozzarella. As a main dish, the salmon Don Diego, grilled with basil and red chili, is especially recommended. The restaurant offers exclusive Italian wines by the glass to introduce diners to interesting bottles. At a poured concrete bar in the center of the large, multilevel room, black-clad young hipsters shout pickup lines at each other; most of the people below are too busy attending to their food to mind.

INEXPENSIVE

Katz's

618 W. Sixth St. ☎ **512/472-2037.** Reservations not accepted downstairs, recommended on weekends at Top of the Marc. Sandwiches $3.95–$8.25; main courses $5.95–$8.95. AE, DC, DISC, MC, V. Downstairs, 24 hours; Top of the Marc, Tues–Sat 5pm–2am. DELI.

If it doesn't quite achieve New York deli status—for one thing, the staff is not nearly rude enough—Katz's is as close as you'll come in Austin. The matzoh balls are as light and the cheesecake as dense as they're supposed to be, and the corned-beef sandwiches come in the requisite gargantuan portions. Offering the same menu, the popular Top of the Marc club upstairs gives this deli the jump on its East Coast rivals in at least one significant aspect: Where else can you enjoy good jazz *and* good blueberry blintzes?

Las Manitas

211 Congress Ave. ☎ **512/472-9357.** Reservations not accepted. Breakfast $3.25–$5.50; lunch $3.50–$6.50. AE, DISC, MC, V. Mon–Fri 7:30am–4pm, Sat–Sun 7am–2:30pm. TEX-MEX.

It's hard to leave town without at least hearing about this funky Mexican diner, decked out with local artwork and colorful tables and chairs. A rack of alternative newspapers at the door sets the political tone, but businesspeople and slackers alike pile into this small place for breakfasts of *migas con queso* (eggs scrambled with corn tortillas, white cheese, and ranchero sauce) or *chilaquiles verdes* (tortilla strips topped with green tomatillo sauce, Jack cheese, and onions). Not all the staff of this family-owned and -operated cafe speak English, but don't worry; if you don't get exactly what you like, you'll like whatever you get.

Mongolian Barbecue

117 San Jacinto Blvd. ☎ **512/476-3938.** Reservations accepted for parties of 10 or more only. Lunch $5; dinner $7. AE, DISC, MC, V. Mon–Fri 11am–3pm, Sat noon–3pm; Mon–Thurs and Sun 5–9:30pm, Fri–Sat 5–10:30pm. ASIAN.

Across the street from the Convention Center, this all-you-can-eat Asian stir-fry buffet is a great place to grab a quick, delicious lunch or a casual dinner. Equipped with a bowl, you'll work your way through a long bar containing a wealth of uncooked vegetables and meats—bell peppers, zucchini, mushrooms, beef, pork, and chicken—to a section displaying such sauces and ingredients as soy, ginger, garlic, and sesame; recipes are posted to guide those seeking traditional tastes like sweet-and-sour or hot garlic Szechuan. Once you've made your final selections, hand them to the nimble chef, who presides over a huge grill. Although he may cook up to 10 dishes at once, he somehow manages to get all of them right all of the time.

✪ Stubb's Bar-B-Q

801 Red River. ☎ **512/480-8341.** Reservations accepted before 6:30pm. Barbecue $5.25–$7.50; main courses $5.50–$11.95. AE, DISC, MC, V. Mon–Sat 11am–11pm, Sun 11am–10pm; live music Mon–Sat until 2am. BARBECUE.

Though C. B. Stubblefield, the Lubbock-based patron saint of Texas barbecue, has gone on to that big smoker in the sky, his vision lives on at this new Austin restaurant, which has become an instant classic. An ornate bar presides over each of the two large levels, which are otherwise basically brick and rough wood; on the first floor, a portrait of Stubbs presides over a lounge with overstuffed couches and chairs. Stubbs was a strong supporter of Texas musicians, so it is fitting that this has become one of the best live-music venues in town.

The food is "big and simple" as Stubbs once put it, not to mention delicious. Barbecued brisket, sausage, chicken, ribs, and turkey come with traditional sides like potato salads and greens. Other options run the gamut from salad to chicken-fried steak. And how can you not love a place that offers Ding Dongs and Twinkies for dessert? (Fresh-baked pies are available too.)

4 Near West Side

EXPENSIVE

✪ Jeffrey's

1204 W. Lynn. ☎ **512/477-5584.** Reservations advised. Main courses $19.75–$27.75; bistro menu $15.75–$18.75. AE, CB, DC, DISC, MC, V. Mon–Thurs 6–10pm, Fri–Sat 6–10:30pm. Closed Sun. SOUTHWESTERN.

David Garrido, Jeffrey's boyish executive chef, exudes culinary passion; you might catch him excitedly explaining to an admiring patron how he went out at dawn to buy just the right mushrooms for one of his daily specials. While his innovative Texas fare is dazzling, the setting for his performance is low-key; people walk into this three-room former storefront, in the artsy Clarksville neighborhood, wearing anything from a T-shirt to a tux.

You can't tell what'll turn up on the ever-changing menu, but you can depend on flavors and textures to dance wildly together without falling down. Among the appetizers I tried were a wonderful goose liver pâté served with mustard and blueberries and crispy oysters topped with a five-alarm honey garlic butter. Elk loin with mango sauce is a tempting recent addition to the entree list. Jeffrey's lower-priced bistro menu might include such lighter and smaller entrees as shrimp salad with baby artichokes. Desserts such as Chocolate Intemperance live up to their diet-destroying promise.

MODERATE

Castle Hill Cafe

1101 W. Fifth St. ☎ **512/476-0728.** Reservations not accepted. Main courses $9–$15. AE, MC, V. Mon–Fri 11am–2:30pm; Mon–Sat 6–10pm. NEW TEXAN.

Surrounded on three sides by trees, Castle Hill gives the illusion of being tucked away somewhere remote, but it's just a block beyond downtown's western border, near two major thoroughfares. With its dark-wood tables, rich southwestern tones, and abundant Oaxacan folk art, this favored yuppie haunt balances comfort and creativity.

A panoply of exciting flavors emerges from the kitchen, a different array for each season. The empañadas filled with curried lamb and raisins and topped with a cilantro yogurt sauce make a superb appetizer, perhaps followed by one of the entree salads such as the Szechuan hacked chicken with cream cheese–stuffed dumplings. Imaginatively conceived and beautifully arranged dinners include beef tenderloin marinated in herbs and served with garlic whipped potatoes; and roasted duck enchiladas with goat cheese, tomatillos, and wild mushrooms.

Hula Hut

3826 Lake Austin Blvd. ☎ **512/476-4852.** Reservations not accepted. Main courses $7–$17. AE, DC, DISC, MC, V. Sun–Thurs 11am–11pm, Fri–Sat 11am–midnight. MEXICAN/POLYNESIAN.

The Hula Hut has perfected the technique of cross-Polynesation: It's mixed Mexican and Pacific Island cooking, added decks reaching out over Lake Austin, and arrived at the formula for fun. This place is especially cheerful if you come with a group ready to experiment with different platters. The Huli Huli Luau Mexicano includes generous portions of smoked ribs, grilled chicken nachos, chicken tacos, garlic roasted potatoes, and an array of delicious sauces such as ranch with jalapeños. The Pescado Platter offers an array of fresh fish and garlic roasted potatoes. At $19.95 and $21.95, respectively, these platters easily satisfy two for lunch or dinner; four could—and often do—enjoy them as appetizers.

Shady Grove

1624 Barton Springs Rd. ☎ **512/474-9991.** Reservations taken weekends only, as needed. Main courses $7–$10. AE, DC, DISC, MC, V. Sun–Thurs 11am–10pm, Fri–Sat 11am–11pm. TEX-AMERICAN.

If your idea of comfort food involves chile peppers, don't pass up Shady Grove. The inside dining area, with its Texas kitsch roadhouse decor and cushy booths, is plenty comfortable, but most people head for the large, tree-shaded patio when they can (it hosts a good "unplugged" music series on Thursday night from May to October). After a day of fresh air at nearby Barton Springs, Freddie's Airstream chili, cooked with 10 different peppers, might be just the thing. All the burgers are made with high-grade ground sirloin, and if you've never had a frito pie (chili in a corn-chip bowl), this is a good place to try one. Large salads—among them, noodles with snow peas—or the Hippie sandwich (grilled eggplant, veggies, and cheese) will satisfy less hearty appetites.

✪ Zoot

509 Hearn. ☎ **512/477-6535.** Reservations advised, especially on weekends. Main courses $12.95–$21.95. AE, CB, DC, DISC, MC, V. Sun–Thurs 5:30–10:30pm, Fri–Sat 5:30–11pm, Sun brunch 11am–2pm. NEW AMERICAN.

Texas chauvinism, eco-consciousness, and 1990s belt tightening have come together in a number of dining rooms around the state to produce a cuisine that's delicious, fresh, and affordable. Zoot is a prime example of this propitious trend. This cozy Enfield restaurant, set in a 1920s cottage, uses only organic vegetables, and designs its dishes around ingredients grown in the area.

There's not a leaf of iceberg lettuce in the house salad, a delightful mix of mustard greens, arugula, and radicchio. And the wonderful deep-fried oysters, served on cellophane noodles as an appetizer, come straight from the Gulf. The menu changes seasonally, but you'll be sure to encounter roast chicken with smoked corn custard, and grilled beef tenderloin among the entrees; regulars complained too loudly when those items were rotated off. Vegetarians will be thrilled to find something to eat besides pasta—perhaps a vegetable napoleon with wild mushrooms, whipped sweet potatoes, and carrots. Zoot also appeals to other senses besides taste: Presentations are gorgeous and soft jazz plays in the background.

INEXPENSIVE

Chuy's

1728 Barton Springs Rd. ☎ **512/474-4452.** Reservations accepted for parties over 12 for weekday lunch only. Main courses $5.75–$7.95. AE, CB, DC, DISC, MC, V. Sun–Thurs 11am–10:30pm, Fri–Sat 11am–midnight. TEX-MEX.

One of the row of low-priced, friendly restaurants that line Barton Springs Road just east of Zilker Park, Chuy's stands out for its determinedly wacky decor—hubcaps

---

🏠 Family-Friendly Restaurants

Chuy's *(p. 161)*   Teens and aspiring teens will enjoy this colorful, inexpensive restaurant with its cool T-shirts, Elvis kitsch, and green iguanas crawling up the walls.

Threadgill's *(p. 163)*   This bustling, cheerful diner has an impressive music history—surely you've told your kids about Janis Joplin?—and an inexpensive ($2.45 to $3.45) "miniature" menu for ages 12 and under.

Mongolian Barbecue *(p. 159)*   Children are bound to find something they like among the many mix-and-match ingredients here. They'll also be fascinated by the whirling dervish of a chef. Best yet, kids' dinners cost only $5.25.

---

lining the ceiling, Elvis memorabilia galore—and its sauce-smothered Tex-Mex fare. You're not likely to leave hungry after scarfing specials such as southwestern enchiladas, piled high with smoked chicken and topped with a fried egg; or a huge sopaipilla stuffed with grilled sirloin, among other things. The margaritas are good and the T-shirts, designed by local artists, even better.

There's another Chuy's in north Austin, 10520 N. Lamar Blvd. (☎ **512/836-3218**).

West Lynn Cafe

1110 West Lynn. ☎ **512/482-0950.** Reservations accepted for dinner only. Main courses $5.50–$8.95. AE, DC, DISC, MC, V. Mon–Thurs 11:30am–10pm, Fri 11:30am–10:30pm, Sat 11am–10:30pm, Sunday 11am–9:30pm. VEGETARIAN.

Although this sunny, soaring-ceiling restaurant, part homey, part techo-chic, is totally vegetarian, it doesn't attract only a Birckenstocks-with-socks crowd. Health-conscious sophisticates and artsy neighborhood locals also come to enjoy well-prepared dishes that range over the world's cuisine. You can enjoy everything from Indonesian curried tofu and Szechuan stir-fry to pesto primavera, mushroom stroganoff, spanikopita, and guacamole enchiladas. Some dishes are rich, but many nondairy, low-cholesterol selections are highlighted, too. Soft background jazz helps create a soothing atmosphere.

5 University / North Central

EXPENSIVE

Ruth's Chris

3010 Guadalupe St. ☎ **512/477-RUTH.** Reservations recommended. Main courses $17.95–$30. AE, CB, DC, MC, V. Mon–Thurs 5:30–10:30pm, Fri–Sat 5:30–11pm, Sun 5:30–10pm. STEAKS/AMERICAN.

It's been said that dressing up in Austin means ironing creases in your jeans, and that the town's upscale restaurants serve chicken-fried chateaubriand. The steaks at Ruth's Chris are sizzled in butter, not batter; many of the diners show up in suits; and there are even white cloths on the tables. Still, with its wooden booths and wide-screen TV in back, this could well be the most casual of Ruth Fartel's franchises. Housed in a former stagecoach stop that dates back more than 100 years, it could also be one of the most fitting settings for consuming large quantities of beef.

If the food here is expensive—mainly because everything, including vegetables, is à la carte—the quality is consistently high. Thick cuts of New York strip, filet, rib eye, and porterhouse steaks are unwaveringly tender, the taste seared in by extra-high cooking temperatures. Service is superb, but, as you might have surmised, not stiflingly formal.

MODERATE

Eastside Cafe

2113 Manor Rd. ☎ **512/476-5858.** Reservations advised. Main courses $5.50–$10.95. AE, CB, DC, DISC, MC, V. Mon–Thurs 11am–10pm, Sat 10am–11pm, Sun 10am–10pm (brunch Sat–Sun 10am–3pm). AMERICAN.

Located in a nondescript neighborhood not far from the airport, the Eastside Cafe is nonetheless popular with locals; it's just east of the university and northeast of the capitol. Diners enjoy eating on a tree-shaded patio or in one of a series of cheery, intimate rooms in a classic turn-of-the-century bungalow.

This restaurant gears its menu to the size of its patrons' appetites; you can get half orders of all the pasta dishes, including an excellent artichoke manicotti, and of some salads, such as the mixed field greens topped with goat cheese. The main course emphasis is on light meats and fish—sesame-breaded catfish, say, or szechuan chicken. Each morning, the gardener informs the head chef which of the vegetables in the restaurant's large organic garden are ready to be pulled up into service. The restaurant's new store carries gardening tools and restaurant cookware.

Granite Cafe

2905 San Gabriel St. ☎ **512/472-6483.** Reservations recommended on weekends. Main courses $9–$19. AE, CB, DC, DISC, MC, V. Mon–Fri 11:30am–10pm, Sat–Sun 11:30am–11pm (brunch served instead of lunch on weekends, 11am–3pm). SOUTHWESTERN.

With its dusty tones, diffused lighting, and global-consciousness-with-money folk art, the Granite Cafe brings the sophistication—and high noise level—of downtown up to the west U.T. campus area. Warm sourdough bread with garlic herb butter arrives immediately after you're seated. The stylish menu changes daily, but you'll always find creative appetizers like soft-shell crab with banana chutney and black-bean salad. An array of wood oven–baked pizzas play variations on classic topping themes; one comes with bacon, onions, red peppers, pine nuts, and sardo cheese. If you're lucky, tomato-basil fondue with grilled shrimp over cappellini or wood-grilled gulf snapper served on basmati rice might appear among the entrees.

INEXPENSIVE

Mother's Cafe & Garden

4215 Duval St. ☎ **512/451-3994.** Reservations taken for parties of six or more only. Soups and salads $2.50–$4.95; main courses $4.25–$7.50. CB, DC, DISC, MC, V. Mon–Fri 11:15am–10pm, Sat–Sun 10am–10pm. VEGETARIAN.

If you want to treat your body right, but don't want to risk a revolt from your taste buds, head over to Mother's. The Save the Earth crowd that frequents this Hyde Park eatery enjoys an international array of veggie dishes, but the inspiration for most of the mainstays comes from south of the border: You'll find classic chili rellenos, burritos, and nachos, along with the more unusual tofu enchiladas. A three-cheese spinach lasagna is especially popular. The tropical shack-style back garden is appealing; the young staff is friendly, but not nauseatingly so; and there's a good, inexpensive selection of local beers and wines.

⑤ Threadgill's

6416 N. Lamar Blvd. ☎ **512/451-5440.** Reservations not accepted. Sandwiches and specials $3.95–$5.45; main courses $4.95–$16.95. MC, V. Daily 11am–10pm. AMERICAN/SOUTHERN.

When Kenneth Threadgill got Travis County's first legal liquor license after the repeal of Prohibition in 1933, he turned his Gulf gas station into a club. His

Wednesday night hootenannies became legendary in the 1960s, with performers like Janis Joplin turning up regularly. The southern-style diner added on in 1980 continues in the tradition of the adjoining club—it's down-home casual and good. If Threadgill's is famous for its $4.95 blue-plate specials and its huge chicken-fried steaks, it's also renowned for its vegetables: You can get jalapeño jambalaya, squash casserole, garlic cheese grits, and Cajun Italian eggplant in combination plates or as sides to the other dishes (seconds are free).

Eddie Wilson, the current owner of Threadgill's, was the founder of the now defunct Armadillo World Headquarters, Austin's most famous music venue—which is why, when he opened a downtown branch in October 1996, he called it Threadgill's World Headquarters, 301 West Riverside (☎ 512/472-9304). Right next door to the old Armadillo, it's filled with music memorabilia from the club. Although it has the same menu, this Threadgill's is larger than the original one and has a state-of-the-art sound system; there's music here on Monday night, uptown on Wednesday.

6 South Austin

EXPENSIVE

Green Pastures

811 W. Live Oak Rd. ☎ **512/444-4747.** Reservations advised for lunch and dinner Thurs.-Sat. Main courses $12-$25. AE, DC, DISC, MC, V. Daily 11am–2pm and 6–10pm. CONTINENTAL.

Peacocks strut their stuff among the 225 live oaks surrounding this mansion, which was built in 1894 and has remained in the hands of the same renowned Austin family since 1916; the current owner's mother turned it into a restaurant in 1945. You'll find southern comfort in the gracious setting and polite service, as well as in a continental menu that nods only gently toward current culinary trends. The lunch crowd may be a bit blue haired, but nighttime draws in Austinites of all stripes; everyone from Van Cliburn to James Michener has dined here.

The creamy lobster crêpes or baked Brie in puff pastry go far to enhance the feeling of well-being brought on by the lovely surroundings. Although the menu changes seasonally, you'll always find two popular dishes on it: duck Texana, wrapped in bacon and served with black-currant sauce, and snapper Florentine, topped with hollandaise and shrimp. The Texas pecan ball (vanilla ice cream rolled in nuts and dripping fudge) is enough to weaken the strongest resolve, but you may want to go for baroque—flaming bananas Foster for two.

MODERATE

Matt's El Rancho

2613 S. Lamar Blvd. ☎ **512/462-9333.** Reservations not accepted after 5pm on weekends, except for large groups. Main courses $6-$9. AE, CB, DC, DISC, MC, V. Mon, Wed–Thurs, and Sun 11am–10pm; Fri–Sat 11am–11pm. Closed Tues. TEX-MEX.

Lyndon Johnson hadn't been serving in the U.S. Senate very long when Matt's El Rancho first opened its doors. Although owner Matt Martinez outlived LBJ and other early customers, plenty of his original patrons followed when he moved his restaurant south of downtown in 1986. They came not out of habit, but because Matt has been dishing up consistently good food since 1952.

Some of the items show the regulars' influence; you can thank former land commissioner Bob Armstrong for the tasty cheese, guacamole, and spiced-meat dip that bears his name. Chile rellenos and grilled shrimp seasoned with garlic and soy are among everyone's perennial favorites. Although the place can seat almost 500, you might still have to wait for an hour on weekend nights. Just sit out on the terrace, sip a fresh-lime margarita, and chill.

INEXPENSIVE

✪ Güero's

1412 S. Congress. ☎ **512/447-7688.** Reservations not accepted. Main courses $5.75–$9.95. AE, DC, DISC, MC, V. Mon–Fri 7am–10pm, Sat–Sun 8am–10pm. MEXICAN.

This sprawling converted feed store has become the center of the newly hip South Austin scene, but it's fine for families, too; there's a children's plate for the under-12 set. And although menu listings are stylishly tongue-in-cheek—the entry for one pork dish describes it as being the same as the beef version "except piggish"—the food is seriously good. You can enjoy health-conscious versions of Tex-Mex standards as well as of some dishes from the interior of Mexico: snapper *à la veracruzano* (with tomatoes, green olives, and jalapeños), say, or Michoacán-style tamales. Lots of plates come topped with cheese, guacamole, and sour cream, but you can also get delicious, low-fat entrees like the chicken *al carbon* (breast meat grilled in achiote, a Yucatán spice), served with whole-wheat tortillas and nonrefried beans. There's live music on Sunday afternoon.

7 East Austin

MODERATE

Mexico Tipico

1707 E. Sixth St. ☎ **512/472-3222.** Reservations accepted. Main courses $6–$14. AE, CB, DC, MC, V. Mon–Thurs 8am–3pm, Fri–Sun 8am–10pm. MEXICAN.

Owned by the friendly Valera family, Mexico Tipico is among the most popular of the informal restaurants dotting the residential neighborhood east of I-35, the unofficial dividing line between Anglo and Hispanic Austin. Diners from both sides of the divide pile into the red leather booths of this large, cheerful room for authentic versions of such specialties as *caldo,* hearty beef soup heaped with potatoes and vegetables, or *rajas con queso,* a dip of poblano peppers, ham, onions, and cheese served with hot corn tortillas. The *cabrito* (kid) is out of this world. Huge inexpensive margaritas in cactus-shaped glasses will complement whatever you order. A $5.95 all-you-can-eat buffet is served Monday through Friday from 11am to 3pm, and there's live Latin-beat entertainment on Friday and Saturday evening—flamenco, conjunto, and mariachi.

8 North / Airport

EXPENSIVE

Dan McKlusky's

10,000 Research Blvd. (Arboretum). ☎ **512/346-0780.** Reservations recommended. Main courses $10.75–$29.95. AE, DC, DISC, MC, V. Mon–Thurs 11:15am–2pm and 5–10pm; Fri 11:15am–2pm and 5–11pm; Sat noon–11pm; Sun noon–9pm. Jazz bar Thurs, Fri, and Sat nights, usually stays open until around 1am. STEAKS.

A bastion of traditionalism in a town fast turning California trendy, Dan McKlusky's offers sanctuary to folks tempted to say "gesundheit" when they hear the word "achiote." Good, old-fashioned surf and turf—especially turf—draws people into these dimly lit dining rooms with exposed-brick walls.

An on-premises butcher cuts fresh, corn-fed beef to your specifications, so you can adjust the size and price of your steak to your appetite; you can also order as many chops or chicken breasts as you like, or customize an entire dinner, combining six fried shrimp, say, with an eight-ounce rib eye. A jazz bar on Friday, Saturday, and Sunday nights stays open until 1am.

The original Dan McKlusky's is downtown (301 E. Sixth St. ☎ **512/473-8924**).

MODERATE

✪ Fonda San Miguel

2330 W. North Loop. ☎ **512/459-4121.** Reservations advised. Main courses $9.95–$17.95. AE, CB, DC, DISC, MC, V. Sun–Thurs 5:30–9:30pm, Fri–Sat 5:30–10:30pm; Sun brunch 11:30am–2pm. MEXICAN REGIONAL.

Like American Southwest chefs who look to Native American staples such as blue corn for inspiration, Mexico City chefs have had their own back-to-the-roots movement, which might involve including ancient Aztec ingredients in their dishes. Such trends are carefully tracked and artfully translated by Ricardo Muñoz at Fonda San Miguel, the best place in town for Mexican regional cuisine. You'll discover that food from the northern Mexico state of Sonora, on which most Tex-Mex fare is based, represents Mexico in the same way that hearty midwestern cooking represents the United States—in a very limited fashion.

The huge dining room, with its carved wooden doors, colorful paintings, and live ficus tree, is a gorgeous backdrop to such appetizers as Veracruz-style ceviche or quesadillas with *huitlacoche,* a corn fungus as rare as French truffles. *Conchinita pibil,* pork baked in banana leaves, is one of the Yucatán offerings; hearty appetites will also enjoy the grilled beef tenderloin from the Tampico region. Familiar northern Mexican fare, extremely well prepared, is offered, too.

Taj Palace

6700 Middle Fiskville Rd. ☎ **512/452-9959.** Reservations advised on weekends. Main courses $5.95–$11.95; all-you-can-eat lunch buffet Mon–Fri $6.50, Sat–Sun $7.95; Mon night dinner buffet $9.95. AE, DC, DISC, MC, V. Mon–Fri 11am–2pm, Sat–Sun 11:30am–2:30pm; Sun–Thurs 5:30–10pm, Fri–Sat 5:30–10:30pm. INDIAN.

In a strip center off I-35, just north of Highland Mall, statues of Ganesh, Krishna, and other Hindu deities preside over dining rooms decorated with colorful masks and Japoori-style wall hangings. Order a bread basket to try such treats as naan or *aloo paratha,* baked in a tandoor oven. The oven also produces such low-fat specialties as fish *tikka,* which is skewered into kabobs. Dishes like *malai kofta,* cheese and vegetable dumplings in a cream and almond sauce, or *murg tikka makhni,* chicken in an herb and tomato sauce with a bit of butter, are richly delicious. This restaurant has another location in south Austin, Brodie Oaks Center, 4141 Capital of Texas Hwy. (☎ 512/447-1997).

Z'Tejas Grill

9400 Arboretum Blvd. ☎ **512/346-3506.** Reservations recommended. Main courses $7.95–$15.95. AE, DC, DISC, MC, V. Mon–Fri 11am–11pm, Sat 10am–midnight, Sun 10am–10pm. SOUTHWESTERN.

An offshoot of a popular downtown eatery, this northwest branch improves a bit on the original. Not that the food is different here—both share a terrifically zippy Southwest menu—but the room is a lot more open, with a soaring ceiling, sophisticated Santa Fe–style decor, and a fireplace. Fish tacos served with avocado vinaigrette dipping sauce make a great starter, and, if you see it on a specials menu, go for the smoked chile rellenos, made with apricots and goat cheese. As an entree, the blackened Voodoo Tuna is as captivating as its name suggests; the Navajo Taco—

made with a variety of exotic but tasty ingredients (such as crunchy fried spinach) heaped atop Indian herb bread—is well worth a try, too.

INEXPENSIVE

ⓢ Kim Phung

7601 N. Lamar Blvd., No. 1. ☎ **512/451-2464.** Reservations not accepted. Lunch special $3.25–$4.25; main courses $4.25–$8.50. DISC, MC, V. Mon–Thurs 10:30am–9pm, Fri–Sun 10:30am–10pm. VIETNAMESE/CHINESE.

The rest of Austin has caught on to what the Asian community to the north has known for some time: Kim Phung is one of the best, most efficient, and least expensive restaurants in town. The low-key strip mall setting doesn't detract from the main draw: huge portions of terrific Vietnamese and Chinese food. Perfectly crisp spring rolls come topped with a thick peanut sauce that's hard to stop sampling. Entrees such as kung pao shrimp or rice with shredded pork skin and crab cakes are good, but most outstanding are the noodle dishes. Particularly recommended are those heaped with chicken, garlic, and hot peppers; grilled tofu; and charbroiled shrimp. The house specialty *pho* noodle soup allows you to tailor your dinner: You choose the main ingredients and then add cilantro, basil, jalapeño, lime, or sprouts to taste. Thai-style coffee, served thick and dark over ice and a dollop of condensed milk, ends the meal with a delicious caffeine jolt.

9 Far West Side

VERY EXPENSIVE

✪ Hudson's on the Bend

3509 Hwy. 620 north. ☎ **512/266-1369.** Reservations recommended, required on weekends. Main courses $19.95–$35. AE, DC, MC, V. Sun–Thurs 6–9pm, Fri–Sat 5:30–10pm (closing times may be earlier in winter; call ahead). SOUTHWESTERN.

If you're game for things that once roamed the wild, served in a very civilized setting, come to Hudson's. Soft candlelight, fresh flowers, fine china, and attentive service combine with out-of-the-ordinary cuisine to make this worth a special-occasion splurge. Sparkling lights draped over a cluster of oak trees draw you into the romantic dining room, set in an old house some 1 1/2 miles southwest of the Mansfield Dam, near Lake Travis.

The *chipotle* cream sauce on top was sufficiently spicy that I couldn't tell whether or not Omar's rattlesnake cakes tasted like chicken, but they were very good, as were the black-bean ravioli and smoked-shrimp quesadilla appetizers. Javelina stuffed with boar and pecans and a mixed grill of antelope, venison, and lamb were available when I visited, but I opted for a superb trout served with tangy mango chili butter. Although portions are more than generous, finishing a slice of key lime pie with graham-cracker crust posed no problem.

One caveat: Its popularity and its charming but acoustically poor setting can make Hudson's very noisy on weekends; opt for the terrace when the weather is nice enough.

MODERATE

County Line on the Hill

6500 W. Bee Cave Rd. ☎ **512/327-1742.** Reservations not accepted. Plates $9.45–$16.95. AE, CB, DC, DISC, MC, V. Summer, Sun–Thurs 5–9:30pm, Fri–Sat 5–10pm; closes half an hour earlier in winter. BARBECUE.

Some critics deride the County Line chain for its "suburban" barbecue, but Austinites have voted with their feet (or, rather, their cars); if you don't get here before 6pm, you can expect to wait as long as an hour and a half to eat. Should this happen, sit out on the deck and soak in the views of the Hill Country, or look at the old advertising signs hung on the knotty-pine planks of this 1920s roadhouse, formerly a speakeasy and a brothel. In addition to the barbecue—oh-so-slowly-smoked ribs, brisket, chicken, or sausage—skewered meat or vegetable plates are available. County Line on the Lake, near Lake Austin, 5204 F.M. 2222 (☎ 512/346-3664), offering the same menu, is open for lunch as well as dinner.

The Oasis
6550 Comanche Trail, near Lake Travis. ☎ **512/266-2441.** Reservations not accepted. Main courses $6.95–$18.95. AE, DISC, MC, V. Daily 11:30am–10pm. AMERICAN.

This is the Austinite's premier place to take out-of-town guests to at sunset: From the multilevel decks nestled into the hillside hundreds of feet above Lake Travis, visitors and locals alike cheer—both with toasts and applause—as the fiery orb descends behind the hills on the opposite bank. No one ever leaves unimpressed. The Oasis's standard American fare, with lots of Tex-Mex selections, is not nearly as inspiring. If you're not starving after a day of water sports on the lake, consider just sitting out on one of the 28 decks and having a margarita, and maybe some chips and salsa. It doesn't get much mellower.

○ The Salt Lick
Hwy. 1826, Driftwood, TX. ☎ **512/858-4959.** Reservations only for large occasions. Main courses $7–$16, depending on nightly menu. Cash only. Tues–Sun noon–10pm. BARBECUE.

It's $11^1/_2$ miles from the junction of 290 west and F.M. 1826 (turn right) to The Salt Lick, but you'll start smelling the smoke during the last 5 miles. Moist chicken, beef, and pork, as well as terrific homemade pickles, more than justify the drive. You're faced with a tough decision here: If you have the all-you-can-eat platter of brisket, sausage, and ribs, you might have to pass on the fresh-baked peach or blackberry cobbler, which would be a pity. In warm weather, seating is outside at picnic tables under live oak trees; in winter, the tables are set down near blazing fireplaces inside. Unlike lots of Texas barbecue places, The Salt Lick prides itself on its sauce, which has a sweet and sour tang (the owner is from Hawaii). And yes, they ship.

INEXPENSIVE

Rosie's Tamale House
13436 Hwy. 71, Bee Cave. ☎ **512/263-5245.** Reservations not accepted. Main courses $4.45–$9.15. No credit cards. Sun–Mon and Wed–Thurs 11am–10pm, Tues 5–10pm, Fri–Sat 11am–10:30pm. TEX-MEX.

When Willie Nelson first started coming to Rosie's in 1973, he always asked for a taco, a beef enchilada, chile con queso, and guacamole. Rosie has moved to a larger place, down the road from her original converted gas station, and Nelson's standing order is now enshrined on the menu as Willie's Plate, but the singer still drops by and Rosie is still here to greet him—and everyone else who comes in. The food's not fancy, but it's filling and good. Before you leave, take out a dozen fresh tamales ($4.75) for a midnight snack and check out the back wall, lined with photos of famous and not-so-famous regular customers. The two other Austin restaurants that bear Rosie's name are run by family members.

10 Only in Austin

For information on Austin's funky, totally original cafe scene, see "Late-Night Bites," in chapter 16.

Reel Barbecue

Forget cheap labor and right-to-work laws: One of the less-publicized inducements for filmmakers to come to Austin is barbecue—slow-cooked over a wood-fueled fire and so tasty it doesn't need sauce. The Austin Barbecue Loop, an unoffical feeding arena, transcribes a rough 30-mile radius from the state capitol. Sometimes the meat in these rib joints comes on butcher paper rather than plates, and usually there's little ceremony in the service—if there's any service at all. But who cares about amenities when you're dealing with this kind of flavor and aroma?

Gary Bond, film liaison for the Austin Convention and Visitors Bureau, has the celluloid/barbecue connection skinny. According to Bond, the eastern portion of the loop, where rolling prairies, farmland, and small towns pass for Everywhere, USA, has gotten especially rave reviews from location scouts, stars, and producers alike. **Rudy Mikeska's,** in downtown Taylor, was featured in *The Hot Spot* as The Yellow Rose, the racy hangout of the Don Johnson character, while less than a block away, **Louie Mueller Barbecue** served as a location for *Flesh and Bone,* starring Dennis Quaid and James Caan. To the south, in Elgin, crews from movie segments, music videos, and commercials have happily hit **Southside Market and Barbecue** on breaks. Still farther south, three hot meat purveyors in Lockhart have Hollywood dealmakers bickering about which is best: **Kreutz Market, Black's Barbecue,** or **Chisolm Trail.**

As for the west loop, the guys scouting for *Lolita* loved **Cooper's** open pit in Llano, while **The Salt Lick,** near Driftwood (see review above), has hosted lots of wrap parties. In Austin itself, Nora Ephron couldn't tear herself away from **The Green Mesquite.**

DINING WITH A VIEW OF THE BATS

In late March through mid-November, when thousands of bats fly out from under the Congress Avenue Bridge to seek a hearty bug dinner, the most coveted seats in town are the ones with a view of the astounding phenomenon. The **Shoreline Grill** (see above) and the **Cafe at the Four Seasons,** 98 San Jacinto Blvd. (☎ 512/478-4500), are the two most toney spots for observing the little critters. **La Vista** at the Hyatt Regency Austin on Town Lake, 208 Barton Springs Rd. (☎ 512/477-1234), and **TGIF's** at the Radisson Hotel on Town Lake, 11 E. First St. (☎ 512/478-9611), both offer casual, collegial roosts from which to watch the bats depart for their sunset food forage.

COFFEE SHOPS

Austin has often been compared to Seattle for its music scene and its green, college-town atmosphere; although the city isn't quite up to speed when it comes to coffee-houses, there are a sufficient number these days to constitute a respectable scene. Recommended are **Little City,** 916 Congress Ave. (☎ 512/476-2489), for its ultrachic design and its proximity to the downtown tourist sights—it's the only place where you can get a java fix near the capitol on Sunday (a new location, at 3403 Guadalupe, near the U.T. campus, ☎ 512/467-2326, roasts its own beans); **Mozart's,** 3825 Lake Austin Blvd. (☎ 512/477-2900), for its terrific views of Lake Austin and its white-chocolate almond croissants; and **Ruta Maya,** 218 W. Fourth St. (☎ 512/472-9637), for its funky atmosphere, live Latin music (4 nights a week), and perfectly brewed coffee.

14

What to See & Do in Austin

Stroll up Congress Avenue and you'll see much the same sight as visitors to Austin did more than 100 years ago: a broad thoroughfare gently rising to the grandest of all state capitols. Obsessed from early on with its place in history, the city is not neglecting it now, either. The capitol recently underwent a complete overhaul and presents a better face than ever to the public, while downtown's historic Sixth Street is continually turning back the clock with ongoing restorations.

But it is Austin's myriad natural attractions that put the city on all the "most livable" lists. From bats and birds to Barton Springs, from the Highland Lakes to the hike-and-bike trails, Austin lays out the green carpet for its visitors. You'd be hard-pressed to find a town that has more to offer fresh-air enthusiasts.

Bicycling is not the only free ride in Austin; there's no charge for transportation on the city's three 'Dillo lines, which cover most of the downtown tourist sites as well as the University of Texas. Other freebies include the Convention and Visitors Bureau's excellent guided walks and the state-sponsored tours of the governor's mansion and the state capitol.

SUGGESTED ITINERARIES

If You Have 1 Day

You'll see much of what makes Austin unique if you spend a day downtown. You might start out with a cup of coffee and pancakes at Kerbey Lane Cafe or a Mexican breakfast at Las Manitas. Then head over to the Old Land Office Building, interesting in itself and, as an information center, the ideal place to begin your tour of the Capitol Complex. The capitol itself and its new extension are next; you'll be impressed by results of the costly restoration. After that it's on to the Governor's Mansion; keep in mind that the last tour is at 11:40am. If you still have the strength and want to see how the other half lived in the late 19th century, walk west to the nearby historic Bremond block; otherwise, head south toward historic Sixth Street where, after getting fortified with some lunch, you can stroll. Still south but not very far is the north shore of Town Lake; rest here under the shade of a cherry tree or join the athletic hordes in perpetual motion on the hike-and-bike trail. If you're in town from late

March through October, book a table at the Shoreline Grill and watch the bats take off at dusk from under the Congress Avenue Bridge. Devote any energy you have left to the live music scene back on Sixth Street, which takes on an entirely new character at night.

If You Have 2 Days

Day 1   Follow the itinerary outlined in "If You Have 1 Day," above.
Day 2   In the morning, head out to the National Wildflower Research Center, where Texas's bountiful natural blooms are the stars. In the afternoon, go to the LBJ Library, Texas Memorial Museum, and the Huntington Art collection on the University of Texas campus (if you're traveling with youngsters, substitute the excellent Children's Museum or the Jourdan Bachman Pioneer Farm). At night, get your music fix away from the Sixth Street mob—try Antone's for blues or Liberty Lunch for rock or reggae.

If You Have 3 Days

Days 1–2   Same as Days 1 and 2 in "If You Have 2 Days."
Day 3   Scope out the cityscape at Mt. Bonnell, the highest point in Austin; then head down to the Austin Museum of Art at Laguna Gloria, at the foot of the mount. If the weather is nice, have lunch at one of the restaurants along Barton Springs Road and then spend the afternoon in Zilker Park: Go for a stroll at the lovely Botanical Gardens and afterward dip into the Barton Springs pool. Interested in history? In the afternoon, substitute the sights on Austin's east side—the George Washington Carver Museum, the State Cemetery, and the French Legation; there are a number of good, inexpensive Mexican restaurants in the area.

If You Have 4 Days

Days 1–3   Same as Days 1–3 in "If You Have 3 Days."
Day 4   Take a day trip to Fredericksburg or New Braunfels in the Hill Country. Fredericksburg lays on the Germanic charm a bit more, but New Braunfels competes with a discount mall and lots of river-rafting options.

If You Have 5 Days or More

Days 1–3   Follow the strategy in "If You Have 3 Days," above.
Days 4–5   Stay overnight at a bed-and-breakfast in Fredericksburg, and visit the LBJ Ranch, Enchanted Rock State Park, and some nearby Hill Country towns (see chapter 17).

1 The Top Attractions

✪ Barton Springs Pool

Zilker Park, 2201 Barton Springs Rd. ☎ **512/476-9044.** Admission $2.50 adults Mon–Fri, $2.75 Sat–Sun; 50¢ children 12–17, 25¢ children 11 and under; free (no lifeguards present) 5am–9am Memorial Day–Labor Day, off-season 5am–9am and dusk–10pm. Tues–Wed and Fri–Sun 5am–10pm, Mon and Thurs 5am–7:30pm; gift shop and information center (☎ 512/481-1466) open daily 10am–5pm. Bus 30 (Barton Creek Square).

If the University of Texas is the seat of Austin's intellect and the state capitol its political pulse, Barton Springs is the city's soul. The Native Americans who settled near these waters believed they had spiritual powers; today's residents still place their faith in the abilities of the spring-fed pool to soothe them as well as cool them.

Each day, approximately 32 million gallons of water from the underground Edwards Aquifer bubble to the surface here; at one time, this force powered several

Going Batty

Austin has the largest urban bat population in North America—much to the delight of Austinites. Some visitors are a bit dubious at first, but it's impossible not to be impressed by the sight of 1.5 million emerging en masse from under the Congress Avenue Bridge.

Each March, free-tailed bats migrate from central Mexico to various roost sites in the Southwest. In 1980, when a deck reconstruction of Austin's bridge created an ideal environment for bringing up babies, some 750,000 pregnant females began settling in every year. Each bat gives birth to a single pup; by August, these offspring can take part in nightly forays west for bugs, usually around dusk. Depending on the group's size, the bats might munch on anywhere from 10,000 to 30,000 pounds of insects a night—one of the things that makes them so popular with Austinites. By November, they're old enough to hitch a ride back south with the group on the winds of an early cold front.

When the bats are in town, an educational kiosk designed to dispel some of the more popular myths about them is set up each evening on the north bank of the river, just east of the bridge. You'll learn, for example, that bats are not rodents; that they're not blind; and that they're not in the least interested in getting in anyone's hair. **Bat Conservation International** (☎ 512/327-9721), based in Austin, has lots of information, too, and you can call the *Austin American-Statesman* **Bat Hotline** (☎ **512/415-5700,** category 3636) to find out when the bats are going to emerge from the bridge.

Austin mills. Although the original limestone bottom remains, concrete was added to the banks to form uniform sides to what is now a swimming pool of about 1,000 feet by 125 feet. Maintaining a constant 68° temperature, the amazingly clear water is bracing in summer and warming in winter, when many hearty souls brave the cold for a dip. Lifeguards are on duty for most of the day, and a large bathhouse operated by the Parks and Recreation Department offers changing facilities and an information center/gift shop.

LBJ Library and Museum

University of Texas, 2313 Red River. ☎ **512/916-5136.** Free admission. Daily 9am–5pm. Closed Christmas. Bus: Convention Center/U.T. Campus 'Dillo, U.T. Shuttle.

Set on a hilltop commanding an impressive campus view, the LBJ Library contains some 40 million documents relating to the colorful 36th president, along with gifts, memorabilia, and other historical objects. Johnson himself kept an office here from 1971, when the building was dedicated, until his death in 1973. Photos trace his long political career, starting with his early successes as a state representative and continuing through to the Kennedy assassination and the Civil Rights movement; LBJ's success in enacting social programs is depicted in an Alfred Leslie painting of the Great Society. Johnson loved political cartoons, even when he was their target; examples from his large collection are among the museum's most interesting exhibits.

✪ State Capitol

11th and Congress Sts. ☎ **512/463-0063.** Free admission. Mon–Fri 7am–10pm, Sat–Sun 9am–5pm; 24 hours a day during legislative sessions (held in odd years, starting in Jan, for 140 straight days; 30-day special sessions are also called sometimes). Hour-long free guided tours given every 15 minutes Mon–Fri 8:30am–4:30pm, every 30 minutes Sat–Sun 9:30am–4:30pm. Bus: All three 'Dillo lines.

Downtown Austin Attractions & Shopping

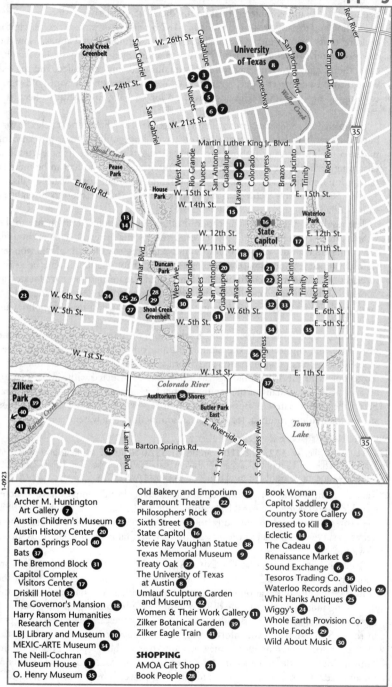

ATTRACTIONS

Archer M. Huntington Art Gallery **7**
Austin Children's Museum **23**
Austin History Center **20**
Barton Springs Pool **40**
Bats **37**
The Bremond Block **31**
Capitol Complex Visitors Center **17**
Driskill Hotel **32**
The Governor's Mansion **18**
Harry Ransom Humanities Research Center **7**
LBJ Library and Museum **10**
MEXIC-ARTE Museum **34**
The Neill-Cochran Museum House **1**
O. Henry Museum **35**

Old Bakery and Emporium **19**
Paramount Theatre **22**
Philosophers' Rock **40**
Sixth Street **33**
State Capitol **16**
Stevie Ray Vaughan Statue **38**
Texas Memorial Museum **9**
Treaty Oak **27**
The University of Texas at Austin **8**
Umlauf Sculpture Garden and Museum **42**
Women & Their Work Gallery **11**
Zilker Botanical Garden **39**
Zilker Eagle Train **41**

SHOPPING

AMOA Gift Shop **21**
Book People **28**

Book Woman **13**
Capitol Saddlery **12**
Country Store Gallery **15**
Dressed to Kill **3**
Eclectic **14**
The Cadeau **4**
Renaissance Market **5**
Sound Exchange **6**
Tesoros Trading Co. **36**
Waterloo Records and Video **26**
Whit Hanks Antiques **25**
Wiggy's **24**
Whole Earth Provision Co. **2**
Whole Foods **29**
Wild About Music **30**

Begun in 1990 and completed in time for the 1995 legislative session, a massive renovation and expansion—to the tune of $187.6 million—restored Texas's capitol building to its former glory and added a striking new underground annex. Now the capitol grounds are being torn apart in order to return them to the past, too. Among other things, tall Victorian-era drinking fountains are being reinstalled, and the old wrought-iron perimeter fence, painted back to its original black with gold stars, is going up again (though the doors will no longer have to be shut to keep the cattle out).

Completed in 1888, the current capitol replaced an 1852 limestone statehouse that burned down in 1881; a land-rich but otherwise impecunious Texas government traded 3 million acres of public lands to contractors to finance its construction. Gleaming pink granite was donated to the cause, but a railroad had to be built to transport the material some 75 miles from Granite Mountain, near Marble Falls, to Austin. Texas convicts labored on the project alongside 62 stonecutters brought in from Scotland.

The result was the largest state capitol in the country, second only in size to the U.S. capitol—but measuring 7 feet taller. The building covers 3 acres of ground; the cornerstone alone weighs 16,000 pounds, and the total length of the wooden wainscoting runs approximately 7 miles. A splendid rotunda and dome lie at the intersection of the main corridors; the House and Senate chambers are located at opposite ends of the second level. The legislative sessions are open to the public; go up to the third-floor visitors' balcony if you want see how Texas-style politics are conducted.

Almost 700,000 tons of rock were chiseled from the ground to make way for the new extension, connected to the capitol and four other state buildings by tunnels. Skylights let in natural illumination and afford spectacular views of the capitol dome. To complement the 1888 building, the annex was constructed with similar materials and incorporates many of the capitol's symbols and styles. The design of what has been called the "inside-out, upside-down capitol" is extremely clever; the large brass star on the outdoor rotunda, for example, also functions as a water drain.

National Wildflower Research Center

4801 La Crosse Ave. ☎ **512/292-4100.** Admission $3.50 adults, $2 students and seniors 60 and older, $1 children 18 months–5 years. Tues–Sun 9am–5:30pm. Take Loop 1 (Mo-Pac) south to Slaughter Lane; drive eight-tenths of a mile to La Crosse Ave.

Talk about fieldwork: The researchers at this lovely, colorful complex have 42 acres of wildflowers for their personal laboratory. Founded by Lady Bird Johnson in 1982, the center is dedicated to the study and preservation of native plants—and where better to survey them than in the Texas Hill Country, famous for its glorious spring blossoms?

A new facility, opened in 1995, expands an earlier site. The main attractions are naturally the display gardens and meadow, but the native stone architecture of the visitors center and observation tower is attention-grabbing, too. Included among the interesting indoor displays is one of Lady Bird's wide-brimmed gardening hats and a talking lawn mower with a British accent. The facility's research library is the largest in the U.S. for native plant information; you can buy a packet that includes the recommended species for your home state, as well as a bibliography of books on the subject. Many of these books are sold at the gift shop, which also carries lots of locally made items. The admission and gift shop proceeds help fund the nonprofit organization.

2   More Attractions

ARCHITECTURAL HIGHLIGHTS

Moore/Andersson Compound

2102 Quarry Rd. ☎ **512/477-6660**. Tours $6. By appointment only.

Architecture buffs won't want to miss the hacienda-like compound where Charles Moore spent the last decade of his life—when he wasn't traveling, that is. The peripatetic American architect, who kept a low profile but had a great influence on postmodernism, built five homes; this one, which he designed with Arthur Andersson, perfectly demonstrates his combination of controlled freedom, whimsical imagination, and connection to the environment. The wildly colorful rooms are filled with folk art from around the world; odd angles, bunks, and dividers render every inch of space fascinating.

Moonlight Towers

In May 1895, the first dam-generated electric current illuminated four square blocks around each of Austin's 31 new moonlight towers. Some residents of the still-rural town worried that these 165-foot-high spires would confuse the roosters, who wouldn't be able to figure out when the sun was coming up. Seventeen of these cast-and wrought-iron towers, most of them downtown, remain part of Austin's street-lighting system; you can also see one in Hyde Park, at 41st Street and Speedway.

A CEMETERY

State Cemetery

E. Seventh Street at Comal St. ☎ **512/478-8930**. Free admission. Mon–Fri 8am–5pm, Sat–Sun 9am–6pm. Bus 4–18 stops nearby.

The city's namesake, Stephen F. Austin, is the best-known resident of this east-side cemetery, established by the state in 1851. Judge Edwin Waller, who laid out the grid plan for Austin's streets and later served as the city's mayor, also rests here, as do eight former Texas governors, various fighters in Texas's battles for independence, and a woman who lived to tell the tale of the Alamo. Barbara Jordan recently became the first African-American to be interred at the cemetery. Perhaps the most moving monument, sculpted by Elisabet Ney (see "Museums/Galleries," below), commemorates General Albert Sidney Johnston, who died for the Confederacy at the Battle of Shiloh. An excellent self-guided tour pamphlet, available from the Austin Convention and Visitors Bureau, details headstone highlights. If you don't feel like walking around this historic boneyard, you can visit its Web site at www.gsc.state.ex.us; features include a list of past and future occupants, as well as biographies of over 200 of the more famous ones.

HISTORIC SITES

Capitol Complex Visitors Center

112 E. 11th St. (southeast corner of capitol grounds). ☎ **512/305-8400**. Free admission. Tues–Fri 9am–5pm, Sat 10am–5pm. Free tours of the building given every half hour on the hour. Bus: All three 'Dillo lines.

The capitol wasn't the only important member of the state complex to undergo a face-lift: Texas also spent $4 million to gussy up its oldest surviving office building, the 1857 General Land Office. If the imposing German Romanesque structure looks a bit grand for the headquarters of an administrative agency, keep in mind that land has long been the state's most important resource. Among the employees of this important—and very political—office, in charge of maintaining records and surveying holdings, was the writer O. Henry, who worked as a draftsman from 1887 to 1891; he based two short stories on his experiences here.

The building was rededicated as a visitors' center for the Capitol Complex in 1994; the Texas Department of Transportation also distributes state travel information here. A Walter Cronkite–narrated video tells the history of the complex, and changing exhibits on the first floor highlight the Capitol Preservation Project; upstairs, displays focus on the Land Office and other aspects of Texas's past.

Driskill Hotel

604 Brazos St. ☎ **512/474-5911.** Bus: Convention Center/U.T. Campus 'Dillo, Congress/ Capitol 'Dillo.

Colonel Jesse Driskill was not a modest man; when he opened a hotel in 1886, he named it after himself, put busts of himself and his two sons over the entrances, and installed bas-relief sculptures of longhorn steers—to remind folks how he had made his fortune. Nor did he build a modest property: The ornate four-story structure, which originally boasted a skylit rotunda, has the largest arched doorway in Texas over its east entrance. So posh that the state legislature met here while the 1888 capitol was being built. The hotel has had its ups and downs over the years, but it remains *the* place for Austin politicos to host their grand events. You can pick up a self-guided tour brochure at the front desk, or make an appointment with the concierge for a guided walk-through.

French Legation

802 San Marcos. ☎ **512/472-8180.** Admission $3 adults, $2 seniors, $1 students (under 18). Tues–Sun 1–5pm. Go east on Seventh St., then turn left on San Marcos St.; the parking lot is behind the museum on Embassy and Ninth Sts.

The oldest residence still standing in Austin was built in 1841 for Compte Alphonse Dubois de Saligny, France's representative to the fledgling Republic of Texas. Although his home was very extravagant for the then primitive capital, the flamboyant de Saligny didn't stay around to enjoy it for very long; he left town in a huff after his servant was beaten in retaliation for making bacon out of some pigs that had dined on the diplomat's linens. In the back of the house, considered the best example of French colonial–style architecture outside Louisiana, is a re-creation of the only known authentic Creole kitchen in the United States. A gift shop focuses on Texas history from the time of the republic to the present.

Governor's Mansion

1010 Colorado St. ☎ **512/463-5518.** Free admission. Tours scheduled every 20 minutes Mon–Fri 10am–11:40am; closed weekends, some holidays, and at the discretion of the governor. Bus: Congress/Capitol 'Dillo, ACC/Lavaca 'Dillo.

If the governor of Texas happens to be hosting a luncheon, members of the last tour of the mansion might notice warm smells wafting from the kitchen. Although it's one of the oldest (1856) buildings in the city, this opulent house is far from a museum piece: State law requires that the governor live here whenever he or she is in Austin.

This is not exactly a hardship, although the mansion was originally built by Abner Cook without any indoor toilets (there are now seven). The house was beautifully restored in 1979, but you can still see the scars of nails hammered into the bannister of the spiral staircase in order to break Governor Hogg's young son Tom of the habit of sliding down. The nation's first female governor, Miriam "Ma" Ferguson, entertained her friend Will Rogers in the mansion, and Governor John Connally recuperated here from gunshot wounds received when he accompanied John F.

Kennedy on his fatal motorcade through Dallas. Among the many historical artifacts on display are a desk belonging to Stephen F. Austin and portraits of Davy Crockett and Sam Houston.

Come as close to opening time as you can; only a limited number of people are allowed to tour the mansion during the few hours it's open to the public. If you arrive later, you might either have a long wait or not get in at all.

Neill-Cochran Museum House

2310 San Gabriel St. ☎ **512/478-2335.** Admission $2 adults, children under 10 free. Wed–Sun 2–5pm, guided tour only. Bus: ACC/Lavaca 'Dillo, U.T. shuttle.

Abner Cook, the architect-contractor responsible for the governor's mansion and many of Austin's other gracious Greek revival mansions, built this home in 1855; it bears his trademark portico with six Doric columns and a balustrade designed with crossed sheaves of wheat. Almost all of its doors, windows, shutters, and hinges are the originals—which is rather astonishing when you consider that the house was used as the city's first Blind Institute in 1856 and then as a hospital for Union prisoners near the end of the Civil War. The beautifully maintained 18th- and 19th-century furnishings are interesting, but many people come just to see the painting of blue-bonnets that helped influence legislators to designate these native blooms the state flower.

Old Bakery and Emporium

1006 Congress Ave. ☎ **512/477-5961.** Free admission. Mon–Fri 9am–4pm, first three Sat in Dec 10am–3pm. Bus: Congress/Capitol 'Dillo.

On the National Register of Historic Landmarks, the Old Bakery was built in 1876 by Charles Lundberg, a Swedish master baker, and continuously run as a confectionery until 1936; you can still see the giant oven and wooden baker's space inside. Rescued from demolition by the Austin Heritage Society, the brick-and-limestone building is one of the few unaltered structures on Congress Avenue. It now houses a gift shop, selling crafts handmade by seniors; a reasonably priced lunchroom; and a hospitality desk with visitors' brochures.

Paramount Theatre

713 Congress Ave. ☎ **512/472-5470** (box office) or 512/472-5411.

The Marx Brothers, Sarah Bernhardt, Helen Hayes, and Katharine Hepburn all entertained at this former vaudeville house, which opened as the Majestic Theatre in 1915 and functioned as a movie palace for 50 years. Restored to its original opulence, the Paramount now hosts Broadway shows; visiting celebrity performers; local theatrical productions, including an impressive Kids Classic series; and, in the summer, old-time films.

Treaty Oak

503 Baylor St., between W. Fifth and Sixth Sts.

Legend has it that Stephen F. Austin signed the first boundary treaty with the Comanches under the spreading branches of this 500-year-old live oak, which once served as the symbolic border between Anglo and Indian territory. Whatever the case, this is the sole remaining tree in what was once a grove of Council Oaks—which made the well-publicized attempt on its life in 1989 especially shocking. But almost as dramatic as the story of the tree's deliberate poisoning by an attention-seeking Austinite is the tale of its rescue by an international team of foresters. The dried wood from a major limb that they removed has been allocated to local artists, who are creating public artworks celebrating the tree. You can also buy items such as pen sets, gavels, clocks, and wooden boxes made out of the tree's severed limbs. They're a bit pricey (the least expensive item is $69) but the proceeds go to the forestry unit of the City of Austin Parks and Recreation Department; call 512/499-6745 for more information.

LAKES

Highland Lakes

The six dams built by the Lower Colorado River Authority in the late 1930s through the early 1950s not only controlled the flooding that had plagued the areas surrounding Texas's Colorado River (not to be confused with the more famous river of the same name to the north), but also transformed the waterway into a sparkling chain of lakes, stretching some 150 miles northwest of Austin. The narrowest of them, Town Lake, is also the closest to downtown; the heart of urban recreation in Austin, it boasts a shoreline park and adjacent hike-and-bike trail. Lake Austin, the next in line, is more residential, but offers Emma Long Park as a public shore. Serious aquatic enthusiasts keep going until they reach Lake Travis, the longest lake in the chain and the one that offers the most possibilities for playing in the water. Together with the other Highland Lakes—Marble Falls, LBJ, Inks, and Buchanan—these comprise the largest concentration of freshwater lakes in Texas. See also "Staying Active," below, for activity and equipment rental suggestions.

LIBRARIES/RESEARCH CENTERS

Austin History Center/Austin Public Library

810 Guadalupe St. ☎ **512/499-7480.** Free admission. Mon–Thurs 9am–9pm, Fri–Sat 9am–6pm, Sun noon–6pm; closed most holidays. Bus: ACC/Lavaca 'Dillo.

Built in 1933, the Renaissance revival–style public library not only embodies some of the finest architecture, ironwork, and stone carving of its era, but also serves as the best resource for information about Austin from before the city's founding in 1839 to the present. The center often hosts exhibitions drawn from its vast archives of historical photographs and sketches.

Harry Ransom Humanities Research Center

University of Texas. Harry Ransom Center, 21st and Guadalupe Sts.; Flawn Academic Center, west of the main tower. ☎ **512/471-8944.** Free admission. Exhibitions Mon–Fri 9am–4:30pm. Closed university holidays. Bus: Convention Center/U.T. Campus 'Dillo, U.T. Shuttle.

The special collections of the Harry Ransom Center (HRC) contain approximately 1 million rare books, 36 million manuscripts, 5 million photographs, and more than 100,000 works of art. Most of this wealth is stashed away for scholars' use, but permanent and rotating exhibits of HRC holdings are held in two buildings: the Harry Ransom Center and the Leeds Gallery of the Flawn Academic Center. A Gutenberg Bible—one of only five complete copies in the United States—is always on display on the first floor of the former, and you never know what else you might see: Costumes from the movie *Gone with the Wind,* the original manuscript of Arthur Miller's *Death of a Salesman,* or letters written by novelist Isaac Bashevis Singer.

MUSEUMS/GALLERIES

Archer M. Huntington Art Gallery

University of Texas. Harry Ransom Center, 21st and Guadalupe Sts.; Art Building, 23rd Street and San Jacinto Boulevard. ☎ **512/471-7324.** Free admission. Mon–Sat 9am–5pm, Sun 1–5pm. Closed university holidays. Bus: Convention Center/U.T. Campus 'Dillo, ACC/Lavaca 'Dillo, U.T. Shuttle.

Ranked among the top-10 university art museums in the United States, the Huntington hosts an eclectic variety of work. Among the permanent exhibits in the Harry Ransom Center are the Mari and James Michener collection of 20th-century

American masters; the largest gathering of Latin American art in the U.S.; and a rare display of 19th-century plaster casts of monumental Greek and Roman sculpture. The gallery in the Art Building is used for touring shows and student/faculty art exhibitions.

Austin Museum of Art at Laguna Gloria

3809 W. 35th St. ☎ **512/458-8191.** Admission $2 adults, $1 seniors and students with ID, children under 16 free; free all day Thurs. Tues, Wed, Fri, Sat 10am–5pm, Thurs 10am–9pm, Sun 1–5pm. Bus 9 (Sat–Sun only). One mile past west end of 35th St., at the foot of Mt. Bonnell.

This intimate art museum sits on 28 palm- and pecan-shaded acres overlooking Lake Austin; they're believed by some to be part of a claim staked out for his retirement by Stephen F. Austin, who didn't live to enjoy the view. The lovely Mediterranean-style villa that houses the exhibits was built in 1916 by Austin newspaper publisher Hal Sevier and his wife, Clara Driscoll, best known for her successful crusade to save the Alamo from commercial development. Dedicated to 20th-century American art, the gallery hosts seven to ten shows a year; they might feature the work of Austin and central Texas artists or contemporary Mexican photographers. Construction on a large new downtown facility, designed by architect Robert Venturi, is scheduled to start in 1997. Local politics have held up this project for years, however, so stay tuned.

Elisabet Ney Museum

304 E. 44th St. ☎ **512/458-2255.** Free admission. Wed–Sat 10am–5pm, Sun noon–5pm. Bus 1 or 5.

Strong-willed and eccentric, German-born sculptor Elisabet Ney nevertheless charmed Austin society in the late 19th century; when she died, her admirers turned her Hyde Park studio into a museum. In the former loft and working area—part Greek temple, part medieval battlement—visitors can view plaster replicas of many of her pieces. Drawn toward the larger-than-life figures of her age, Ney had created busts of Schopenhauer, Garibaldi, and Bismarck by the time she was commissioned to make models of Texas heroes Stephen F. Austin and Sam Houston for an 1893 Chicago exposition. William Jennings Bryan, Enrico Caruso, Jan Paderewski, and four Texas governors were among the many visitors to her Austin studio.

George Washington Carver Museum

1165 Angelina St. ☎ **512/472-4089.** Free admission. Tues–Thurs 10am–6pm, Fri–Sat noon–5pm. Bus 2.

The many contributions of Austin's African-American community are highlighted at this museum, the first one in Texas to be devoted to black history. Rotating exhibits of contemporary artwork share the space with photographs, videos, oral histories, and other artifacts from the community's past. Cultural events are often held here, too. The museum's collection is housed in the city's first public library building, opened in 1926 and moved to this site in 1933; the newer George Washington Carver branch of the public library is next door.

MEXIC-ARTE Museum

419 Congress Ave. ☎ **512/480-9373.** Admission $2 suggested donation. Mon–Sat 10am–6pm. Bus: Congress/Capitol 'Dillo.

The first organization in Austin to promote multicultural contemporary art when it was formed in 1983, MEXIC-ARTE has a small permanent collection of 20th-century Mexican art, including a fascinating array of masks from the state of Guerrero. It's supplemented by visiting shows, including some from Mexico, such as a major retrospective of the work of muralist Diego Rivera. The museum also programs an average of two music, theater, and performing arts events each month, and runs mural tours to Mexico.

O. Henry Museum

409 E. Fifth St. ☎ **512/472-1903.** Free admission. Wed–Sun noon–5pm. Closed Thanksgiving, Christmas, New Year's Day. Bus: Convention Center/U.T. Campus 'Dillo.

When William Sidney Porter, better known as O. Henry, lived in Austin (1884–98), he published a popular satirical newspaper called the *Rolling Stone.* He also held down an odd string of jobs, including a stint as a teller at the First National Bank of Austin, where he was later accused of embezzling funds. It was while he was serving time for this crime that he wrote the 13 short stories that established his literary reputation. The modest Victorian cottage in which O. Henry lived with his wife and daughter from 1893 to 1895 recently underwent a major restoration. Inside are the family's bedroom furniture, silverware, and china, as well as the desk at which the author wrote copy for the *Rolling Stone.*

Texas Memorial Museum

University of Texas, 2400 Trinity St. ☎ **512/471-1604.** Free admission, donations appreciated. Mon–Fri 9am–5pm, Sat 10am–5pm, Sun 1–5pm. Bus 27.

During a whistle-stop visit to Austin in 1936, Franklin Roosevelt broke the ground for this museum, built to commemorate the centennial of Texas independence. Whatever your age, you'll probably remember going on a class trip to a place like this, with dioramas, stuffed animals, and other displays detailing the geology, anthropology, and natural history of your home state.

Three things make this museum well worth a visit: an intriguing exhibit on the history of firearms; the original zinc goddess of liberty that once sat on top of the capitol; and a good gift shop, with lots of ethnic crafts and educational toys.

Umlauf Sculpture Garden and Museum

605 Robert E. Lee Rd. ☎ **512/445-5582.** Admission $2 adults, $1 students, children 6 and under free. Thurs, Sat–Sun 1–4:30pm, Fri 10am–4:30pm (open Sat in June, July, and Aug 10am–4:30pm); Tues–Wed by appointment. Closed Mon. Bus 29 or 30.

This is a very user-friendly museum, one for people who don't enjoy being cooped up in a stuffy, hushed space. An art instructor at the University of Texas for 40 years, Charles Umlauf donated his home, studio, and more than 250 pieces of artwork to the city of Austin, which maintains the lovely native garden where much of the sculpture is displayed. Umlauf, whose pieces reside in such places as the Smithsonian Institution and New York's Metropolitan Museum, worked in many media and styles. He also used a variety of models; you'll probably recognize the portrait of Umlauf's most famous U.T. student, Farrah Fawcett.

Women & Their Work Gallery

1710 Lavaca St. ☎ **512/477-1064.** Free admission. Mon–Fri 10am–5pm, Sat 1–5pm. Bus: Congress/Capitol 'Dillo.

Founded in 1978, this gallery is devoted to more than visual art—it also promotes and showcases women in dance, music, theater, film, and literature. Regularly changing exhibits have little in common except innovation; you may not always like what you see, but you're unlikely to be bored. The gift shop is a good place to pick up unusual dishes or jewelry created by female artists.

NEIGHBORHOODS/HISTORIC BLOCKS

Bremond Block

Between Seventh and Eighth, San Antonio and Guadalupe Sts.

"The family that builds together, bonds together" might have been the slogan of Eugene Bremond, an early Austin banker who established a mini–real-estate monopoly for his own kin in the downtown area. In the mid-1860s, he started

investing in land on what was once Block 80 of the original city plan; in 1874 he moved into a Greek revival home made by master builder Abner Cook. By the time he was through, he had created a family compound, purchasing and enlarging homes for himself, two sisters, a daughter, a son, and a brother-in-law. Some were destroyed, but those that remain on what is now known as the Bremond Block are exquisite examples of elaborate late 19th-century homes. One of the homes is a bed-and-breakfast; the others are offices, not open to the public.

Hyde Park
Between E. 38th and E. 45th, Duval and Guadalupe Sts.

Unlike Eugene Bremond (see above), developer Monroe Martin Shipe built homes for the middle, not upper, classes. In the 1890s, he created—and tirelessly promoted—a complex-cum-resort at the southwest edge of Austin; he even built an electric streetcar system to connect it with the rest of the city. By the middle of this century, Austin's first planned suburb had become somewhat shabby, but recent decades of gentrification have turned the tide. Now visitors can amble along pecan-shaded streets and look at beautifully restored residences, many in pleasing combinations of late Queen Anne and early craftsman styles. Shipe's own architecturally eclectic home, at 3816 Ave. G, is a bit grander than some of the others, but not much.

Sixth Street
Between Lavaca Ave. and I-35.

Formerly known as Pecan Street—all the east–west thoroughfares in Austin were originally named for trees—Sixth Street was once the main connecting road to the older settlements east of Austin. During the Reconstruction boom of the 1870s, the wooden wagon yards and saloons of the 1850s and 1860s began to be replaced by the more solid masonry structures you see today.

After the grand, new state capitol was built in 1888, the center of commercial activity began shifting toward Congress Avenue; by the middle of the next century, Sixth Street had become a skid row. Restoration of the nine blocks designated a National Register District began in the late 1960s; in the 1970s, the street blossomed into a live-music center. Now lined with more than 70 restaurants, galleries, theaters, nightspots, and shops, Austin's former main street is still rather sedate during the day, but it comes alive on weekend nights when a (mostly young) crowd throngs the sidewalks for some serious club crawling.

PANORAMA

Mt. Bonnell
3800 Mt. Bonnell Rd. Free admission. Daily 5am–10pm. Take Mt. Bonnell Road 1 mile past the west end of W. 35th St.

For the best views of the city and Hill Country, ascend to this mountaintop park, the highest point in Austin at 785 feet and the oldest tourist attraction in town. It has long been a favorite spot for romantic trysts; rumor had it that any couple who climbed the 106 stone steps to the top together would fall in love (an emotion often confused with exhaustion). The peak was named for George W. Bonnell, Sam Houston's commissioner of Indian affairs in 1836.

PARKS & GARDENS

Emma Long Metropolitan Park
1600 City Park Rd. ☎ 512/346-1831. Admission $3 per vehicle Mon–Thurs, $5 Thurs–Sun and holidays. Daily 7am–10pm. Exit I-35 at 290 west, then go west (street names will change

Greater Austin Attractions and Shopping

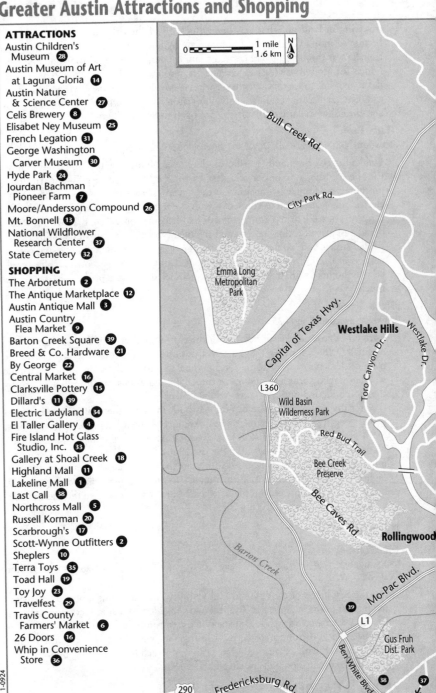

ATTRACTIONS

Austin Children's
  Museum **28**
Austin Museum of Art
  at Laguna Gloria **14**
Austin Nature
  & Science Center **27**
Celis Brewery **8**
Elisabet Ney Museum **25**
French Legation **31**
George Washington
  Carver Museum **30**
Hyde Park **24**
Jourdan Bachman
  Pioneer Farm **7**
Moore/Andersson Compound **26**
Mt. Bonnell **13**
National Wildflower
  Research Center **37**
State Cemetery **32**

SHOPPING

The Arboretum **2**
The Antique Marketplace **12**
Austin Antique Mall **3**
Austin Country
  Flea Market **9**
Barton Creek Square **39**
Breed & Co. Hardware **21**
By George **22**
Central Market **16**
Clarksville Pottery **15**
Dillard's **11** **39**
Electric Ladyland **34**
El Taller Gallery **4**
Fire Island Hot Glass
  Studio, Inc. **33**
Gallery at Shoal Creek **18**
Highland Mall **11**
Lakeline Mall **1**
Last Call **38**
Northcross Mall **5**
Russell Korman **20**
Scarbrough's **17**
Scott-Wynne Outfitters **2**
Sheplers **10**
Terra Toys **35**
Toad Hall **19**
Toy Joy **23**
Travelfest **29**
Travis County
  Farmers' Market **6**
26 Doors **16**
Whip in Convenience
  Store **36**

1-0924

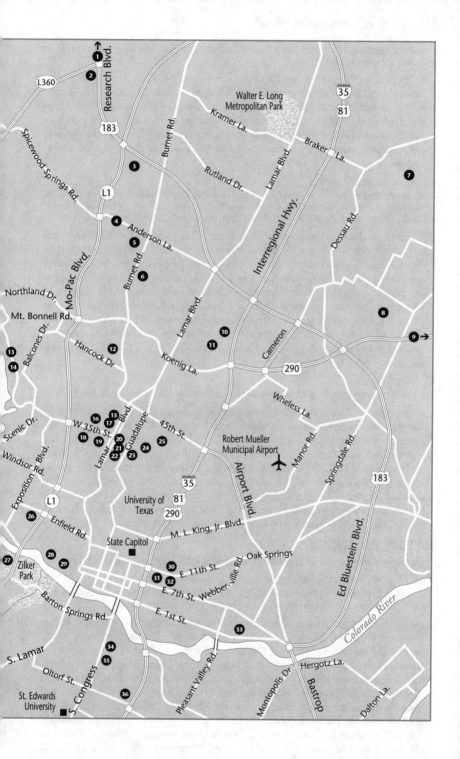

to Koenig, Allendale, Northland, and F.M. 2222) to City Park Rd. (near Loop 360); turn south and drive 6.2 miles to park entrance.

More than 1,000 acres of woodland and a mile of shore along Lake Austin make Emma Long Park—named for the first woman to sit on Austin's city council—a most appealing metropolitan space. Water activities are centered around two boat ramps and a fishing dock; there's also a protected swimming area, guarded by lifeguards on summer weekends. Camping permits are available. If you hike through the stands of oak, ash, and juniper to an elevation of 1,000 feet, you'll see the city spread out before you.

Zilker Botanical Garden

2220 Barton Springs Rd. ☎ 512/477-8672. Free admission; dinosaur-track tours $2 adults, $1 students, preschoolers free. Grounds open daily 8am–7pm. Garden center open Mon–Fri 8:30am–4:30pm; Sat 1–5pm (Jan–Feb), 10am–5pm (Mar–Dec); Sun 1–5pm. Bus 30.

There's bound to be something blooming at the Zilker Botanical Garden from March to October, but no matter what time of year you visit, you'll find this a soothing spot. The Oriental Garden created by Isamu Taniguchi is particularly peaceful; ask someone at the garden center to point out how Taniguchi landscaped the word *Austin* into his design. A butterfly garden attracts gorgeous winged visitors during April and October migrations, and you can poke and prod the plants in the herb garden to get them to yield up their fragrances. One-hundred-million-year-old dinosaur tracks were discovered on the grounds in January 1991; you can view them only on tours given on Saturday morning, May through November—call the garden (☎ 512/251-1816) for times.

✪ Zilker Park

2201 Barton Springs Rd. ☎ 512/476-9044. Free admission. Daily 5am–10pm. Bus 30.

Comprising 347 acres, the first 40 of which were donated to the city by the wealthy German immigrant for whom the park is named, this is Austin's favorite public playground. Its centerpiece is Barton Springs (see "The Top Attractions," above), but visitors and locals also flock to the Zilker Botanical Garden, the Austin Nature Preserves, and the Umlauf Sculpture Garden and Museum, all described in this chapter; see also the "Especially for Kids" and "Staying Active" sections, below, for details about the Austin Nature and Science Center, the Zilker Eagle Train, and Town Lake canoe rentals. In addition to its athletic fields (eight for soccer, two for softball, and one for rugby), the park also hosts a nine-hole disk (Frisbee) golf course.

NATURE PRESERVES

For information on Wild Basin Preserve, see "Special-Interest Sightseeing," below.

City of Austin Nature Preserves

301 Nature Center Dr. ☎ 512/327-5437 or 512/327-5478. Free admission. Daily, dawn to dusk. To locate the city's preserves, phone one of the numbers listed above.

Austin boasts a remarkably diverse group of natural habitats in its city-run nature preserves. At **Blunn Creek** (1100 block of St. Edward's Drive), 40 acres of upland woods and meadows are traversed by a spring-fed creek; one of the two lookout areas is made of compacted volcanic ash. The 500-acre **Forest Ridge** (8000 N. Capital of Texas Hwy.) affords wonderful views of surrounding Hill Country and Bull Creek waterfalls. Spelunkers will like **Karst** (3900 Deer Lane), which is honeycombed with limestone caves and sinkholes. Lovely **Mayfield Park** (3505 W. 35th St.) directly abuts the Barrow Brook Cove of Lake Austin; peacocks and hens roam freely around lily ponds, and trails cross over bridges in oak and juniper woods. Visitors to the rock-walled ramada at the **Zilker Preserve** (Barton Springs Road and Loop 1), with its meadows, streams, and cliff, can look out over downtown Austin. All the preserves are maintained in a primitive state with natural surface trails and no restrooms.

Westcave Preserve

Star Rte. 1, Dripping Springs. ☎ **210/825-3442.** Free admission. Sat–Sun, for tours at 10am, noon, 2 and 4pm (weather permitting). Take Hwy. 71 to Ranch Rd. 3238; follow the signs 15 miles to Hamilton Pool, which is across the Pedernales River Bridge from the preserve.

If you don't like the weather in one part of Westcave Preserve, you might like it better in another: Up to 25° difference in temperature has been recorded between the highest area of this natural habitat, an arid Hill Country scrub, and the lowest, a lush riparian woodland spread across a canyon floor. Because the ecosystem here is so delicate, the 30 acres on the Pedernales River may be entered only by guided tour. No reservations are taken; the first 30 people to show up at the allotted times are allowed in.

OUTDOOR ART

Philosophers' Rock

Zilker Park, 2201 Barton Springs Rd., just outside the entrance to Barton Springs Pool.

Glenna Goodacre's wonderfully witty bronze sculpture of three of Austin's most recognized personalities from mid-century—naturalist Roy Bedichek, humorist J. Frank Dobie, and historian Walter Prescott Webb—captures the essence of the three friends who used to shmooze together at Barton Springs Pool. No heroic posing here: Two of the three are wearing bathing trunks, which reveal potbellies, wrinkles, and sagging muscles, and all three are sitting down in mid-discussion. But the intelligence of their expressions and the casual friendliness of their pose have already made this 1994 piece an Austin favorite.

Stevie Ray Vaughan Statue

South side of town lake, adjacent to Auditorium Shores.

In contrast to the Philosophers' Rock (see above), Ralph Roehming's bronze tribute to Austin singer/songwriter Stevie Ray Vaughan is artificial and awkward. Although he's wearing his habitual flat-brimmed hat and poncho, the stiffly posed Stevie Ray looks more like a frontiersman with a gun than a rock star with a guitar. But his devoted fans don't care; flowers and messages can almost always be found at the foot of the statue.

A UNIVERSITY

University of Texas at Austin

Guadalupe and I-35, Martin Luther King Jr. Blvd. and 26th St. ☎ **512/471-3434.**

In 1883, the 221 students and 8 teachers that made up the newly established University of Texas in Austin had to meet in makeshift classrooms in the town's temporary capitol; at the time, the 2 million acres of dry west Texas land that the higher educational system had been granted barely brought in 40¢ an acre for grazing. Now nearly 50,000 students occupy 120 buildings on U.T.'s main campus alone; and that arid west Texas land, which blew a gusher in 1923, has raked in more than $4 billion of oil money—two-thirds of it directed to the U.T. school system.

Two visitors' centers, one at Sid Richardson Hall, next to the LBJ Library, and the other in the Arno Nowotny Building, at I-35 and Martin Luther King Jr. Boulevard, offer maps and other campus information; they're open weekdays from 8am to 4:30pm (☎ **512/471-6498**). Free campus tours designed for prospective students leave from the Main Tower information desk weekdays at 11am and 2pm (only at 2pm in December and May) and Saturday at 2pm; call **512/475-7399** for details.

See "The Top Attractions," above, for details on the LBJ Library and Museum; listings in this section for the Harry Ransom Humanities Research Center, Archer M. Huntington Art Gallery, and the Texas Memorial Museum; and the Walking Tour of university sights, below.

WINERIES & BREWERIES

Celis Brewery

2431 Forbes Dr. ☎ **512/835-0884.** Free admission. Tours, followed by samplings, conducted Tues–Sat at 2 and 4pm, and Fri at 5:30pm. Take U.S. 290 east, just past its crossing with U.S. 183; turn left at Cross Park Dr. and take it north to Forbes Dr.

Those with a taste for highly prized Belgian beers will want to tour the Celis Brewery, on the northeast side of Austin. Pierre Celis, who had made "white" (wheat) beer in the village of Hoegaarden, found the spring-fed water and limestone terrain of the Austin area conducive to reproducing the beverage that had been brewed for 500 years in his native Belgian town. The brewery was built around two huge, hand-hammered copper drums that Celis imported to give his beer the desired flavor.

Fall Creek Vineyards

2.2 miles northeast of Tow. ☎ **915/379-5361.** Free admission. Mar–Oct Mon–Fri 11am–3pm for tasting and sales, Sat noon–5pm tours, tasting, and sales, Sun noon–4pm tasting and sales. Closed Sun from Nov–Feb. For the most scenic route, take Hwy. 71 (Ben White Boulevard) west to Marble Falls, and pick up Hwy. 1431 west; it'll dead-end into 261 north (called Lakeshore Dr. at Lake Buchanan); when you get to 2241, take it north past Tow, where it will trail off at the vineyards.

The wines sold at this 65-acre vineyard, praised by critics around the country, amply reward the long drive up to the northwest shore of Lake Buchanan. You may have already tried a glass or two at fine restaurants in Austin; here you can sample the full range of award winners, including carnelians, Rieslings, and zinfandels. Special tours can be arranged through the Austin office (☎ **512/476-4477**).

Hill Country Cellars

U.S. Hwy. 183 north, Cedar Park. ☎ **512/259-2000.** Free admission. Tasting room open daily noon–5pm; winery tours given Fri–Sun 1–4pm on the hour (or by appointment). Take U.S. Hwy. 183 north, four-fifths of a mile past F.M. 1431.

Stroll under a trellised wood arbor and then enjoy the chardonnay and cabernet sauvignon grapes grown on the premises of this vineyard/winery, about 20 minutes northwest of Austin. A 200-year-old native grapevine is the centerpiece of the picnic area where various seasonal festivals are held. Winemaker Russell Smith moved back from Napa Valley to work here in his native Texas, which is newly developing a wine industry.

Slaughter Leftwich Vineyards

4209 Eck Lane. ☎ **512/266-3331.** Free admission. Daily 1–5pm for free tastings and sales; winery tours given Fri–Sun at 1:30 and 3:30pm (from June–Sept tours given every day except Mon). Take R.R. 620 one mile past Mansfield Dam, turn right onto Eck Lane at intersection of Hudson Bend Rd. and R.R. 620.

The Slaughter Leftwich vineyards produced Texas's first chardonnays in the high-plains region of Texas, but you don't have to travel out to the Lubbock area to try these award-winning bottles; just take a scenic drive to a shady lane near Austin's Lake Travis. The winery and tasting room are in a native stone structure, built to resemble

> ### ❓ Did You Know?
>
> - Austin is the only city in the world to preserve its first public electric lights; 17 of the original 31 moonlight towers are still operating around the city. (A special moonlight tower was erected for scenes in the movie *Dazed and Confused* when it was filmed in Austin.)
> - Sixty percent of Austinites use computers, making Austin the most computer-literate city in the United States. The city is also home to the most highly educated people per capita, and has the highest bookstore sales per capita of the U.S.'s 50 largest cities.
> - The University of Texas's Buford H. Jester Center, which hosts the college dormitories, has the largest kitchen in Texas, capable of serving more than 13,000 students a day.
> - The world's first photograph, created by Joseph Nicèphore Nièpce in 1826, is at U.T.'s Harry Ransom Humanities Research Center.
> - There are jackrabbits living at Austin's Robert Mueller Airport.

those popular in the last century. If you like whites, the chardonnay is your best bet; but all the wines are reasonably priced, so it's hard to go very wrong.

3 Especially for Kids

Most children will like the machine that turns pennies into capitol-dome souvenirs at the **Capitol Complex Visitors Center,** but unless your offspring are especially history minded, outdoor attractions are Austin's biggest kiddie draw. There's lots of room for children to splash around at **Barton Springs,** and even youngsters who thought **bats** were creepy are likely to be converted on further acquaintance with the critters. The **dinosaur tracks** at the **Zilker Botanical Garden** are particularly popular with kids. The following attractions are especially geared toward children.

Austin Children's Museum

1501 W. Fifth St. ☎ **512/472-2499.** Admission $2.50 adults, $2 children 2–17, children under 2 free. Free on Sun 4–5pm and Wed 5–8pm; inquire about the Open Door Policy (free admission to all who ask). Tues–Sat 10am–5pm, Sun noon–5pm. Closed Mon and Easter. Bus 21.

Offering everything from tools for tots to a soundstage for teens, this museum appeals to a wide range of ages and interests. Subtly instructive interactive exhibits include Stuffee, a huge cloth doll that can be unzipped for anatomy lessons, and plastic versions of a supermarket. Many children like to manipulate the vacation-creating computers; if you ask nicely, your offspring might show you how to use them. Along with permanent playscapes, there are also visiting exhibits, such as movable kinetic sculptures. Dance, music, or dramatic performances are held in the museum's gallery on weekends.

Austin Nature and Science Center

Zilker Park, 301 Nature Center Dr. ☎ **512/327-8181.** Donations requested; occasional special exhibits charge separately. Mon–Sat 9am–5pm, Sun noon–5pm. Closed Thanksgiving, Christmas. Bus 63.

A working beehive and ant farm are among the displays in the hands-on Discovery Lab at Austin's 80-acre Nature Center; the tortoises, lizards, porcupine, and vultures in the Wildlife Exhibit—among more than 50 creatures brought here because they've been orphaned or injured in the wild—also hold kids' attention.

Jourdan Bachman Pioneer Farm

11418 Sprinkle Cut Off Rd. ☎ **512/837-1215.** Admission $3 adults, $2 children over 3. June–Aug Sun 1–5pm, Mon–Thurs 9:30am–3pm; Sept–May Sun 1–5pm, Mon–Wed 9:30am–1pm. Take exit 243 east off I-35 to Dessau Rd., turn left, and go a half mile to Sprinkle Cut Off Rd. and take a right.

Traveling back in time to the rural 1880s might make kids appreciate the simplicity of such modern chores as having to clear the dinner table—at least temporarily. When Harriet Bachman and Frederic Jourdan set up housekeeping in northeast Austin in 1852, cattle herders drove past their property on the Chisholm Trail. Today's visitors to what was once their farm can enter into the worlds of three typical Texas families of the late 19th century: wealthy cotton farmers, homesteaders from Appalachia, and freed slaves turned tenant farmers. On Sunday afternoon, there's always something interactive for kids to do, from making sausage to milking cows. Elroy, a former area sharecropper who now works on the farm, is a wonderful storyteller, and he gets the young'uns moving when he summons them with his cowhorn.

Zilker Eagle Train

Zilker Park, 2100 Barton Springs Rd. ☎ **512/478-8167.**

The operator of Zilker Park's narrow-gauge, light-rail miniature train lost its city contract in 1996; it's due to reopen in the spring or summer of 1997. When you visit, phone ahead to confirm if that's happened and to check on current admission and opening hours.

4 Special-Interest Sightseeing

FOR TRAVELERS INTERESTED IN AFRICAN-AMERICAN HERITAGE

The George Washington Carver Museum (see "More Attractions," above) is the best place to learn about Austin's African-American past, but a number of other sites in east Austin are worth visiting, too. Less than two blocks from the Carver Museum, on the corner of Hackberry and San Bernard Streets, stands the **Wesley United Methodist Church.** Established at the end of the Civil War, it was one of the leading black churches in Texas. Catercorner across the street, the **Zeta Phi Beta Sorority,** Austin's first black Greek letter house, occupies the Thompson House, built in 1877; it's also the archival center for the Texas chapter of the sorority. Nearby, at the State Cemetery (see "More Attractions," above), you can visit the gravesite of Barbara Jordan, the first African-American to be buried here.

About half a mile away, the sparsely furnished **Henry G. Madison Cabin** was built around 1863 by a black homesteader; when it was donated to the city in 1873, it was relocated to the grounds of the **Rosewood Park and Recreation Center,** 2300 Rosewood Ave. (☎ **512/472-6838**). (The cabin is locked, so you need to ask someone at the center to open it.) You'll have to go across town, to the near west side, to explore the neighborhood known as Clarksville, founded by a former slave in 1871 as a utopian community for freed blacks; it's an almost entirely white artists' enclave now, however.

For a more up-to-date look at the Austin scene, visit **Mitchie's Fine Black Art Gallery & Bookstore,** 5312 Airport Blvd. (☎ **512/323-6901**), and **Bydie Arts & Gifts,** 412 E. 6th St. (☎ **512/474-4343**), both offering a good selection of African-American painting and sculpture. **Folktales,** 1806 Nueces St. (☎ **512/472-5657**),

and **Just for Us,** 9616 N. Lamar Blvd. (☎ **512/837-1488**), specialize in black literature; they often host readings and book signings.

SKY GAZING

Wild Basin Wilderness Preserve

805 N. Capital of Texas Hwy. ☎ **512/327-7622.** Admission $3 adults, $1.50 ages 5–12, children under 5 free. Tours twice monthly, weather permitting, generally 8 or 8:30pm to 9:30 or 10pm.

Sitting on a 227-acre peninsula high above Loop 360, the Wild Basin Wilderness Preserve is a perfect place to watch the moon rise over Austin; the clarity of the night sky from here is, well, stellar. In addition to its daytime nature walks, given every weekend, Wild Basin sponsors moonlighting and stargazing tours twice a month. Call ahead for exact dates: The moonlighting tour coincides with the full moon, and stargazing is scheduled for 3 or 4 days after the new moon. This popular heavenly peak is limited to 20; make reservations as far in advance as possible.

5 Walking Tour—University of Texas

Start: The Arno Nowotny Visitors Center.
Finish: The Littlefield Fountain.
Time: 1 hour, not including food breaks or visits to the museums.
Best Times: On the weekends, when the campus is less crowded (and more parking is available).
Worst Times: Morning and midday during the week when classes are in session and parking is impossible to find (beware: those tow-away zone signs mean business).

No ivy tower—although it hosts some—the University of Texas is as integral to Austin's identity as it is to its economy. To explore the vast main campus is to glimpse the city's future as well as its past: Here state-of-the-art structures—including recently installed information kiosks able to play the school's team songs for you—sit cheek by jowl with elegant examples of 19th-century architecture. The following tour points out many of the most interesting spots on campus; unless you regularly trek around the Himalayas, however, you'll probably want to drive or take a bus between some of the first seven sights (parking limitations were taken into account in this initial portion of the circuit). For a walking tour alone, begin at stop no. 8.

Note: Stops 2, 5, 6, 12, and 20 are also discussed earlier in this chapter, where their entrance hours are listed.

In 1839, the Congress of the Republic of Texas ordered a site set aside for the establishment of a "university of the first class" in Austin. Some 40 years later, when the flagship of the new University of Texas system opened, its first two buildings went up on that original 40-acre plot, dubbed College Hill. Although there were attempts to establish master-design plans for the university from the turn-of-the-century onward, they were only carried out in bits and pieces until 1930, when money from an earlier oil strike on U.T. land allowed the school to begin building in earnest. Between 1930 and 1945, consulting architect Paul Cret put his mark on 19 university buildings, most of which show the influence of his education at Paris's Ecole des Beaux-Arts. If the entire 357-acre campus will never achieve stylistic unity or anything close to it, its earliest section has a grace and cohesion that makes it a delight to stroll.

Although we start out at the oldest building owned by the university, this tour begins far from the original campus. At the frontage road of I-35 and the corner of Martin Luther King Jr. Boulevard, you can pull into the parking lot of:

1. **The Arno Nowotny Building.** In the 1850s, many state-run asylums for the mentally ill and the physically handicapped arose on the outskirts of Austin. One of these was the State Asylum for the Blind, built by Abner Cook around 1856. The ornate Italianate-style structure soon became better known as the headquarters and barracks of General Custer, who had been sent to Austin in 1865 to reestablish order after the Civil War. Incorporated into the university and restored for its centennial celebration, the building is now one of U.T.'s two visitors' bureaus.

   Take Martin Luther King Jr. Boulevard to Red River, then drive north to the:

2. **LBJ Library and Museum,** which offers another rare on-campus parking lot; you'll want to leave your car here while you look at sights 3 through 6. The first presidential library to be built on a university campus, the huge travertine marble structure oversees a beautifully landscaped 14-acre complex. Among the museum's exhibits is a seven-eighths scale replica of the Oval Office as it looked when the Johnsons occupied the White House. In the adjoining Sid Richardson Hall are the Lyndon B. Johnson School of Public Affairs; the Barker Texas History Center, housing the world's most extensive collection of Texana; and the second of U.T.'s visitors' bureaus.

   Stroll down the library steps across East Campus Drive to 23rd Street, where, next to the large Burleson bells on your right, you'll see the university's $41 million:

3. **Performing Arts Center,** which includes the 3,000-seat Bass Concert Hall, the 700-seat Bates Recital Hall, and other College of the Fine Arts auditoriums. The state-of-the-art acoustics at the Bass Concert Hall enhance the sounds of the largest tracker organ in the U.S.: Linking contemporary computer technology with a design that goes back some 2,000 years, it has 5,315 pipes—some of them 16 feet tall—and weighs 48,000 pounds.

   From the same vantage point to the left looms the huge:

4. **Darrell K. Royal/Memorial Stadium,** where the first of the traditional U.T.–Texas A&M Thanksgiving Day games was played in 1924; the upper deck directly facing you was added in 1972. In a drive to finance the original stadium, female students sold their hair, male students their blood; U.T. alum Lutcher Stark matched every $10,000 they raised with $1,000 of his own funds. The stadium's 1995 name change (from Texas Memorial Stadium) to honor legendary Longhorns football coach Darrell K. Royal angered some who wanted the stadium to remain solely a memorial to Texas veterans, and confused others who wonder if the very active Royal is still alive.

   Continue west on 23rd; at the corner of San Jacinto, a long staircase marks the entrance to the:

5. **Art Building,** home to the Archer M. Huntington Art Gallery. The permanent collections are in the Harry Ransom Center (see no. 20, below); this smaller space features touring exhibitions and student/faculty shows.

   Walk a short distance north on San Jacinto. A stampeding group of bronze mustangs will herald your arrival at the:

6. **Texas Memorial Museum,** a monumental art moderne building designed by Paul Cret. Inside, on the first floor, the 16-foot-tall Goddess of Liberty defines the term *statuesque.* Liberty, who reigned atop the state capitol dome until 1986, was designed to be viewed from more than 300 feet away; up close and personal, she's a bit crude. The museum also houses a fascinating collection of antique firearms, some carved into exotic animal shapes.

Walking Tour—The University of Texas

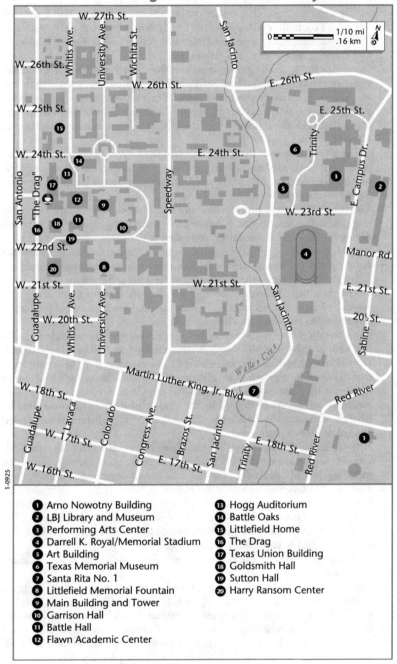

0   1/10 mi
    .16 km

1. Arno Nowotny Building
2. LBJ Library and Museum
3. Performing Arts Center
4. Darrell K. Royal/Memorial Stadium
5. Art Building
6. Texas Memorial Museum
7. Santa Rita No. 1
8. Littlefield Memorial Fountain
9. Main Building and Tower
10. Garrison Hall
11. Battle Hall
12. Flawn Academic Center
13. Hogg Auditorium
14. Battle Oaks
15. Littlefield Home
16. The Drag
17. Texas Union Building
18. Goldsmith Hall
19. Sutton Hall
20. Harry Ransom Center

When you exit the building, take Trinity, which, curving into 25th Street, will bring you back to the parking lot of the LBJ Library and to your car. Retrace your original route along Red River until you reach Martin Luther King Jr. Boulevard. Drive west; at the corner of San Jacinto, you'll see:

7. **Santa Rita No. 1,** an oil rig transported here from west Texas, where liquid wealth first spewed forth from it on land belonging to the university in 1923. The money was distributed between the University of Texas system, which got the heftier two-thirds, and the Texas A&M system. Though not its main source of income, this windfall has helped make the U.T. system the second richest next to Harvard.

There's no parking in the area, so it's best to pay passing obeisance to the oil god, continue on to University Avenue, and then hang a left. There are public parking places around 21st Street and University, where you'll begin your walking tour at the:

8. **Littlefield Memorial Fountain,** built in 1933. Pompeo Coppini, sculptor of the magnificent bronze centerpiece, believed that the rallying together of the nation during World War I marked the final healing of the wounds caused by the Civil War. He depicted the winged goddess Columbia riding on the bow of a battleship sailing across the ocean—represented by three rearing sea horses—to aid the Allies; the two figures on the deck represent the army and the navy.

This three-tiered fountain graces the most dramatic entrance to the university's original 40 acres. Behind you lies the state capitol. Directly ahead of you, across an oak-shaded mall lined with heroic statues, the:

9. **Main Building and Tower** rests on the site of the university's first academic building, built in 1884. The 307-foot-high structure that now rises above the university was created by Paul Cret in 1937; it's a fine example of the beaux arts style, particularly stunning when lit to celebrate a Longhorn victory. Sadly, the tower's many notable features—the small classical temple on top, say, or the 17-bell carillon—will always be dogged by the shadow of the carnage committed by Charles Whitman, who, in August 1966, killed 16 people before he was himself gunned down by a sharpshooter.

If you ascend the staircase on the east (right) side of the tower to the stone balustrade, you can see the dramatic sweep of the entire eastern section of campus, including the LBJ Library. The first building in your direct line of vision is:

10. **Garrison Hall,** named for one of the earliest members of the U.T. faculty, and home to the department of history. Important names from Texas's past—Austin, Travis, Houston, and Lamar—are set here in stone. The walls just under the building's eaves are decorated with cattle brands; look for the carved cow skulls and cactuses on the balcony window on the north side.

If you retrace your steps to the western (left) side of the Main Building, you'll see:

11. **Battle Hall,** regarded by many as the campus's most beautiful building. Designed in 1911 by Cass Gilbert, architect of the U.S. Supreme Court building, this hall was the first to be done in the Spanish Renaissance style that came to characterize so many of the structures on this section of campus; note the terracotta-tiled roof and broadly arched windows. On the second floor, you can see the grand reading room of what is now the Architecture and Planning Library.

When you exit Battle Hall, go left to the northern door, which faces the much newer:

12. **Flawn Academic Center.** A 200,000-volume undergraduate library shares space here with exhibits from the archives of the Humanities Research Center

(see no. 20, below). Among the permanent displays in the Academic Center's Leeds Gallery is a cabin furnished with the effects of Erle Stanley Gardner, Perry Mason's creator. In front of the building, Charles Umlauf's *The Torch Bearers* symbolizes the passing of knowledge from one generation to the next.

If you continue walking along the eastern side of the Academic Center, you'll pass:

13. The Hogg Auditorium, another Paul Cret building, designed in the same monumental art moderne mode as his earlier Texas Memorial Museum.

Go a few steps farther and you'll come to a group of trees that have been dubbed the:

14. Battle Oaks. The three oldest members of this small grove are said to predate the city of Austin itself. They survived the destruction of most of the grove to build a Civil War fortress, as well as a later attempt to displace them with a new Biology Building. It was this last, near-fatal skirmish that earned them their name: Legend has it that Dr. W. J. Battle, a professor of classics and an early university president, holed up in the largest oak with a rifle to protect the three ancient trees.

Just across the street at the corner of 24th and Whitis is the impressive:

15. Littlefield Home, built in 1894 in high Victorian style. Major George W. Littlefield, a wealthy developer, cattle rancher, and banker, bequeathed more than $1 million to the university on the condition that its campus not be moved to land that his rival, George W. Brackenridge, had donated. During the week, when the U.T. Development Office is open, you can enter through the east carriage driveway to see the house's gorgeous gold-and-white parlors, griffin-decorated fireplace, and other ornate details.

Walk west about a block to Guadalupe to reach:

16. The Drag—as its name suggests, the main off-campus action strip. Bookstores, fast-food restaurants, and shops line the thoroughfare, which is usually crammed with students trying to grab a bite or a book between classes. On weekends, the pedestrian mall set aside for the 23rd Street Renaissance Market overflows with crafts vendors.

☕ **TAKE A BREAK   Texas French Bread,** 2270 Guadalupe St., at 23rd Street (☎ **512/474-2785**), next door to the Co-op, is just the spot for a healthy salad or sandwich and a good cup of coffee.

To get back to the university, cross Guadalupe at the traffic light in front of the huge Co-op, between 24th and 22nd Streets. You'll now be facing the west mall. On your left is the:

17. Texas Union Building, another Paul Cret creation. A beautifully tiled staircase leads up to the second level where, through the massive carved wooden doors, you'll see the Cactus Cafe, a popular coffeehouse and music venue. This bustling student center hosts everything from a bowling alley to a formal ballroom.

Immediately across the mall to the right is:

18. Goldsmith Hall, one of two adjacent buildings where architecture classes are held. Also designed by Paul Cret, this hall has beautifully worn slate floors and a palm tree–dotted central courtyard.

Walk through the courtyard and go down a few steps; to your right is the second component of the School of Architecture:

19. Sutton Hall, designed by Cass Gilbert in 1918. Like his Battle Hall, it is gracefully Mediterranean, with terracotta moldings, a red-tile roof, and large Palladian windows.

If you enter Sutton Hall through the double doors at the front and exit straight through the back, you'll be looking directly at the chunky, contemporary:

20. Harry Ransom Center, home to both the Humanities Research Center (HRC) and the Huntington Art Collection. The satirical portrait of a rich American literary archive in A. S. Byatt's best-selling novel *Possession* is widely acknowledged to have been based on HRC. On the first floor of this building, the center's rare Gutenberg Bible sits in front of the Huntington galleries, which host an array of 20th-century, western, classical, and Latin American art.

When you leave the building, you'll be back on 21st Street, facing the fountain where the walking tour began.

6 Organized Tours

BUS TOURS

Gray Line

P.O. Box 9802-557, Austin, TX 78766. ☎ **512/345-6789.** Tickets $22 adults, $19 seniors, $11 children 5–11. Tours Mon, Wed, Fri (pick up 9–9:30am, return 12:30–1pm).

In 3½ hours, Gray Line's coach tours touch on Austin's highlights, including the state capitol, the University of Texas, Barton Springs, Treaty Oak, and more. The company provides complimentary pickup and return to most motels and hotels in town.

LAKE TOURS

Capital Cruises

Hyatt Regency Town Lake boat dock. ☎ **512/480-9264.** Bat and sightseeing cruises, $8 adults, $6.50 seniors, $5 children 4–12; dinner cruises, $22 adults, $15 children. Bat cruise, daily at sunset (call ahead for exact time), weather permitting; sightseeing cruise, Sat–Sun at 1pm; dinner cruise, Fri–Sun at 6pm. Reservations required for dinner cruises; for bat and sightseeing cruises, show up at the dock a minimum of 30 minutes in advance.

From March through October, Capital Cruises plies Town Lake with electric-powered boats heading out on a number of popular tours. The bat cruises are especially big in summer, when warm nights are perfect for the enjoyable and educational hour-long excursions; the high point is seeing thousands of bats stream out from under their Congress Avenue Bridge roost. Dinner cruises, featuring fajitas from the Hyatt Regency's La Vista restaurant, are also fun on a balmy evening, and the afternoon sightseeing tours are a nice way to while away an hour on the weekend.

Lone Star River Boat

South shore of Town Lake, between the Congress Ave. and South First St. Bridges. ☎ **512/327-1388.** $9 adults, $6 children under 12, $7 senior citizens; half-price fares Jun–Aug on Wed. Tours Mar–May and Sept–Oct Sat–Sun 3pm; June–Aug Tues–Sun 5:30pm, also Fri at 10:30pm. No tours Nov–Feb.

You'll set out against a backdrop of Austin's skyline and the state capitol on this riverboat cruise and move upstream past Barton Creek and Zilker Park; 100-feet-high cliffs and million-dollar estates are among the sights you'll glimpse along the way. These scenic tours, accompanied by knowledgeable narrators, last 1½ hours. Slightly shorter bat-watching tours, which cost $1 less, are available from April through October. Times vary, so call ahead.

Vanishing Texas River Cruise

P.O. Box 901, Burnet, TX 78611. ☎ **512/756-6986.** $15 adults; $13 seniors, students, active military; $10 children 6–12; children 5 and under free. Tours every day at 11am (contingent on reservations), except Tues.

It's about 1¹/₂ hours from Austin to the Lake Buchanan dock from which these fascinating naturalist tours depart; at Burnet, drive 3 miles west on Hwy. 29 to R.R. 2341, turn right, and go 13.5 miles. A guide narrates the history of the area and points out the seasonal flora and fauna, among them bald eagles (November to March), migratory birds and wildflowers (March to May), and wild deer and turkey (June to October). There's a full-service snack bar aboard the vessel, and on Saturday nights from May through October, a sunset dinner cruise departs at 6pm ($25 including the cruise and the meal).

TRAIN TOURS

Hill Country Flyer Steam Train Excursion

☎ **512/477-8468.** Coach, $24 adults, $10 children 13 and under; first class, $38 adults, $19 children. Tours Sat–Sun 10am (return 5:30pm); 2-week advance reservations strongly suggested in high season.

The Austin Steam Train Association restored the five historic coaches and the 1916 locomotive that you'll board for a leisurely 33-mile excursion from Cedar Park, northwest of Austin. After crossing the South San Gabriel River, the train whistles past scenic Hill Country vistas, especially pretty in spring and fall; at the end of the line— the town of Burnet, near Lake Buchanan—an Old West gunfight is staged for passengers. Special events include murder mystery excursions and, on the first Saturday of each month at 7pm, the 2-hour Twilight Flyer coach, which includes snacks. The Hill Country Flyer picks up passengers at the Capitol Metro Park & Ride Lot at Hwy. 183 and Farm Road 1431 in Cedar Park.

WALKING TOURS

Whatever price you pay, you won't find better guided walks than the informative and entertaining ones offered, gratis, by the **Austin Convention and Visitors Bureau (ACVB),** 201 E. Second St., 78701 (☎ **800/926-2282** or 512/478-0098), from March through November. Tours of the historic Bremond Block leave every Saturday and Sunday at 11pm; Congress Avenue/East Sixth Street is explored on Thursday, Friday, and Saturday starting at 9am, Sunday at 2pm. The Capitol Complex tour is conducted on Saturday at 2pm and Sunday at 9am. All tours depart *promptly* from the south entrance of the capitol; come even a few minutes late, and you'll miss out. The ACVB also publishes four excellent self-guided tour booklets, including one of Hyde Park and another of the state cemetery; they make for interesting reading, even if you don't have time to follow the routes.

7 Staying Active

BALLOONING   For an uplifting experience, consider a hot-air balloon ride over Hill Country. **Aeronauts Hot Air Balloons** (☎ 512/440-1492), **Airwolf Adventures** (☎ 512/836-2305), **Balloon Port of Austin** (☎ 512/835-6058), **Hill Country Balloons** (☎ 512/345-1575), and **Sundance Balloon Adventures** (☎ 512/990-8183) are all reputable operators with FAA licensed pilots. Their scenic excursions, including champagne breakfast, generally last about an hour.

BICYCLING   A city that has a "bicycle coordinator" on its payroll, Austin is a cyclist's dream. Contact **Austin Parks and Recreation,** 200 S. Lamar Blvd. (☎ 512/499-6700), for information on the city's more than 25 miles of scenic paths, the most popular of which are the Barton Creek Greenbelt (7.8 miles) and the Town Lake Greenbelt (10.1 miles). The **Veloway** (☎ 512/480-3032), a 3.1-mile paved loop in Slaughter Creek Metropolitan Park, is devoted exclusively to bicyclists. You can rent bikes and get maps and other information from **University Cyclery,** 2901 N. Lamar

Blvd. (☎ 512/474-6696); a number of downtown hotels rent or provide free bicycles to their guests. For information on weekly road rides, phone the **Austin Cycling Association,** P.O. Box 5993, 78763 (☎ 512/477-0776; e-mail bikinfred@aol.com), which also publishes a monthly newsletter, *Austin Cycling News.* For rougher mountain-bike routes, try the **Austin Ridge Riders** (☎ 512/454-3959).

BIRD WATCHING   Endangered golden-cheeked warblers and black-capped vireos are among the many species you might spot around Austin. The **Travis Audubon Society** (☎ 512/926-8751) organizes regular birding trips and even has a rare-bird hot line. The various parks and preserves (see "More Attractions," above) can also tell you who's flown into town.

CANOEING   You can rent canoes at **Zilker Park,** 2000 Barton Springs Rd. (☎ 512/478-3852), for $6 an hour; **Capital Cruises,** Hyatt Regency boat dock (☎ 512/480-9264), also offers hourly rentals on Town Lake. If your paddling skills are a bit rusty, the **Austin Nature and Science Center** (☎ 512/327-8180) and **U.T. Recreational Sports Outdoor Program** (☎ 512/471-6045) give instructional courses.

FISHING   The focus is on fly-fishing at downtown's **Austin Angler,** 312¹/₂ Congress Ave. (☎ 512/472-4553), an excellent place to pick up a license, tackle, and information on where to find the big ones. **Git Bit** (☎ 512/280-2861) provides guide service for half- or full-day bass-fishing trips on Lake Travis; prices, including equipment, start at $125 per person.

GOLF   For information about Austin's five **municipal golf courses,** call 512/480-3020; all offer pro shops and equipment rental, and their greens fees are very reasonable. Among them are the 9-hole Hancock, which was built in 1899 and is the oldest course in Texas; and the 18-hole Lions, where Tom Kite and Ben Crenshaw played college golf for the University of Texas.

HIKING   Austin abounds in nature trails in its parks and preserves; see "More Attractions," above, for additional information. Contact the **Colorado River Walkers of Austin** (☎ 512/280-2952 or 512/326-5701) or the **Sierra Club** (☎ 512/472-1767) if you're interested in organized hikes.

ROCK CLIMBING   Those with the urge to hang out on cliffs can call **Mountain Madness** (☎ 512/292-6624), which holds weekend rock-climbing courses at Enchanted Rock, a stunning granite outcropping in the Hill Country. **Texas Mountain Guides** (☎ 512/482-9208) let you choose between outdoor and indoor courses in the Austin area.

SAILING   Lake Travis is the perfect place to let the wind drive your sails; among the operators offering instruction and boat rentals in the Austin area are **Commander's Point Yacht Basin** (☎ 512/266-2333), **Dutchman's Landing** (☎ 512/267-4289), and **Texas Sailing Academy** (☎ 512/261-6193).

SCUBA DIVING   The clarity of the limestone-filtered waters of Lake Travis makes it ideal for peeking around underwater. Boat wrecks and metal sculptures have been planted on the lake bottom of the private portion of **Windy Point Park** (☎ 512/266-3337), and Mother Nature has provided the park's advanced divers with an unusual underwater grove of pecan trees. Equipment rentals and lessons are available nearby from **Pisces** (☎ 512/258-6646) and **Scuba International** (☎ 512/219-9484).

SPELUNKING   The limestone country in the Austin area is rife with dark places in which to poke around; in the city, two wild caves that you can crawl into with the proper training are **Airman's Cave** on the Barton Creek Greenbelt and **Goat Cave**

Preserve in southwest Austin. See also chapter 17 for other caves in nearby Hill Country.

SWIMMING   The best known of Austin's natural swimming holes is **Barton Springs** (see "The Top Attractions," above), but it's by no means the only one: Other scenic outdoor spots to take the plunge include **Deep Eddy Pool,** 401 Deep Eddy Ave. at Lake Austin Boulevard (☎ 512/472-8546), and **Hamilton Pool Preserve,** off Texas 71 on R.M. 3238 (☎ 512/264-2740). For lakeshore swimming, consider **Hippie Hollow** on Lake Travis, 2¹/₂ miles off R.M. 620 (☎ 512/473-9437), where you can let it all hang out in a series of clothing-optional coves; or **Emma Long Metropolitan Park** on Lake Austin (see "More Attractions," above). You can also get into the swim at a number of **free neighborhood pools;** phone 512/476-4521 for information.

TENNIS   The very reasonably priced **Austin High School Tennis Center,** 2001 W. First St. (☎ 512/477-7802), **Caswell Tennis Center,** 2312 Shoal Creek Blvd. (☎ 512/478-6268), **Pharr Tennis Center,** 4201 Brookview Dr. (☎ 512/477-7773), and **South Austin Tennis Center,** 1000 Cumberland Dr. (☎ 512/442-1466), all have enough courts to give you a good shot at getting one. To find out about additional public courts, call 512/420-3020.

WINDSURFING   If you catch them at the right time, **U.T. Recreational Sports** (☎ 512/471-1093) can help you brush up on your windsurfing technique. At Lake Travis, **Beach Front Boat Rentals** (☎ 512/258-8400) loans sailboats and motorboats in addition to sailboards.

8 Spectator Sports

There are no professional or minor-league teams in Austin, but college sports are very big, particularly when the University of Texas Longhorns are playing. For information about schedules, call the **U.T. Athletics Ticket Office** (☎ 512/471-3333); to order tickets, contact **UTTM Charge-A-Ticket** (☎ 512/477-6060).

BASEBALL   The **Longhorn baseball** team goes to bat from February through May at Disch-Falk Field (just east of I-35, at the corner of Martin Luther King Jr. Boulevard and Comal). Many players from this former NCAA championship squad have gone on to the big time—for example, Roger Clemens, two-time Cy Young award winner for the Boston Red Sox.

BASKETBALL   The **Lady Longhorn basketball** and **Longhorn basketball** teams, both Southwest Conference champions, play in the Frank C. Erwin Jr. Special Events Center (just west of I-35 on Red River between Martin Luther King Jr. Boulevard and 15th Street) from November through March.

FOOTBALL   It's hard to tell which is more central to the success of an Austin Thanksgiving: the turkey or the U.T.–Texas A&M game. Moved in 1996 to the Big 12 Conference, the **Longhorn football** team often fills the huge Darrell K. Royal/Texas Memorial Stadium (just west of I-35 between 23rd and 21st Streets, East Campus Drive and San Jacinto Boulevard) during home games, played from August through November.

Fans also turn out in droves each summer to watch the Super Bowl champion **Dallas Cowboys** in summer training camp at St. Edwards University, 3001 S. Congress. The players arrive in mid-July and stay around 5 to 6 weeks, generally practicing twice a day from Monday through Friday. Dates and local contact numbers for the team change each year; for the most up-to-date information, phone the Cowboys' office in Dallas (☎ 214/556-9327).

GOLF   Celebrities such as Joe Namath and Dennis Quaid tee off for a good cause at the **East Austin Youth Classic,** held at Barton Creek Resort (☎ 512/329-4000) in June. Classic in its own way is the **Cow Patty Open,** played—where else?—in a cow pasture. The hilarious mid-October event raises money for various children's projects; contact the Greater Austin Chamber of Commerce, P.O. Box 1967, 78767 (☎ 512/322-5659), for details.

HORSE RACING   Pick your ponies at **Manor Downs,** 8 miles east of I-35 on U.S. 290 east (☎ 512/272-5581). The track is open Friday to Sunday, March through June; gates open at 11:30am, with the first post at 1:30pm. The rest of the year, you can see simulcast racing from Wednesday through Sunday in the works; call for the current schedule.

Austin Shopping

15

When it comes to items intellectual, musical, or ingestible, Austin is a match for cities twice its size. Shopping here has not otherwise evolved into an art, but you'll find outstanding stores in all areas.

1 The Shopping Scene

Specialty shops and art galleries are slowly filtering back to the renovated 19th-century buildings along **Sixth Street** and **Congress Avenue,** but much of Austin's shopping has moved out to the malls. Bargain hunters go farther afield to the huge collections of factory outlet stores in San Marcos and New Braunfels; see chapter 17 for details. Little enclaves offering more intimate retail experiences can be found on **Sixth Street west of Lamar** and, nearby, north of 12th Street and West Lynn. In the vicinity of **Central Market,** between West 35th and 40th Streets and Lamar and Mo-Pac, such small shopping centers as 26 Doors and Jefferson Square are similarly charming settings for acquisition. Many stores on **the Drag**—the stretch of Guadalupe Street between Martin Luther King Jr. Boulevard and 26th Street, across from the University of Texas campus—are student oriented, but a wide range of clothing, gifts, toys, and, of course, books can also be found here. Below Town Lake, **South Congress Avenue,** from Riverside south to Annie Street, has long been a fun place to seek vintage clothing and antiques, and it's lately been revitalized, as lots of hip restaurants and cafes open in the area.

HOURS   Specialty shops in Austin tend to open around 9 or 10am, Monday through Saturday, and close at about 5:30 or 6pm; many have Sunday hours from noon until 6pm. Malls tend to keep the same Sunday schedule, but Monday through Saturday they don't close their doors until 9pm.

2 Shopping A to Z

ANTIQUES

In addition to the one-stop antique markets listed below, a number of smaller shops line Burnet Road north of 45th Street.

Austin Antique Mall
8822 McCann Dr. ☎ **512/459-5900.**

You can spend anything from a fiver to thousands of dollars in this megacollection of past-oriented stores. More than 100 dealers in a 30,000-square-foot indoor space sell Roseville pottery, Fiesta dishes, Victorian furniture, costume jewelry, and much, much more. Think this is big? About 20 minutes north of Austin, the Antique Mall of Texas, 1601 S. I-35 (☎ 512/218-4290), in Round Rock, run by the same people, has double the number of stalls.

Antique Marketplace
5350 Burnet Rd. ☎ 512/452-1000.

For people who like antiques but don't enjoy speaking in hushed tones, the Antique Marketplace offers bargains and treasures in a friendly, relaxed atmosphere. You'll find a little bit of everything under the roof of this large warehouse-type building in central Austin—a lamp-restoration specialist, Czech glass, funky collectibles, and expensive furnishings.

Whit Hanks Antiques
1009 W. Sixth St. ☎ 512/478-2101.

More than 50 high-quality dealers gather at toney Whit Hanks, just across the street from Treaty Oak. Even if you can't afford to buy anything, stop in to see the various craftspeople—ironsmiths, stone carvers, and cabinetmakers among them—at work. It's also fun to ogle items from fine crystal and vases to antique Chinese cabinets and neoclassical columns. Two blocks west of the original store, the new Whit Hanks Consignment, 1214 W. Sixth St. (☎ 512/478-2398), offers 15,000 square feet of additional space.

ART GALLERIES

Country Store Gallery
1304 Lavaca St. ☎ 512/474-6222.

Occupied by the architect and the superintendent of the state capitol during its construction in the late 19th century, this former boardinghouse now hosts the oldest art gallery in Austin and maybe all of Texas. The deer heads and branding irons on the walls complement bronzes and action paintings by well-known western artists such as Olaf Wieghorst, and provide interesting contrasts to the French impressionists and landscapes also sold here. All told, more than 2,500 pieces of all styles are available in this 7,000-square-foot space.

El Taller Gallery
8015 Shoal Creek Blvd., Suite 109. ☎ 800/234-7362 or 512/302-0100.

Located off Mo-Pac near Northcross Mall, this appealing showcase for southwestern art sells Santa Fe pieces at Austin prices. Amado Pena, who once owned the gallery, is represented here exclusively; you'll also find work by R. C. Gorman and other Native American artists. Handmade Pueblo pottery, Zapotec Indian weavings, and "critter" jewelry by Richard Lindsay are among the gallery's other interesting offerings.

Gallery at Shoal Creek
1500 W. 34th St. ☎ 512/454-6671.

Since it opened in 1965, Shoal Creek has moved away from an exclusive emphasis on western art to encompass work from a wide range of American regions. The focus is on contemporary painting in representational or Impressionist styles—for example, Jerry Ruthven's Southwest landscapes or Nancy McGowan's naturalist watercolors. Like El Taller, this is an Austin outlet for many artists who also have galleries in Santa Fe.

Wild About Music
710 W. Sixth St. ☎ **512/708-1700.**

Austin's commitment to music makes it a perfect location for this new gallery and shop, strictly devoted to art with a musical theme. Some of the pieces are expensive, but nearly all of them are fun. Come in to see the whimsical aquariums by local artist Larry Plitz, the life-size cardboard cutouts of President Clinton playing the sax, and the unique Texas music T-shirt collection. Gift items run the gamut from books and bola ties to watches and wind chimes.

BOOKS

As might be expected, many of Austin's best bookstores are concentrated in the University of Texas area, and specifically on the Drag. Along with discounted reading matter, new and used, **Half-Price Books,** 3110 Guadalupe St. (☎ **512/451-4463,** two other locations), also carries CDs, cassettes, and videos. The **University Co-Op,** 2246 Guadalupe St. (☎ **512/476-7211**), opened in 1898, has many volumes of general interest; in addition, it has the most orange-and-white Longhorn T-shirts and mugs and other U.T. souvenirs in town.

Book People
603 N. Lamar Blvd. ☎ **512/472-5050.**

In early 1995, the conjunction of Sixth Street and Lamar Boulevard acquired seriously good vibes when this expanded version of what was once primarily a New Age bookstore opened up next to a huge new whole-foods supermarket (see "Food," below). Now stocking more than 300,000 titles ranging over a wide variety of subjects, Book People also has an extensive array of self-help videos and books on tape. Lots of intimate sitting areas and an espresso bar prevent this huge store from feeling overwhelming.

Book Woman
918 W. 12th St. ☎ **512/472-2785.**

Offering the largest selection of books by and about women in Austin, this store is also one of Texas's best feminist resource centers, the place to find out about women's organizations and events statewide. Book Woman also carries a great selection of T-shirts, cards, and posters, including a blowup of the *Texas Monthly* magazine cover of a white-leather-clad Governor Ann Richards straddling a B-I-G motorcycle.

CHILDREN'S BOOKS

Toad Hall
1206 W. 38th St. (26 Doors). ☎ **512/323-2665.**

You'll find excellent reading material for toddlers to teens here, as well as a friendly staff who can offer advice about what might best suit your child's interests. One of the largest children's bookstores in the Southwest, Toad Hall also carries lots of kiddie tapes, CDs, and videos.

CRAFTS

Eclectic
916 W. 12th St. ☎ **512/477-1816.**

A dazzling panoply of furniture, crafts, pottery, and paintings from around the world is beautifully presented at Eclectic, with the muted tones of antiques counterpointing the more brightly colored contemporary work. An outstanding jewelry section includes Native American pieces as well as bracelets, pins, and necklaces from

Portugal, Thailand, and many other exotic places. Different countries are featured on a rotating basis.

Tesoros Trading Co.
209 Congress Ave. ☎ **512/479-8377.**

Colorful handwoven cloth from Guatemala, intricate weavings from Peru, glassware and tinwork from Mexico, metal-and-stone jewelry from Thailand, sequined banners from Haiti, wood carvings from Kenya . . . all these and more are available at Tesoros, which, in addition to its high-quality folk art, also offers a limited amount of furniture, dishes, and housewares from around the world. Reasonably priced items mingle with expensive treasures. Visiting artists turn up to give lectures, workshops, and craft demonstrations.

A DEPARTMENT STORE

Dillard's
Highland Mall. ☎ **512/452-9393;** Barton Creek Mall, ☎ **512/327-6100.**

This Little Rock–based chain, spread throughout the Southwest, carries a nice variety of mid- to high-range merchandise. The Barton Creek store is slightly larger than the one in Highland Mall, but both have Texas shops with good selections of stylish western fashions.

DISCOUNT SHOPPING

Last Call
Brodie Oaks Shopping Center, Ben White Blvd. at South Lamar. ☎ **512/447-0701.**

Neiman Marcus fans will want to take advantage of Last Call, which consolidates fashions from 27 of the high-toned department stores and sells them for 50% to 75% off. Different merchandise shipments arrive every week. Not only can you find great bargains, but you needn't sacrifice the attention for which Neiman Marcus is famous by coming here; the staff is as helpful as at all the other branches, and personal shopper service is available.

FASHIONS

Scott-Wynne Outfitters
The Arboretum, 10000 Research Blvd., Suite 127. ☎ **512/346-7012.**

Whether it's checked flannel hunting shirts or colorful fringed dancing skirts you're seeking, Scott-Wynne's got 'em. This large, privately owned Austin outlet features upscale outdoor lines such as Woolrich and Patagonia, as well as chic southwestern casual clothing for men and women. Attractive accessories—hats, belts, American Indian jewelry—will complement any well-dressed Texan's wardrobe.

The Whole Earth Provisions Co.
2410 San Antonio St. ☎ **512/478-1577.**

Austin's large population of outdoor enthusiasts come here to be outfitted in the latest earth-friendly fashions. From thermal underwear made of organically grown, unbleached cotton to state-of-the-art synthetic jackets and all the layers in between, campers, hikers, and climbers will find any item of clothing they might need, as well as the gear to go along with it. Housewares, toys, and travel books are also sold here. There's another location in south Austin at 4006 S. Lamar Blvd. (☎ 512/444-9974); a new store should be open by the time you read this at 1014 N. Lamar Blvd.

VINTAGE

Dressed to Kill
2418 Guadalupe St. (The Drag). ☎ **512/476-3148.**

An entire wall of well-preserved dresses faces one of vintage cowboy shirts, topcoats, and vests at Dressed to Kill, offering the largest and highest-quality selection of vintage clothing in town; in between are hats, scarves, shoes, and a variety of funky accessories. If you covet an item you can't afford, you might be able to work out a trade for some of your own already worn clothes.

Electric Ladyland/Lucy in Disguise with Diamonds
1506 S. Congress Ave. ☎ **512/444-2002.**

Feather boas, tutus, flapper dresses, angel wings, and the occasional gorilla suit overflow the narrow aisles of Austin's best-known costume and vintage clothing outlet. The owner, who really *does* dress like that all the time, is a walking advertisement for her fascinating store. You can buy everyday clothes here like floral-print dresses and striped shirts—though even these require some degree of flamboyance—but you're likely to get sidetracked by rack after rack of outrageousness.

WOMEN

See also The Cadeau, listed under "Gifts/Souvenirs," below.

By George
2905 San Gabriel St. ☎ **512/472-5951.**

Because it has suits and dressy clothes, as well as lots of pamper-yourself potpourri and bath oils, 30- and 40-somethings tend to frequent this By George store, while the college set stick with the more casual outlet on the Drag, 2324 Guadalupe St. (☎ 512/472-2731). But both shops offer hip, contemporary fashions in natural fabrics, and great purses and shoes to match. Don't feel neglected, guys: There's a By George for men two doors down from the Drag woman's store, 2346 Guadalupe St. (☎ 512/472-5536).

Scarbrough's
4001 N. Lamar Blvd. (Central Park). ☎ **512/452-4220.**

Opened in 1894 on the then prime corner of Sixth and Congress, Scarbrough's has moved around a bit since then, but it's still in the hands of the same family, now the fourth generation of Scarbroughs. If the store has achieved dowager status, its clothing is far from dowdy; women in Austin have long relied on Scarbrough's to outfit them in the latest fashions, from boot-scootin' boogie finery to glamorous gowns for the governor's ball.

FOOD

Central Market
40th and Lamar. ☎ **512/206-1000.**

All Austin was abuzz when this huge Central Market complex opened in 1994; now it's an integral part of town. More than just a place to buy every imaginable food item—fresh or frozen, local or imported—this gourmet megamarket also has a restaurant section, with separate areas offering cowboy, bistro, Italian, and vegetarian cuisine. A weekly newsletter announces what's fresh in the produce department, which jazz musicians are entertaining on the weekend, and which gourmet chef is holding forth at the market's cooking school.

Travis County Farmers' Market
6701 Burnet Rd. ☎ **512/454-1002.**

Not only does this market offer great fresh fruit and vegetables from all around the Austin area, but it also hosts monthly festivals honoring particular crops and/or growing seasons. April, for example, honors the 1015 "Y" onion, lauded as sweet, mild, and tear-free, while June celebrates peaches with contests for the best peach cobbler, peach ice cream, and peach preserves.

Whole Foods
601 N. Lamar Blvd. ☎ **512/476-1206.**

From chemical-free cosmetics to frozen tofu burgers, Whole Foods covers the entire (organic) enchilada; it's the place to find anything edible or applicable that comes in a low-fat or otherwise pure version. If you need to fortify yourself before shopping this huge food emporium or want to try well-prepared versions of some of the store's products, head upstairs to the reasonably priced Clearwater cafe and juice bar (☎ 512/476-0902), open daily from 11am to 10pm. The northwest store in Gateway Market, 9607 Research Blvd. (☎ 512/345-5003), is slightly smaller but also has a cafe.

HARDWARE, ETC.

Breed & Co. Hardware
718 W. 29th St. ☎ **512/474-6679.**

You don't have to be a power-drill freak to want to visit Breed & Co.: How many hardware stores, after all, have bridal registries where one can sign on for Waterford crystal? This darling of Austin do-it-your-selfers has everything from nails to tropical plants, organic fertilizer, gardening and cookbooks, pâté molds, and cherry pitters. You're sure to find something here that you never knew you needed but—now that you know it exists—you have to have. The new branch in the chic Westlake Hills area, 3663 Bee Cave Rd. (☎ 512/328-3960), is the only store in Austin that carries Tiffany china.

GIFTS/SOUVENIRS

See also Wild About Music, listed under "Art Galleries," above.

Capitol Complex Visitors Center
112 E. 11th St. ☎ **512/305-8400.**

Over the years, visitors have admired—sometimes excessively—the intricately designed door hinges of the capitol. The gift shop at the new visitors' center sells brass bookends made from the original molds used, during the capitol's renovation, to cast replacements for the hinges that had been cadged. Other terrific Texas items sold here include paperweights made from reproductions of the capitol's Texas-seal doorknobs, local food products, beautiful leather purses, and a variety of educational toys. The shop also has an excellent selection of historical books.

The Cadeau
2316 Guadalupe St. (The Drag). ☎ **512/477-7276.**

"Cadeau" means gift in French, and this is the perfect place to find one, whether it be beautiful contemporary kitchenware, pottery, jewelry, clothing, bibelots, chatchkes, or knickknacks. Be forewarned: Just when you think you've got your choice narrowed down, you may suddenly realize there are two more rooms chock-full of goodies to choose from. To add to the dilemma, there's a newer location, at 4001 N. Lamar Blvd. (☎ 512/453-6988), near 38th Street.

GLASS & POTTERY

Clarksville Pottery & Gallery
4001 North Lamar, Suite 200. ☎ **512/454-9079.**

This pottery emporium, filled with lovely pieces created by local artisans, has moved from its namesake location in the artsy section of downtown to a prime spot near Central Market (see "Food," above). You'll find everything that might come in ceramic, from candleholders to bird feeders, as well as handmade kaleidoscopes and contemporary jewelry in a variety of media. There's also an outlet in the Arboretum, 9722 Great Hills Trail, Suite 380 (☎ 512/794-8580).

Fire Island Hot Glass Studio, Inc.
3401 E. Fourth St. ☎ **512/389-1100.**

This glassblowing studio, about 2 miles east of I-35, is a bit off-the-beaten track, but it's a treat to watch the owners/artists, Matthew LaBarbera and his wife, Teresa Ueltschey, at their delicate craft. Demonstrations are given every Saturday morning (September through January and March through May) from 9am to noon; other times are available by appointment. You'll find the couple's elegant perfume bottles, oil lamps, bowls, and paperweights in fine galleries around Austin, but this showroom naturally has the largest selection. If you have a certain design in mind, you can special order a set of goblets.

JEWELRY

Russell Korman
3806 N. Lamar Blvd. ☎ **512/451-9292.**

You'd never know it from his current elegant digs, but Russell Korman got his start in Austin's jewelry trade by selling beads on the Drag. Although he's moved on to fine 14-karat gold, platinum, and diamond pieces, his store still has a considerable collection of more casual sterling silver from Mexico. Prices are very competitive, even for the most formal baubles.

AMOA Gift Shop
823 Congress Ave. ☎ **512/495-9224.**

The interim exhibition space and gift shop of the Austin Museum of Art (the new Venturi building is going up three blocks away) boasts a fine array of distinctive hand-made jewelry, glassware, and pottery. A lot of local artists are featured, but you can also pick up Frank Lloyd Wright–designed merchandise. This is the place, too, for your artsy T-shirts, posters, and mugs.

MALLS/SHOPPING CENTERS

The Arboretum
10000 Research Blvd. (Hwy. 183 and Loop 360). ☎ **512/338-4437.**

It's worth a trip to the far northwest part of town to a shopping center so chic that it calls itself a market, not a mall. This two-level collection of outdoor boutiques sur-rounding the toney Renaissance hotel doesn't include any department stores. Tasteful upscale clothing—Polo-Ralph Lauren, Jaeger—as well as specialty gift and craft shops, are featured. Dining options, including a sub shop and a TGI Friday's, tend to be on the casual side; there's an outlet for Amy's, Austin's favorite locally made ice cream.

Barton Creek Square
2901 S. Capital of Texas Hwy. ☎ **512/327-7040.**

Set on a bluff with a view of downtown, Barton Creek tends to be frequented by upscale west siders; the wide-ranging collection of more than 180 shops is anchored by Dillard's, Foley's, Sears, J. C. Penney, and Montgomery Ward. One of the newest malls in Austin, it's refined and low-key, but the fact that it includes both Frederick's of Hollywood and Victoria's Secret lingerie boutiques makes one wonder if the daytime soaps might not be onto something about the bored rich.

Highland Mall
6001 Airport Blvd. ☎ **512/454-9656.**

Austin's first mall, built in the 1970s, is still one of the city's most popular places to shop; it's located at the south end of the hotel zone near the airport, just minutes north of downtown on I-35. Reasonably priced casual clothing stores like the Gap and Express vie with high-end shops such as Laura Ashley and Pappagallo, while Dillard's, Foley's, and J. C. Penney department stores coexist with specialty stores— Out of Africa Gifts, say, and the Warner Bros. Studio Store. The tonier Lincoln Plaza shops are just to the south, on I-35. The food court is impressive.

Lakeline Mall
11200 Lakeline Mall Dr., Cedar Park. ☎ **512/257-SHOP.**

Austin's newest shopping mecca, in an upscale far northwest location, is notable for its attention-grabbing design, featuring lots of colorful reliefs and murals of the city. The shops, including Foley's, Dillard's, Mervyn's, and J. C. Penney, are not nearly so unusual, but there are some interesting specialty shops: Perfumania, offering designer fragrances at up to 50% off, and The Stockpot, with state-of-the art cookware.

Northcross Mall
2525 W. Anderson Lane. ☎ **512/451-7466.**

Smaller than Highland and Barton Creek malls, Northcross is Austin's recreational shopping center, with the city's only ice-skating rink, a six-screen movie theater, and a large food court; there's even a special number that details mall events (☎ **512/459-FFUN**). It's also home to Oshman's Super Sport, a huge sporting-goods emporium where customers can try out equipment at a batting cage, basketball court, and roller-blading surface. Specialty shops include Aaron's Rock and Roll and Chantal's antiques.

26 Doors
1206 W. 38th St. ☎ **512/477-1212.**

Not all the shops in 26 Doors boast the exquisite wooden antique entryways that give this Spanish-style shopping center its name, but all are intimate and charming. Among the items sold in the specialty stores arrayed around a tiled, tree-shaded courtyard are crafts, clothing, children's books, and cheesecake.

MARKETS

Renaissance Market
West 23rd and Guadalupe Sts. (The Drag).

Flash back to tie-dye days at this open-air market, selling some good-quality handmade crafts and jewelry along with cheesy, commercial items. It's theoretically open all the time, but vendors generally turn out in force on weekends only. The kids will like the jugglers, magicians, and kaleidoscopes.

A FLEA MARKET

Austin Country Flea Market
9500 Hwy. 290 east (4 miles east of I-35). ☎ **512/928-2795** or 512/928-4711.

Every Saturday and Sunday year-round, more than 550 covered spaces are filled with merchants purveying anything you might imagine—new and used clothing, fresh herbs and produce, electronics, antiques. This is the largest flea market in central Texas, covering more than 130 paved acres. There's live music every weekend—generally a spirited Latino band to step up the shopping pace.

MUSIC

Sound Exchange
2100A Guadalupe St. (The Drag). ☎ **512/476-8742.**

Come to the Sound Exchange for hard-to-find older music, imports, and releases by local bands, especially in the rock-and-roll and punk-rock genres; the walls are plastered with posters announcing upcoming Austin shows. You can get some pretty good bargains in vinyl, tape, and CDs here, and browse obscure music magazines to your heart's content.

Waterloo Records and Video
600 N. Lamar Blvd. ☎ **512/474-2500.**

Carrying a huge selection of sounds of all sorts, Waterloo is always the first in town to get the new releases; if they don't have something on hand, they'll order it for you promptly. The store offers preview listening, compilation tapes of Austin groups, and tickets to all major-label shows around town; it also hosts frequent in-store promotional performances by both local and midsized national bands. For purists, there's a vinyl annex.

TOYS

Terra Toys
1708 S. Congress Ave. ☎ **800/247-TOYS** or 512/445-4489.

Steiff teddy bears, the wooden Playmobil world, and other high-quality imported toys are among the kiddie delights at Terra, just south of the river. The store also carries a variety of miniatures, train sets, books, and dress-up clothes. For everyday children's apparel, try the owners' other place, Dragonsnaps, 1700 S. Congress (☎ 512/445-4497), just down the block.

Toy Joy
2900 Guadalupe St. ☎ **512/320-0090.**

The name says it all; the only question is whether kids or grown-ups will have more Toy Joy here. Ambi and San Rio are among the appealing children's lines sold in the large back room; up-front things like lava lamps and cartoon character watches keep both generation Xers and baby boomers endlessly fascinated. This store has some great Japanese toys, but for the full range—including a 4-foot-high radio-controlled Godzilla and Astro Boy videos—check out the newer branch, down the road on the Drag, 2100B Guadalupe St. (☎ 512/472-2262). Both stores stay open until midnight on Friday and Saturday.

TRAVEL

Travelfest
1214 W. Sixth St. ☎ **800/590-3378** or 512/469-7906.

A concept whose time has clearly come, the country's first all-inclusive travel shop offers guidebooks, luggage, cameras, binoculars, over-the-counter medicines, travel-sized containers, and a full-service travel agency under one roof. Those planning a trip of any sort can come in and browse various useful directories or attend the free travel-related seminars held 3 or 4 nights a week. The first store, 9503 Research Blvd. (☎ 512/418-1515), was so successful that the owner opened this second, larger one in downtown's West End.

WESTERN STORES

Capitol Saddlery
1614 Lavaca St. (between 16th and 17th Sts). ☎ **512/478-9309.**

The custom-made boots of this classic three-level western store near the capitol were immortalized in a song by Jerry Jeff Walker. Run by the same family for decades, this place is a bit chaotic, but it's worth poking around here to see the hand-tooled saddles, belts, tack, and altogether unyuppified cowboy gear.

Sheplers
6001 Middle Fiskville Rd. ☎ **512/454-3000.**

Adjacent to Highland Mall and especially convenient to those staying in the hotel zone north of the airport, Austin's huge branch of this growing chain of western-wear department stores has everything the well-dressed urban cowboy or cowgirl could require. If you get a sudden urge for a concho belt or bola tie when you get back home, call 800/835-4004 for a mail-order catalog.

WINE & BEER

Whip in Convenience Store
1950 S. I-35. ☎ **512/442-5337.**

Be it lager or stout, produced in Hill Country or New Delhi—if it's legally imported into Texas, you can get it here. At a conservative estimate, the cooler is filled with almost 300 different types of beer at any given time, with even more come Oktoberfest or other special beer-producing seasons. Wines are also beginning to make a strong showing here, and imported cigars have recently started to be sold. You can pick up munchies to go with your brews at this large convenience store on the frontage road of I-35.

Wiggy's
1130 W. Sixth St. ☎ **512/474-WINE.**

If liquor and tobacco are among your vices, Wiggy's can help you indulge in high style. In addition to its extensive selection of wines (more than 1,500) and single-malt scotches, this friendly west-end store also carries a huge array of imported smokes, including humidified cigars. Prices are reasonable and the staff is very knowledgeable.

Austin After Dark

16

Given the long reach of its body of performing arts, it would be hard to imagine an itch for entertainment, high or low, that Austin couldn't scratch. Live-music freaks enjoy a a scene that rivals those of Seattle and Nashville, while culture vultures have local access to everything from classic lyric opera to high-tech modern dance. (Ironically, the source of much of the city's high culture is literally crude: When an oil well on land belonging to the University of Texas system blew in a gusher in 1923, money for the arts was assured.)

The best sources for what's on around town are the *Austin Chronicle* and *XLent,* the entertainment supplement of the *Austin-American Statesman;* both are free and available in hundreds of outlets every Thursday.

Two music hot lines offer quick takes on the local club action: **KLBJ** at ☎ **512/832-4094** and **KGSR** at ☎ **512/478-2842.**

The **Austin Circle of Theaters Hotline** (☎ **512/320-7168**) can tell you what's on the boards each week. If you want to know who's kicking around, phone **Danceline** (☎ **512/474-1766**).

The **TicketMaster** number for the University of Texas, the locus for most of the city's performing-arts events, is **512/477-6060;** **Paramount Theatre** events can also be booked at this number. The Box Office (☎ **512/499-TIXS**) handles phone charges for many of the smaller theaters in Austin and can give you supplementary information—what to wear, for example, or what restaurants are nearby—about all of them.

You can call **AusTix** (☎ **512/397-1450**), the city's half-price theater and performing arts outlet, for a recorded listing of what's currently being discounted, and then buy tickets at **Book People,** 603 North Lamar Blvd. (Wednesday through Saturday from 11:30am to 6:30pm), or at the **Austin Visitors Center,** 201 E. Second St. (Thursday, Friday, and Saturday from 11:30am to 1:30pm).

FREE ENTERTAINMENT

Starting in late April or early May, the city sponsors 10 weeks of no-cost Wednesday night concerts at Auditorium Shores, and Sunday afternoon concerts at the Zilker Hillside Theater. Barring classical, they run the gamut of musical styles, from rock and reggae to country and western and Latin. Call **512/442-2263** for current schedules of these two series and of the free **Zilker Park Jazz Festival** in September. Every other Wednesday night from June through August, the upscale Arboretum shopping center (10000 Research Blvd.) hosts a **Blues on the Green** concert series in their open-air courtyard; call **512/338-4437** for details. Some 70,000 people turn out to cheer the *1812 Overture* and the fireworks at the Austin Symphony's **Fourth of July Concert** at Auditorium Shores (☎ **512/476-6064**).

PBS's longest-running show (it first aired in 1965), *Austin City Limits* has showcased such major country-and-western talent as Lyle Lovett, Garth Brooks, Reba McEntire, and Mary Chapin Carpenter. It's taped live from August through December at the KLRU-TV studio. Free tickets are distributed on a first-come, first-served basis, 1 to 3 days before each taping. Phone the show's hot line at **512/475-9077** for details.

From mid-July through late August, the Zilker Hillside Theater, across from Barton Springs Pool, hosts a **summer musical series** (☎ **512/397-1463**); featuring *Barnum* in 1997, the series started in the late 1950s and is the longest-running one in the United States. The summer **Austin Shakespeare Festival** is often held at the theater, too; call **512/454-BARD** for up-to-date information about locations and dates. More than 5,000 people can perch on the theater's natural grassy knoll to watch performances. Seating is first-come, first-served; bring your own blanket or lawn chairs.

The first weekend in June, the **Austin Contemporary Ballet** plié for the nonpaying public. Performances usually take place at the Zilker Hillside Theater; call **512/892-1298** for details.

1 The Club & Music Scene

The 1972 appearance at the Armadillo World Headquarters of country-and-western "outlaw" Willie Nelson, uniting hippies and rednecks in a common musical cause, is often credited with the birth of the live-music scene on Austin's Sixth Street. The city has since become an incubator for a wonderfully vital, cross-bred alternative sound that mixes rock, country, folk, and blues. Although the Armadillo is defunct and Sixth Street is past its creative prime—with some notable exceptions, it caters pretty much to a rowdy college crowd—live music in Austin is very much alive, just more geographically diffuse. Some clubs, like Antone's, have always been off-the-beaten path; others, like the Backyard, are newly expanding the boundaries of Austin's musical terrain. Poke around; you can never tell which dive might turn up the latest talent (Janis Joplin, Stevie Ray Vaughan, and Jimmie Dale Gilmore all played local gigs). If you're here during SXSW (see box, below), you'll see the town turn into one huge, music-mad party.

Categories of clubs in a city known for crossover are often very rough approximations; those that completely defy typecasting are dubbed "eclectic." Cover charges range from $2 to $8, with free or cheap drinks usually included when prices are at the high end.

FOLK & COUNTRY

Broken Spoke

3201 S. Lamar Blvd. ☎ **512/442-6189.**

This is the genuine item, a western honky-tonk dating from 1964 with a wood-plank floor and a cowboy-hatted, two-steppin' crowd. Still, it's in Austin, so don't be surprised if the band wears Hawaiian shirts, or if tongues are firmly in cheek for some of the songs. Photos of Hank Williams, Tex Ritter, and other country greats line the walls of the club's "museum." You can eat in a large, open room out front, or bring your long necks back to a table overlooking the dance floor.

Label It Successful—Austin's SXSW Music Conference

In 1996, Austin's SXSW (South by Southwest) Music and Media Conference celebrated its 10th anniversary. More than 5,500 industry professionals and 7,000 fans registered for a program that included 80 panels and workshops and 675 appearances by bands at more than 40 music venues around town, while thousands more bought $40 wristbands that entitled them to see the live shows. The total impact of the 5-day event on the Austin economy was estimated at $15 million.

When SXSW started out in 1987 as an offshoot of New York City's now defunct New Music seminar, it was primarily a way to showcase unsigned Texas bands. In only a decade, it has become the most anticipated convention on the industry calendar. Speakers and panelists over the years have included everyone from Johnny Cash and Bob Guccione, publisher of *Spin* magazine, to Anne Richards, the governor of Texas. Ry Cooder, Arlo Guthrie, Iggy Pop, Michelle Shocked, Soul Asylum, Toad the Wet Sprocket, and Lucinda Williams have been among the featured artists.

Fledgling musicians from around the world come here now to shmooze with A&R reps, publicists, journalists, radio personalities, managers, and other industry suits—with good reason. In the past, now-popular bands and singers like the Presidents of the United States of America, Lisa Loeb, and Letters to Cleo were signed by major labels after impressing the right people.

Some who have attended the conference from the start complain that it's changed, that it's no longer a showcase for new bands but a forum for groups that recording companies have already signed and want to publicize. So many hot names turn out now, too, that the unknown have a hard time getting audience attention. The festival has also gotten more diffuse: In recent years, a film festival and conference and multimedia component have been added.

And, for the 1997 festival, the wristbands that allowed access to all the live shows were no longer sold in advance to the public; the only way to get admission to the shows now is to register for the entire conference—in 1997, the cost ran from $230 to $450, depending on how early you signed on.

Still interested? The conference is held annually the third week of March. Contact **SXSW Music Festival,** P.O. Box 4999, Austin, TX 78765 (☎ **512/467-7979;** fax 512/451-0754; e-mail sxsw@sxsw.com).

Cactus Cafe
Texas Union, University of Texas campus. ☎ **512/475-6515.**

A small, dark cavern with great acoustics and a fully stocked bar, U.T.'s Cactus Cafe is singer/songwriter heaven, a place where dramatic stage antics take a back seat to engaged showmanship. The attentive listening vibes attract talented solo artists like Jimmy LaFave and nationally recognized Austin native Shawn Colvin, along with well-known acoustic combos. Monday nights are set aside for open-mike performances.

✪ Continental Club
1315 S. Congress Ave. ☎ **512/441-2444.**

Although it also showcases rock, rockabilly, and new-wave sounds, the Continental Club holds on to its roots in traditional country, celebrating events such as Hank Williams's birthday. A small, smoky club with high stools and a pool table in the back room, this is a not-to-be-missed Austin classic. It's considered by many to have the best happy hour music in town, and the folksy Tuesday blues with Toni Price is a real crowd pleaser.

Hang 'Em High Saloon
201 E. Sixth St. ☎ **512/322-9143.**

A welcome alternative to Sixth Street's rock scene, this large country bar and dance hall does the Wild West bit well. Willie Nelson and Jerry Jeff Walker have both come by, conferring the town's most prestigious seal of approval. This is the place to come for country-and-western boogeying, but remember: There's no line dancing allowed.

JAZZ & BLUES

✪ Antone's
2915 Guadalupe St. ☎ **512/474-5314.**

Clifford Antone's place is as open-minded as any in Austin; Willie Nelson celebrated his 60th birthday here and country-and-western crossover bands like the Lounge Lizards turn up all the time. But in this dark, cavernous room, where Stevie Ray Vaughan was once a regular, the strains of a blues guitar are still the most likely to be heard. When major blues artists venture down this way—for example, Buddy Guy, Etta James, or Edgar Winter—you can be sure they'll either be playing Antone's or stopping by for a surprise set.

Elephant Room
315 Congress Ave. ☎ **512/473-2279.**

Film stars on location in Austin mingle with T-shirted students and well-dressed older aficionados at this intimate downtown venue, as dark and as smoky as a jazz bar should be. The focus is on contemporary and traditional jazz, though the bill branches out to rock on occasion.

Pearl's Oyster Bar
9003 Research Blvd. ☎ **512/339-7444.**

Some jazz acts join Texas rhythm-and-blues bands 7 nights a week in a funky New Orleans atmosphere. Settle in here for some good seafood and beer along with the blues.

Top of the Marc
618 W. Sixth St. ☎ **512/472-9849.**

A standout in a town surprisingly weak on jazz, Top of the Marc draws a sophisticated crowd to hear artists like the Duke Ellington Orchestra as well as favorite local bands. You can enjoy hot pastrami (see "Katz's" in chapter 13) and cool sounds in a chic black-and-white room or on an outdoor roof deck.

ROCK

Electric Lounge
302 Bowie St. ☎ **512/476-FUSE.**

The barometer of Austin's rock/pop scene, the Electric Lounge is the town's main showcase for local up-and-coming bands. If you squint at the dimly lit corner stage and concrete-block walls, you'll have no trouble imagining you're in someone's garage.

Emo's
603 Red River St. ☎ **512/477-EMOS.**

Austin's last word in alternative music, Emo's draws acts of all sizes and flavors. It primarily attracts a college crowd, but you won't feel really out of place if you graduated a long time ago. The front room holds the bar, pool tables, and pinball machines. You'll have to cross the outside patio to reach the back room where the bands play.

Liberty Lunch

405 W. Second St. ☎ **512/477-0461.**

This huge converted warehouse, with a concrete floor sloping down to a large stage, has a longstanding reputation for presenting the widest range of midscale rock and roll of any club in Austin. Expect to see acts ranging from Los Lobos to the Cowboy Junkies and the Wallflowers; hardcore, metal, and reggae bands turn up, too. Be sure to check out the great tropical mural.

Maggie Mae's

512 Trinity St. ☎ **512/478-8541.**

Good rock cover bands, a great selection of beers, and plenty of space set Maggie Mae's apart from the collegiate-crowded clubs lining Sixth Street. Five separate bars make ordering easy, and the live music plays upstairs and down; the outside courtyard is generally reserved for the blues.

ECLECTIC

❍ The Backyard

Hwy. 71 west at R.R. 620, Bee Cave. ☎ **512/236-4146.** Tickets $6–$8 local acts, $12–$39 national acts.

A terrific sound system and a casual country atmosphere have helped make this one of the hottest new venues in town. Since it opened in 1993, the Allman Brothers, Chet Atkins, Joan Baez, Jimmy Cliff, Leonard Cohen, Chick Corea, Warren Zevon, the Band, and k.d. lang have all played the terraced outdoor amphitheater, which is shaded by ancient live oaks. Come early for dinner; a committedly Texas menu (barbecue, Tex-Mex, steaks, and burgers) is reasonably priced and good.

Hole in the Wall

2538 Guadalupe St. ☎ **512/474-5314.**

This intimate club, on the Drag just off the U.T. campus, has a longstanding tradition of trying anything once. It's a great coup for local performers to be booked here, and the audience often gets to say, "We saw them when" about popular Texas bands that later hit it big. There's a good bar food menu, and pool tables in back.

La Zona Rosa

612 W. Fourth St. ☎ **512/472-9075.**

Another Austin classic, LZR mixes a Tex-Mex menu with high-quality music ranging from Latino and alternative country to punk rock. A renovated garage brightly painted with monsters and filled with kitschy memorabilia is an appropriately outrageous setting for the club's cutting-edge sounds. There's no cover Sunday through Thursday.

CABARET

Café Bremond

404 W. Seventh St. ☎ **512/482-0411.**

This new cabaret confirms all those rumors that romance has made a comeback. From Wednesday through Sunday, balladeers dressed to the nines belt their hearts out to audiences sipping champagne in a dimly lit room. The only thing missing is the thick haze of smoke—this is Austin in the 1990s, after all.

COMEDY CLUBS

Esther's Follies
525 E. Sixth St. ☎ 512/320-0553. Performances Thurs 8pm, Fri–Sat 8 and 10pm. Tickets $10 Thurs, $12 Fri, $14 Sat; $4 off for students.

You might miss a couple of the punchlines if you're not in on the latest twists and turns of local politics, but the no-holds-barred Esther's Follies doesn't spare Washington, either. It's very satirical, very irreverent, very Austin.

Velveeta Room
525 E. Sixth St. ☎ 512/469-9116. Performances Thurs 9pm, Fri–Sat 8, 9, and 11:30pm. Tickets $4 Thurs and Fri, $6 Sat.

For one-stop comedy consumption, go straight from Esther's to the Velveeta Room next door. This deliberately cheesy club serves more standard stand-up, local as well as national. Thursday is Monk's Night Out, improv with lots of audience participation, while Friday and Saturday include open mikes.

Capitol City Comedy
8120 Research Blvd., Suite 100. ☎ 512/467-2333. Performances nightly 8:30pm, Fri and Sat also 10:45pm. Tickets $7 Sun, Wed, and Thurs; $2 Mon; $3.50 Tues; $10 Fri and Sat.

Top ranked on the stand-up circuit, Cap City books nationally recognized comedians like Bobcat Goldthwait and Jeff Foxworthy. The cream of the crop turn up on Friday and Saturday, of course, but you'll find plenty to laugh at (including lower prices) the rest of the week.

DANCE CLUBS & DISCOS

Dancing fools head for Sixth Street, where they can hop from one club to another within a five-block radius. Gays and straights mix it up at **Ohms,** 611 E. Seventh St. (☎ 512/472-7136), a great dance club. **Proteus,** 501 E. Sixth St. (☎ 512/472-8922), often holds raves. **Eden 2200,** 614 E. Sixth St. (☎ 512/499-8700) draws mostly 18- to 26-year-olds, while the crowd at **Abrattos,** 318 E. Fifth St. (☎ 512/477-1641), tends to be 21 and older. **Paradox,** 311 E. Fifth St. (☎ 512/469-7615), often hosts high-profile acts like Blondie and the Beastie Boys. **5th St. Station,** 505 E. Fifth St. (☎ 512/478-6065), and **Planet Austin,** 505 E. Fifth St. (☎ 512/708-0678), are also very popular.

2 The Performing Arts

In addition to having its own symphony, theater, ballet, lyric opera, and modern dance companies, Austin draws major international talent to town. Much of the action, local and imported, goes on at the University of Texas's Performing Arts Center, but some terrific outdoor venues take advantage of the city's abundant greenery and mild weather.

MAJOR PERFORMING ARTS COMPANIES
OPERA & CLASSICAL MUSIC

Austin Chamber Music Center
4930 Burnet Rd., Suite 203. ☎ 512/454-7562.

This teaching and performing group features an Intimate Concert series, open to the public but held at elegant private homes. They also host visiting national and international artists—for example, the Maia Quartet from Juilliard.

Now that you know your way around, let's move on to something simple.

For card and collect calls.

1 800 CALL ATT is the only number you need to know when you're away from home. Dial it from any phone, anywhere* and your calls will always go through to AT&T.

*Available in U.S. and Canada. © 1997 AT&T

Austin Lyric Opera

1111 W. Sixth St. ☎ **800/31-OPERA,** 512/472-5992 (box office), or 512/472-5927. Tickets $12–$80.

Austin's first professional opera company, started in 1985, presents three productions a year at the Bass Concert Hall. Major international artists as well as performers of national stature hit the high notes in such operas as Mozart's *The Magic Flute* and Puccini's *La Bohéme,* which are on the program for the 1996–97 season.

Austin Symphony

1101 Red River St. ☎ **888/4-MAESTRO** or 512/476-6064. Tickets: Classical, $11–$25; Pops, $15 and $25.

A resident in Austin since 1911, the symphony performs most of its classical works at Bass Concert Hall; guest artists in the 1996–97 season included Nadja Salerno-Sonnenberg and Doc Severinson. The informal Pops shows, which featured Van Cliburn in the same season, play to a picnic table–seated crowd at the Palmer Auditorium. In summer at Symphony Square, every Wednesday from 9:30 until about 11:30am, kids can try out various orchestral instruments in the symphony's version of a petting zoo. Symphony Square is a complex comprising an outdoor amphitheater and four historic structures dating from 1871 to 1877; narrow Waller Creek runs between the seats and the stage of the amphitheater.

Maestro Sung Kwak, the resident conductor, is leaving at the end of the 1996–97 season; 1997–98 will be devoted to finding his replacement, with auditioning guest conductors running the show.

THEATER

Frontera Hyde Park Theatre

511 W. 43rd St. ☎ **512/419-7408** (box office) or 512/499-8497 (theater). Tickets $8–$10.

An intimate neighborhood theater in Austin's historic Hyde Park district presents the innovative, contemporary work of the Frontera theater company. Genres range from music and dance to performance art, subjects from baseball to racism and lesbianism, but you can expect whatever you see to be intellectually engaging. The annual month-long FronteraFest, called "the most exciting theatrical event in Austin" by the *Austin Chronicle,* showcases local talent of all kinds.

Live Oak Theatre

State Theatre, 719 Congress St. ☎ **512/472-5143** (box office) or 512/472-7134. Tickets $15–$18.

Austin's most professional theater puts on a wide variety of work, from acclaimed classics like Oscar Wilde's *The Importance of Being Ernest* to contemporary works such as Edward Albee's *Three Tall Women.* In 1996, the theater saw the premiere of the *Dead Presidents' Club* by Larry L. King, who wrote *The Best Little Whorehouse in Texas.* Readings from nationwide participants in the Harvest Festival of New Plays are held in the fall; the play that wins the contest is produced during the season.

Mary Moody Northen Theatre of St. Edward's University

3001 S. Congress Ave. ☎ **512/448-8484** (box office) or 512/448-8483. Tickets $10 adults, $8 seniors, $5 students.

U.T.'s College of Fine Arts is not the only act in town: St. Edward's University also has a thriving theater department, which gets support for its performances from a variety of professional directors and guest actors. The 1996–97 season ranged from the rock classic *Grease* to *Twelfth Night* by Shakespeare.

Vortex Repertory Company

Planet Theatre, 2307 Manor Rd. ☎ **512/499-TIXS** (box office) or 512/478-LAVA. Ticket prices average around $11, with discounts available for students and seniors.

A converted warehouse with an outdoor courtyard and cafe, the Planet Theatre (just east of the University of Texas and I-35) complements Vortex's avant-garde program. Names of such 1996-97 productions as *Lucifa, Panoptikon,* and *Pitchfork Disney* may be familiar only to the initiated, but you might want to check it out for something different.

Zachary Scott Theatre Center

1510 Toomey Rd. (John E. Whisenhunt Arena Stage) or 1421 W. Riverside Dr. (Kleberg Stage). ☎ **512/476-0541** (box office) or 512/476-0594. Tickets $13–$25.

Austin's oldest theater, incorporated in 1933, features such Broadway and off-Broadway fare as *The Heiress, Jelly Roll,* and *Sylvia,* as well as holiday specials like *A Christmas Carol.* Works are performed at two adjacent theaters—one a three-sided thrust stage, the other in the round—at the edge of Zilker Park; it's a sneaker's throw from the parking lot to the hike-and-bike trail.

DANCE

Ballet Austin

3004 Guadalupe St. ☎ **512/476-2163** (box office) or 512/476-9051. Tickets $8–$39.

This company's 20 professional dancers leap and bound in such classics as *The Nutcracker* and *Coppelia,* as well as in such pieces as *Three of Hearts,* a suite of three modern ballets. Among the many places Ballet Austin has toured is Cyprus, where artistic director Lambros Lamrou was born. When in town, they perform at Bass Concert Hall or, for children's shows, the Paramount Theatre.

Sharir Dance Company

3724 Jefferson St., Suite 201. ☎ **512/458-8158.** Tickets $14 (students and senior discounts available).

An aptly high-tech ensemble for on-line Austin, Sharir first stretched the boundaries of dance toward virtual reality in 1994 when the company included video projections and computer-generated images in its choreography; it has been continuing its exploration of new technologies ever since. This exciting postmodern troupe, in residence at the University of Texas's College of Fine Arts, holds most of its Austin performances at the college's Performing Arts Center, but also offers site-specific environmental pieces.

3 The Bar Scene

BREW PUBS

Copper Tank Brewing Company

504 Trinity St. ☎ **512/478-8444.**

Within the confines of these thick limestone walls, sports fans wanting to catch the game on one of the two large screens, couples dining from an eclectic menu, and singles hoping to meet that certain someone mingle with beer aficionados, who come to savor the light Whitetail Ale or the Big Dog Stout. Wednesday nights all drafts are only a dollar. A small courtyard provides a haven from the crowd.

Waterloo Brewing Company
401 Guadalupe St. ☎ **512/477-1836.**

The first brew pub in Texas—do-it-yourself suds weren't legal in the state until late 1993—Waterloo has a decent dining room on the first floor, a noisy game room upstairs, and six good microbrews on tap. The pale ale is excellent and the full-bodied O. Henry's Porter is practically a meal in itself.

BRITISH BAR

Dog & Duck Pub
406 W. 17th St. ☎ **512/479-0598.**

We've had it verified by Brits that this is the real McCoy, a comfy local with a relaxing atmosphere. You'll be touring all the British Isles with the mix of darts, Irish jams, bagpipes, and hearty brews. The bangers and mash taste authentic, too—not that this is necessarily a good thing.

CIGAR BAR

Cedar Street
208 W. Fourth St. ☎ **512/708-8811.**

The martini and cigar crowd hang out here. Actor Denzel Washington has visited, as has musical legend Bob Dylan. When the weather's warm, the courtyard area provides more space as well as live music, usually jazz or acoustic; otherwise it's pretty close quarters—not ideal if you don't like cigar smoke. There's usually a cover.

GAY BAR

Oilcan Harry's
211 W. Fourth St. ☎ **512/320-8823.**

This is the place to come to find a buttoned-down, Brooks Brothers kind of guy; its name notwithstanding, this slick warehouse district bar attracts a clean-cut, upscale crowd. There's dancing here, but not with the same frenzy as at many of the other clubs.

HISTORIC BAR

Scholz Garten
1607 San Jacinto Blvd. ☎ **512/474-1958.**

Since 1866, when councilman August Scholz first opened his tavern near the state capitol, every Texas governor has visited it at least once (and many quite a few more times). Recently, new owners, who also run the popular Green Mesquite BBQ, have given Texas's oldest operating biergarten new life. The extensive menu now combines barbecue favorites with traditional bratwurst and sauerkraut; a new sound system cranks out the polka tunes; and new patio tables as well as a few stragetically placed TV sets help Longhorn fans cheer on their team—a Scholz's tradition in and of itself. All in all, this is a great place to drink in some Austin history.

LOCAL FAVORITE

Cedar Door
910 W. Cesar Chavez. ☎ **512/473-3712.**

"Cheers" with a redwood deck looking out on Town Lake, the Cedar Door is Austin's favorite local, drawing a group of potluck regulars ranging from hippies to journalists and politicos. The beer's cold, the drinks are strong, and to lots of folks it feels like home.

PIANO BAR

Driskill Hotel
604 Brazos St. ☎ 512/474-5911.

Sink into one of the plush chairs arrayed around a grand piano and enjoy everything from blues to show tunes in the opulent upper-lobby bar of Austin's only historic hotel. A pianist accompanies the happy-hour hors d'oeuvres munching (nightly from 5 to 7pm), but the ivory thumping doesn't get going in earnest until 9pm on Thursday, Friday, and Saturday, when people start singing along.

SPORTS BAR

BW3 Grille
218 E. Sixth St. ☎ 512/472-7227.

With 18 regular sets, three big screens, and two satellite hookups, BW3 is the place to catch your favorite team. A few pool tables upstairs and down, as well as the popular NTN Trivia game help to round out the action. The name refers to the bar menu's specialty, buffalo wings, which come with a choice of 12 sauces. *Beware:* When they say hot, they really mean it.

4 Movies

Local theaters screen the most foreign films in the state. It's almost harder to find mainstream movies in Austin than it is to locate foreign films in most other cities; nearly every cinema in town devotes at least one screen to something off Hollywood's beaten track. In the university area, the largest concentration of art films can be found at the **Dobie Theatre,** 2021 Guadalupe St., on the Drag (☎ 512/472-FILM), and at the two venues of the **Texas Union Film Series,** U.T. campus: Texas Union Building and Hogg Auditorium (☎ 512/475-6666). The **Village Cinema Art,** 2700 W. Anderson Lane (☎ 512/451-8352), across from Northpark Mall, also exclusively showcases independent and imported fare. Those looking for something Hollywood usually head for **Highland Pavilion 10,** I-35 at Middle Fiskville Road (☎ 512/454-9562).

5 Late-Night Bites

If it's 3am and you have a hankering for a huge stack of pancakes to soak up that last shiner you probably shouldn't have drank, Austin has you covered. Part Texas roadhouse, part all-night diner, Austin's cafes are characterized by extra late hours, funky atmosphere, and large quantities of hippie food. To call them cafes is a bit misleading—there's nothing remotely resembling Gallic chic here—but it's as good a term as any for these Austin originals.

One of the earliest on the scene and still hugely popular is **Kerbey Lane,** 3704 Kerbey Lane (☎ 512/451-1436); come Sunday morning, locals spill out on the porch of the comfortable old house, waiting for a table so they can order the signature "pancakes as big as your head." Musicians finishing up late-night gigs at the Continental Club usually head over to the **Magnolia Cafe South,** 1920 S. Congress Ave. (☎ 512/445-0000); the Love Veggies sautéed in garlic butter and the

Deep Eddy burrito go over big here. Although it's relatively new on the scene, the **Austin Java Co.,** 1206 Parkway (Lamar and Enfield) (☎ **512/476-1829**), is already developing a loyal after-hours clientele; portions of everything from hummus dip to creamy tomatillo crawfish pasta are gigantic. **Momma's,** 314 N. Congress (☎ **512/469-9369**), a recently opened bastion of political incorrectness, is also a comer. Not far from the Sixth Street music strip, this is the place where bartenders go for some good ol' country cooking and a smoke after their clubs close. Magnolia Cafe and Kerbey Lane are open 24 hours daily; Momma's is open round the clock on Thursday through Saturday; and Austin Java Co., an early bird, shuts down at 4am Saturday and Sunday, earlier during the week. Both Austin Java Co. and Magnolia Cafe have outdoor decks.

17

Touring the Texas Hill Country

A rising and falling dreamscape of lakes and rivers, springs and caverns, the Hill Country is one of Texas's prettiest regions, especially in early spring when wildflowers daub it with every pigment in nature's palette. Dotted with old dance halls, country stores, and quaint Teutonic towns—more than 30,000 Germans emigrated to Texas during the great land-grant years of the Republic—and birthplace to one of the U.S.'s more colorful recent presidents, the region also presents a riveting tableau of the state's history.

San Antonio lies at the southern edge of the Hill Country, while Austin is the northeastern gateway to the region. The following tour traces a roughly circular route from San Antonio, but it's only 80 miles between the two cities; distances in this area are sufficiently short that you can design excursions based on your point of origin and your particular interests. The highlights are covered here, but those with extra time will find far more to explore. Contact the **Hill Country Tourism Association,** 1700 Sidney Baker, Suite 200, Kerrville, 78028 (☎ **210/895-5505**), for a packet of information about additional things to see and do in the area; you'll also receive a schedule of the many food and music fests celebrated here throughout the year.

Note: Driving in the Hill Country can be a delight, but the speed limit on a number of roads without passing lanes is 70 mph. If you want to meander and enjoy the scenery, be prepared to pull over and let other cars pass, or you'll have a retinue of annoyed locals on your tail.

1 Boerne

From downtown San Antonio, it's a straight shot, 30 miles north on I-10 to Boerne (rhymes with "journey"); this is a good base for those who want to be near a big city as well as to some very rural areas. A popular health resort in the 1880s, the little (2.2-mile) town was first settled 30 years earlier by freedom-seeking German intellectuals; it was named after German firebrand journalist Ludwig Börne. A gazebo with a Victorian cupola in the center of the main plaza often hosts concerts by the Boerne Village Band, the oldest continuously operating German band in the world outside Germany (it first tuned up in 1860). A number of the town's 19th-century limestone buildings house small historical museums, boutiques, and restaurants, but

Boerne's biggest draw for many is its antique shops—more than 20 line the "Hauptstrasse," or main street. For a self-guided tour, stop in at the **Boerne Chamber of Commerce,** 1 Main Plaza, 78006 (☎ **210/249-8000**).

SEEING THE SIGHTS IN & AROUND BOERNE

Those who want to spend their time outdoors can explore four distinct ecosystems— grassland, marshland, woodland, and river bottom—via short treks on the **Cibolo Wilderness Trail,** City Park Road (☎ **210/249-4616**). If you like to stroll carrying golf clubs, the top-rated **Tapatio Springs,** Johns Road exit off I-10 west (☎ **800/ 999-3299**), is the place.

One of the most popular close-by attractions is **Cascade Caverns,** about 2 miles south of Boerne, exit 543 on I-10 (☎ **210/755-8080**). This active cave boasts huge chambers, a 90-foot underground waterfall, and comfortable walking trails. It's also easy to tour the stalactite- and stalagmite-filled **Cave Without a Name,** 325 Kreutzberg Rd., 12 miles northeast of Boerne (☎ **210/537-4212**); a naming contest held when the cavern was discovered in 1939 was won by a little boy who wrote that it was too pretty to name (the $500 he earned put him through college).

Rafters and canoers like **Guadalupe River State Park,** some 13 miles east of Boerne, off Hwy. 46 on P.R. 31 (☎ **210/438-2656**), comprising more than 1,900 acres surrounding a lovely, cypress-edged river. Keep an eye out: You might spot white-tailed deer, coyotes, armadillos, or even a rare golden-cheeked warbler here.

Those whose tastes run to the above-ground, indoors, and epicurean will want to drive 12 miles north of Boerne on F.M. 1376 to the **Sister Creek Vineyards** (☎ **210/324-6704**), located in a converted century-old cotton gin on the main— actually the only—street in Sisterdale (population 25). Among the bottles available for sampling, the 1994 Texas cabernet sauvignon is especially good. Weave down the road afterward to the **Sisterdale General Store,** opened in 1954 and not changed very much since then. Cowboy art, a beautiful handcrafted bar made of East Texas pine, and down-home hospitality are among the reasons to set here a while.

WHERE TO STAY

Now a lovely Victorian-style B&B, **Ye Kendall Inn,** 128 W. Blanco, Boerne, 78006 (☎ **210/249-2138**), opened as a stagecoach lodge in 1859. The rooms ($80) and suites ($125) are beautifully appointed, but the former have their bathtubs in the center, near the bed, and commodes behind a screen. If you're traveling with a companion with whom you're not willing to be that intimate, book a suite.

You'll have all the privacy you like at the **Boerne Lake Lodge,** 310 Lakeview Dr., Boerne, 78006 (☎ **210/249-9555**), where rooms ($150 per night for two, $250 for four including breakfast) are in spacious and light-filled Hill Country–style houses. The woodsy lakeside setting is idyllic and the lodge has its own river barge.

The **Guadalupe River Ranch,** P.O. Box 877, Boerne, 78006 (☎ **800/460-2005; e-mail grranch@connecti.com**), was owned by actress Olivia de Haviland in the 1930s and served as an art colony for a while. This gorgeous spread offers abundant opportunities for activities ranging from river rafting to porch sitting. Rates with breakfast run $150 a night for two; with three meals, $218.

WHERE TO DINE

Scuzzi, in Ye Kendall Inn (see above), 128 W. Blanco (☎ **210/249-8886**), serves good northern Italian cuisine in an elegant atmosphere. Try the linguini alla Scuzzi, heaped with shrimp and three types of peppers.

The more casual **Bear Moon Bakery,** 401 S. Main St. (☎ **210/816-BEAR**), is ideal for a hearty breakfast, light lunch, or early dinner. Organic ingredients and

The Texas Hill Country

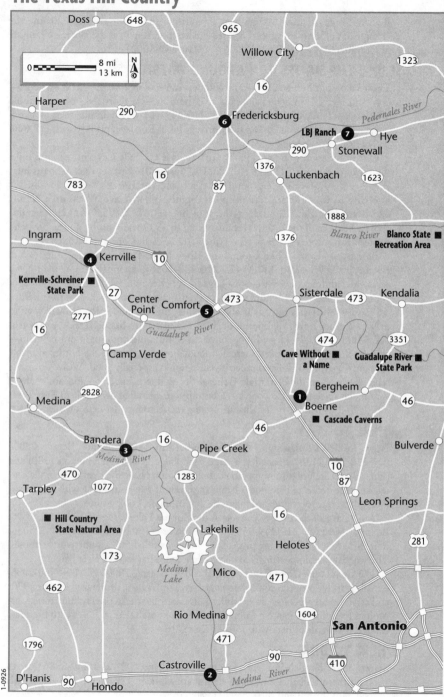

Doss 648
965
Willow City
1323
16
Harper
290
Fredericksburg 6
Pedernales River
LBJ Ranch 7 Hye
290 Stonewall
1376
Luckenbach
1623
783
16
87
1888
1376
Blanco River Blanco State ■
Recreation Area
Ingram
Kerrville 4
10
Kerrville-Schreiner ■
State Park
27
Center
Point Comfort 473
5
Sisterdale 473 Kendalia
2771
Guadalupe River
474 3351
16
Camp Verde
Cave Without ■ Guadalupe River ■
a Name State Park
Medina
2828
Bergheim
Boerne 1
46
Bandera 3 16
Medina River
Pipe Creek
Cascade Caverns ■
46
Bulverde
470
1077
1283
10
Tarpley
87
Hill Country ■
State Natural Area
16
Leon Springs
Lakehills
281
173
Helotes
Mico
462
Medina
Lake
471
Rio Medina
1604
San Antonio
1796
471
Castroville 2
90
410
D'Hanis 90
Hondo
Medina River

0 8 mi
13 km
N

1-0926

222

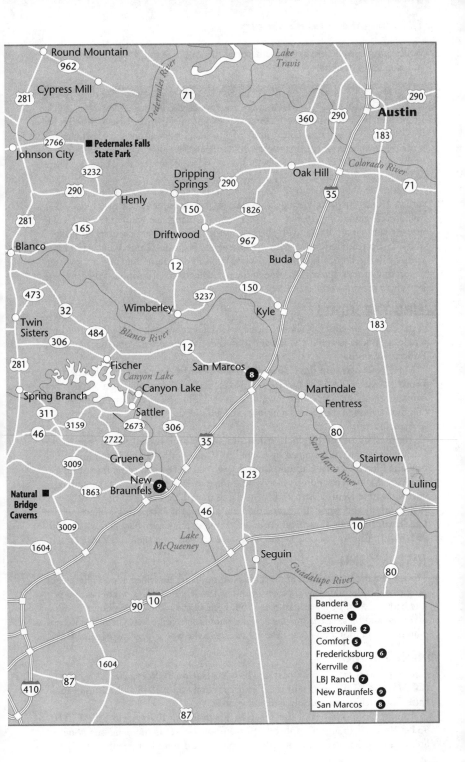

Round Mountain
962
Cypress Mill
281
Pedernales River
71
Lake Travis
360
290
290 **Austin**
183
2766
■ Pedernales Falls State Park
Johnson City
3232
Colorado River
71
290
Dripping Springs
290
Oak Hill
Henly
150
35
281
165
Driftwood
1826
Blanco
12
967
Buda
473
32
Wimberley
3237
150
Kyle
183
Twin Sisters
484
Blanco River
306
12
281
Fischer
Canyon Lake
San Marcos ❽
Martindale
Fentress
Spring Branch
Canyon Lake
311
3159
Sattler
2673
306
80
46
2722
35
Stairtown
Gruene
San Marco River
123
Luling
Natural ■ Bridge Caverns
3009
1863
New Braunfels ❾
46
10
3009
Lake McQueeney
Seguin
80
1604
Guadalupe River
90 10
1604
Bandera ❸
Boerne ❶
Castroville ❷
Comfort ❺
Fredericksburg ❻
Kerrville ❹
LBJ Ranch ❼
New Braunfels ❾
San Marcos ❽
87
410
87

223

locally grown produce enhance the flavor of the inventive soups, salads, sandwiches, and wonderful desserts.

2 Castroville

Even though Castroville is even closer to San Antonio than Boerne—20 miles via U.S. 90 west—it has maintained more of a pristine, rural atmosphere, perhaps because the town doesn't encourage growth. Residents who are not descended from one of the founding families often feel a bit like outsiders, even after they have lived here for more than 20 years.

Castroville was founded on a scenic bend of the Medina River in 1844. Two years earlier, Henri Castro, a Portuguese-born Jewish Frenchman, had received a 1.25-million-acre grant from the Republic of Texas in exchange for a commitment to colonize the land. Second only to Stephen F. Austin in the number of settlers he brought over, Castro recruited most of his 2,134 émigrés from the Rhine Valley, and especially from the French province of Alsace. You can still hear Alsatian, an unwritten dialect of German, spoken by some of the older members of town, but the language is likely to die out of the area when they do.

SEEING THE SIGHTS

Note: Castroville closes down on Monday and Tuesday, and some places are shuttered on Sunday as well. If you want to find everything open, come on Thursday, Friday, or Saturday.

Make your first stop the **Castroville Chamber of Commerce,** 802 London St., 78009 (☎ **800/778-6775** or 210/538-3142), where you can pick up a booklet that contains a walking tour of the town's historical buildings, as well as a map that details the location of the various boutiques and antique shops (they're not concentrated in a single area).

Almost 100 of the original settlers' unevenly slope-roofed houses remain in Castroville, some still occupied by the builders' ancestors; the oldest standing structure, the **First St. Louis Catholic Church,** went up in 1846 on the corner of Angelo and Moy. Many of the European-style headstones in the **cemetery** at the western edge of town, where Henri Castro's wife, Amelia, is buried, date back to the 1840s.

A gristmill and wood-and-stone dam are among the interesting artifacts at the **Landmark Inn State Historical Park,** 402 Florence St., Castroville, 78009 (☎ **210/931-2133**); Robert E. Lee is said to have stayed at what was then the Vance Hotel.

A HISTORIC INN

The **Landmark Inn** (located in the State Historical Park described above) offers eight simple rooms decorated with pieces from the 1940s. Prices for a double with a private bath are $55; with a shared bath, $50; none of the rooms have phones or TVs. A continental breakfast is included in the rate. Don't come here for luxurious appointments, but for a uniquely peaceful setting in the woods near the Medina River.

WHERE TO DINE

Get a delicious taste of the past at **Haby's Alsation Bakery,** 207 U.S. 90 east (☎ **210/538-2118**), owned by the Tschirhart family since 1948 and featuring apple fritters, strudel, stollen, breads, and coffee cakes.

Among the specialties of the **Alsatian Restaurant,** 403 Angelo St. (☎ **210/931-3260**), set in an atmospheric 19th-century house, is the delicious boneless Strasbourg chicken seasoned with curry; recommended accompaniments from a good wine cellar are noted on the menu. The biergarten-style outdoor patio is delightful for lunch.

The more formal **Normandie Restaurant,** 1302 Fionella St. (☎ 210/538-3070), features a classic French menu, including escargot and coq au vin. Strains of songs from Normandy, homeland of one of the propieter/chefs, float through the pretty, lace-curtained cottage.

3 Bandera

North of Castroville and west of Boerne, Bandera is a slice of life out of the Old West; everything and everybody here seems to have come straight off a John Ford film set. Established as a lumber camp in 1853, this popular guest-ranch center still has the feel of the frontier: Not only are many of its historic buildings intact— including **St. Stanislaus** (1855), the second-oldest Polish church in the country— but people are as genuinely friendly as any you might imagine from America's small-town past.

WHAT TO SEE & DO IN BANDERA

Take your time strolling along Main Street, where you can watch craftspeople create traditional cowboy gear. Be sure to stop in at the **Bandera Forge** (☎ 210/796-7184), a working blacksmith shop (you can design your own branding iron); **Sim's Spur Company** (☎ 210/796-3716), which sells intricate spurs and bits; and **Kline Saddlery** (☎ 210/796-3399), where those who don't have horses can buy a hand-tooled belt or wallet. If all this puts you in the mood to mount your own nag, the **Bandera County Convention and Visitors Bureau,** P.O. Box 171, 1808 Hwy. 16 south, 78003 (☎ 800/364-3833 or 210/796-3045), can help you find an outfitter. It's also the place to check whether any rodeos or roping exhibitions are in the area (you're especially likely to catch them in summer) and to pick up a pamphlet detailing the town's many historic buildings and stores.

If your relation to the ponies tends toward the monetary, **Bandera Downs** (☎ 800/572-2332 or 210/796-7781), on Hwy. 16 approximately a mile south of town, offers parimutuel betting on all its live events as well as on simulcast satellite races.

ENJOYING THE GREAT OUTDOORS

You can canter through the **Hill Country State Natural Area,** 10 miles southwest of Bandera (☎ 210/796-4413), the largest state park in Texas allowing horseback riding; the nearest outfitter is the helpful and reliable **Running R Ranch,** Route 1 (☎ 210/796-3984). A visit to the nonprofit **Brighter Days Horse Refuge** in Pipe Creek, about 9 miles northeast of Bandera (☎ 210/510-6607), will warm any animal lover's heart. The price of admission to this rehab center for abandoned and neglected horses is only a bag of carrots or apples, but donations are most welcome.

About 20 miles southeast of town (take Hwy. 16 to R.R. 1283), **Medina Lake** is the place to hook crappie, white or black bass, and, especially, huge yellow catfish; the public boat ramp is on the north side of the lake, at the end of P.R. 37. The Bandera Convention and Visitors Bureau can provide names of various outfitters to those who want to kayak, canoe, or tube down the Medina River.

Most people visit the **Lost Maples State Natural Area,** about 40 miles west of Bandera in Vanderpool (☎ 210/966-3413), in autumn, when the leaves put on a brilliant show, but birders come in winter to look at bald eagles, hikers like the wild-flower array in spring, and anglers try to reduce the Guadalupe bass population of the Sabinal River in summer. Those seeking accommodations more upscale than the campground should try the **Texas Stagecoach Inn,** HC-02, Box 166, Vanderpool, 78885 (☎ **210/966-6272**), a huge (6,000-square-foot) 1885 house done in 1950s ranch style. The views are lovely, the breakfasts elaborate, and the rates ($70 to $90) reasonable.

STAYING AT A GUEST RANCH

For the full flavor of this region, plan to stay at one of Bandera's many guest ranches.

At the **Dixie Dude Ranch,** P.O. Box 548, Bandera, 78003 (☎ **800/375-Y'ALL** or 210/796-4481), you're likely to see white-tailed deer or wild turkeys as you trot on horseback through a 725-acre spread; the down-home, friendly atmosphere keeps folks coming back year after year.

Tubing on the Medina River is among the many things you might do during the day at the **Mayan Ranch,** P.O. Box 577, Bandera, 78003 (☎ **210/796-3312** or 210/460-3036), another well-established family-run place; corporate groups often do a bit of loosening up here. Both ranches provide lots of additional western fun for their guests during high season—maybe two-step lessons, cookouts, hayrides, singing cowboys, or trick-roping exhibitions. Adult rates (at the Dixie Dude Ranch, $80 to $90 per person per night, at the Mayan Ranch, $102 to $125 per person per night) include three home-cooked meals, two trail rides, and most of the other activities.

Serious equestrians or wanna-bes might try the more upscale **Bald Eagle,** P.O. Box 1177, Bandera (☎ **210/460-3012**), where riding time is limited only by seat soreness (the ranch's hot tub might help). Rates for accommodations in the modern western cabins, including meals and rides, run from $242 per person for a (minimum) 2-night stay off-season. No children under 16 allowed.

WHERE TO DINE

When you're ready to put on the feed bag, try Main Street's **O.S.T.** (☎ **210/ 796-3636**), named for the Old Spanish Trail that used to run through Bandera; serving up down-home Texas and Tex-Mex victuals since 1921, this cafe has a room dedicated to the Duke and other cowboy film stars.

Just down the block, **Harvey's Old Bank Steakhouse** (☎ **210/796-8486**) puts out its salad bar in the former vault of the 1910 building. The huge lunch buffets, which usually include fried chicken and other country-style selections, are a steal.

A HONKY-TONK

Don't miss **Arkey Blue's Silver Dollar Saloon** (☎ **210/796-8826**), a genuine spit-and-sawdust cowboy honky-tonk on Main Street; Hank Williams, Sr., carved his name on one of the tables. When there's no band on, plug a quarter in the old jukebox and play a country ballad by owner Arkey.

EN ROUTE TO KERRVILLE

Both of the roads from Bandera to Kerrville are scenic and each has its distinct allure. If you take the longer Hwy. 16 route—37 miles compared to 26—you'll pass through **Medina.** You won't doubt the little town's claim of being the Apple Capital of Texas when you come to Love Creek Orchards Cider Mill and Country Store on the main street; along with apple pies and other fresh-baked goods, you can buy apple cider, apple syrup, apple butter, apple ice cream . . . you can even have an apple sapling shipped back home to you.

Military buffs might want to take the more direct Hwy. 173, which passes through **Camp Verde** (1856–69), the former headquarters of the short-lived U.S. Army camel cavalry. Widespread ignorance of their habits and the onset of the Civil War led to the abandonment of the attempt to introduce "ships of the desert" into dry Southwest terrain, but the commander of the post had great respect for his humpbacked recruits. There's little left of the fortress itself, but the old General Store and Post Office (1877), chock-full of camel memorabilia and artifacts from the past, remains intact. Buy some postcards and the fixings to have a picnic at the pleasant roadside park nearby.

4 Kerrville

With a population of about 20,000, Kerrville is larger than the other Hill Country towns so far explored. Now a popular retirement and tourist area, it was founded in the 1840s by Joshua Brown, a shingle-maker attracted to the area's many cypresses. A rough-and-tumble camp surrounded by more civilized German towns, Kerrville soon became a ranching center for longhorn cattle and, more unusually, for Angora goats, eventually turning out the most mohair in the United States. After it was lauded in the 1920s for its healthful climate, Kerrville began to draw youth camps, sanitoriums, and artists.

SEEING THE SIGHTS IN KERRVILLE

The newly restored downtown area, flanked by the Guadalupe River and a pleasant park, is the most interesting part of town. For a glimpse of affluent Hill Country life in the early days, visit the **Hill Country Museum,** 226 Earl Garrett St. (☎ **210/ 896-8633**), a mansion built by Alfred Giles of native stone for pioneer rancher Capt. Charles Schreiner. **Old Republic Square** (off Lemos, between Main and Water Streets) hosts a collection of quaint gift shops and boutiques. Many of them specialize in antiques, but **Artisan Accents,** 826 Water St. (☎ 210/896-4220), sells beautiful contemporary crafts.

The **Cowboy Artists of America Museum,** 1550 Bandera Hwy. (☎ **210/ 896-2553**), just outside the main part of town, displays various visions of the West in a striking southwestern-style building. Outdoor enthusiasts will enjoy the nearby **Kerrville-Schreiner State Park,** 2385 Bandera Hwy. (☎ **210/257-5392**), a 500-acre green space boasting 7 miles of hiking trails, as well as swimming and boating on the Guadalupe River.

Sika deer, Corsican sheep, and the rare scimitar-horned oryx are among the species you can capture for your photo album on the **Kerrville Camera Safari,** 2301 Sidney Baker north (☎ **210/792-3600**), a drive-through wildlife ranch. The **Kerrville Convention and Visitors Bureau** (1700 Sidney Baker, Suite 200, 78028; ☎ **800/221-7958** or 210/792-3535), can give you a map and clue you into more of the town's attractions; ask about the huge Kerrville Folk Festival, which draws fans from around the country.

A NEARBY RANCH

You'll have to make a reservation to visit the **Y. O. Ranch,** 32 miles from Kerrville, off Hwy. 41, Mt. Home, 78058 (☎ **210/640-3222**). Originally comprising 550,000 acres purchased by Charles Shreiner in 1880, the Y. O. Ranch is now a 40,000-acre working ranch known for its exotic wildlife as well as for its Texas longhorn cattle. You can go out for a horseback ride and lunch during the day or stay overnight, if you don't mind sleeping under a furry hunting trophy.

WHERE TO STAY

The **Holiday Inn Y. O. Ranch Hotel and Conference Center,** 2033 Sidney Baker, Kerrville, 78028 (☎ **800-HOLIDAY** or 210/257-4440)—not near the Y. O. Ranch (see above) but in Kerrville itself—offers large and attractive western-style quarters; its Sam Houston dining room features wild game and big steaks, and the saloon occasionally serves up live music with its whisky. Doubles range from $68 to $99, depending on the season.

WHERE TO DINE

Combine lunch with antiquing at the **Water Street Antique Co.,** 820 Water St. (☎ **210/257-5044**), a restored turn-of-the-century building with a charming tearoom.

At **Pampell's Fountain,** 701 Water St. (☎ **210/257-8454**), you can enjoy a brown cow (coke, chocolate syrup, and chocolate ice cream) and then comb the former confectionery and opera house for items dating back to the era when such ice-cream sodas were the rage.

5 Comfort

The most direct route from Kerrville to Fredericksburg is via Hwy. 16 north, but it's well worth detouring 18 miles southeast along Hwy. 27 to seek Comfort. True to its name, it's one of the most pleasant of the Hill Country towns. It has been said that the freethinking German immigrants who founded Comfort in 1852 were originally going to call it *gemütlichkeit*—a more difficult-to-pronounce native version of its current moniker—when they arrived at this welcoming spot after an arduous journey from New Braunfels. The story is probably apocryphal, but it's an appealing explanation, especially as no one is quite sure what the truth is.

The rough-hewn limestone buildings in the center of Comfort may comprise the most complete 19th-century business district in Texas; some of the offices were designed by architect Alfred Giles, who also left his distinctive mark on San Antonio's streets. The earliest church in town was built some 40 years after the first settlers arrived; during the initial period, the founders' antireligious beliefs, for which they had been persecuted in the old country, prevailed. Most of the settlers were also opposed to the Confederacy during the Civil War. The **Treue der Union (True to the Union) Monument** (High Street, between Third and Fourth Streets) was erected in 1866 to commemorate 36 antislavery settlers who were killed by Confederate soldiers when they tried to defect to Mexico.

ANTIQUING

A majority of the town's antique shops (high-quality, but also high-priced) are in the limestone buildings along High Street. Make your first stop the **Ingenhuett Store,** 830 High St. (☎ **210/995-2149**), set in an Alfred Giles building and operated by the same German-American family since 1880; along with groceries, outdoor gear, and sundries, it carries maps and other sources of tourist information.

It's open far more frequently than the **Comfort Chamber of Commerce,** P.O. Box 777, Comfort, 78013 (☎ **210/995-3131**), on Seventh and High Streets, which has very limited hours.

WHERE TO STAY

One of the largest and most interesting antique shops in town, **Comfort Common,** 818 High St., Comfort, 78013 (☎ **210/995-3030**), doubles as a bed-and-breakfast. Reasonably priced accommodations in what was once the 19th-century Faust-Ingenhuett Hotel, built by Alfred Giles, are imaginatively decorated; all have private baths and look out onto a peaceful garden. Rates run from $55 to $75 for the rooms,

$75 to $80 for the suites; there's also a separate cottage and log cabin for $90 and $95, respectively.

WHERE TO DINE

The chef/owner of **Arlene's,** 426 Seventh St., just off High Street (☎ **210/ 995-3330**), used to be the food critic for the *San Antonio Express-News.* Her freshly made soups, quiches, sandwiches, and desserts prove she knew whereof she wrote.

The **Café on High Street,** 814 High St. (☎ **210/995-3470**), also specializes in light repasts prepared on the premises. The German chocolate pie, based on a recipe from Brenham, Germany, is divine. Both restaurants are open only Thursday through Sunday from 11am to 4pm.

BATS & OSTRICHES ALONG A BACKROAD TO FREDERICKSBURG

If you missed the **bats** in Austin, you've got a chance to see even more in an abandoned railroad tunnel supervised by the Texas Parks and Wildlife Department. From Comfort, take Hwy. 473 north 4 or 5 miles. When the road winds to the right toward Sisterdale, keep going straight on Old Highway 9; in another 8 or 9 miles, you'll spot a parking lot and a mound of large rocks on top of a hill. During migration season (May to November), you can watch as many as $2^1/_2$ million Mexican free-tailed bats set off on a food foray at around dusk. In past years, state-sponsored naturalist tours have been given on Thursday and Saturday evenings from June through October; call **800/792-1112** (punch in the "Parks" selection) to find out if they're still offered.

Even if you don't stop for the bats, this is a wonderfully scenic route to Fredericksburg. You won't see any road signs—have faith, this really will take you to a town, eventually—but you'll spot grazing goats and cows and even some strutting ostriches.

6 Fredericksburg

San Antonians and Austinites flock to Fredericksburg on the weekends, and with good reason. The town offers fine shopping, interesting historic attractions, and some of the most unusual accommodations around—all in a lovely rural setting.

Fredericksburg may be getting a bit trendy—film star spottings are increasingly common these days—but it also remains devoted to its European past. Baron Ottfried Hans von Meusebach was one of 10 nobles who formed a society designed to help Germans resettle in Texas, where they would be safe from political persecution and economic hardship. In 1846, he took 120 émigrés in ox-drawn carts from New Braunfels to this site, which he named for Prince Frederick of Prussia; the town's mile-long main street is still wide enough for a team of oxen to turn around in. The permanent peace treaty Meusebach negotiated with the Comanches in 1847 (the only one in the U.S. that was ever honored!), and the gold rush of 1849—Fredericksburg was the last place the California-bound prospectors could get supplies—both helped the town thrive.

SEEING THE SIGHTS

The **Convention and Visitors Bureau,** 106 N. Adams, 78624 (☎ **210/997-6523**), can direct you to the many points of interest in the town's historic district. These include a number of little **Sunday Houses,** built by German settlers in distant rural areas because they needed a place to stay overnight when they came to town to trade or attend church. You'll also notice many homes built in the Hill Country version of the German *fachwerk* design, made out of limestone with diagonal wood supports.

The unusual octagonal **Vareins Kirche (Society Church)** in Market Square (☎ 210/997-7832) once functioned as a town hall, school, and storehouse; a 1935 replica of the original 1847 building now holds the archives of the Gillespie County Historical Society.

The Historical Society also maintains the **Pioneer Museum Complex,** 309 W. Main St. (☎ 210/997-2835), anchored by the 1849 Kammlah House, which was a family residence and general store until the 1920s; among the other historical structures here are a one-room schoolhouse and a blacksmith's forge.

The 1852 Steamboat Hotel, originally owned by the grandfather of World War II naval hero Chester A. Nimitz, is now home to the exhibits of the **Admiral Nimitz Museum State Historical Park,** 340 E. Main St. (☎ 210/997-4379); also in the park are the Japanese Garden of Peace and the History Walk of the Pacific War—3 acres of large World War II relics.

SHOPPING

If you're pressed for time, Main Street between Elk and Milam is the town's most concentrated shopping area, but other sections are worth exploring, too. More than 100 specialty shops, many of them in mid-19th-century houses, feature work by Hill Country artisans; you can take a tour of a **dulcimer factory** (715 S. Washington), see a **glassblowing studio** (109 E. Main St.), or watch **candles** being made (151 and 121 E. Main St.). The biggest draw for many, however, are the five **Homestead Stores,** four on Main Street and one on Lincoln. People from all over Texas come here to shop for fashionable home furnishings, which combine European and Hill Country styles. One of the stores is devoted entirely to white things. Also becoming increasingly well known via its mail-order business is the **Fredericksburg Herb Farm,** 402 Whitney St. (☎ 800/259-HERB). There's an outlet on Main Street, but it's worth the short trip south of town to see the flower beds that produce salad dressings, teas, fragrances, and air fresheners (including an incredible chocolate mint scent). The grounds also host a restaurant and B&B.

WHAT TO SEE & DO NEARBY

One of the many attractions in the Fredericksburg vicinity is **Lady Bird Johnson Municipal Park,** 2 miles southeast on Hwy. 16 (☎ 210/997-4202), with an 18-hole golf course, a tennis court, and a 17-acre lake for fishing.

Lots of well-known performers turn up in the dance hall of **Luckenbach** (11 miles southeast on R.R. 1376), immortalized in a song by Waylon Jennings and Willie Nelson. There's not much else in the tiny town—listed under "L" in the Fredericksburg section of the county telephone directory—except a general store with a bar, but it's a great place to hang out on a weekend afternoon; someone's almost always strumming the guitar.

Three wineries near Fredericksburg all offer tastings and tours: **Oberhellmann Vineyards,** 14 miles north on Hwy. 16 (☎ 210/685-3297), **Grape Creek Vineyard,** 9 miles east on Hwy. 290 (☎ 210/644-2710), and Becker Vineyards, 1 mile farther east on 290 (☎ 210/644-2681).

For a **scenic loop drive,** head northwest to Willow City; the 13-mile route, which leads back to Hwy. 16, is especially spectacular in wildflower season.

Take F.M. 965 some 18 miles north to reach **Enchanted Rock State Park** (☎ 915/247-3903), a 640-acre, pink-granite dome that draws thousands of hikers each year. The creaking noises that emanate from it at night—likely caused by the cooling of the rock's outer surface—led the area's Indian tribes to believe the rock was inhabited by evil spirits.

GUEST COTTAGES IN FREDERICKSBURG

Fredericksburg is known for its *gastehauses* (guest cottages); many historic homes have been converted into romantic havens replete with robes, fireplaces, and even spas. You can book anything from an 1865 homestead with its own wishing well to a bedroom above an old bakery to a limestone Sunday House. Unlike most B&Bs, these places ensure privacy; breakfast is provided the night before (the perishables are left in a refrigerator). For a booklet detailing some of the most interesting ones, contact **Gastehaus Schmidt,** 231 W. Main St., Fredericksburg, 78624 (☎ **210/997-5612**). **Bed & Breakfast of Fredericksburg,** 619 W. Main St., Fredericksburg, 78624 (☎ **210/997-4712**), **Be My Guest,** 402 W. Main St., Fredericksburg, 78624 (☎ **210/997-7227**), and **Hill Country Lodging Service** (☎ **800/745-3591** or 210/990-8455) include more traditional bed-and-breakfasts among their listings.

DINING IN & AROUND FREDERICKSBURG

The **Altdorf Biergarten,** 301 W. Main St. (☎ **210/997-7865**), and **Friedhelm's Bavarian Inn,** 905 W. Main St. (☎ **210/997-6300**), both feature hearty German schnitzels, dumplings, and sauerbraten, and large selections of beer.

For good home brews and friendly atmosphere, the **Fredericksburg Brewing Co.,** 245 E. Main St. (☎ **210/997-1646**), is hard to beat; book one of the rooms upstairs, and you can relax in your own bed after a pizza and a pint of Pedernales Pilsner.

For an entirely different atmosphere and menu, stop in at the popular **Peach Tree Tea Room,** 210 S. Adams St. (☎ **210/997-9527**); the quiches and salads are super, the ice cream pie heavenly. Browsing the gift gallery afterward won't really burn off too many calories, but it's always a good rationalization.

About 11 miles north of Fredericksburg on I-87, the **Hill Top Cafe** (☎ **210/997-8922**) serves excellent Cajun and Greek food (a new chef from Dallas's famed Cafe Annie is just settling in); you might find the owner, a former member of the band Asleep at the Wheel, very much awake at the piano.

7 Lyndon B. Johnson Country

Welcome to Johnson territory, where the forebears of the 36th president settled almost 150 years ago. Even before he attained the country's highest office, Lyndon Johnson was a local hero whose successful fight for funding of a series of dams provided the region with inexpensive water and power. If you can, make a day out of a visit to LBJ's boyhood home and the sprawling ranch that became known as the Texas White House; even those who don't usually feel drawn to the past are likely to find themselves fascinated by Johnson's frontier lineage. Consider bringing along a picnic to enjoy at the state park; there are also quite a few restaurants in Johnson City.

A HISTORICAL PARK

From Fredericksburg, take U.S. 290 east for 16 miles to the entrance of the **Lyndon B. Johnson State and National Historical Parks at LBJ Ranch,** Box 238, Stonewall, 78671 (☎ **210/868-7128** or 210/644-2252), co-run by the Texas Parks and Wildlife Department and the National Park Service. Tour buses depart regularly from the Visitors Center to the still-operating Johnson Ranch; you probably won't spot Lady Bird Johnson, who spends about a third of her time here, but don't be surprised to see longhorn cattle being grazed.

Crossing over the swift-flowing Pedernales River to fields filled with phlox, Indian blanket, and other wildflowers, one can easily see why Johnson used the ranch as a second, more comfortable White House, and why, discouraged from running for a second presidential term, he came back here to find solace and, all too soon, to die. A reconstructed version of the former president's modest birthplace lies close to his final resting place, shared with five generations of Johnsons. On the side of the river from which you started out, period-costumed guides at the Sauer-Beckmann Living History Farm give visitors a look at typical Texas–German farm life at the turn of the century; the midwife who attended LBJ's birth grew up here. Nearby, you can take advantage of a swimming pool (open only in summer) and lots of picnic spots; bring your pole if you want to fish in the Pedernales River.

Admission is $3 per person for bus tours; all other areas are free. All state park buildings, including the Visitors Center, are open daily from 8am to 5pm except Christmas; the Sauer-Beckmann Living History Farm is open daily from 8am to 4:30pm except Christmas; the Nature Trail, grounds, and picnic areas are open until dark daily. National Park Service tours of the LBJ Ranch, lasting from 1 to $1^1/_2$ hours, depart from the State Park Visitors Center daily from 10am to 4pm except Christmas (tours may be shortened or canceled due to excessive heat and humidity).

JOHNSON CITY

It's 14 miles farther east along U.S. 290 to Johnson City, a pleasant agricultural town named for founder James Polk Johnson, who was LBJ's second cousin. The **Johnson City Tourism and Visitors Bureau,** P.O. Box 485, Johnson City 78636 (☎ 210/868-7684), can provide information about dining, lodging, and shopping in Johnson City. Those interested in staying at a local B&B should call **210/868-7684.**

The Boyhood Home—the house on Ninth Street where Lyndon was raised after age 5—is the centerpiece of this unit of the **Lyndon B. Johnson National Historical Park,** P.O. Box 329, Johnson City, 78636 (☎ 210/868-7128). The modest white clapboard structure that the family occupied from 1913 on was a hub of intellectual and political activity: LBJ's father, Sam Ealy Johnson, Jr., was a state legislator, and his mother, Rebekah, was one of the few college-educated women in the country at the time. From here, be sure to walk over to the Johnson Settlement, where LBJ's grandfather, Sam Ealy Johnson, Sr., and his great uncle, Jessie, engaged in successful cattle speculation in the 1860s. The rustic dogtrot cabin out of which they ran their business is still intact. Before exploring the two sites, stop at the new Visitors Center (take F Street to 10th Street; you'll see the signs), where a number of excellent displays and a moving film about Johnson's presidency provide background for the buildings you'll see.

Admission is free. The Boyhood Home, Visitors Center, and Johnson Settlement are all open 9am to 5pm daily except Christmas and New Year's Day.

EN ROUTE TO AUSTIN

If you're heading on to Austin, take a short detour from U.S. 290 to **Pedernales Falls State Park,** 8 miles east of Johnson City on F.R. 2766 (☎ 210/868-7304). When the flow of the Pedernales River is normal to high, the stepped waterfalls that give the 4,860-acre park its name are dramatic.

8 San Marcos

It's a quick 26 miles south via I-35 from Austin to San Marcos. The temporary site of two Spanish missions in the late 1700s, the town was settled by Anglos in the middle of the 19th century and is now home to Southwest State University, the alma mater of Lyndon Johnson and of singer George Strait.

WHAT TO SEE & DO

Few people come to San Marcos to see the historic sights. In the center of town, clear, cool springs, which keep a constant temperature of 72°, well up from the Balcones Fault to form Spring Lake. On its shores sits **Aquarena Springs Resort,** 1 Aquarena Springs Dr. (☎ **800/999-9767** or 512/396-8900), renowned for glass-bottomed boats from which you can view some of the rare flora and fauna that the springs support, as well as for Ralph the Swimming Pig, who performs at a submarine theater (actually, there have been a series of Ralphs).

The **San Marcos River,** which begins at Spring Lake, attracts many canoers and rafters; between May and September, the local Lions Club (☎ **512/396-LION**) rents inner tubes and operates a river shuttle at City Park.

When the Balcones Fault was active some 30 million years ago, an earthquake created the cave at the center of the rather tacky **Wonder World,** 1000 Prospect St., off Bishop (☎ **800/782-7653, ext. 2283,** or 512/392-3760); in addition to the cave, you can see water flowing upward at an Anti-Gravity House.

OUTLET SHOPPING

If truth be told, lots of people bypass San Marcos altogether and head straight for the two factory outlet malls a few miles south of downtown; it's the biggest discount shop fest in Texas. Take exit 200 from I-35 for both the **Tanger Factory Outlet Center** (☎ **800-4TANGER** or 512/396-7444) and the larger and tonier **San Marcos Factory Shops** (☎ **800/628-9465** or 512/396-7183), across the street. Among the almost 150 stores, you'll find everything from Donna Karan, Anne Klein, and Brooks Brothers to American Tourister and Mikasa. There's also a new Saks Fifth Avenue outlet.

The **San Marcos Convention and Visitors Bureau,** 202 N. C. M. Allen Pkwy., 78666 (☎ **800/782-7653, ext. 177,** or 512/393-5900), can provide you with information on mall bus transportation, as well as a complete list of places to eat and stay in town.

A SPECTACULAR DRIVE

San Marcos is a convenient jumping-off point for one of Texas's most breathtaking drives; take R.R. 12 west to R.R. 32 to reach the **Devil's Backbone,** a 30-mile, switchback-filled route affording spectacular Hill Country views.

WHERE TO STAY & DINE

Try the friendly **Crystal River Inn,** 326 W. Hopkins, San Marcos, 78666 (☎ **512/396-3739**). Rooms in this Victorian bed-and-breakfast run from $75 to $100, suites from $90 to $125. Guests can also book ladies-only and murder-mystery weekends.

Pepper's at the Falls, 100 Sessoms Dr. (☎ **512/396-5255**), serving burgers, grilled chicken, fajitas, and the like, offers great views of the San Marcos River.

IN NEARBY WIMBERLY

On the first Saturday of each month from April through December, a huge gathering of craft booths on Market Day draws Austinites to Lion's Field in **Wimberly,** some 15 miles northwest of San Marcos.

Most of the shops and boutiques in the town itself are nothing special, but **Sable V Fine Art Gallery** (☎ **512/847-8868**) and **Teeks Gallery and Gifts**

(☎ 512/847-8975), both on the town square, are high-quality exceptions. **Wimberly Glass Works,** Spoke Road, 1.6 miles south of the town square (☎ 512/847-9348), stands out for its rainbow-like array of blown glassware (you can watch artist Tim de Jong at work much of the time).

Right next door is perhaps the best reason to come to Wimberly: The **Blair House,** No. 1 Spoke Hill Rd., Wimberly, 78676 (☎ 512/847-8828), a luxurious inn on 85 Hill Country acres, offers beautifully decorated rooms in a Texas limestone ranch complex. Talk about relaxing: Four of the six have Jacuzzis, and there's a massage room and sauna on the property. Innkeeper Jonnie Stansbury is a gourmet chef and rates ($135 for a double) include her elaborate breakfasts. Most Saturday nights, she also offers outstanding, multicourse dinners that draw people all the way from Austin (book ahead).

If you're interested in other places to stay, eat, or shop in Wimberly, the **Chamber of Commerce** (1400 R.R. 12, just north of the town square; ☎ 512/847-2201) can help.

PICKING OUT A HAT IN BUDA

There's not a whole lot happening in the town of Buda, but if you get off I-35 at the Buda exit (exit 220, about halfway between Austin and San Marcos), you'll see **Texas Hatters** (☎ 512/295-HATS or 512/441-HATS) on the access road on the east side of the highway. In business for more than 50 years, this western hatter has had an unlikely mix of famous customers, from Tip O'Neill, George Bush, and the king of Sweden to Al Hirt, Willie Nelson, and Arnold Schwarzenegger—to name just a few.

9 New Braunfels

Some 16 miles south of San Marcos on I-35, New Braunfels sits at the junction of the Comal and Guadalupe Rivers. German settlers were brought here in 1845 by Prince Carl of Solms-Braunfels, the commissioner general of the Society for the Protection of German Immigrants in Texas; members of the same group continued on to found Fredericksburg. Although Prince Carl returned to Germany within a year to marry his fiancée, who refused to join him in the wilderness, his colony prospered; by the 1850s, New Braunfels was the fourth-largest city in Texas after Houston, San Antonio, and Galveston. New Braunfels is not nearly as large today, but it's not one of Hill Country's quainter towns, either.

WHAT TO SEE & DO IN & AROUND NEW BRAUNFELS

At the **New Braunfels Chamber of Commerce,** 390 S. Seguin, 78130 (☎ 800/572-2626 or 210/625-2385), you can pick up a pamphlet mapping out an antique-lovers' crawl. Those who want to remain in the modern world of retail can explore more than 40 shops in **Mill Store Plaza,** 651 Business Loop I-35 north (☎ 210/620-6806), another popular factory outlet mall.

Of note on the 39-point historic walking tour of midtown, also available at the Chamber of Commerce, are the ornate Romanesque gothic Comal County Courthouse (1898) on Main Plaza and the nearby Jacob Schmidt Building (193 W. San Antonio), built on the site where William Gebhardt, of canned chili fame, perfected his formula for chili powder in 1896. The **Hummel Museum,** 199 Main Plaza (☎ 800/456-4866 or 210/625-5636), displays the world's largest collection of drawings by Sister M. I. Hummel; the popular German figurines they inspired can be purchased in the museum's gift shop. Prince Carl never did build a planned castle for his sweetheart, Sophia, on the elevated spot where the **Sophienburg Museum,** 401 W. Coll St. (☎ 210/629-1572), now stands, but it's nevertheless an excellent place to learn about the history of New Braunfels and other Hill Country settlements. The **Museum of Texas Handmade Furniture,** 1370 Church Hill Dr. (☎ **210/ 629-6504**), also sheds light on local domestic life of the last century. You can tour some of the historic homes on **Conservation Plaza;** ask for directions at the Chamber of Commerce, or call **210/629-2943.**

HISTORIC GRUENE

You can get a more concentrated glimpse of the past, however, at Gruene (pro- nounced "Green"), 4 miles northwest of downtown New Braunfels. It was first settled by German farmers in the 1840s, but was virtually abandoned during the Depres- sion in the 1930s. It remained a ghost town until the mid-1970s, when two inves- tors realized the value of its intact historic buildings and sold them to businesses rather than razing them. These days tiny Gruene is crowded with day-trippers browsing the specialty shops in the wonderfully restored structures; try **H. P. Gruene Antique Mall** (☎ **210/629-7781**) for reasonably priced and fun nostalgia.

WATER SPORTS

Gruene also figures among the area's impressive array of places to get wet, most of them open only in summer. Outfitters who can help you ride the Guadalupe River rapids on raft, tube, canoe, or inflatable kayak include **Rockin "R" River Rides** (☎ **800/553-5628** or 210/629-9999) and **Gruene River Company** (☎ **210/ 625-2800**), both on Gruene Road just south of the Gruene Bridge.

Those who want to get wet without riding the rapids should head for downtown New Braunfels' **Landa Park** (☎ **210/608-2165**), where you can either swim in the largest spring-fed pool in Texas or calmly float in an inner tube down the state's smallest (2¹/₂ miles) river; you can also rent paddleboats or glass-bottomed boats here. **Schlitterbahn,** 305 W. Austin St. (☎ **210/625-2351**), Texas's biggest water park, features gigantic slides, rides, and pools, as well as the world's first uphill water coaster. Even if you don't want to immerse yourself, you might take the lovely 22-mile drive along the Guadalupe River from downtown's Cypress Bend Park to Canyon Lake, which is perfect for scuba diving because of its clarity.

NEARBY CAVERNS

Natural Bridge Caverns, 26495 Natural Bridge Caverns Rd. (☎ **210/651-6101**), 12 miles west of New Braunfels, is named for the 60-foot limestone arch spanning its entryway. More than a mile of huge rooms and passages are filled with stunning, multihued formations.

STAYING IN NEW BRAUNFELS

The **Prince Solmes Inn,** 295 E. San Antonio St., New Braunfels, 78130 (☎ **800/ 624-9169** or 210/625-9169), has been in continuous operation since it opened its doors to travelers in 1898. A prime downtown location, tree-shaded courtyard, and florid, high-Victorian–style sleeping quarters have put rooms ($60 to $80) and suites ($100 to $130) at this bed-and-breakfast in great demand.

For a river view, consider the **Gruene Mansion Inn,** 1275 Gruene Rd., New Braunfels, 78130 (☎ **210/629-2641**). The barns that once belonged to the opulent 1875 plantation house were converted to rustic elegant cottages with decks; some also offer romantic lofts (if you don't like stairs, request a single-level room). Accommo- dations for two go from $85 to $125 per night. Breakfast, served in the plantation house, is $5 extra.

If you're planning to come to town during *wurstfest* (late October through early November), be sure to book far in advance.

DINING IN NEW BRAUNFELS & GRUENE

The oldest restaurant in New Braunfels, **Krause's Cafe,** 148 S. Castell St. (☎ 210/625-7581), serves substantial German dishes and blue-plate specials in a diner-type setting.

In Gruene, the **Gristmill Restaurant,** 1287 Gruene Rd. (☎ 210/625-0684), a converted 100-year-old cotton gin, has a Texas casual menu including catfish, burgers, and chicken-fried steak and good views of the Guadalupe River.

The more upscale **Restaurant at Gruene Mansion,** 1275 Gruene Rd. (☎ 210/620-0760), serving everything from Cajun to German and continental cuisine, was built recently but looks like an old European hall; it offers an outside deck overlooking the river.

GRUENE AFTER DARK

Lyle Lovett and Garth Brooks are among the big names who've played at **Gruene Hall,** Gruene Road, corner of Hunter Road (☎ 210/606-1281), the oldest country-and-western dance hall in Texas and still one of the most mellow places to listen to music.

Appendix for Foreign Visitors

Although American fads and fashions have spread across Europe and other parts of the world so that America may seem like familiar territory before your arrival, there are still many peculiarities and uniquely American situations that any foreign visitor will encounter.

1 Preparing for Your Trip

ENTRY REQUIREMENTS

DOCUMENT REGULATIONS   Canadian citizens may enter the United States without visas; they need only proof of residence.

Citizens of the United Kingdom, New Zealand, Japan, and most Western European countries traveling on valid national or European Community passports may not need a visa for fewer than 90 days of holiday or business travel to the United States, providing that they hold a round-trip or return ticket and enter the United States on an airline or cruise line participating in the visa-waiver program.

Note: Citizens of these visa-exempt countries who first enter the United States may then visit Mexico, Canada, Bermuda, and/or the Caribbean islands and then reenter the United States, by any mode of transportation, without needing a visa. Further information is available from any U.S. embassy or consulate.

Citizens of countries other than those stipulated above, including citizens of Australia, must have two documents:

- a valid **passport,** with an expiration date at least 6 months later than the scheduled end of the visit to the United States; and
- a **tourist visa,** available without charge from the nearest U.S. consulate. To obtain a visa, the traveler must submit a completed application form (either in person or by mail) with a $1^{1}/_{2}$-inch square photo and demonstrate binding ties to a residence abroad.

Usually you can obtain a visa at once or within 24 hours, but it may take longer during the summer rush from June to August. If you cannot go in person, contact the nearest U.S. embassy or consulate for directions on applying by mail. Your travel agent or airline office may also be able to provide you with visa applications and instructions. The U.S. consulate or embassy that issues your visa will determine whether you will be issued a multiple- or single-entry visa and if there will be any restrictions regarding the length of your stay.

MEDICAL REQUIREMENTS   No inoculations are needed to enter the United States unless you are coming from, or have stopped over in, areas known to be suffering from epidemics, particularly cholera or yellow fever.

If you have a disease requiring treatment with medications containing narcotics or drugs requiring a syringe, carry a valid signed prescription from your physician to allay any suspicions that you are smuggling drugs.

CUSTOMS REQUIREMENTS   Every adult visitor may bring in free of duty: 1 liter of wine or hard liquor; 200 cigarettes or 100 cigars (but no cigars from Cuba) or 3 pounds of smoking tobacco; $100 worth of gifts. These exemptions are offered to travelers who spend at least 72 hours in the United States and who have not claimed them within the preceding 6 months. It is altogether forbidden to bring into the country foodstuffs (particularly cheese, fruit, cooked meats, and canned goods) and plants (vegetables, seeds, tropical plants, and so on). Foreign tourists may bring in or take out up to $10,000 in U.S. or foreign currency with no formalities; larger sums must be declared to Customs on entering or leaving.

INSURANCE   There is no national health system in the United States. Because the cost of medical care is extremely high, we strongly advise every traveler to secure health coverage before setting out.

You may want to take out a comprehensive travel policy that covers (for a relatively low premium) sickness or injury costs (medical, surgical, and hospital); loss or theft of your baggage; trip-cancellation costs; guarantee of bail in case you are arrested; costs of accident, repatriation, or death. Such packages (for example, Europe Assistance, 252 High St., Croydon, Surrey CRO 1NF, England; ☎ **01/680-1234**), are sold by automobile clubs at attractive rates, as well as by insurance companies and travel agencies.

MONEY

CURRENCY & EXCHANGE   The U.S. monetary system has a decimal base: one American **dollar ($1)** = 100 **cents (100¢).**

Dollar bills commonly come in $1 ("a buck"), $5, $10, $20, $50, and $100 denominations (the last two are not welcome when paying for small purchases and are not accepted in taxis or at subway ticket booths). There are also $2 bills (seldom encountered).

There are six denominations of coins: 1¢ (one cent or "a penny"), 5¢ (five cents or "a nickel"), 10¢ (ten cents or "a dime"), 25¢ (twenty-five cents or "a quarter"), 50¢ (fifty cents or "a half dollar"), and the rare $1 piece.

TRAVELER'S CHECKS   Traveler's checks denominated in U.S. dollars are readily accepted at most hotels, motels, restaurants, and large stores. But the best place to change traveler's checks is at a bank. Do not bring traveler's checks denominated in other currencies.

CREDIT CARDS   The method of payment most widely used is the credit card: VISA (BarclayCard in Britain), MasterCard (Eurocard in Europe, Access in Britain, Chargex in Canada), American Express, Diners Club, Discover, and Carte Blanche. You can save yourself trouble by using "plastic money" rather than cash or traveler's checks in most hotels, motels, restaurants, and retail stores (a growing number of food and liquor stores now accept credit cards). You must have a credit card to rent a car. It can also be used as proof of identity (often carrying more weight than a passport), or as a "cash card," enabling you to draw money from banks that accept them.

Note: The "foreign-exchange bureaus" so common in Europe are rare even at airports in the United States, and nonexistent outside major cities. Try to avoid having to change foreign money, or traveler's checks denominated other than in U.S. dollars, at a small-town bank, or even a branch in a big city; in fact, leave any currency other than U.S. dollars at home—it may prove more nuisance to you than it's worth.

SAFETY

GENERAL While tourist areas are generally safe, crime is on the increase everywhere, and U.S. urban areas tend to be less safe than those in Europe or Japan. Visitors should always stay alert. This is particularly true of large U.S. cities. It is wise to ask the city's or area's tourist office if you're in doubt about which neighborhoods are safe. Avoid deserted areas, especially at night. Don't go into any city park at night unless there is an event that attracts crowds—for example, visiting the Christmas tree in Austin's Zilker Park. Generally speaking, you can feel safe in areas where there are many people and many open establishments.

Avoid carrying valuables with you on the street, and don't display expensive cameras or electronic equipment. Hold on to your pocketbook, and place your billfold in an inside pocket. In theaters, restaurants, and other public places, keep your possessions in sight.

Remember also that hotels are open to the public, and in a large hotel, security may not be able to screen everyone entering. Always lock your room door—don't assume that once inside your hotel you are automatically safe and no longer need be aware of your surroundings.

DRIVING Safety while driving is particularly important. Question your rental agency about personal safety, or ask for a brochure of traveler safety tips when you pick up your car. Obtain written directions, or a map with the route marked in red, from the agency showing how to get to your destination. And, if possible, arrive and depart during daylight hours.

Recently more and more crime has involved cars and drivers. If you drive off a highway into a doubtful neighborhood, leave the area as quickly as possible. If you have an accident, even on the highway, stay in your car with the doors locked until you assess the situation or until the police arrive. If you are bumped from behind on the street or are involved in a minor accident with no injuries and the situation appears to be suspicious, motion to the other driver to follow you. *Never* get out of your car in such situations. You can also keep a premade sign in your car that reads: PLEASE FOLLOW THIS VEHICLE TO REPORT ACCIDENT. Show the sign to the other driver and go directly to the nearest police precinct, well-lighted service station, or all-night store.

If you see someone on the road who indicates a need for help, do *not* stop. Take note of the location, drive on to a well-lighted area, and telephone the police by dialing **911.**

Park in well-lighted, well-traveled areas if possible. Always keep your car doors locked, whether attended or unattended. Look around you before you get out of your car, and never leave any packages or valuables in sight. If someone attempts to rob you or steal your car, do *not* try to resist the thief/carjacker—report the incident to the police department immediately.

You may wish to contact the San Antonio Convention and Visitors Bureau, P.O. Box 2277, San Antonio, TX 78298 (☎ **800/447-3372**), or the Austin Convention and Visitors Bureau, 201 E. Second St., Austin TX 78701 (☎ **800/926-2282**), before you go for advice on safety precautions.

2 Getting to the U.S.

Travelers from overseas can take advantage of the APEX (Advance Purchase Excursion) fares offered by all the major U.S. and European carriers. Aside from these, attractive values are offered by Icelandair on flights from Luxembourg to New York and by Virgin Atlantic Airways from London to New York/Newark.

Houston is the hub for international flights into Texas. **Air Canada** (☎ **800/776-3000**) offers direct flights from Toronto to Houston; **Continental** (☎ **800/231-0856**) and **British Airways** (☎ **800/247-9297**) both have daily nonstop service from London.

Some large American airlines (for example, TWA, American Airlines, Northwest, United, and Delta) offer travelers on their transatlantic or transpacific flights special discount tickets under the name **Visit USA,** allowing travel between any U.S. destinations at minimum rates. They are not on sale in the United States, and must, therefore, be purchased before you leave your foreign point of departure. This system is the best, easiest, and fastest way to see the United States at low cost. You should obtain information well in advance from your travel agent or the office of the airline concerned, since the conditions attached to these discount tickets can be changed without advance notice.

The visitor arriving by air, no matter what the port of entry, should cultivate patience and resignation before setting foot on U.S. soil. Getting through Immigration control may take as long as 2 hours on some days, especially summer weekends. Add the time it takes to clear Customs and you'll see that you should make very generous allowance for delay in planning connections between international and domestic flights—an average of 2 to 3 hours at least.

In contrast, travelers arriving by car or by rail from Canada will find border-crossing formalities streamlined to the vanishing point. And air travelers from Canada, Bermuda, and some places in the Caribbean can sometimes go through Customs and Immigration at the point of departure, which is much quicker and less painful.

For further information about travel to San Antonio and Austin, see the "Getting There" sections of chapters 2 and 10, respectively.

3 Getting Around the U.S.

Without a doubt, the easist ways to travel within the U.S. are by car and by air for longer distances. All the major car-rental companies are represented in Texas; for details about San Antonio and Austin, see the "Getting Around" sections of chapters 3 and 11, respectively.

Visitors should be aware of the limitations of long-distance rail travel in the United States. With a few notable exceptions (for instance, the Northeast Corridor line between Boston and Washington, D.C.), service is rarely up to European standards: Delays are common, routes are limited and often infrequently served, and fares are rarely significantly lower than discount airfares. Thus, cross-country train travel should be approached with caution. If you do decide to travel by train, international visitors can buy a **USA Railpass,** good for 15 or 30 days of unlimited travel on Amtrak. The pass is available through many foreign travel agents. Prices in 1994 for a 15-day pass are $208 off-peak, $308 peak; a 30-day pass costs $309 off-peak, $389 peak. (With a foreign passport, you can also buy passes at some Amtrak offices in the United States, including locations in San Francisco, Los Angeles, Chicago, New York,

Miami, Boston, and Washington, D.C.) Reservations are generally required and should be made for each part of your trip as early as possible.

The cheapest way to travel the United States is by bus. Greyhound (☎ **800/ 231-2222**), a nationwide bus line, offers an **Ameripass** for unlimited travel for 7 days ($179), 15 days ($289), and 30 days ($399). Bus travel in the United States can be both slow and uncomfortable, so this option is not for everyone.

FAST FACTS: For the Foreign Traveler

Automobile Organizations Auto clubs will supply maps, suggested routes, guide-books, accident and bail-bond insurance, and emergency road service. The major auto club in the United States, with 955 offices nationwide, is the American Auto-mobile Association (AAA). Members of some foreign auto clubs have reciprocal arrangements with the AAA and enjoy its services at no charge. If you belong to an auto club, inquire about AAA reciprocity before you leave. The AAA can provide you with an International Driving Permit validating your foreign license. You may be able to join the AAA even if you are not a member of a reciprocal club. To inquire, call **800/336-4357**. In addition, some automobile-rental agencies now provide these services, so you should inquire about their availability when you rent your car.

Automobile Rentals To rent a car you need a major credit card. A valid driver's license is required, and you usually need to be at least 25. Some companies do rent to younger people but add a daily surcharge. Be sure to return your car with the same amount of gas you started out with; rental companies charge excessive prices for gasoline. All the major car-rental companies are represented in Texas; for details about San Antonio and Austin, see the "Getting Around" sections of chap-ters 3 and 11, respectively.

Business Hours Banks are open weekdays from 9am to 3 or 4pm, although there's 24-hour access to the automatic tellers (ATMs) at most banks and other outlets. Generally, offices are open weekdays from 9am to 5pm. Stores are open 6 days a week, with many open on Sunday, too; department stores usually stay open until 9pm at least 1 day a week.

Climate See "When to Go," in chapter 2.

Currency See "Money" in "Preparing for Your Trip," above.

Currency Exchange You'll find currency-exchange facilities at the San Antonio International Airport. In Austin, a number of Bank One branches around town provide this service; there's also an American Express Travel Service Office at 2943 W. Anderson Lane (☎ **512/452-8166**).

Drinking Laws See "Liquor Laws" in "Fast Facts: San Antonio," chapter 3, and "Fast Facts: Austin," chapter 11.

Electricity The United States uses 110 to 120 volts, 60 cycles, compared to 220 to 240 volts, 50 cycles, as in most of Europe. In addition to a 100-volt converter, small appliances of non-American manufacture, such as hair dryers or shavers, will require a plug adapter, with two flat, parallel pins.

Embassies & Consulates All embassies are located in the national capital, Wash-ington, D.C.; some consulates are located in major cities, and most nations have a mission to the United Nations in New York City. Foreign visitors can obtain telephone numbers for their embassies and consulates by calling "Information" in Washington, D.C. (☎ 202/555-1212).

There's a Canadian consulate in Dallas, 750 N. St. Paul St., Suite 1700, 75201 (☎ 214/922-9806). Houston is home to consulates for the United Kingdom, 1000 Louisiana St., 77002 (☎ 713/659-6270), and for Australia, 1990 Post Oak Blvd., Suite 800, 77056 (☎ 713/629-9131).

Emergencies   Call **911** to report a fire, call the police, or get an ambulance.

If you encounter traveler's problems, check the local directory to find an office of the Traveler's Aid Society, a nationwide, nonprofit, social-service organization geared to helping travelers in difficult straits. Their services might include reuniting families separated while traveling, providing food and/or shelter to people stranded without cash, or even emotional counseling. If you're in trouble, seek them out.

Gasoline (Petrol)   One U.S. gallon equals 3.75 liters, while 1.2 U.S. gallons equals 1 imperial gallon. You'll notice there are several grades (and price levels) of gasoline available at most gas stations. And you'll also notice that their names change from company to company. The unleaded ones with the highest octane are the most expensive (most rental cars take the least expensive "regular" unleaded) and leaded gas is the least expensive, but only older cars can take this, so check if you're not sure.

Holidays   On the following legal national holidays, banks, government offices, post offices, and many stores, restaurants, and museums are closed: New Year's Day (January 1); Martin Luther King Day (third Monday in January); President's Day (third Monday in February); Memorial Day (last Monday in May); Independence Day (July 4); Labor Day (first Monday in September); Columbus Day (second Monday in October); Veteran's Day (November 11); Thanksgiving Day (last Thursday in November); Christmas Day (December 25). During presidential-election years, Election Day is a national holiday (the Tuesday following the first Monday in November).

Languages   Major hotels may have multilingual employees. Unless your language is very obscure, they can usually supply a translator on request. Many people in San Antonio are fluent in Spanish.

Legal Aid   The foreign tourist, unless positively identified as a member of the Mafia or of a drug ring, will probably never become involved with the American legal system. If you are pulled up for a minor infraction (for example, of the highway code, such as speeding), never attempt to pay the fine directly to a police officer; you may wind up arrested on the much more serious charge of attempted bribery. Pay fines by mail, or directly into the hands of the clerk of the court. If accused of a more serious offense, it's wise to say and do nothing before consulting a lawyer. Under U.S. law, an arrested person is allowed one telephone call to a party of his or her choice. Call your embassy or consulate.

Mail   If you want your mail to follow you on your vacation and you aren't sure of your address, your mail can be sent to you, in your name, c/o General Delivery at the main post office of the city or region where you expect to be. The addressee must pick it up in person and produce proof of identity (driver's license, credit card, passport, etc.).

Generally to be found at intersections, mailboxes are blue with a red-and-white stripe and carry the inscription U.S. MAIL. If your mail is addressed to a U.S.

destination, don't forget to add the five-figure postal code, or ZIP (Zone Improvement Plan) Code, after the two-letter abbreviation of the state to which the mail is addressed (CA for California, FL for Florida, NY for New York, and so on).

Newspapers and Magazines   National newspapers include the *New York Times, USA Today,* and the *Wall Street Journal.* National news weeklies include *Newsweek, Time,* and *U.S. News & World Report.* There's only one major daily newspaper in San Antonio and Austin: the *San Antonio Express-News* and the *Austin-American Statesman,* respectively.

Radio & Television   Audiovisual media, with three full-time coast-to-coast networks—ABC, CBS, NBC—and three newer networks offering limited, prime-time-only programming—Fox, UPN, and the WB—along with the Public Broadcasting System (PBS) and a large number of cable networks—including CNN, MTV, and TBS—play a major part in American life. In big cities, televiewers have a choice of about a dozen channels (including the UHF channels), most of them transmitting 24 hours a day, without counting the pay-TV channels showing recent movies or sports events. All options are usually indicated on your hotel TV set. You'll also find a wide choice of local radio stations, each broadcasting particular kinds of talk shows and/or music—classical, country, jazz, pop, gospel—punctuated by news broadcasts and frequent commercials.

Safety   See "Safety" in "Preparing for Your Trip," above.

Taxes   In the United States there is no VAT (Value-Added Tax) or other indirect tax at a national level. Every state, and each city in it, has the right to levy its own local tax on all purchases, including hotel and restaurant checks, airline tickets, and so on. In San Antonio, the sales tax is $7^3/4$%; in Austin, it's 8%.

Telephone, Telegraph, Telex   The telephone system in the United States is run by private corporations, so rates, especially for long-distance service, can vary widely—even on calls made from public telephones. Local calls in the United States usually cost 25¢. Generally, hotel surcharges on long-distance and local calls are astronomical. You are usually better off using a public pay telephone, which you will find clearly marked in most public buildings and private establishments as well as on the street. Outside metropolitan areas, public telephones are more difficult to find. Stores and gas stations are your best bet.

Most long-distance and international calls can be dialed directly from any phone. For calls to Canada and other parts of the United States, dial 1 followed by the area code and the seven-digit number. For international calls, dial 011 followed by the country code, city code, and the telephone number of the person you wish to call.

For reversed-charge or collect calls, and for person-to-person calls, dial 0 (zero, *not* the letter "O") followed by the area code and number you want; an operator will then come on the line, and you should specify that you are calling collect, or person-to-person, or both. If your operator-assisted call is international, ask for the overseas operator.

For local directory assistance ("information"), dial 411; for long-distance information, dial 1, then the appropriate area code and **555-1212.**

Like the telephone system, telegraph and telex services are provided by private corporations like ITT, MCI, and above all, Western Union, the most important. You can bring your telegram in to the nearest Western Union office (there are hundreds across the country), or dictate it over the phone (a toll-free call, **800/ 325-6000**). You can also telegraph money, or have it telegraphed to you, very quickly over the Western Union system.

Telephone Directory   There are two kinds of telephone directories available to you. The general directory is the so-called White Pages, in which private and business subscribers are listed in alphabetical order. The inside front cover lists the emergency number for police, fire, and ambulance, and other vital numbers (like the Coast Guard, poison-control center, crime-victims hot line, and so on). The first few pages are devoted to community-service numbers, including a guide to long-distance and international calling, complete with country codes and area codes.

The second directory, printed on yellow paper (hence its name, Yellow Pages), lists all local services, businesses, and industries by type of activity, with an index at the back. The listings cover not only such obvious items as automobile repairs by make of car, or drugstores (pharmacies), often by geographical location, but also restaurants by type of cuisine and geographical location, bookstores by special subject and/or language, places of worship by religious denomination, and other information that the tourist might otherwise not readily find. The Yellow Pages also include city plans or detailed area maps, often showing postal ZIP Codes and public transportation routes.

Time   The United States is divided into four time zones (six, if Alaska and Hawaii are included). From east to west, these are: eastern standard time (EST), central daylight time (CDT), mountain standard time (MST), Pacific standard time (PST), Alaska standard time (AST), and Hawaii standard time (HST). Always keep changing time zones in mind if you are traveling (or even telephoning) long distances in the United States. For example, noon in New York City (EST) is 11am in Chicago (CDT), 10am in Denver (MST), 9am in Los Angeles (PST), 8am in Anchorage (AST), and 7am in Honolulu (HST).

Most of Texas, including San Antonio and Austin, is on Central Time; the far western part of the state, around El Paso, observes Mountain Time (clocks are set 1 hour earlier). Daylight saving time is in effect from the last Sunday in April through the last Saturday in October (actually, the change is made at 2am on Sunday) except in parts of Arizona, Hawaii, part of Indiana, and Puerto Rico. Daylight saving time moves the clock 1 hour ahead of standard time.

Tipping   Service in America is some of the best in the world, and is rarely included in the price of anything. The amount you tip should depend on the service you have received. Good service warrants the following tips: bartenders, 15%; bellhops, $2 to $4; cab drivers, 15%; cafeterias and fast-food restaurants, no tip; chambermaids, $1 per person per day; checkroom attendants, 50¢ to $1 (unless there is a charge, then no tip); gas station attendants, no tip; hairdressers, 15% to 20%; parking valets, $1; redcaps (in airports and railroad stations), $2 to $4; restaurants and nightclubs, 15%.

Toilets   Foreign visitors often complain that public toilets are hard to find in most U.S. cities. True, there are none on the streets, but the visitor can usually find one in a bar, restaurant, hotel, museum, department store, or service station—and it will probably be clean (although the last-mentioned sometimes leaves much to be desired). Note, however, a growing practice in some restaurants and bars of displaying a notice that "toilets are for the use of patrons only." You can ignore this sign, or better yet, avoid arguments by paying for a cup of coffee or soft drink, which will qualify you as a patron. The cleanliness of toilets at railroad stations and bus depots may be more open to question, and some public places are equipped with pay toilets, which require you to insert one or more coins into a slot on the door before it will open.

THE AMERICAN SYSTEM OF MEASUREMENTS

Length

1 inch (in.)			=	2.54cm			
1 foot (ft.)	=	12 in.	=	30.48cm	=	.305m	
1 yard (yd.)	=	3 ft.			=	.915m	
1 mile (m)	=	5,280 ft.					= 1.609km

To convert miles to kilometers, multiply the number of miles by 1.61. Also use to convert speeds from miles per hour (mph) to kilometers per hour (kmph).

To convert kilometers to miles, multiply the number of kilometers by .62. Also use to convert kmph to mph.

Capacity

1 fluid ounce (fl. oz.)			=	.03 liter		
1 pint (pt.)	=	16 fl. oz.	=	.47 liter		
1 quart (qt.)	=	2 pints	=	.94 liter		
1 gallon (gal.)	=	4 quarts	=	3.79 liters	=	.83 Imperial gal.

To convert U.S. gallons to liters, multiply the number of gallons by 3.79.

To convert liters to U.S. gallons, multiply the number of liters by .26.

To convert U.S. gallons to Imperial gallons, multiply the number of U.S. gallons by .83.

To convert Imperial gallons to U.S. gallons, multiply the number of Imperial gallons by 1.2.

Weight

1 ounce (oz.)			=	28.35g		
1 pound (lb.)	=	16 oz.	=	453.6g	=	.45 kg
1 ton	=	2,000 lb.	=		907 kg	= .91 metric ton

To convert pounds to kilograms, multiply the number of pounds by .45.

To convert kilograms to pounds, multiply the number of kilograms by 2.2.

Area

1 acre			=	.41ha	
1 square mile	=	640 acres	=	2.59ha	= 2.6 sq. km

To convert acres to hectares, multiply the number of acres by .41.

To convert hectares to acres, multiply the number of hectares by 2.47.

To convert square miles to square kilometers, multiply the number of square miles by 2.6.

To convert square kilometers to square miles, multiply the number of square kilometers by .39.

Temperature

To convert degrees Farenheit to degrees Celsius, subtract 32 from °F, multiply by 5, then divide by 9 (example: 85°F − 32 × $^5/_9$ = 29.4°C).

To convert degrees Celsius to degrees Fahrenheit, multiply °C by 9, divide by 5, and add 32 (example: 20°C × $^9/_5$ + 32 = 68°F).

Index

SAN ANTONIO ACCOMMODATIONS INDEX

SAN ANTONIO RESTAURANT INDEX

FROMMER'S COMPLETE TRAVEL GUIDES

*(Comprehensive guides to destinations around the world, with
selections in all price ranges—from deluxe to budget)*

Acapulco/Ixtapa/Taxco
Alaska
Amsterdam
Arizona
Atlanta
Australia
Austria
Bahamas
Bangkok
Barcelona, Madrid & Seville
Belgium, Holland & Luxembourg
Berlin
Bermuda
Boston
Budapest & the Best of Hungary
California
Canada
Cancún, Cozumel & the Yucatán
Caribbean
Caribbean Cruises & Ports of Call
Caribbean Ports of Call
Carolinas & Georgia
Chicago
Colorado
Costa Rica
Denver, Boulder & Colorado Springs
Dublin
England
Florida
France
Germany
Greece
Hawaii
Hong Kong
Honolulu/Waikiki/Oahu
Ireland
Italy
Jamaica/Barbados
Japan
Las Vegas
London
Los Angeles
Maryland & Delaware
Maui

Mexico
Mexico City
Miami & the Keys
Montana & Wyoming
Montréal & Québec City
Munich & the Bavarian Alps
Nashville & Memphis
Nepal
New England
New Mexico
New Orleans
New York City
Northern New England
Nova Scotia, New Brunswick & Prince
    Edward Island
Paris
Philadelphia & the Amish Country
Portugal
Prague & the Best of the Czech Republic
Puerto Rico
Puerto Vallarta, Manzanillo & Guadalajara
Rome
San Antonio & Austin
San Diego
San Francisco
Santa Fe, Taos & Albuquerque
Scandinavia
Scotland
Seattle & Portland
South Pacific
Spain
Switzerland
Thailand
Tokyo
Toronto
U.S.A.
Utah
Vancouver & Victoria
Vienna
Virgin Islands
Virginia
Walt Disney World & Orlando
Washington, D.C.
Washington & Oregon

FROMMER'S FRUGAL TRAVELER'S GUIDES

(The grown-up guides to budget travel, offering dream vacations at down-to-earth prices)

Australia from $45 a Day

Berlin from $50 a Day

California from $60 a Day

Caribbean from $60 a Day

Costa Rica & Belize from $35 a Day

Eastern Europe from $30 a Day

England from $50 a Day

Europe from $50 a Day

Florida from $50 a Day

Greece from $45 a Day

Hawaii from $60 a Day

India from $40 a Day

Ireland from $45 a Day

Italy from $50 a Day

Israel from $45 a Day

London from $60 a Day

Mexico from $35 a Day

New York from $70 a Day

New Zealand from $45 a Day

Paris from $65 a Day

Washington, D.C. from $50 a Day

FROMMER'S PORTABLE GUIDES

(Pocket-size guides for travelers who want everything in a nutshell)

Charleston & Savannah

Las Vegas

New Orleans

San Francisco

FROMMER'S IRREVERENT GUIDES

(Wickedly honest guides for sophisticated travelers)

Amsterdam

Chicago

London

Manhattan

Miami

New Orleans

Paris

San Francisco

Santa Fe

U.S. Virgin Islands

Walt Disney World

Washington, D.C.

FROMMER'S AMERICA ON WHEELS

(Everything you need for a successful road trip, including full-color road maps and ratings for every hotel)

California & Nevada

Florida

Mid-Atlantic

Midwest & the Great Lakes

New England & New York

Northwest & Great Plains

South Central &Texas

Southeast

Southwest

FROMMER'S BY NIGHT GUIDES

(The series for those who know that life begins after dark)

Amsterdam

Chicago

Las Vegas

London

Los Angeles

Miami

New Orleans

New York

Paris

San Francisco

WHEREVER YOU TRAVEL, *H*ELP IS NEVER FAR AWAY.

From planning your trip to providing travel assistance along the way, American Express® Travel Service Offices are always there to help.

San Antonio

Rennert World Travel, Inc. (R)
116 North Star Mall
San Antonio
210/349-2761

Rennert World Travel, Inc. (R)
Windsor Park Mall
San Antonio
210/654-6310

Rennert World Travel, Inc. (R)
8103 Broadway
San Antonio
210/828-4809

Rennert World Travel, Inc. (R)
13418 San Pedro
San Antonio
210/494-5533

Austin

American Express Travel Service
2943 West Anderson Lane
Austin
512/452-8166

Accent Travel (R)
5521 Balcones Drive
Austin
512/451-6591

Accent Travel (R)
9722 Great Hills Trail
Austin
512/338-0444

Accent Travel (R)
3737 Executive Center Drive #100
Austin
512/338-2828

Travel

http://www.americanexpress.com/travel